Voice of the Living Light

Voice of the Living Light

Hildegard of Bingen and Her World

Edited by

Barbara Newman

UNIVERSITY OF CALIFORNIA PRESS
Berkeley · Los Angeles · London

University of California Press
Berkeley and Los Angeles, California

University of California Press, Ltd.
London, England

© 1998 by
The Regents of the University of California

Library of Congress Cataloging-in-Publication Data

Voice of the living light : Hildegard of Bingen and her world / edited
  by Barbara Newman.
    p.   cm.
    Includes bibliographical references and index.
    ISBN 0-520-20826-9 (alk. paper)
    ISBN 0-520-21758-6 (pbk. : alk. paper)
    1. Hildegard, Saint, 1098–1179. 2. Germany—Intellectual life.
I. Newman, Barbara, 1953– .
BX4700.H5V65   1998
282′.092—dc21
  [b]   98-14149
                                 CIP

Printed in the United States of America

9 8 7 6 5 4 3 2 1

Contents

Illustrations

following page 118

Figs. 15–17 are reproduced by permission of the Biblioteca Governativa, Lucca. Figs. 1, 2, 3, 5, 6, 8, 10, 11, and 12 are reproduced by permission of the Rheinisches Bildarchiv, Cologne. Other sources are acknowledged below.

Acknowledgments

Multiple authors incur multiple debts, and in a collaborative volume such as this one it is scarcely possible to thank all who have contributed at every stage of the way. Our special gratitude goes to Douglas Abrams Arava of the University of California Press: without his zeal and unflagging commitment, this volume would never have seen the light of day. We would like to thank Grover Zinn, Bernard McGinn, and two anonymous press readers for their painstaking review of the entire volume. Joan Cadden, Monica Green, Richard Kieckhefer, Rachel Koopmans, Maryna Mews, Lorene Pouncey, and Lisa Wolverton offered valuable help and advice on individual essays. E. Randolph Daniel and Sabina Flanagan graciously shared their forthcoming work with us. Thanks are due to Cynthia Abbott for help in assembling the illustrations, to Richard Boursey for preparing camera-ready copies of the music, and to Barbara Abou-El-Haj, Walter Cahn, and Clifford and Audrey Ekdahl Davidson for the loan of photographs. Librarians at several institutions, including the Yale Divinity School, the Institute for Advanced Study, and Northwestern University, have gone out of their way to help. Some of the research for this book was generously funded by the Institute for Advanced Study and the National Endowment for the Humanities. Kathleen Daniels of Northwestern University patiently and knowledgeably assisted us with software conversions. Peter Jeffery, Gale Pollen, and Cheryl Serviss helped with formatting and clerical details, and Maeve Callan spent many meticulous hours in the "reveal codes" mode, helping our computers if not our minds to achieve perfect harmony.

ONE

"Sibyl of the Rhine"

Hildegard's Life and Times

Barbara Newman

Hildegard of Bingen (1098–1179), mistress of St. Rupert's Monastery and "Sibyl of the Rhine," would have been extraordinary in any age.[1] But for a woman of the twelfth century, hedged by the constraints of a misogynist world, her achievements baffle thought, marking her as a figure so exceptional that posterity has found it hard to take her measure. For centuries she was ignored or forgotten, like so many accomplished women of the past. A skeptical historian in the nineteenth century tried to explain her away by casting doubt on the authenticity of her books, imagining a male ghostwriter behind her mask.[2] A fideist countered by reading her prophetic claims in a naively literal way, making God the ghostwriter who dictated every word she set down and Hildegard but a passive and uncomprehending tool.[3] Even now, despite enormous advances in scholarship on medieval women, she is still portrayed at times as an anomaly. Some books give the impression that she dropped into her world like a meteorite from a late-twentieth-century sky, proclaiming enlightened postmodern views on gender, ecology, ecumenism, and holistic health to an uncomprehending age.[4]

The purpose of this book is to set Hildegard in context, but this project will in no way diminish her exceptionality. Among the countless "firsts" and "onlies" to her credit, Hildegard was the only woman of her age to be accepted as an authoritative voice on Christian doctrine; the first woman who received express permission from a pope to write theological books; the only medieval woman who preached openly, before mixed audiences of clergy and laity, with the full approval of church authorities;[5] the author of the first known morality play[6] and the only twelfth-century playwright who is not anonymous; the only composer of her era (not to mention the only medieval woman) known both by name and by a large corpus of surviving music; the first scientific writer to discuss sexuality and gynecology from a female perspective;[7] and the first saint whose official biography includes a first-person memoir.[8]

Yet exceptionality is only half the picture, for to study Hildegard's complete oeuvre is also to study the entire sweep of twelfth-century culture and society. Her prophetic career and her vast correspondence contribute to but also need to be illumined by a knowledge of all the burning religious and political issues of her day: the conflict between empire and papacy, the territorial ambitions of Frederick Barbarossa, the ravages of schism and civil war, the careerism of contemporary prelates, the rising threat of the Cathar heresy, the Second Crusade, the invigorating developments and crises in monastic reform, the nascent evangelical poverty movement, the competition for lucrative endowments and relics, the struggle over clerical celibacy. To understand Hildegard's massive visionary trilogy, readers need to be aware of twelfth-century developments in sacramental theology, the emerging doctrine of purgatory, Christian-Jewish relations, biblical exegesis, and cosmology, to name only a few of the topics she covers. Her medical and scientific writings present a body of encyclopedic lore about animals, birds, fishes, herbs, trees, gemstones, metals, nutrition, sexuality, disease, and therapeutics. To hear or perform her music and drama is to enter the rich and, for most of us, exotic world of Benedictine liturgy. Beyond their remarkable beauty, Hildegard's chants can offer insight into matters ranging from the self-image of consecrated women to the nature of devotion directed toward Mary and the saints. Her illuminated manuscripts, unique in twelfth-century iconography, raise a host of questions about the work of women as artists, producers, and patrons of deluxe books. Even her vita, or saintly biography, sheds light on the politics of canonization and new trends in women's spirituality.

Given the scope of Hildegard's accomplishments, an introduction to *all* the dimensions of her life and creativity lies beyond the competence of any individual scholar. Hence this book is a collaborative effort by specialists in many fields, ranging from medieval theology to medicine to music. Attentive readers will note that in some areas Hildegard's teaching proves to be socially and religiously conservative, while in others she stood at the vanguard of twelfth-century thought or developed wholly original ideas. Only contextual study can distinguish what is typical or atypical, idiosyncratic or commonplace, in such a large and bewilderingly diverse oeuvre. It should be stated at the outset, however, that although Hildegard was in many ways "transgressive," breaking her society's gender taboos with impunity, she was in no sense heretical.[9] To be sure, she named and fiercely challenged the abuses of power that she saw around her, writing to archbishops and kings with a truly prophetic, sometimes shocking candor. And she made enemies, among them the abbot who resented her bid for monastic independence, the unnamed detractors who felt sure she was deceived by demons, the reform-minded canoness who penned a withering critique of her elitism, and the prelates who slapped an interdict on her monastery when she was eighty years old and ailing. Yet her career as a whole testifies to the farthest limits of acceptable behavior in the twelfth century, including the degree and ferocity of criticism that powerful churchmen might be willing to tolerate. What Hildegard "got away with" must be finally explained not only by her energy and ability but also by her contemporaries' genuine belief that she was inspired by God, no matter how uncomfortable she made them feel. But had she voiced any genuine heresy, that is, doctrinal error in matters pertaining to the faith, there is no question that she would have been promptly silenced, her books condemned, and her unusual activities brought to a swift and if need be violent end.[10] Doctrinal orthodoxy, in short, was not only a matter of deep-seated conviction for the seer but also a necessary condition for her survival.

Our principal source for her biography is the *Vita Sanctae Hildegardis* (*Life of St. Hildegard*), a book whose title reveals its purpose: to secure her veneration as a saint and, if possible, her canonization by the church.[11] Like other hagiographic texts, therefore, it does not pretend to offer an "objective," even-handed treatment of its subject. The *Vita* pursues its religious goal by ascribing as many events as possible to supernatural rather than natural causes, discerning the hand of God in all of Hildegard's motivations and actions, and emphasizing her official validation as a prophet, which is attested not only by miracles but also by an ascending chain of authorities: her teacher, her abbot, the archbishop of Mainz, a synod of bishops at Trier, St. Bernard of Clairvaux, and finally Pope Eugene III. Once these churchmen had certified Hildegard's visionary gift as authentic and God-given, the path was cleared for two major undertakings: the completion and publication of her first book, called *Scivias* (an abridgment of *Scito vias Domini*, or know the ways of the Lord), and the founding of her new monastery on the desolate site of the Rupertsberg, or St. Rupert's Mount. Given the importance of these initiatives, the *Vita* focuses intensely on the period between Hildegard's "prophetic call," which she experienced in 1141 at the age of forty-three, and the secession of the Rupertsberg from its motherhouse, the male monastery of St. Disibod, in 1155. The life has much less to say about Hildegard's early years and her final decades.

A monk named Godfrey of St. Disibod, who served as provost at the Rupertsberg late in Hildegard's life (1174–1176), began to compose her *Vita* even before she died, anticipating that the community would want to promote her as a saint. Unfortunately Godfrey predeceased Hildegard, leaving his work unfinished. Several years after Hildegard's death in 1179, her friends commissioned another monk, Theoderic of Echternach, to finish the task. But Theoderic was apparently chosen more for his literary reputation than his personal interest in the saint; he seems to have had no direct acquaintance with Hildegard and little knowledge of her works.[12] So instead of resuming the narrative where Godfrey had left off, Theoderic made an extraordinary choice: he decided to fill book 2 of the *Vita* with memoirs that Hildegard herself had dictated to help her earlier biographer, interspersing his own awed if sometimes uncomprehending comments. Thus the *Vita* permits us to compare three diverse perspectives on Hildegard's life: her own, the perceptions of a monk who worked for her, and the imagination of a more distant admirer who, having only secondhand knowledge, tried to fit her life into the stereotyped pattern of female sanctity fashionable in his own age. Fortunately, however, the *Vita* is not our only source for Hildegard's life. We can supplement and, if necessary, correct it with the information provided by another fragmentary vita,[13] Hildegard's letters,[14] the autobiographical prefaces of her books, a series of charters and other official documents pertaining to her monasteries,[15] and (with greater caution) an account of miracles prepared for her canonization.[16]

All of these sources have been known since the nineteenth century. In 1992, however, surprising light was shed on Hildegard's early life by the discovery of another vita: that of her teacher, Jutta of Sponheim, who was herself considered a saint.[17] It is fitting, then, to begin the account of Hildegard's life with a look at these two women's intertwined destinies.[18] Born in 1098, Hildegard was the daughter of a Rhenish nobleman, Hildebert of Bermersheim, and his wife, Mechthild. Little is known of this couple except that they were wealthy and prolific: Hildegard was the youngest of ten children.[19] Jutta, six years older than Hildegard, was born in 1092 to Count Stephen of Sponheim and his Bavarian wife, Sophia. Although the Sponheim family was more exalted than that of Bermersheim, the two clans were affiliated and may have been distantly related. So when the teenaged Jutta made a precocious decision to enter the religious life, Hildegard's parents strengthened this advantageous alliance by offering their youngest child—their "tithe to God," as one biographer put it—to be her companion.

Europe at the turn of the twelfth century was aglow with a revival of the eremitic life, a cherished ascetic ideal dating back to the desert fathers and mothers of the early Christian era. In growing numbers men and women alike were forsaking not only marriage but even the security of established monasteries to live an austere, solitary life as free-roaming hermits (the preferred option for men) or as enclosed recluses (the lifestyle recommended for women).[20] Young girls in particular might go to extraordinary lengths to adopt such a life, resisting parental demands with all the determination of martyrs. When the twelve-year-old Jutta became ill, she vowed to become a nun if she survived and thereafter refused all her suitors *viriliter* ("like a man"), much to her family's disgust. Her biographer says Jutta "endured great perils" to preserve her chastity, and although he does not elaborate, we might recall the trials of her English contemporary, Christina of Markyate. Forced into an arranged marriage, Christina steadfastly refused to sleep with her husband, although he and her parents tried everything from sorcery to attempted rape. At last she fled the family home, disguised as a man, and took refuge in a hermit's cell, where she remained in hiding for years, even though the enclosure was too small for her to stand in and she could only go out to answer nature's call under cover of night.[21]

Jutta seems to have been equally fierce and independent. From about 1106 she embarked on an unvowed religious life in the house of Lady Uda, a widow of Göllheim, possibly with the eight-year-old Hildegard already in tow.[22] After Uda died Jutta expressed a desire to go on pilgrimage, further indicating her spirit of adventure. But her brother Meinhard, later count of Sponheim, thwarted that plan and persuaded her, at age twenty, to settle at the monastery of St. Disibod. Thus on All Saints' Day, November 1, 1112, the young noblewoman was formally enclosed as a recluse and took her monastic vows, together with Hildegard (then fourteen) and one or two other girls who also bore the name of Jutta.[23] Since their ordinary prelate, Archbishop Adalbert I of Mainz, was at that time a political prisoner of the emperor Henry V, the girls' vows were received by Otto, bishop of Bamberg.[24]

Some accounts of Hildegard give the impression that when she and Jutta joined the community at St. Disibod it was already a well-established house. But this was not the case. Although the Disibodenberg was indeed an ancient religious site, allegedly founded by a wandering Irish hermit in the seventh century, the monastery had passed through many vicissitudes and stood vacant for several years during the political exile of Archbishop Ruthard of Mainz (reigned 1089–1109). He returned in 1106 and refounded the community two years later, restoring the dilapidated site and staffing it with monks who may have been affiliated with the reformed Benedictine congregation of Hirsau.[25] When Jutta and Hildegard arrived, then, the existing monastery was quite new and still under construction. Thus the young Hildegard grew up surrounded by the noise and bustle of masons and carpenters, an experience reflected in the ubiquitous architectural metaphors of her *Scivias*.[26] We know little about the space occupied by the women; it is unclear, for example, whether they had their own chapel for singing the Divine Office or participated along with the men.[27] What is clear, however, is that the well-born and distinguished Jutta (unlike Hildegard) enjoyed an excellent relationship with the monks, who lost no time in promoting her sainthood when she died (22 December 1136).

Jutta's *Vita* describes her as an ascetic par excellence, using conventional terms borrowed from the life of the sixth-century St. Radegund of Poitiers.[28] We are told that Jutta devoted herself to prayer, fasting, vigils, nakedness, and cold; she tortured her body with a hairshirt and an iron chain, which she removed only on great festivals; and she refused meat for eight years in defiance of her abbot, who urged moderation. At least once a day she recited the entire Psalter, which in wintertime she often said barefoot. As *magistra*, mistress or teacher, of the girls under her tutelage, Jutta would certainly have taught Hildegard to chant the Psalter and thus to read Latin at an elementary level. It is interesting that Hildegard, in a laconic and somewhat backhanded reference to her foster mother, says that she herself had "scarcely any knowledge of letters, as an uneducated woman had taught" her.[29] Jutta's biographer, in contrast, praises her capable intellect and tenacious memory, describes her as a ready teacher who refused to play favorites, and casually alludes to her literacy when he remarks that she received many letters from devotees seeking her prayers. In addition, the *Life of Lady Jutta* repeatedly presents the recluse as a teacher and her companions as *discipulae,* or students, at one point referring to the women's hermitage as a *schola,* or school.[30] Although these references to learning need not be exaggerated, they should incline us to take Hildegard's lifelong protestations of ignorance with more than a grain of salt.

When the adult Hildegard described herself as *indocta* ("uneducated"),[31] she was in one sense telling the truth. Unlike boys of her vocation and status, she did not have the opportunity to attend a cathedral school or to follow itinerant masters as a wandering scholar.[32] Nor had she studied at a convent with a splendid library, as did her contemporary Heloise, who received an outstanding classical education at Argenteuil,[33] or Abbess Herrad of Hohenbourg, who was to compile an encyclopedia of patristic learning from the rich store of books at her disposal.[34] Since Hildegard never had occasion to study the trivium, or literary arts, her command of Latin grammar would always remain shaky, and she developed a style that could be awkward and idiosyncratic rather than urbane and polished.[35] But if her early education paled by comparison with others', Hildegard was to amass prodigious learning by the end of her life.[36] By midcentury, too, St. Disibod had acquired a substantial library of its own, though its destruction during the Reformation era makes it difficult to know for certain what books Hildegard might have read there. The main purpose of her apparent self-deprecation, however, was not to belittle herself or comment on the faults of her early training but to emphasize that the source of her revelations was divine, not human. Without this indispensable claim to prophecy, her career as a writer and preacher would have been unthinkable.[37]

Other indications in Jutta's life suggest a degree of continuity between the two holy women. We learn that Jutta herself was endowed with prophetic powers: when an abbot died, God showed her who his successor would be. Like Hildegard, too, she earned a reputation as a healer and made St. Disibod into a mecca for pilgrims, who are said to have revered her "as a heavenly oracle."[38] It appears, then, that Hildegard learned considerably more than the Psalter from Jutta. She also saw firsthand what an unusually gifted and energetic nun might make of her vocation. Yet the delicate girl's temperament was very different from the recluse's. A savage ascetic, Jutta died at forty-four, worn out by her austerities, while Hildegard, though of fragile health, prized the classic Benedictine virtue of moderation and lived to be eighty-one. In addition, her visionary bent was all her own. From Hildegard's *Vita* we learn that as a tiny child she beheld "a light so dazzling that [her] soul trembled," but she had no words to speak of it.[39] Another source recounts a story of childhood clairvoyance: seeing a pregnant cow, the girl accurately predicted the color and markings of her calf.[40] As both women's biographies confirm, Hildegard continued to have visions under Jutta's tutelage, culminating in a hair-raising account of the soul's journey after death. Then thirty-eight, she watched as her teacher's spirit in the hands of angels passed close by the flames of purgatory and endured false accusations from the devil before being received by St. John the Evangelist and led into paradise.[41] This, Hildegard's earliest recorded vision, anticipates certain passages from her *Scivias* and especially her book on purgatory, the *Liber vite meritorum* (*Book of Life's Merits*).

Jutta at the time of her death had ten disciples, of whom Hildegard was said to be the "first and most intimate . . . flourishing in a holy way of life, the acme of all virtues."[42] Not surprisingly, she was soon elected *magistra* in her teacher's stead. As the *Life of Jutta* states, "After her passing [Hildegard] took over the administration of her school."[43] It is odd, though, that the seer's own memoirs say nothing of her election to leadership but skip ahead to the "great pressure of pains" she experienced in her early forties, when God first commanded her to "cry out and write" what she saw in her visions.[44] This moment, rather than Jutta's death or her election as mistress, represented the first major crisis in Hildegard's life. As the now famous story runs, she initially confided only in the monk Volmar, who had been her teacher and would become her lifelong friend, secretary, and confidant. In all likelihood he was her confessor as well. Despite Volmar's support, however, Hildegard felt so daunted by the prospect of writing and the concomitant fear of ridicule that she became severely ill. This would become a recurrent pattern both in her own life and in the narratives of countless female visionaries in the later Middle Ages. A vision or divine command to write so terrifies the woman that it brings on a sickness, at once punitive and motivating, which will in turn become a catalyst for action: the would-be prophetess cannot be cured until she obeys the heavenly voice.[45] In Hildegard's case, Volmar's encouragement and the cautious support of Kuno, abbot of St. Disibod, enabled her eventually to surmount her fears and embark on the task. The famous authorportraits of Hildegard present an idealized picture of her at work in her scriptorium. Her face uplifted toward heaven, she receives streams of fire from on high, signifying divine inspiration, as she writes with her own hand on wax tablets—or perhaps, as the art historian Madeline Caviness suggests, sketches the visionary forms unfolding before her eyes. Separated by a partition, Volmar makes a fair copy of her text on parchment, and one of Hildegard's nuns—perhaps her favorite, Richardis of Stade—stands by to assist her (see figure 16).[46]

It is quite possible to read the *Scivias* simply as a work of Christian theology, including material on ethics, biblical commentary, sacred history, and cosmology as well as thorough discussions of the Trinity and redemption through Christ. To understand the power and distinctiveness of this book, however, we must look more closely at its genesis in what Hildegard called her *visio* ("vision," in the singular, rather than "visions"). In many so-called visionary writings from the Middle Ages, visual description plays only a minor role, while the bulk of the text is given over to conversations between the seer and a heavenly figure like Christ, Mary, or an angel.[47] But Hildegard was a visionary in the strictest sense. Not in ecstasy or trance or dream but wide awake, she retained the full use of her senses and yet "saw things" in living color—mountains, cosmic eggs, spheres of shimmering light, colossal figures, towering walls and pillars—sometimes in static tableaux and sometimes in dynamic motion. Late in her life a distant admirer asked Hildegard to explain how she received her revelations, and she enlightened him in a now famous letter.[48]

"I have always seen this vision in my soul," she wrote, and in it "my soul, as God would have it, rises up high into the vault of heaven and into the changing sky and spreads itself out among different peoples, although they are far away." The light that illumined her, she added, was "not spatial, but far, far brighter than a cloud that carries the sun . . . And as the sun, the moon, and the stars appear in water, so writings, sermons, virtues, and certain human actions take form for me and gleam within it." Hildegard insisted that this "shadow of the Living Light" was never absent from her field of vision, and when she received revelations within it, the words that came to her were "not like words uttered by the mouth of man, but like a shimmering flame, or a cloud floating in a clear sky." Moreover, on rare occasions she saw within this "shadow" or "reflection" another light, "the Living Light" itself, by which she seems to have meant a direct experience of God. "I cannot describe when and how I see it, but while I see it all sorrow and anguish leave me, so that then I feel like a simple girl instead of an old woman."

What are we to make of this account? Certainly it is not conventional. Twelfth-century authors were familiar with several theories of visionary experience, including those of St. Augustine, Dionysius the Areopagite, and Hildegard's contemporary Richard of St.-Victor. These theorists distinguished among several kinds of vision—such as imaginative, intellectual, and spiritual—and established hierarchies among them, always representing pure, imageless contemplation as higher than the more "corporeal" types of vision.[49] But none of their descriptions closely match Hildegard's, and her insistence that she remained awake and lucid during her visions is virtually unique. Her correspondent, the monk Guibert of Gembloux, had asked whether the visions appeared to her in ecstasy or in dreams, as these were the only possibilities he could imagine; but she replied, in effect, "none of the above." Nor can modern theories fully account for her experience. David Baumgardt, a scholar of mysticism, noticed the synaesthetic quality of Hildegard's visions and described her inspiration as a kind of "intellectual downpour," comparable to that experienced by her countryman and kindred spirit Jakob Boehme (1575–1624).[50] At the height of the psychedelic era, Kent Kraft compared the seer's visions with reports of mescalin hallucinations, using the theories of Timothy Leary to account for what he took to be parallel psychosomatic processes.[51] But this hypothesis has won few adherents.

Since the early twentieth century a growing number of scholars have ascribed Hildegard's visions, or at least the physical aspect of them, to migraine. Charles Singer, a historian of science, long ago pointed out that the classical migraine aura can produce disturbances of the visual field ("scintillating scotomata") much like what Hildegard experienced in her visions of shimmering lights, falling stars, and "fortification figures," perceived by her as the crenellated walls and turrets common in Romanesque architecture.[52] Moreover, in describing her chronic illnesses, she mentions symptoms like temporary blindness and an oppressive, paralyzing sense of heaviness, which would be consistent with severe migraine attacks. Yet by no means all of her visions fit the model of migraine auras, nor would such a diagnosis account for the *constant* presence of the "shadow of the Living Light." Whether or not Hildegard had migraine—and it seems plausible that she did—that condition no more "explains" her prophetic vocation than Dostoevsky's epilepsy explains his literary genius (even if he wrote brilliantly about the disorder in *The Idiot*). We may come closest to Hildegard's experience if we understand her discrete "visions" as incidental to her overarching "vision," and in that respect, she recalls William Blake.[53] The eighteenth-century maverick had in common with Hildegard a powerful and distinctive sense of the divine, coupled with a prophetic outrage against evil (especially the evil in religious institutions). In addition, both had a penchant for constructing dense and difficult mythopoeic systems, and both conveyed their vision in a more accessible way through lyrics as well as brilliantly painted images that could not possibly be mistaken for the work of any other.

With the loyal assistance of Volmar, Hildegard continued to labor at her *Scivias* until 1146 or 1147. At that time the fiery St. Bernard, Cistercian abbot of Clairvaux, undertook a preaching tour to promote the Second Crusade against Islam, and his travels eventually brought him to the Rhineland.[54] There his preaching was received with adulation as throngs gathered to witness miraculous cures. Among his many admirers was Hildegard, who not only endorsed the crusading effort but wistfully contrasted her own timidity ("wretched and more than wretched in the name of woman") with the abbot's bold courage ("like an eagle gazing straight into the sun"). In the first of several hundred letters ascribed to her, she confided to Bernard the whole story of her visions, seeking his consolation and advice. The abbot responded briefly but to the point, urging Hildegard to "rejoice in the grace of God" she had received, though with all humility, and to pray for his sinful self.[55] About a year later "the grace of God" brought Bernard along with his former disciple, Pope Eugene III, to the Rhineland city of Trier for a synod of bishops (November 1147–February 1148). It was this meeting that would set the apostolic seal of approval on Hildegard's visions. In the intervening years the ambitious Henry, archbishop of Mainz, had learned of her revelations from Abbot Kuno, and—perhaps sensing a means to enhance the prestige of his diocese—saw fit to raise the matter with the assembled prelates.

Pope Eugene, guided by Bernard of Clairvaux, advanced the reforming agenda of the late-eleventh-century popes by doing all he could to centralize and consolidate papal authority. In particular, he responded to the perceived threat of heresy by undertaking to investigate and pass judgment on potentially controversial books of theology.[56] Informed of Hildegard's revelations, therefore, he appointed a papal commission to visit her at the Disibodenberg and secure a manuscript of the still unfinished *Scivias*. Having attained the book, as the seer herself says, the pope "had it read before many and himself read from it," whereupon he sent her a letter "commanding" her to continue recording her visions. Godfrey expands on this account: "The pope commanded the blessed Hildegard's writings to be brought to him . . . and, taking them up with his own hands, he himself read publicly in lieu of a reciter before the archbishop, the cardinals, and all the clergy who were present . . . and stirred the minds and voices of all to rejoicing and praise of the Creator." Bernard too is said to have spoken out in the seer's favor.[57] No doubt the prelates were motivated in part by the staunch orthodoxy of the *Scivias*, in which Hildegard stresses precisely those doctrines, such as the divine origin of marriage, the sanctity of the Eucharist, and the dignity of the priesthood, that the Cathars most vehemently denied.

About sixty years later Cardinal Jacques de Vitry would similarly promote the cult of another holy woman, Marie of Oignies, because he saw her and the movement she represented as a bastion of orthodox fervor against the growing allure of heresy.[58]

For Hildegard's nuns at St. Disibod, the papal validation came as a mixed blessing. Word of the pope's decree traveled fast, making Hildegard a celebrity and spreading her fame throughout Europe. In the twelve years since Jutta's death the community had grown to include eighteen or twenty women, who had brought with them rich dowries and donations, and the number of pilgrims had multiplied. For Kuno and the monks the now celebrated visionary nun represented both a material and a spiritual asset, perhaps even rivaling the cult of the sainted Jutta. But for Hildegard herself, dependence on the men's community was beginning to rankle. The nuns' living conditions were increasingly crowded, while their wealth remained firmly under the abbot's control. Perhaps the visionary felt a need for spiritual as well as financial independence in order to grow into the fullness of her talents. In any case, sometime in 1148 she received a new revelation declaring that she and her "girls" must move to their own house, which she was called to establish on Mount St. Rupert. But this unexpected vision was hardly received with joy. Many of the nuns, their families, and their patrons objected to the hardship and poverty such a move would entail, while Kuno was livid at the prospect of the nuns' secession. In this spiritual emergency Hildegard took once again to her bed, this time with a paralyzing illness. According to her memoirs, she was unable to rise or work until the resistance to God's call had been overcome, while according to Godfrey the outcome was settled by a miracle. Kuno, says the *Vita*, physically tried to lift the ailing seer from her bed but, finding her "like a stony rock," acknowledged that she was suffering no human illness but a divine chastisement, and he grudgingly released her to depart.[59]

In the meantime, Hildegard had been busily negotiating to buy the Rupertsberg land, which she secured with the help of Henry of Mainz and her most important patron, the marchioness Richardis of Stade. This noblewoman, the scion of an exalted Saxon family, was a cousin of Jutta of Sponheim and mother of Hildegard's favorite nun, likewise named Richardis.[60] Only a few years after the move, however, Hildegard would pay the cost of such lofty patronage. For a time all had gone uncommonly well for her. Title to the land was gained, detractors were gradually won over, and in 1150 she and her nuns left St. Disibod for their new home, making an epic journey that she would later compare to the exodus of Israel from Egypt. By 1151 the *Scivias* was at last complete, its decade-long composition delayed by the tumultuous move. But in the same year an unexpected blow fell as if from heaven. Archbishop Hartwig of Bremen, son of the marchioness and brother of Hildegard's protégée Richardis, invited his sister to accept the vacant post of abbess at the aristocratic nunnery of Bassum, far to the north. Humanly, spiritually, and politically, Hildegard felt crushed by the "defection" of her favorite. In a frantic letter-writing campaign that would extend all the way to Pope Eugene, she tried in vain to quash the election, charging with some plausibility that it was motivated by family politics rather than the will of God and even hinting darkly at simony.[61] Perhaps she also begrudged the younger but more highborn woman the title of "abbess," a dignity Hildegard herself coveted but could not attain, given the newness of her foundation.[62]

To Richardis herself, however, Hildegard wrote in an exceptionally candid and intimate mode, voicing all the passion of a bereft lover. "Woe is me, your mother, woe is me, daughter—why have you abandoned me like an orphan? I loved the nobility of your conduct, your wisdom and chastity, your soul and the whole of your life, so much that many said: What are you doing?" Her overpowering love for Richardis contrasts tellingly with the proper but much cooler sentiment she expressed in her commendation of Jutta. In thus revealing the depths of her soul, Hildegard shows for once the human face behind the "trumpet of the Living Light."[63] At the same time she affords an early glimpse into the kind of chaste but troubled, intensely erotic bond between nuns that later spiritual directors would call "particular friendship"—and sternly forbid.[64] In the event, the Richardis affair had a tragic dénouement. Hildegard's pleading persuaded the young abbess to return to Bingen, if only for a visit, but she was carried off by a sudden fever in 1152 before she could do so. The bereft Hildegard consoled herself with the thought that God, the true lover of virgins, had taken Richardis for himself before her beauty could be corrupted by the world. Not long afterward Hildegard paid her daughter a last memorable tribute in her play, the *Ordo virtutum* (play of virtues), where the character Chastity proclaims: "O Virginity, you stand in the royal bridal chamber. How tenderly you burn in the King's embraces when the sun shines through you, so that your noble flower shall never wilt!"[65]

The death of Richardis was the first of several losses Hildegard experienced around this time. In 1153 both Pope Eugene and St. Bernard

died, as did her patron Henry of Mainz, after being deposed for embez-
zling—despite her last-ditch attempts to intercede for clemency on his
behalf.[66] Closer to home Hildegard was embroiled in a long struggle
with the monks of St. Disibod over possession of the endowments, primarily land holdings, which had been donated on profession of her
nuns. Visiting the Disibodenberg in 1155, she threatened a dying Kuno
in God's name, announcing that if the monks continued to withhold the
women's property they were "the worst of robbers," and if they recalled Volmar to his abbey—evidently another point of contention—
they would be "sons of Belial."[67] Hildegard later reported this embassy
to her daughters as a great success, but it should be noted that she did
not get quite everything she wanted. Her declaration of independence
required not only prophetic denunciations but also a substantial payment in cash,[68] and throughout her lifetime she remained officially subject to the abbot of St. Disibod. Not until the thirteenth century did the
decline of that community enable her successors to claim the title of
abbess.

In the meantime Hildegard had much work to do to establish the
Rupertsberg on a firm monastic footing. On the practical side there was
constant construction to supervise; on the spiritual, the nuns' liturgical
life required care and nurture. Hildegard may have composed her *Ordo
virtutum,* a drama of the pilgrim soul's progress from the buoyancy of a
youthful conversion, through temptation and sin, to a sadder but wiser
maturity and a final triumph over Satan, as a festival play for the profession of novices, of whom she had many.[69] By the end of her life her
monastery housed up to fifty nuns. But since their patron was St. Rupert, an obscure ninth-century nobleman rather than some great apos-
tle, Hildegard first needed to revive his long-forgotten cult, for a
monastery required strong patrons both on earth and in heaven. She attended to this need by writing a hagiographic life of Rupert[70] as well as
a stunning musical sequence and a series of antiphons for his feast day.
These liturgical pieces were only a few of more than seventy that she
eventually gathered in her song cycle under the title *Symphony of the
Harmony of Celestial Revelations.*[71]

While the arrangement of liturgical music in cycles was not altogether new, as a generic device it was gaining renewed popularity in
Hildegard's lifetime. Abelard had assembled such a cycle for the use of
Heloise's nuns at the Paraclete, and the canon Adam of St.-Victor composed another.[72] In a departure from common practice, however, Hildegard did not follow the procedure of *contrafactura,* setting new words

to existing melodies or composing tunes that could be sung with a variety of lyrics. Instead, all of her pieces combine words and melody to form inseparable wholes. They are exceptional in other ways as well. For instance, to consider only their formal properties, Hildegard wrote her lyrics in Latin "free verse" rather than in classical quantitative meters or the newly fashionable rhymed stanzas, and her melodies are considerably more rhapsodic and wide-ranging than traditional Gregorian chant.[73] She always maintained that her musical gift, like her visions and her understanding of Scripture, came to her "without any human instruction": she recorded the songs and taught them to her nuns just as she had heard them sung by celestial voices.

Aside from praying the Divine Office, reading and copying books, and providing for their material needs, the Rupertsberg nuns would have maintained a hospice for their many guests and pilgrims, perhaps including an infirmary for the sick. Most ordinary health care in the twelfth century was provided by men's and women's monasteries, along with village healers and herbalists. Although some men acquired professional training at medical schools, like the famous one at Salerno, the treatment provided by such physicians was accessible only to the rich. Monasteries, however, not only offered hospitality to all but held out hope of both natural and supernatural healing. Pilgrims who came to venerate the tombs and relics of saints, praying for miraculous cures, might at the same time benefit from nursing care and treatment offered by the religious.[74] Monks and nuns dispensed remedies based on a core of medical knowledge handed down from Greco-Roman antiquity, augmented by centuries of practice but limited by the local availability of herbs. As mistress of the Rupertsberg, Hildegard took an ardent interest in healing. No doubt she was prompted by the suffering of pilgrims, as well as by her own chronic ill health, to investigate the wholesome and toxic properties of plants, animals, gemstones, foods and beverages, and other aspects of her environment. But while her scientific and medical writings are extensive, they differ from her other books in that they have probably not come down to us in the form she intended.[75]

Hildegard notes in the preface to her *Liber vite meritorum* (1158), where she lists her previous books, that she had recently completed one with the intriguing title of *Subtilitates diversarum naturarum creaturarum* (*Subtleties of the Different Natures of Creatures*). The *Vita* mentions a work with a similar title. Typically Hildegardian is this concentration on the intricacies and providential uses of God's creation. Yet what the surviving manuscripts transmit is not this book but two others, one called *Physica* or *Liber simplicis medicinae* (*Book of Simple Medicine*), the other entitled *Liber compositae medicinae* (*Book of Compound Medicine*) or *Causae et curae* (*Causes and Cures*).[76] One controversial explanation is that copyists, sometime in the late twelfth or early thirteenth century, may have lifted materials from Hildegard's original book and arranged them in separate compilations corresponding to established genres of medical writing.[77] "Simples" were remedies employing a single ingredient, such as an herb, mineral, or animal part, whereas "compound medicine" dealt in recipes concocted from numerous ingredients, many of them exotic or hard to procure. The *Book of Simple Medicine* describes the physical properties of an enormous number of items, ranging from rye bread and beer to elephants to rubies, in nine encyclopedic sections. Not all of this material is intended for practical use; much of it attests to learning gleaned from books, personal observation, and, above all, Hildegard's all-encompassing fascination with the cosmos as the work of God.[78] In *Causes and Cures,* however, therapeutic needs come to the fore. Here the material is organized not by ingredients but by diseases, arranged according to the parts of the body they afflict. The book is nonetheless something of a hodgepodge, interspersing the medical portions with remarkable but disorganized material on human sexuality, the fall of Adam and Eve, male and female personality types,[79] musings on the weather and the planets, and even lunar horoscopes. The thirteenth-century compiler or copyist of *Causes and Cures* was more concerned with the usefulness of his text than with its "authenticity," and it is possible (though not certain) that he inserted material from a variety of authors. Conversely, excerpts from Hildegard's known medical writings have begun to surface in a few other medieval compilations.[80] Much textual scholarship remains to be done, therefore, before this aspect of her work is fully understood.

Hildegard's writing in the mid-1150s can be seen as a vast, multifaceted work of celebration. In the *Symphonia* she celebrated the Trinity, the Virgin Mary, and the saints; in the *Play of Virtues,* the spiritual triumph of virginity; in the *Life of St. Rupert,* her patron saint and, by extension, her own community; in the *Subtleties,* the wonders of the natural world. She also found time for a more mysterious project, her so-called *Lingua ignota* (*Unknown Language*)—a glossary of about a thousand imaginary nouns, complete with their own "secret alphabet" (*litterae ignotae*). No one knows precisely what Hildegard meant to do with this language. It may have been an attempt to reproduce the pure, virginal tongue spoken by Adam and Eve in paradise, thus a kind of sacred game, a quirky and playful way to heighten the camaraderie of her nuns.[81] For twelfth-century monks the exchange of letters of friendship, composed in the urbane and elegant Latin of the schools, served a similar purpose,[82] but Hildegard had quite literally to forge her own language. By 1158–1159, however, she had moved into a darker and more urgent phase of her career: the confrontation with personal and systemic evil.

As abbess in all but name, Hildegard bore full responsibility for the spiritual growth and discipline of her daughters. But we must not imagine the Rupertsberg under her direction as an idyll of harmonious sisterhood. To be sure, twelfth-century monastic writers sometimes called the cloister a "paradise of delights," but they also called it a prison, a military training camp, and a purgatory.[83] Women might enter nunneries for several reasons other than sheer devotion, among them parental vows, the companionship of their female kin, lack of a dowry sufficient to marry well, desire to escape marriage altogether, a thirst for learning, a disability, a secure retirement home in old age.[84] But once there, they were sworn in principle to constant warfare against the world, the flesh, and the devil. Temptations lay in wait around every corner, and even in the cloister salvation was not automatic but had to be earned by heroic struggle. In her *Scivias* Hildegard had given pride of place to the Virtues, a troupe of allegorical virgins whom she envisioned in radiant beauty and resplendent apparel, first deploying them along the pillars and ramparts of what she called the "Edifice of Salvation," later bringing them onstage to be enfleshed by her women in the *Ordo virtutum*. But Chastity, Charity, Humility, and the rest were not mere personifications for Hildegard, though similar characters appear in countless medieval allegories. She perceived them rather as living emanations of the Divine, powerful energies streaming down from God to animate human moral striving. The Virtues are both a choir of celestial beings and an army massed against Satan.[85]

In the second volume of her trilogy, the *Book of Life's Merits* (written 1158–1163), Hildegard directed her vision to the devil's side and gave form and voice to the Vices.[86] In medieval literary tradition, all virtues and vices were conventionally female, chiefly because the abstract Latin nouns that designate them are feminine in gender. Hildegard departed from this convention so as to avoid demeaning representations of women, instead portraying her Vices as grotesque, parodic creatures, part human and part animal, to make sin as ugly as possible. Yet the brilliance of the work lies in their seductive speeches, since the business of the Vices is to make sin attractive. In a sequence of debates where the alluring, self-excusing, or whining Vices are rebutted by the sober, undeceived Virtues of the *Scivias,* Hildegard dramatizes her conviction that self-knowledge, or what Genesis calls "the knowledge of good and evil," is the root of moral discernment and right action.[87] The overall tone of this book is austere, even somber, reflecting Hildegard's experience and realism as a spiritual director, and it is quintessentially monastic. Even its construction in brief, self-contained snippets suggests that Hildegard meant it to be used for reading in chapter or as an edifying text to accompany the otherwise silent meals of monks or nuns in their refectory. Evidence from the 1170s indicates that it was in fact used this way by the monks in two Belgian monasteries, Gembloux and Villers, where the mistress of Rupertsberg was highly esteemed.[88]

Beyond its dramatized ethical instruction, the *Book of Life's Merits* has another dimension. Along with the centralization of papal power, twelfth-century clerical reformers concerned themselves increasingly with the pastoral care and thoroughgoing conversion of the laity. One aspect of this reform was a continuing struggle to take marriage out of the hands of parents and establish it firmly as part of the church's sacramental system, with all matrimonial disputes and impediments to come under the jurisdiction of canon law. Another closely related development was the rapid expansion of the penitential system, culminating in the decree of the Fourth Lateran Council (1215) that every Christian must confess his or her sins privately to a priest and receive Communion at least once a year. The pastoral genre of confessors' manuals supplied priests with detailed guides on how to interrogate penitents about the nature and severity of their sins, after which they were to assign an appropriate penance for each.[89] The *Book of Life's Merits* has much in common with such manuals, for Hildegard recommends the proper remedies of prayer, fasting, almsgiving, and more stringent penances (like the wearing of hairshirts) to atone for every sin she describes. If a sinner should die repentant but without completing the necessary penance on earth, he or she would have to pay a debt to God in purgatory before attaining the purity of soul required to enter heaven.[90] In the *Book of Life's Merits* Hildegard was among the first authors to give a detailed account not only of the specific torments of purgatory (envisioned as a lake of fire or a stinking, oozing marsh) but also of their theological rationale.[91] Her promotion of all aspects of the penitential system—careful and thorough instruction about sins, auricular confession, penance, and purgatory—shows once again that she was no rebel but a staunch ally of the Gregorian reform movement.

Zealous clerics often defined their aim as "reform of the church in head and members," a total purification of Christ's body from the pope down to the meanest peasant. More visible than the gradual reform of the members was the intense controversy that swirled around the head. Hildegard, no stranger to politics, noted darkly on a few occasions that she had been born "in an effeminate age" under the reign of "a certain tyrant," by whom she meant the German king (or Holy Roman Emperor) Henry IV.[92] Henry had been locked at the time in a relentless struggle with Pope Urban II over investiture, the right to appoint (and thus dominate) the powerful prince-bishops of the empire. This controversy and the warfare it generated were ostensibly ended by the Concordat of Worms in 1122, an agreement whereby bishops would be canonically elected and invested by the pope with ring and staff (symbols of their spiritual office), while emperors retained the right to intervene in disputed elections and to invest bishops with their "regalia" (symbols of their secular, feudal role as barons of the realm). The compromise was inherently unstable, however, since the prelates' political allegiance to the empire remained in conflict with their ecclesiastical obedience as long as emperors and popes continued to struggle for dominance.[93] Strong emperors tried to control the papacy itself by naming "antipopes" of their own choosing to that office, while "legitimate" popes retaliated by excommunicating emperors and appointing "antikings." One of the longest and bitterest of these schisms broke out in 1159, when Frederick Barbarossa challenged Pope Alexander III by supporting the election as antipope first of Victor IV, then of two successors on his death.[94]

Soon after Frederick's coronation in 1152 he had summoned Hildegard to an audience at his palace of Ingelheim, not far from the Rupertsberg, where he apparently asked her to prophesy the fortunes of his reign.[95] Its beginning looked promising indeed, as Frederick successfully mustered his royal authority to quell private warfare in Germany, but his imperial ambitions in Italy soon stirred up even greater strife, and he proved himself determined to regain control of the German episcopacy. From Hildegard's papalist viewpoint, the subservience of the emperor's bishops was as bad as the Roman schism itself. While the mighty prelates of Cologne, Mainz, and Trier engaged in political intrigues, supported Frederick's Italian wars, and amassed land and riches for their personal aggrandizement, the church as Hildegard saw it suffered persecution from within. Christ's beleaguered bride appeared to her in grave distress, like a virgin threatened with rape: her face spattered with dust, her silken robe in tatters, her shoes mired with grime.[96] The apocalyptic symbol carried an all too obvious meaning. In defiance of the reformers' agenda, priests deprived of their right to marry were taking concubines instead; ecclesiastical offices were freely bought and sold (the sin of simony); greedy prince-bishops neglected the task of preaching; and the most fervent laity, disgusted with clerical corruption, threw off the dust of the Catholic church and flocked to join the impressively chaste, ascetic Cathars. These religious dissidents were dualists who rejected the material world and the body as creations of an evil god, whom they renounced by abstaining from procreation, following a strict vegetarian diet, and, ideally, ending their lives in a sacramental act of self-starvation.[97]

It is in this context that we must understand both Hildegard's correspondence and her extraordinary preaching. Like her protégée and fellow prophet Elisabeth of Schönau, Hildegard urged vigorous pastoral action against the Cathars and denounced them in visions and sermons, not long before several were burned alive at Cologne in August 1163.[98] Recognizing that the dissident movement profited from the chaos of the Catholic church, she blamed the rapid spread of heresy chiefly on negligent prelates. Thus she broke with, even threatened, Barbarossa for persisting in his schismatic policies, and in a flood of letters she tirelessly harangued the bishops themselves, exhorting them to fairness and vigilance in pastoral care, warning them against schism and heresy, reminding them of their duty to obey God rather than man, and calling them sternly to judgment. Although her visionary and allegorical language is often obscure, the dominant message comes through clearly enough. Hildegard's public sermons, especially the ones she preached at Trier (Pentecost 1160) and Cologne (1163), represent the apex of her prophetic politics.[99] Using the mysterious, highly charged imagery of the apocalypse, and speaking at times in the awesome first person for God, she summoned up remembrance of all his mighty deeds—the wonders of creation, the lessons of sacred history, the shedding of Christ's blood—only to highlight the enormity of the clerics' betrayal. Like the final portions of the *Scivias* and of her last book, the *Liber divinorum operum* (*Book of Divine Works*), these sermons prophesy disaster, including anticlerical riots and secular confiscation of the church's wealth, if prelates failed to repent while they still had time. Of all her multifarious writings, it was Hildegard's apocalyptic prophecies that made the keenest impression on her age and held the longest gaze of posterity.[100]

Perhaps most astonishing of all is the response of the very prelates she attacked so vehemently. Not only did they fail to invoke St. Paul's authority against her, as one might have expected ("I permit no woman to teach or to have authority over men; she is to keep silent")[101] but they actually *invited* her to preach and then wrote to her afterward, begging for transcripts of her sermons. Although the texts come down to us in Latin, we do not know what language Hildegard actually used. If she did preach in the learned tongue it may have helped to ensure her safety, since the use of Latin would have aimed her critique straight at its clerical targets without stirring up the dangerous hornets' nest of lay anticlericalism. The monk Caesarius of Heisterbach, writing around 1225, records that Hildegard preached her solemn anti-Cathar sermon to the priests of Cologne in Latin. Yet she may well have preached in German when she addressed mixed audiences of clergy and laity.[102] The evidence is inconclusive because sermons delivered in the vernacular were frequently taken down in shorthand, to be polished after the event and set down for posterity in Latin.

But the majority of Hildegard's sermons and letters were directed to a different audience—her fellow monastic superiors. While the twelfth century is often regarded as a golden age of monasticism, it was an age rife with conflict on that front as well. New monastic orders, especially the Cistercians under the magnetic leadership of Bernard of Clairvaux, challenged the more solidly entrenched Benedictines by their emphasis on poverty, fasting, manual labor, and stricter observance of the Benedictine Rule. Other reformers experimented with new forms of collaboration between religious women and men, to the scandal of purists like Bernard, who felt certain the reformers were playing into the devil's hands because it was easier to raise the dead than to be always with a woman and not have intercourse.[103] Wandering hermits and itinerant preachers took up the siren call of the "apostolic life," aiming at a literal imitation of Jesus and his earliest disciples—an ideal that would culminate with the founding of the Franciscan and Dominican orders in the early thirteenth century.[104] In contrast to these movements, Hildegard's foundation preserved the aristocratic character of the traditional "black monks," or Benedictines, an order that had long been enmeshed in the feudal alliances and family strategies of the German nobility. Her unabashed sense of class superiority can be shocking to more democratic sensibilities, and it even shocked some of her contemporaries.

When a fellow *magistra,* Tenxwind of Andernach, questioned the luxurious attire of Hildegard's nuns and challenged her practice of accepting only noble, wealthy girls into her community, reminding her that Jesus chose humble fishermen, Hildegard was not in the least apologetic. God loved all his children regardless of rank, she replied, but people of different social classes could not possibly live together without rancor and envy, any more than sheep, goats, and cattle could be herded into a single barn.[105]

This exchange, though understandably famous, is not typical of Hildegard's monastic epistles. More often, she advanced the cause of moderate reform and played the role of peacemaker in squabbling communities. This portion of her correspondence opens a revealing window onto the inner life of twelfth-century monasticism, less idealized than the picture conveyed by the glowing treatises of St. Bernard and his confreres on the love of God. In some houses, we learn, ambitious members schemed to be elected superior, while in others, harried abbesses and weak abbots yearned to lay down the burdens of office, dreaming of a quiet hermitage or an invigorating pilgrimage to Rome. In one community discipline might be lax and worship slipshod, with individuals doing just as they pleased, while in another the superior imposed a regimen so harsh that the community revolted. Writing to her fellow monastic leaders, Hildegard urged discretion on some, renewed zeal on others, using biblical exegesis, analogies from nature, and home-grown parables to drive home her points. Many of these letters either preceded or followed personal visits, during which Hildegard probably preached in the chapterhouse or chapel as well as meeting individually with the leaders. By using local monastic archives to determine the regnal years of abbots and abbesses, it is possible to date most of the exchanges roughly and thus to construct a chronology of Hildegard's preaching tours. Beginning in 1158 at the age of sixty, she made four such excursions, the first three mainly by boat along Germany's great rivers—the Main, the Moselle, and the Rhine—and the fourth, a more arduous overland journey in Swabia, when she was well into her seventies.[106] Her health, never robust, deteriorated further with age but could not daunt her formidable spirit.

By the mid-1160s the Rupertsberg nuns had grown so numerous that Hildegard was able to found a daughterhouse at Eibingen across the Rhine. This second foundation is poorly documented, but on the basis of Hildegard's exchange with Tenxwind, some have speculated that its purpose was to house nuns of less exalted social rank. If so, democracy has had the last laugh, for the original Rupertsberg was destroyed by the Swedes in 1632 during the Thirty Years' War, but the monastery at Eibingen, today the Abbey of St. Hildegard, still stands. Although it was dissolved in 1814 with the sweeping secularization of the Napoleonic era, nuns returned to the site in 1907, and for most of the twentieth century the abbey has been a flourishing women's community as well as a center of scholarly research on Hildegard.[107]

One other incident of the 1160s casts an oblique light on the seer's fame. A young lady named Sigewize, native of Cologne, had been suffering for years from a hapless malady: she was possessed, or as Hildegard put it, "overshadowed" by a demon.[108] Like others with the same affliction, she was escorted from town to town by her kinsfolk, visiting the shrine of one saint after another in the hope of a miraculous cure. During an exorcism one day, Sigewize's demon taunted that he could only be cast out by an old woman named "Scrumpilgard," so the priest—it happened to be the abbot of Brauweiler—lost no time in addressing the sibyl of the Rhine. Hildegard, no doubt hoping to avoid a dangerous face-to-face meeting with the demoniac, responded by sending the abbot a theatrical ceremony of exorcism, with the roles of seven biblical characters to be played by seven priests, each pronouncing a different conjuration over the devil.[109] The Brauweiler monks duly performed the rite, but as the demon would not be vanquished so easily, there was nothing for it but to pack Sigewize off to the Rupertsberg, where the nuns welcomed her with mingled compassion and terror. There she remained throughout the season of Lent, 1169, as Hildegard organized a concerted campaign on her behalf, persuading monks, nuns, and layfolk alike to pray, fast, and give alms. In the meantime (for the devil can cite Scripture for his purpose), Sigewize regaled the populace by preaching, her sermons perhaps meant as parodies of Hildegard's own.[110] Finally, at the Easter Vigil when the priest solemnly consecrated the baptismal font, the devil "horribly departed through the woman's shameful parts, along with excrement." The grateful Sigewize, healed and in her right mind, would spend the rest of her short life as a novice at the Rupertsberg.

As for Hildegard, even the combined pressures of travel, ill health, and administration could not keep her long from intellectual work. The decade between 1163 and 1173 witnessed the composition of her last great volume, the *Book of Divine Works,* a masterful study of the harmonies between macrocosm and microcosm.[111] In this vision, the seer wrote in her memoirs, "I saw the height and depth and breadth of the firmament, and how the sun, moon, and stars are arranged in it." But she also saw how all of these are correlated with the proportions and functions of the human body, as well as with the subtle workings of God within the soul. The doctrine of "man the microcosm" animated humanistic thinking from antiquity through the Renaissance and is probably best known today from the famous drawing by Leonardo da Vinci showing a nude, perfectly proportioned man with arms outstretched in the center of a circle. Several of the dazzling illuminations in Hildegard's *Book of Divine Works* are similar, except that just as the human being straddles the cosmos, the universe in its turn is embraced by an enormous, overarching figure of Divinity.[112] This is not God the Father but a flaming winged figure who identifies herself as *Caritas*—Charity or Love—and proclaims:

> I am the supreme and fiery force that kindled every living spark, and I breathed forth no deadly thing . . . And I am the fiery life of the essence of God: I flame above the beauty of the fields; I shine in the waters; I burn in the sun, the moon, and the stars . . . I also am Reason. Mine is the blast of the resounding Word through which all creation came to be, and I quickened all things with my breath so that not one of them is mortal in its kind; for I am Life.[113]

In structure the *Book of Divine Works* continues the pattern established in the *Scivias* and the *Book of Life's Merits,* their common form marking the three works, though disparate in subject, as a unified trilogy. Hildegard begins each major section by introducing a new vision, using a direct experiential formula redolent of the biblical prophets: "And I saw." She then presents the visionary scene in vivid, painterly detail, complete with colors and proportions. If figures such as Virtues or Vices appear, their symbolic attire is described and they make speeches disclosing their essence. After completing the visual portion of her text, which may be far from self-explanatory, the seer marks a transition into the much longer didactic and allegorical portion with words such as, "I heard a voice from heaven saying to me." This "voice," seldom further identified, goes on to gloss each detail of the vision, including the speeches of the dramatis personae; it repeats the earlier descriptions verbatim but adds lengthy explanations. Thus the initial "vision" text plays the same role as a biblical text in a commentary: it is a peg on which the author hangs all the instruction she wants to give. While the visionary report is thus invested with a high degree of authority, Hildegard also feels free to add new material not adumbrated in the original description. Her "heavenly voice" sometimes appears to be the voice of God speaking in the first person (using expressions like "My Son Jesus Christ," for example), but such "prophetic" moments occur only sporadically in the text, where the third-person voice otherwise dominates. Not only is this form itself reminiscent of biblical exegesis but the visionary gloss is frequently interrupted by short exegetical sections, as Hildegard reaches for a scriptural verse to reinforce or amplify her point.[114]

Finally, each vision is brought to a close with a formulaic admonition to the reader. In book 3 of the *Scivias* we read: "Let the one who has ears sharp to hear inner meanings ardently love My reflection and pant after My words, and inscribe them in his soul and conscience." In the *Book of Life's Merits* the recurrent formula runs: "These things uttered about the souls of the penitent . . . are faithful; and let the faithful attend to them and gather them in the memory of good knowledge." The *Book of Divine Works* famously ends with a still more solemn warning: "Let no one be so bold as to add anything to the words of this book or delete anything from it, lest he himself be deleted from the book of life and all the beatitude under the sun. . . . Whoever presumes to do otherwise sins against the Holy Spirit, and will be forgiven neither here nor in the age to come."[115] This impressive threat (compare Revelation 22.18–19) may indeed have militated against the excerpting of Hildegard's works in florilegia, with the exception of one anthology of her apocalyptic prophecies compiled in 1220.[116] Aside from this extremely popular text, entitled *The Mirror of Future Times*, the seer's three theological volumes were seldom abridged and rarely copied, partly no doubt because of their daunting length. They survive in a comparatively small number of medieval manuscripts: ten for the *Scivias* (two of them lost in modern times), five for the *Book of Life's Merits,* and only four for the *Book of Divine Works.*

As Hildegard was preparing to make her final revisions of *Divine Works* in 1173 (and despite her claim to verbal inspiration, she revised meticulously),[117] the work came to a sudden and distressing standstill with the death of Volmar, her lifelong secretary and "only beloved son." Volmar's loss was a blow to the prophet in several ways. Aside from her personal grief, Hildegard had trouble persuading Helengar, then abbot of St. Disibod, to release the monk her nuns had elected to succeed Volmar as their provost, and once again she was compelled to appeal to the pope. While all women's monasteries required the regular assistance of at least one priest to say Mass and hear confessions, the needs at the Rupertsberg were far greater. The ailing Hildegard, now

seventy-five, with a community numbering fifty nuns plus assorted servants and laborers, badly needed administrative as well as secretarial
help. This time her appeal succeeded and for a brief time the nuns were
granted the services of Godfrey, who also began to compose Hildegard's *Vita*. Further assistance was supplied by two kinsmen, her
brother Hugh (who had been cantor of Mainz cathedral) and her
nephew Wezelin (provost of St. Andreas at Cologne). But Godfrey died
in 1176 and Hugh a year later, leaving the seer bereft once again. Fortunately, by this time she had become acquainted through letters with
Guibert, the French-speaking monk of Gembloux, in what is now Bel-
gium. We encountered Guibert earlier as a passionate inquirer into
Hildegard's visionary experience. Responding to her urgent invitation,
he traveled to the Rupertsberg in 1177 and formed a close friendship
with the aged seer, remaining there as secretary until 1180, several
months after her death. It is to Guibert's zeal that we owe Hildegard's
celebrated letter "on the manner of her visions" as well as his unfinished biography of her, several prolix epistles on her reputation and
conditions at the Rupertsberg late in her life,[118] and the project of
preserving all her writings (except her medical works) in a single enormous volume, the so-called *Riesenkodex,* or "giant book" of Wiesbaden.[119]

Even in her seventies, however, the former recluse turned woman of
affairs was not allowed to spend her declining years in peace and quiet.
Doubtless she was overjoyed to receive news of the long-desired end of
the Roman schism, when Barbarossa finally gave up his futile attempts
to control the papacy and made peace with Alexander III in the Treaty
of Venice (1177). But her own fame, as she had discovered many times,
was still a mixed blessing. Hildegard and Guibert had some mutual
friends among the Cistercian monks of Villers, near Gembloux. Like
many others, these monks thought of "the sibyl of the Rhine" as an oracle who could enable them to transcend the uncertainties of human
thought with direct messages from God. Accordingly, they presented
her through Guibert with a list of thirty-eight theological and exegetical
questions and proceeded to pester her without mercy for replies. The
lengthy correspondence between Villers and the Rupertsberg on this
subject makes for both comic and pathetic reading: the monks take an
alternately bullying and obsequious tone, while Hildegard pleads illness
but promises to do the best she can, and Guibert as go-between is torn
between the desperation of his mistress and the demands of his imperi-
ous friends. Ironically, the seer did complete at least perfunctory replies

to all thirty-eight questions before she died, but they were evidently "lost in the mail" so that the monks, for all their importuning, received no satisfaction.[120] The whole incident goes to show how tempting it was to manipulate a prophet's gifts: power-hungry schemers as well as the merely curious, like the Villers monks, all had designs on "the voice of the Living Light." Admittedly, Hildegard's own sometimes heavy-handed use of her prophetic persona could encourage this tendency.

The brouhaha over the Villers questions was but a minor nuisance compared to Hildegard's last great trial. When she founded the Rupertsberg nearly three decades before, she had been delighted that wealthy families coveted the privilege of burying their dead in her churchyard, making appropriate gifts to show their gratitude for the sisters' prayers. Such donations constituted a major source of revenue for all monastics. But one such burial caused Hildegard untold trouble. In 1178 a certain nobleman, whose identity is lost to us, was interred at the Rupertsberg. He had during his lifetime been excommunicated for some grave sin, also unknown, though reliable witnesses eventually proved the noble had been reconciled before his death and had received absolution along with the last rites of the church. But the canons of Mainz, in whose diocese the Rupertsberg lay, were apparently unaware that the anathema had been lifted. It is also possible that they cherished some implacable grievance either against Hildegard herself or against the dead man and his family. In any case, the canons demanded that she have the corpse exhumed as unworthy of burial in sacred ground, and speaking in the bishop's name, they threatened the Rupertsberg with an interdict if she did not comply. But since Hildegard was convinced that yielding to this request would mean inexcusable desecration of the body, she stood her ground, effacing all traces of the grave to prevent others from disturbing it and so incurring the prelates' sanction.[121]

An interdict, the heaviest penalty the church could impose, was a collective excommunication: as long as it lasted, the nuns could neither receive Communion nor sing the Divine Office, which they had to mutter *sotto voce*.[122] Hildegard, torn between her commitment to the deceased and her obedience to the church, obeyed the interdict while protesting it by every means at her disposal. It is significant that she objected to the silencing of chant even more vehemently than she did to loss of the sacrament. In fact, one of her most powerful (though in the event unsuccessful) pleas for release amounted to nothing less than a theology of music, an art that she described to the prelates of Mainz as a reminiscence of Eden and a foretaste of heaven. Before Adam's fall, she wrote, his holy voice had rung with "the sound of every harmony and the sweetness of the whole art of music. And if he had remained in the condition in which he was formed, human frailty could never endure the power and the resonance of that voice." Angels too exult in constant song, whereas Satan—the spirit of discord—"lured humankind away from the celestial harmony" and cannot bear the sound of music. So in silencing her nuns, Hildegard implied, the prelates were doing the devil's work and depriving God of his just praise, for which they would in turn be deprived of his company in heaven.[123] But the canons, unmoved by her threats and her eloquence alike, persevered until Hildegard's friend, Archbishop Philip of Cologne, intervened to produce witnesses who convincingly swore to the dead man's absolution. Thus the interdict was finally lifted, after still further setbacks, in March 1179. On September 17 of the same year, Hildegard herself "made a blessed passing to the celestial Bridegroom" while, as the *Vita* poetically adds, two rainbows crossed in the twilit sky, setting the whole of St. Rupert's Mount aglow with celestial fireworks.[124]

More than forty years earlier, when Jutta died, Hildegard and Abbot Kuno together had commissioned her *Vita*. In those days an authorized biography of some revered founder, along with a well-kept tomb and a community to record the miracles performed there, were sufficient to make a local saint. But in the intervening decades the papacy had centralized its control in yet another way by formalizing and bureaucratizing the process of canonization. To be sure, even in the later Middle Ages, papal canonization was a relative rarity, and the majority of "new saints" were simply venerated locally by people who lacked the clout, expertise, and money required to promote a cause in Rome.[125] Yet Hildegard's friends and daughters decided to make a formal bid for canonization, with every hope of success. After all, she had been a staunch supporter of Pope Alexander III, who still reigned at the time of her death; she numbered bishops and influential nobles among her friends; and she was undeniably famed for her prophetic gifts, her healing powers, and her unwavering defense of orthodoxy. Among the many steps her supporters took toward the goal were preparation of Hildegard's *Vita*, production of deluxe illuminated manuscripts of her *Scivias* and *Book of Divine Works*, encouragement of pilgrimage to her shrine, documentation of all the miracles ascribed to her in life and after death, composition of a hymn and liturgical lessons for her feast day, and embroidery of an altarcloth depicting her with the nimbus of a saint.[126]

Then as now, however, the cause unfolded at a most leisurely pace. Confident in the possession of eternity, Rome seldom hurries. By the time that Pope Gregory IX officially opened the canonization proceedings in 1227, almost half a century had passed since Hildegard's death and most of the witnesses who had known her were also dead. Despite the pope's personal support of her cause and the encouragement of his successor, no official decree of sainthood was ever forthcoming. There is no need to posit any dark political motive for this failure. Pope Gregory's stated reason was mere bureaucratic incompetence: as the commissioners' report lacked sufficient detail and precision in recording Hildegard's miracles, it was not possible to authenticate them, and by the mid-thirteenth century the cures had ceased. More significantly, though, only 50 percent of all canonization processes in the thirteenth century—or for that matter, the entire medieval period—issued in official sainthood. The success rate for women and for monastics was even lower, standing at 46 percent for each category; and between 1198 and 1461 not a single Benedictine nun was raised to the altar.[127] Clearly the politics of sainthood had shifted away from the old, established orders toward the Dominicans and Franciscans and, among women, toward the lay penitents who were closely connected with these orders. Under the circumstances, what is remarkable about Hildegard's cause is not that it failed but that it came so close.

Despite the absence of any papal decree, her cult continued unperturbed.[128] At least six thirteenth-century chronicles from Germany, France, and England refer to her as "St. Hildegard," and by 1324 the Rupertsberg nuns were able to procure from the Avignon papacy a decree of indulgence for pilgrims to her shrine. Several paintings and sculptures from the fifteenth century continue the tradition of representing her as a saint. In the sixteenth century her name was included in the widely used Roman martyrology of Baronius, guaranteeing her continued veneration. Finally, in 1940, the Vatican saintmakers (now called the Sacred Congregation) officially approved the celebration of her feast day in all German dioceses. As of this writing, there has still been no formal canonization, yet some have gone so far as to propose that Hildegard be named a "doctor of the Church" in recognition of her theological achievements—a distinction so far granted to only three women, Saints Catherine of Siena, Teresa of Avila, and recently Thérèse of Lisieux. There we may safely let the matter rest, for our business henceforth concerns not Hildegard's sainthood but the many dimensions of her life, work, and writing in the context of her times.

TWO

Abbess

"Mother and Teacher"

JOHN VAN ENGEN

Born into a free noble family at Bermersheim in 1098, Hildegard was pledged to the religious life at age eight and entrusted to the care of a recluse at fourteen. At age thirty-eight she succeeded Jutta of Sponheim as head of the women attached to St. Disibod. About age fifty-two she seceded with eighteen others to establish a house on Mount St. Rupert at Bingen, and fifteen years later she founded a daughter community at Eibingen across the Rhine; she served as abbess to both houses until her death in 1179. Reared in a noble household for fourteen years and trained as a recluse for twenty-four, Hildegard oversaw monastic women for forty-three years, ruling at the end some eighty nuns. Despite her fame as a visionary, Hildegard acted in her world fundamentally as an abbess. Though she spoke as the mouthpiece of the "Living Light," she understood herself as charged with the care of souls, in her own community and among Christians at large.

Those astonished at Hildegard as visionary and author, including the sisters in her own house, took for granted her role and status as an abbess. In the early 1170s the sisters feared that illness would take from them their "reverend lady, sweetest mother, most holy teacher, and true companion in the mysteries." They had the priest-secretary Volmar draft a letter expressing what would go missing once they no longer saw her each day. They named in order: her responses to people bringing queries, her novel interpretation of Scripture, her unusual melodies and songs, her new sermons on feast days, her insight into the status of the dead, and her peering into times past, present, and future.[1] But Hildegard responded to them as the "mother" they had "elected" and from her "motherly interior." She told her nuns first to remember how she had secured the house and its privileges and second, "after they could no longer suck at her breasts," to keep charity among themselves, stay in the house, and pursue what Benedict taught.[2] Facing death, she focused on their house as a hard-won institutional reality and on what she had imparted as a spiritual caregiver. Earlier too, in autobiographical passages, she had drawn attention to her actions as founder alongside her visionary experiences.[3]

This essay will treat Hildegard as abbess. The first part traces her gradual movement from recluse to head of community, then from subordinate prioress to independent abbess. I focus on those experiences and institutions that contributed to her making as an abbess. Part 2 examines the spiritual care she exercised as a mother and teacher. I draw on what Hildegard herself said about caregiving and especially on the spiritual counsel she offered others, from monks and nuns to abbots and bishops, including the pope himself.

THE MAKING OF AN ABBESS

In religious ideal and social practice monks ranked as the first order of society between the ninth and the mid-twelfth centuries. Women in that era, however, found few opportunities for monastic life, men's houses outnumbering theirs in most regions by more than ten to one. Since the ninth century monasteries had served society as centers of intercession for the living and the dead. That valued purpose was carried out most solemnly—and, it was thought, most effectively—by monk-priests saying Mass. Women religious could pray for family members and benefactors, and they did; but they could not offer up the divine sacrifice. Although contemporaries rarely spoke of women's roles comparatively, it seems that women were valued more as managers of households, mothers of children, and makers of alliances through marriage: acts only they could perform, as only priests could say Mass. To endow a religious house for women or to place a daughter or sister in a monastery represented a sheer gift, with little social or religious recompense. These houses were in consequence nearly all royal or noble foundations, their properties usually retained or overseen by powerful lay families. Women's foundations achieved no independence and produced little documentation, though their abbesses might rank as leaders in society. The women themselves came uniformly from the upper strata of society, whether they were placed in the monastery by families that could afford to make such a gift or sought monastic life in widowhood as a place of refuge or retirement.

Religious devotion and social fashion became inextricably mixed. Whatever the motives of founders or reformers and of those women who entered or were placed in nunneries, connections to the highest

nobility eased the austerities of monastic life. These women knew and
expected steady interaction with privileged relatives, material provi-
sioning of a kind that befitted a residence for ladies, and access to
education, even a mannered "finish." They were not surprised when
families occasionally insisted that they leave the monastery to marry.
Churchmen also believed women generally incapable of sustaining the
regime of fasting, prayer, and vigils imposed on monks, thus opening
the way to further accommodations for nuns. Compromise began with
the monastic rule, since in the early medieval West women lacked a distinctive norm for their religious lives. Most often they adapted the
Benedictine Rule. But in German imperial lands, going back to Carolingian times, the distinction between nuns and canonesses was often
blurred. In theory, nuns were pledged to poverty and to permanency
while canonesses could hold property and leave to marry. In practice,
whether female religious observed such distinctions or even recognized
them depended largely on local custom in their houses. The intervention of bishops or abbots and the attitudes of founding or supporting
families often counted for as much as the purposes of the abbess.[4]

Hildegard, tenth child of a lesser noble family, was bound to the religious life at age eight. Child oblation had provided most monks and
nuns for centuries, and in 1106 the parental act was still deemed irre-
versible. All evidence about her parents' act of dedication comes from
years later: Hildegard's own remarks sixty years afterward and the account of her secretary Guibert of Gembloux in 1177. At age eight her
parents offered her up "with sighs" in Hildegard's words, as a "tithe"
according to Guibert.[5] At age fourteen, on All Saints' Day 1112,[6] they
bound her over to the house of St. Disibod, roughly fifteen miles from
home, as a recluse subject to the spiritual formation of the young noblewoman Jutta. This crucial span of six years, often conflated in later reports, has confused historians.[7] Much is at stake here. As a noble girl
Hildegard remained connected to her familial household in some way
until they could locate a fitting situation. Hildegard thus recalled still
asking "her nursemaid" (*quadam nutrice mea*) about visions she experienced between her "third" and "fifteenth" years. On her reaching
marriageable age, however, as Guibert colorfully put it, "beasts of the
field" threatened to seize what her parents had destined (*mancipaue-
rant*) for religious life.[8] At adolescence they then found for her a holy
refuge and a social alliance. They asked that she be joined to the daughter of the ascendant Count Stephen of Sponheim, to become a recluse at
St. Disibod. These years at home made a difference, even if she was

early set apart in some way. Through her fourteenth year Hildegard experienced the life of a court and a village and ever after possessed an uncommon knowledge of court and family life as well as of nature, agriculture, and sexuality.

Jutta represented a different case, an emblem of the new way. Reformers wanted recruits who "chose" the religious life as "adults," meaning as marriageable adolescents aged fourteen to sixteen. Jutta of Sponheim was daughter and sister to a powerful comital family with expanding territories at the border between Trier and Mainz. Tutored as a child in Latin, she insisted on going her own way: dedicating herself to religious life at age twelve and taking the veil from the archbishop of Mainz against her family's wishes, placed with a religious widow named Uda of Göllheim for three years, then resisting propitious marriages as a teenager and begging to set off as a pilgrim. Her brother, with the help of Bishop Otto of Bamberg and the accompanying gift of an estate and its church, arranged for Jutta, in her twentieth year, to become attached to the regional and recently reformed house of St. Disibod.[9] The family thereby yielded to her adult will. Or, as Hildegard referred to this permanent commitment to chastity, they acknowledged publicly her "betrothal to Christ."

Hildegard, despite parental oblation, may have herself "consented" at age fourteen. In her forties this was her avowed teaching, bolstered perhaps by experience of noble daughters subjected to the religious life against their wills. Her position coincided with that of reformers and canon lawyers (that is, after the pioneering intervention of Gratian, author in the 1130s of the received textbook on church law). Parents who wished to offer their children to the Lord's service, she taught in her *Scivias*, should *promise*—that word suggesting the oblation ceremony itself—to care for them up to the age of reason, all the while exhorting their children to choose the religious life; then the parents should either hurriedly agree when the child consented or consider themselves unbound and blameless if she dissented.[10] Whether or not Hildegard's parents made such a promise or acted in this way, this passage seems to represent how she wished to remember her own transition out of the family household into life as a recluse. Hildegard later commented on the negative effects of coercion: To force children into religious life led "certainly," she noted, to their fleeing "in body or in mind."[11] A girl must want Christ as her "royal husband" over some propertied male. For any man to violate this pledge of chastity, always a risk for young noblewomen, meant, Hildegard declared bluntly, to "break open heaven."[12]

About life at St. Disibod in the twenty-four years during which Hildegard was formed in the religious life, fragmentary detail alone survives. This ecclesiastical site, built on a hill at the confluence of the Nahe and Glan rivers, originally served as a clerical outpost for the archdiocese of Mainz. In the midst of the investiture struggle, Archbishops Ruthard (1089–1109) and Adalbert (1111–1137) safeguarded it by establishing Benedictines there subject directly to them; the monks came from Mainz and Hirsau and the material support from noble allies.[13] During all of Jutta's years and most of Hildegard's, the site was steadily under construction, with regular visits by prelates and princes. In 1138 the tomb of Disibod was opened and an altar to Benedict dedicated just behind it; in 1143 the archbishop of Mainz finally dedicated the new church with its high altar and a marble tomb for Disibod.[14]

Where the women fit into this complex is not known, though later legend placed their space just off the joining point of the monks' choir and the south transept;[15] this suggests a position opposite the monks' cloister to the north. Jutta's family, wealthy and powerful enough to work their will at a house still in the making, had a "cell" built for their daughter. She and two or three other young women (including Hildegard), as it was told much later, were enclosed in this "prison" or "tomb" (*mausoleum*) far from the noisy clamor of lay people (*populari strepitu*). Their cell was a stone structure, with access sealed off except for a window through which they could receive food and at certain hours converse with others. There the women did battle with demonic forces and their own flesh, a battle that the slippery and inconstant nature of woman was commonly thought unable to endure.[16] In less flowery rhetoric the *Life of Jutta*, written by a monk at St. Disibod soon after her death in 1136, described a strict ascetic regime with devotion primarily to praying the Psalter and to contemplation. After Jutta's death at age forty-four, Hildegard, one of three allowed to prepare her body, saw the chain she had secretly worn and the three "grooves" it had cut into her body.[17]

These women were not isolated in reality, however withdrawn and meditative their lifestyle. People of all social classes, her monk-biographer proudly reports, streamed to Jutta as to an oracle of the spiritual life and sent her letters. Acting as a "Martha," she deemed it best not to avoid them but to pour out either the vinegary wine of correction or the oil of healing.[18] Other noble families, beyond Hildegard's, began to present their daughters as adults or oblates, along with gifts, and the community included at least seven more women by Jutta's death. The cell was expanded, in Guibert's rhetoric, to accommodate the "concourse" (*frequentiam*) of a monastery without losing the claustration of a tomb.[19] At her passing Jutta gave a sign to have the monks called and died while they sang litanies over her, her later biographer among them.[20] Jutta asked the abbot that she not be buried in "some sacred space" but in a place where she would be "daily trampled on by passersby"[21]—humility that hinted at her sense of the public. As a young religious, then, Hildegard observed in Jutta a paradigm for the oracular role she would herself play for more than thirty years. But Jutta's stature sprang from a self-imposed ascetic regime, Hildegard's from her experience of divine visions.

The prior at St. Disibod in the early 1150s, not long after Hildegard had left, recalled her early years there (1112–1136): how the monks had known her almost from the cradle, her rearing, education, way of life, her training in "women's work" and the Psalter.[22] Whatever the expectations of their families or of the monks (his reference to "women's work" hints plenty), these noblewomen sheltered at St. Disibod became a community, a *scola* in the words of Jutta's monk-biographer, echoing Benedict's "school of Christ."[23] Jutta instructed her "daughters" in religious practices (*instituta*), forming disciples "trained under her teaching" (*sub magisterio eius educatae*).[24] This Jutta, a person Hildegard described as "unlearned" (*indocta mulier me docuerat*) and as "never giving her body any peace,"[25] aimed not at "learning" but at "institutes" more single-mindedly ascetical. Hildegard herself learned Latin; that is, during those years she deepened a passive reading knowledge into a rough but rich dictational skill, apparently with the help of the monk-priest Volmar. From age fifteen to thirty-eight, in sum, Hildegard lived with other young noblewomen, first as a recluse, then in a communitarian religious regime that formed her ascetically (disciplining the body) and theologically (reading sermons and treatises), as part of a life dedicated to praying the psalms.

At Jutta's death, by the order of Abbot Kuno (1136–1155) and the request of her companions, Hildegard took over this *scola* as "prioress."[26] Whether or not Guibert's title was accurate, Hildegard was subject to the abbot and the women to her. In this setting, neither a full double monastery nor a women's house with an abbess, she learned spiritual leadership. What Guibert praised at Mount St. Rupert in 1177, he ascribed to these early years (1136–1147) at St. Disibod. Hildegard subjected her body to her spirit and proved most austere with herself. With her companions she acted more compassionately according to their needs and limits. Whether Guibert here echoed standard teaching or whether Hildegard perpetuated Jutta's model, one trait anticipated a theme in her own later letters. She oversaw a form of religion, Guibert claims, that was severe without being onerous or insupportable. She admonished and patiently tolerated but did not cut off or bitterly reproach those who rebelled against even this less punishing form of life.[27] Hildegard apparently set aside Jutta's ascetic athleticism but remained intent on forming a community that was spiritual, not social, in purpose.

Yet there was a decidedly social dimension to this religious life. On this front Hildegard moved from an informal arrangement to an enforced stance. Her community increased to eighteen or so, all of them, like Jutta and herself, from noble families. Beyond Hiltrud, a niece of Jutta, the most significant was Richardis, also a relative of Jutta's and daughter to the countess of Stade in Saxony; she became Hildegard's trusted and beloved companion. By about 1140 lords and ladies of nearly equal rank, linked by familial and regional networks, were placing their daughters in this "cell," itself attached to a reformed monastery protected by the archbishop of Mainz. By the later 1140s rumors were rife. Tenxwind of Andernach, a reforming canoness devoted to the new poverty like her Augustinian brother Richard of Springiersbach and connected mostly to ministerials and town burghers, noted the growing fame of Hildegard's community, but snidely. She questioned her practice of allowing only nobles to join, even refusing nonnoble women. Hildegard coolly defended this policy as congruent with God's ordering of the world, drawing on a rural analogy: "Oxen, asses, and sheep are not kept in the same stable." Such separation was necessary for the maintenance of good order, since otherwise nonnobles might join merely out of vainglory or the noble women might sniff at their inferiors.[28] Hildegard thus retained in her community, now as a matter of divine order, the earlier conjunction between nobility and women in monastic life. In an early song, written in this period, she identified apostles as the "noble people of the Savior."[29]

For her noble companions Hildegard began to devise special observances—known in part from Tenxwind's biting critique, thus matters of public knowledge. She endowed her virgin band, handpicked noble servants of the Lord, with special garb, rituals, and songs. While at St. Disibod she began to write original songs and melodies for her women to sing, additions to the Psalter and office. They sang of blessed virgins as noble persons in whom God the King foresaw all celestial beauty.[30] They sang of themselves as "heirs to the Lion, lords in his service between choir and altar." They "discharged their duty to the Lamb" by "singing praises like the angels" and "aiding the people with their presence."[31] Their presence at St. Disibod attracted increased attention for more than the proffered prayers. On feast days Hildegard had the sisters go to church praying the psalms and wearing golden crowns with an emblem of the lamb of God on the front, golden rings on their fingers, and white silken veils that reached to the floor; and they left their hair unbound. Tenxwind's sisters, by contrast, would have had their hair tied up under short black veils. For this eccentric, privileged observance, probably linked to receiving their Lord in Communion, Hildegard defiantly offered theological justification. Virgins, she explained, were not subject to a man, unlike their married counterparts, so the full vitality of each of their selves as manifest in their hair (their "greenness") remained within their own wills. They might choose to cover their hair in humility or to uncover it when they went as brides to meet their Spouse.[32] In retrospect, the new community at St. Disibod, growing out of an informal arrangement for recluses with ties to the local nobility, with the indulgence of her abbot, allowed Hildegard to conceive and put in place a highly personal conception of religious observance.

Roughly a decade into her leadership, Hildegard moved to secede from St. Disibod and set her sisters up in an independent community. This entire move would require five years, from 1147 to 1152. Its circumstances and motivations remain less than clear. A monk of St. Disibod named Godfrey, sent to serve as Hildegard's secretary in 1174 and chief author of book 1 of her vita, ascribed the move to deliberations about how best to enlarge the sisters' houses, presumably for a swelling number of recruits (*transferendis et ampliandis earum mansionibus consilium uersaretur*).[33] Hildegard always ascribed the decision to a vision from God: She suffered intensely when she refrained from telling the monks about it and she became physically paralyzed when they resisted. Abbot Kuno (1136–1155) ardently objected; some whispered that she was deceiving herself with vanity; some even conspired against her.[34] For the monks it meant potentially the loss of a visionary of growing fame, of recluses with strong ties to the local nobility, and of the material gifts they had brought to the house. Hildegard recalled the whole move as miraculous, not least her discovery of a new site (*inueni in euidentibus miraculis per uoluntatem Dei*).[35] This contested revelation was not the first public manifestation of her visionary calling. Five years into her leadership, about 1141, she had gained approval from

Abbot Kuno to begin transcribing her visions (the future *Scivias*) with
the help of the monk-priest Volmar; early in 1147 she felt fully authorized by Bernard of Clairvaux and Pope Eugene III. Just after her interaction with them, as Godfrey narrated it, came this visionary call to
move from the cloister of her oblation. As for the site, Hildegard "saw"
a hill much like St. Disibod, the Rupertsberg, at the point where the
Nahe flowed into the Rhine, roughly twenty miles downstream (six
hours' journey). This hillside, unoccupied apart from a chapel, a farm-
stead, and vineyards, she might have observed on journeys into Mainz.

Founding a house was finally a matter of political influence and
material resources,[36] particularly when the proposal was to break with
a house immediately subject to the archbishop of Mainz. The deci-
sive intervention, in Hildegard's telling,[37] came from the marchioness
Richardis of Stade, mother of Hildegard's favorite and second cousin to
Jutta. She persuaded the archbishop to agree that these noblewomen
could acquire the Rupertsberg, owned then by two brothers, one an
official at Hildesheim and the other provost of the collegiate church
Holy Cross in Mainz. According to a "list of goods" copied about
1195, the site was purchased for twenty marks in 1147.[38] The material
resources came from the network of nobility that had supported these
women: the count palatine Hermann von Stahleck and his wife,
Gertrude (sister to the emperor, Conrad III), Count Meinhard of Sponheim (brother of Jutta and father of Hiltrud), Hildegard's own brothers
(Hugh was chanter at Mainz), and other regional noblemen (probably
with daughters or relatives among the sisters). At least one gift was
specified as given by a widow for her daughter on entry,[39] meaning that
Hildegard maintained a practice reformers increasingly labeled simoniac. So too after a while, Hildegard reports, "rich people buried their
dead by us in honor."[40] That is, she kept up the traditional monastic exchange of material for spiritual benefits, properties noted in the "list of
goods" as "conferred for the souls of the faithful."[41] The chapel to Rupert was rededicated on 1 May 1151 and Archbishop Henry of Mainz
issued the house's founding document early in 1152.[42] At the dedication he himself granted the mill at Binger Loch, since he had learned the
nuns possessed no mill of their own. By the end of Hildegard's life her
house was relatively well endowed, possessing the Rupertsberg and virtually all of her native village (Bermersheim), together with estates and
vineyards in the surrounding region.

When exactly Hildegard moved to Mount St. Rupert is unknown, although the date is usually set at approximately 1150. In one autobio-

graphical passage she claimed to have arrived there to find no suitable dwellings and to have resided initially with "twenty girls born of rich parents" in poor circumstances. Indeed the people of Bingen, the women's relatives, and even several sisters shook their heads—for Hildegard another "affliction"—over such "well-born girls" moving from a place "where they wanted nothing" to a place of such "poverty."[43] Hildegard set about the building of a monastic complex, a process she had witnessed at St. Disibod through most of her adult years. Guibert described the Mount St. Rupert twenty-seven years later (a short construction time, in his view) as a complex not grand but ample and fitting, well laid-out for religious life and never without visitors.[44]

Some women left in those early days, their falsity proved by their later lives, Hildegard noted.[45] Not all of these noblewomen (or their families) were pleased with this move and its hardships. More important, during the same tense period of transition and building (1150–1151) Richardis was forcibly removed to assume a position as abbess.[46] The loss of this most beloved sister, her companion in writing the *Scivias,* unsettled Hildegard deeply. Partly to keep Richardis, partly to shield religious life from such social machinations, she protested loudly. Indeed she remonstrated with the very people who had just made possible the founding of her house. She warned the mother, Marchioness Richardis, that this attempt to promote her daughter would only ruin the nun,[47] pleaded with young Richardis's brother the archbishop of Bremen to intervene (conceding that his mother and sister and the count palatine Hermann would not),[48] implied to the archbishop of Mainz that worldly money and power (thus simony) lay behind all this,[49] even cautiously presented this "blackness" to Pope Eugene.[50] To found her own community on Mount St. Rupert, in sum, Hildegard had to cling to her vision and deploy all her leadership skills in the face of the monks who were her "masters," her noble supporting families, and even some of her sisters.

Once the house was founded and dedicated, Hildegard took up two crucial institutional matters: the dowries or gifts these women had brought to St. Disibod and the freedom of Mount St. Rupert from its abbot. The resolution, achieved after several years, involved a compromise. As Hildegard retold it, she was stricken again with illness, had to be carried into the chapel, and could not move until she had resolved to journey to St. Disibod and lay matters before the abbot and monks.[51] There she harangued them as "despoilers of the temple" if they dared retain for themselves the gifts of the sisters and "sons of Belial" if they dared threaten her with spiritual punishment (withholding pastoral care).[52] Afterward Hildegard wrote the abbot that some of the brothers had raged at her as a "black bird" and a "frightful beast." But she felt convinced that God himself had moved her from their place; her soul had become so shaken that she would have died had she stayed.[53] Abbot Kuno resisted, or he failed to finalize matters before his death (June 1155). So Abbot Helengar (1155–1178) struck the agreement, which Godfrey described as paying off his brothers with cash and leaving them most of what the sisters' families had given, in return for the virtual autonomy of Mount St. Rupert thereafter.[54]

Hildegard insisted that she get the agreement in writing, and Archbishop Arnold of Mainz issued two documents in May 1158, one confirming the properties the house had meanwhile acquired and the other sealing her agreement with St. Disibod.[55] The sisters were to be free (*soluta libere*) of the monks and hold the properties of Mount St. Rupert independently, with all present and future gifts belonging to the sisters; properties the sisters had given on entrance remained with St. Disibod, in exchange (*concambio*) for eight estates (*mansus*) probably closer to Bingen. The monks also agreed to provide spiritual care, religious profession, and ecclesiastical advocacy when the sisters so willed and granted them free election of a successor to Hildegard. Finally, the archbishop of Mainz placed the sisters' house directly under his protection, as St. Disibod was, forbidding any lay advocacy. Ten years after resolving to move Hildegard had thus achieved a virtually independent religious foundation. Moreover, she had regulated in writing those practices—dowry gifts, lay advocacy, spiritual care, and election of a superior—through which princes and prelates regularly reached into women's houses. Five years later Hildegard petitioned the emperor Frederick I in person for his protection. He confirmed the archbishop's privilege and placed her house under the imperial "right arm," warning off all lay advocates and powers.[56]

Information about the house built on Mount St. Rupert and the life conducted within its walls, despite Hildegard's enormous correspondence, is frustratingly sparse. As Guibert observed in 1177, sisters devoted themselves to chant and to reading and learning in silence on feast days; on ordinary days they copied books, wove vestments, and performed manual tasks.[57] Hildegard herself never described the life there, but news of the community she led soon spread. Between 1150 and 1177 the number of sisters increased from twenty to fifty. In 1165 she founded another house at Eibingen across the Rhine, with places for thirty sisters. She reportedly went there two days a week, although almost nothing is known about the circumstances or purposes of this foundation.[58] With women drawn in swelling numbers to her visionary acclaim and religious leadership, Hildegard presumably set at fifty and thirty respectively the number of positions her material resources would allow. Later documents speak of "stipends" at Mount St. Rupert for fifty sisters, two priests, and seven poor women.[59]

To get an understanding of life in Hildegard's monastery, another source may be invoked: the *Life of Disibod,* written in the early 1170s. Years after reconciling with the monks, Hildegard was asked to write a life of their patron, an otherwise unknown Irish monk who had died centuries earlier. With no extant sources, only her own "vision" to rely on, she wrote something of herself into this account. Whether her vita of the saint recalls life at St. Disibod or echoes her later life at Mount St. Rupert, it may be read for its amazing parallels to her experience.[60] The saint, she narrates, gathered a "congregation of fifty perfect brothers in only twelve years," religious whom nearby people generously supported.[61] He converted their hearts to the teachings of Benedict. He taught them to do battle in humility against the hordes of airy spirits that would induce pride and arrogance. He fortified them—verbs she applied to herself!—with the rigor of spiritual discipline, and he rejoiced in any brother who overcame a depraved will.[62] He gathered devoted followers who understood that the life was to be "hard warfare against the self," rejecting people who engaged in religious life only for show in favor of those who sought "the sweet consolation of a quieted mind."[63] Disibod built his monastery atop a hill, she further reports, so that it would not be overrun (*infestarentur*) by people or its rigor in religion softened by daily interaction with visitors. Yet so that he might himself be prepared to meet these people and answer the queries they posed for him, he then took up residence alone in a dwelling and chapel to the east at the bottom of the hill.[64] Whether this particular detail reflected Hildegard's own practice as abbess is unknown but suggestive. Disibod also traveled about to hear the questions and concerns of people, though the monks wanted to have him alone as their teacher. And the people responded with gifts, even estates from the nearby woods.[65] Disibod warned, finally, of his impending end (as Hildegard was doing in the early 1170s) and of troubles to follow, and he admonished his monks to persist in the house. In her narration of Disibod's life Hildegard offered glimpses into her life at Mount St. Rupert—as it was after twenty years or as she wished to think of it.

A monastery founded by a woman, not an emperor, bishop, or prince, and a successful establishment at that, as Guibert noted in 1177, was unprecedented, a miracle.[66] Even the founding document issued in 1152 by the archbishop of Mainz repeated the claim that these women had left St. Disibod for Mount St. Rupert owing to a revelation of the Holy Spirit. Between 1136 and 1158 Hildegard had made herself an "abbess," whatever title she went by: She organized a community, secured its land and incomes, procured and protected its privileges, gathered (and lost) sisters, built a monastic complex, and put in place a distinctive set of religious observances. For the next twenty years, from 1158 onward, while still caring for an ever increasing number of sisters, she acted as a prelate on a public stage, an abbess at large.[67] She set off on preaching missions, first in 1158 to religious houses up the Main river valley, then in 1160 to Trier and up the Moselle river valley, and later still up the Rhine to beyond Cologne. People approached her as a visionary, a prophet in their own times, and she often addressed them in the voice of the "Living Light." But she spoke as an abbess, a person recognized as responsible for the spiritual care of others in body and in soul. One instance may illumine her new standing and round out the story of her making. Sometime in the later 1160s Abbot Helengar of St. Disibod confessed to her that the "fervor of monastic religion was perishing" in his house, the place where she had grown up and from which she had seceded, and he sought her help. Hildegard in reply castigated the monks there for their murmuring spirits and wavering conduct, and she instructed them to subject the "handmaid of their bodies to their souls as to a highly beloved lady"[68]—a familiar image, but striking here. She then prefaced her *Life of St. Disibod,* written near the same time, with a fierce letter-sermon on their falling away from true religious life.[69] No longer the adolescent recluse or the young woman troubled by visions, she counseled the abbot and monks of her home cloister on the nature of the religious life.

THE SPIRITUAL CARE OF A "MOTHER" AND A "TEACHER"

Hildegard considered herself a divinely charged guide for her religious women, not a lady assuming the social privileges of an "abbess." Ordinarily addressed as "mother" or "teacher," she acted in these roles when she instructed sisters, preached in German towns and monasteries, and addressed letters to people across Christendom. What is known about her exercise of spiritual care must be drawn in good part from those letters; people sought her counsel from the time she founded her house, some even before. Her understanding of spiritual care rested most intimately on ten years of leadership at St. Disibod under Abbot Kuno and eventually thirty years at Mount St. Rupert. In these public letters and writings Hildegard nearly always discussed personal situations in terms of types. Communication by correspondence in the Middle Ages reserved specifics for oral exchange, as in the practice of confession. So while Hildegard certainly heard the inner struggles of particular sisters or abbots or houses and offered concrete advice in response, she rarely recorded such details in her writing. Her presentation and conception of religious types, however, was rich.

Hildegard saw the religious persons of her time honestly, without naiveté or false idealism. She knew that people joined the religious life for the wrong reasons: to escape poverty and misery, to turn from some foolishness that had deceived them, to seek help for bodily infirmities, or to elude the oppression of a worldly lord—in other words, not with a genuine change of will and a love of heaven.[70] She knew too as a medical cosmologist that people brought to the cloister the mixture of elements and humors by which they were constituted: the "hard" ones remained sharp, preoccupied with themselves and aloof from others; the "airy" ones blew about in constant vicissitude, fearing God and pressuring themselves for their sins because what they did always displeased them; the "windy" ones mixed all acts with foolishness and reacted with indignity to wise counsel; the "ardent" ones proved zealous for all things worldly and alienated themselves from peace wherever it might be found.[71] To move each of these types toward virtue and a love of heaven required tactful guidance.

Hildegard encouraged and herself exercised empathy toward all human and religious types. But her image of the caregiver must be distinguished from modern paradigms therapeutic in origin. Hildegard expected caregivers to lead, to guide souls toward their heavenly ends. Her most frequent charge against bishops and priests was that they failed to teach or use their authority to shape people in the ways of divine justice. They were supposed to act as pillars, preaching to their charges and doing good works, imbuing and constraining (*perfundere et constringere*) their subjects with divine law. That "law of the Lord," she reminded them, "is rich in discipline through both love and fear," and the whole creature, spiritual and carnal, must be trained to walk the right way.[72] To implement such leadership, to "imbue and constrain" their charges, leaders had first to "discipline" and "coerce" themselves, her most frequent charge to those lamenting the state of their flocks.[73] Early in her public career she even warned Pope Eugene, as one sitting in the place of Christ, to take responsibility for the souls placed in his charge and not to allow their plundering by the powerful prelates around him; on another occasion she admonished him to give commands to the teachers (prelates) in the church and to discipline its subjects, indeed to purify his own eyes and look around his own court.[74]

Hildegard's approach famously balanced correction and mercy in guiding souls. If your daughters weep, she advised one abbess, console them; if they rise up in anger, set them straight; if they act madly (*rabide*), subject them to the discipline of the Rule; if they turn away from you, recall them in person with stories and Gospel words; and if they still do not obey, act firmly in obedience to your supreme teacher.[75] To an abbot who had "cultivated his garden" only to see his monastic congregation "blown apart" again, she counseled that he was still to love the good and right-minded, to reproach the vain and delinquent, and to bear patiently with those hard as stone. He was never to fall on them in harshness or anger but to do everything with moderation lest the flock scatter.[76] While Hildegard boldly sent letters of warning and encouragement to the pope about his flock, especially his curia, much closer to home she instructed the archbishop of Mainz, her superior and protector. He was to "teach" and to "rule" his people in the ways of justice but to exercise that power with a zeal for mercy, for this was the way of God himself.[77] To an abbot zealous to exercise the rod of correction against his wayward monks, she cautioned that he embrace "discretion," imitating God who wanted mercy more than sacrifice.[78]

To recapture Hildegard as "mother" and "teacher" with her own charges is difficult, since her actions inside the community went largely unrecorded. One autobiographical passage offers a telling glimpse into her self-understanding as a caregiver. She linked her task notably to gaining external confirmation of her visionary experiences and of her founding of the monastery:

> Then my mind was firmed up, and I exercised the care of my daughters in all things necessary for both their bodies and their souls, just as it was set for me by my masters [the abbots of Disibodenberg and the archbishops of Mainz]. But in a true vision I saw with great concern how various airy spirits battled against us, and I saw that these same spirits were entangling certain of my noble daughters in various vanities as it were in a net. I made this known to them through a showing of God, and I fortified and entrenched

them with the words of Holy Scripture and the discipline of the Rule and a holy way of life. But some of them, looking on with fierce glances, secretly savaged me with words saying that they were not able to suffer the unbearable pressure ["clanking"] of the Rule's discipline, with which I wished to bind (*constringere uellem*) them. Yet God provided comfort in the form of other good and wise sisters who stood by me in all my sufferings . . .[79]

Hildegard understood caregiving as leadership in a struggle for souls and bodies, and she herself experienced losses. Hers was no finishing school but a battleground. She employed active images, drawn from her social and natural world. True religious were to be "manly," "to act as knights" in strong pursuit of the heavenly life.[80] They were to cultivate the "greenness" of their own fields, vitality in body and spirit.[81] While the sin of the first woman brought darkness, their souls were to radiate God's light.[82] Religious must be dead to this world in their bodies, a "churchyard for sanctification."[83] And they were, above all, to embrace their Spouse in love. In the struggle to "fortify" her own sisters so they could act as warriors or cultivators, radiate light, or experience love, Hildegard aimed to equip them with three resources: Scripture, the Rule, and a way of life.

Scripture filled the lives of sisters by way of the daily office and readings, shaping their memory and language. As a self-conscious *magistra,* Hildegard additionally taught Scripture to her nuns and "preached" to them on feast days, her words to them probably preserved in the so-called "Gospel commentary." That text shows her reviewing basic teachings while glossing the text of the scriptural stories. All her teachings, even in their visionary claims, involved the explication of Scripture. In mid-1153 she explained to her sisters, newly arrived at Mount St. Rupert, the nature of their vital "greenness." She turned to the story of Creation and the Fall, conceded how hard it was to fight off earthly desire once the first woman had turned toward earthly things, urged them to crucify that demonic tyrant and themselves by calling to mind the Son of God, and encouraged them then to "increase and multiply" holy desire so that their "land" would prove spiritually fruitful.[84]

Hildegard went further: she centered monastic life in the Christian story. Christ's incarnation, she consistently taught, introduced the virgin life and authorized this novelty. The conceiving of Christ and the example of his own life overturned the basic desires of this world: "When God was born, the eyes of the church were opened to grasp virginal being."[85] Virgins, as morning stars that show off the rising sun, first appeared at his birth.[86] This teaching came to life in the cloister.

Virgins, after taking vows, were to live with no memory of men, to become as angels. They were to focus on Christ as their master and exemplar, he who died to this world in his passion and rose to God; only thus could they rise from their present valley of humility and ascend without pride the mount of sanctity.[87]

Beyond teaching Scripture, as "mother" Hildegard imposed on her charges the Rule of Benedict as the "law" for their monastic lives. She named Benedict on several occasions a "second Moses," a conviction she had acquired already at St. Disibod, whether from the recently reformed monks or from Jutta.[88] At Mount St. Rupert she declared every word in the Rule to be inspired by the Holy Spirit.[89] In a revealing letter to a fellow *magistra,* she likened the Rule of Benedict to a pilot or rudder that, if obeyed, would guide the entire ship into a "holy way of life" and the "salvation of souls"; the teacher was to impress the Rule on the daughters entrusted to her.[90] Her stance should not be taken as common practice. In the context of all those women's houses that followed no clear rule, her conviction was unique and took on a sharp edge. She wanted religious houses that took Benedict's Rule as a Spirit-given norm, and she never spoke of canonesses, though she certainly knew about them. When the troubles came at St. Disibod twenty years after she had left, she reproached Abbot Helengar for allowing the community to take as one and the same the "pomp of this world" and the "point of their holy way of life [*conversatio*]." Thus they were refusing the law and bending the knee to a strange God. They must now gird themselves like knights. Their sword was to be obedience and the precepts of the Rule; their enemy was disobedience, prideful neglect of the Rule.[91] In the story of medieval monastic life, this was a turnabout, an abbess instructing monks to keep Benedict's Rule.

Hildegard once glossed the Rule in response to a request from another men's house (the place and occasion remain in dispute). She told this community too that nothing need be added to or taken away from Benedict's teaching.[92] While *she* might sound Cistercian in this emphasis, she was probably critiquing various adaptations made in that house. Against the customs or customaries that shaped religious life concretely, especially in women's houses, Hildegard held fast to the Rule in its text. No customary, for instance, is known from her house.[93] Yet she constantly presented the Rule itself as "moderate," as making the virginal life accessible to all people.[94] In practice Hildegard alluded to moderation in balancing sleep and vigils, in allowing certain foods (poultry) while not refraining ostentatiously from food, in adjusting the clothing allowed beyond the Rule's text. She reiterated that oblated children must themselves confirm their religious intentions.[95] Her remarks in this letter-commentary presumed too a multitude of guests visiting the house and the anomalies that might bring to cloistered life.[96] She did not object, only regulated. As in traditional monastic practice, even in withdrawal from the world and submission to the Rule, she expected to maintain contact with the larger world.

At the heart of religious life were the daily rounds of sung prayer. Several contemporary Benedictines commented on the conjunction of prayer and chant as a work of the Spirit lifting the soul to God. By composing new melodies and verses, however, Hildegard contributed directly to the shape of that sung prayer in her house as few abbots ever did. Just as she located the virginal life in a larger theological perspective, so she made universal claims for sung prayer. Articulating her views in 1178–1179 at the end of her life, when an interdict banned the sisters from singing, Hildegard explained to the prelates at Mainz that sung prayer was a work of the Spirit and the prophets. Nuns were to be "exercised outwardly" by way of verses and instruments so they might be "instructed inwardly." These melodies captured, or recaptured, that perfect celestial harmony that Adam had known along with the angels before the Fall, a "knowledge" and "resonant power" that mortal humans could not bear in its pure state. Just as Christ's body was born of the Virgin through the Spirit, so the singing of praises in the church through the Spirit embodied on earth the celestial harmonies.[97] Chanting religious could only sigh when they caught a glimmer in their souls of that original harmony. So then: Anyone who blocked this divine work, Hildegard warned her superiors, contributed to the work of the devil and would not themselves sing with the angels in heaven.[98] For Hildegard the office each day combined the language of Scripture, the instruments of the body, and the breath of the Spirit to instruct inwardly so that a religious might perceive the heavenly harmonies.

The purpose of choosing the virgin way, instruction in Scripture, and observing the Rule was to manifest the virtues in oneself, body and soul. Hildegard did not think of her house as a residence for ladies but as a school for virtue, wherein she saw the interplay of virtues and vices competing to shape a person in the love and fear of God. In Hildegard's visions, these virtues took on a reality larger than life, as beings or forces that each virgin was to appropriate for herself.[99] She often adopted the image of a garden, with the abbess as the gardener and the flowers or herbs cultivated into full bloom as the virtues alive in her subjects.[100] The goal toward which a person was to strive, in herself or in her charges, was "greenness" and "fragrance." Destructive forces overcame them as "gusty tempests," contrary winds that confused and blew down—the vices or evil forces that disquieted human minds.[101]

Benedictines pledged themselves to keep a holy "way of life" (*conversatio*). An abbess held the position of teacher-ruler (*in magisterio*) so as to lead the struggle against the seven plagues (vices) that undid religious souls.[102] Compared to inherited notions of a privileged life, this view of the religious life sounded stern and apparently struck some noblewomen as more than they had sought from Hildegard or religion. Yet Hildegard herself refrained from excesses. She warned against an "unreasonable abstinence" that yielded only pride and vainglory.[103] An abbess who had dried out her own "field" (Hildegard's image) with excessive abstinence was more likely to fly off in anger at the failings of her sisters.[104] Moderation was the key, neither too much nor too little food.[105] To a prioress who had fallen into sin, she conceded the whip of penance, but discretely applied so as not to kill the body; the better way was gently to pray God for a better life rather than to entreat him by way of this "excess of sadness."[106]

Hildegard had a realistic understanding of the waywardness of humans, and she emphasized too the need to purge evil through penance and to meet the demands of divine justice. Indeed her entire second book, begun just after she had securely established her house on Mount St. Rupert, centered on that theme. In the *Book of Life's Merits* she "saw" and explicated elaborate, sometimes horrifying visions of the punishments meted out for particular sins. While she appears to address the faithful generally, Hildegard wrote as someone who knew first the hearts of her women charges. The saints are those whose flesh is wholly subjugated to their spirits—the ideal that Christ realized in the Incarnation and that virgins now intended.[107] Those who despair in the midst of temptation and trouble, who even lose confidence in the goodness of God, should persist in good will with pure prayer on bent knees—but not in some burdensome fashion, lest heavy labors further increase the despair and despair injure the body, depriving the person of all "greenness."[108]

In her epistolary counsel Hildegard occasionally dealt more intimately with various states of soul and body. To an abbot who had disclosed that the monastic life now lacked all fervor for him (as it must have at times for sisters), she observed that when he presumed to be full of understanding, he prayed only indifferently, then experienced tedium in prayer, finally not even finishing his prayers but allowing his body, not wholly cut off as yet, to pursue its tastes. Hildegard interpreted this experience for him as the justice of God testing and purging his soul. He should embrace it, so as to be embraced by God, and to believe confidently still in the wondrous ways of the divine.[109] To a provost at Bonn she wrote that his mind, clouded and heavy and divided from the sun, must be tested and tried so that he might come always to burn with the fire of the Spirit, desire God's justice each day, and ascend from virtue to virtue.[110] Hildegard expected and saw in her sisters the testing of will and desire as part of religious life.

To understand Hildegard as caregiving mother and teacher, exposition must move from the universal, the virginal life as grounded in and living out the incarnate passion, to the particular, the shaping of that life by Scripture, Rule, and virtue, and then to the universal again. For virginal life fit centrally into the universal order. Divine laws governed all created being, in Hildegard's vision: the order put into the nature of things at Creation, the Mosaic law to guide the moral lives of God's people, and the "new law" of charity to orient Christians. Hildegard understood each as obligatory. When lay people kept the laws set for them and obeyed their masters, they thereby adorned the church and embraced their God.[111] But in real practice the world contained a spectrum of law keepers and law breakers, with people outside this ordering at either end. At one extreme, many rejected God's law and became a law to themselves, with no zeal for the divinely ordained just way.[112] Virgins, at the other end, chose a way, of their own free will, which went beyond the law, transcended strict obligation.[113] Once chosen, however, this way could not be revoked but had to be kept. Theirs was nonetheless a choice of freedom—freedom from a man for a virgin, freedom from the world for all religious.[114] This choice is what Hildegard put on ritual display, already at St. Disibod, when her virgins entered church on feast days with golden crowns and unbound hair. But they could sully this freedom. What great nobility it is, she instructed one community of nuns, for a woman to withdraw from being joined to a man, to refuse copulating with men and become betrothed to Christ. This way is hard, she conceded, even bitter. Do not then succumb to secret embraces with a peasant, she warned, but embrace your King in his heavenly bed with the sweetest charity. For any fleshly embrace after vowing virginity, with prince or with peasant, secretly or in the open, was to turn noble freedom into a dancing whore.[115]

By acting as a "teacher/master" Hildegard embodied what she urged on bishops, a vision of ruling by way of teaching, of justice combined with mercy. In a striking parallel with the new schoolmen, she conceived the care of souls as animated as much by teaching as by ruling. An abbess was doing right when "her sheep wanted to hear God's admonition through her teaching."[116] An abbess must provide "rain" for her charges, Hildegard explained, and this nourishment will come properly if she "plows" her own heart with a knowledge of Scripture.[117] Hildegard also consciously employed the mother image. She advised another abbess to embrace Christ and then to experience the Scriptures flowing from the divine font as breasts offered to be sucked.[118] For herself, as a caregiver, Hildegard assumed not only the authority to wield the staff of correction against the wayward and to pour the oil of mercy on the wounded. She positioned herself in the community as a "mother-teacher": She imagined her sisters sucking at her breasts when she taught the virginal way.

Hildegard saw herself as called to uphold and foster the "virginal" and "just" ways in this "most vile of times," as she characterized her era in a letter to the abbot of her home abbey.[119] In her sixties she looked back on her lifetime as traversing a period of spiritual decline, a slowing in fervor that had begun, she thought, about the time of her birth.[120] In these "womanish" times, she warned repeatedly, a terrible purge was about to begin.[121] Scholars, however, have positioned Hildegard most often in a period of historic renewal, the "reformation of the twelfth century." A new and expanded demand by women for a place in religious life marked that era like none earlier.[122] With her guidance of the community at St. Disibod and then her founding of the houses at Mount St. Rupert and Eibingen, Hildegard uniquely responded to that aspiration with independent establishments for women. Yet her actions and teachings as an abbess reveal in her outlook aspects of both the old and the new.

Without deep links to reform figures or movements, Hildegard nonetheless paralleled in her acts and ideas many of theirs. She saw the "virginal way" as the heart of Christian life, like most twelfth-century reformers. She urged compliance with Benedict's Rule as the guide, much like Cistercians. She seceded to establish an independent house, as reformers often did. She insisted on "adult" vocations, like reformers and canon lawyers. She encouraged and exemplified the teaching of the Christian people as the heart of pastoring, like the new schoolmen. She saw a just universe as ruled everywhere by law, like canon lawyers.

She expected leadership from Rome but believed that real renewal began with disciplining the self—as did most reformers in this era.

And yet Hildegard was an imperial abbess and a female caregiver. She came to religious life as an oblate and later accepted oblates. She admitted only noblewomen into her circle. She built an independent house on the gifts and protection of the highest circles, reaching to the archbishop of Mainz and the emperor. She retained the practices of offering prayers in return for gifts or burial and of accepting gifts in return for entry. She added to the Divine Office and religious ritual compositions and observances of her own devising. She maintained contact judiciously with prelates and princes from all parties and circles. She offered counsel to nearly all interested individuals, in person and by letter. She undertook extended preaching tours. Only with the independence and recognition achieved as an imperial abbess and a visionary caregiver could she have fulfilled these roles, never as a recluse attached to a new reform order.

As abbess at Mount St. Rupert, Hildegard came to act as a caregiver to caregivers, or in her language, as a teacher to teachers. Bishops, abbots, priests, and princes sought her advice, and she counseled them, often on matters they dared not take up with people around them, such as a wish to resign their office. To Bishop Henry of Liège, who described himself as overwhelmed (*fluctuanti*), she advised that he "be a good pastor and noble in conduct," that he recall to the homeland the lazy and the wandering, correct the erring, and fight on, so that his soul might one day flash like a victorious knight saluted by comrades.[123] To Pope Anastasius IV (1153–1154), whom she addressed as the instituted spouse of Christ, she lamented that he allowed a "peasant" and "depraved" way of life among his charges and warned that the present "wanton" times would soon give way to "sorrow" and then "terror."[124] She spoke thus to the pope and to all others because the "Living Light" had revealed in visions what to say and emboldened her to say it. Yet she spoke fundamentally as a recognized caregiver, at home and at large. Whether apart from the experience of her visions she could have achieved all she did as abbess, whether she would have had the confidence to act and speak, whether contemporaries would have listened and lent support—all this remains unanswerable, for finally the "mother-teacher" cannot be divided from the visionary prophet. But for purposes of historical understanding, her ruling and teaching roles as abbess must come into their own.

THREE

Religious Thinker

"A Frail Human Being" on Fiery Life

CONSTANT MEWS

I, the Living Light who illumines what is obscure, have
placed the human being whom I have willed, and whom I
have wonderfully afflicted as it pleased me, in the midst of
wonderful things, beyond the reach of human beings in the
past, who did see in Me many hidden things; but I have laid
her low on the ground, so that she may not set herself up in
any boldness of mind.[1]

Hildegard of Bingen never explicitly identified herself as a theologian.
The image she most often uses of herself is that of a frail human being
(*homo fragilis*), no more than ash and filth, not endowed with any formal education. Yet she is quite conscious that she has glimpsed something beyond the reach or "boundary" of human beings in the past
(*trans metam antiquorum hominum*), as she puts it in her opening declaration in *Scivias*. Through this realization she finds an explanation for
the physical distress of her own body. While Hildegard always emphasizes the primacy of her mystical experience, are we able to consider her
as a religious thinker who develops her own theology? What is the
essence of her flash of insight?

Hildegard's writings have been interpreted from a variety of perspectives, both religious and nonreligious. Developing suggestions of the
historian of science Charles Singer and the neurologist Oliver Sacks,
Sabina Flanagan has argued that Hildegard's visions were provoked by
a fusion of physical and psychological factors: migraine attacks, characterized by flashes of light in her visual field, which, after a long period
of frustration and illness in her early life, she came to interpret as hav-

ing a profound spiritual significance.[2] Hans Liebeschütz considered her as a literary genius whose claims to mystical experience masked a sophisticated familiarity with literary traditions—a line of inquiry taken much further by Peter Dronke.[3] In publications directed to an audience interested in popular theology, Matthew Fox has presented Hildegard as an exponent of "creation spirituality," in which emphasis is placed not on the contrast between original sin and man's need for redemption but on the way God works through creation as a whole.[4] Barbara Newman has offered a rather different interpretation of Hildegard's thought as "a theology of the feminine," structured around a succession of feminine images.[5] While all these interpretations offer valuable insights into Hildegard's creative output, they are all necessarily selective in their focus. Hildegard writes about much more than the natural world or feminine images. Claims that her thought is directed toward affirmation of nature or the feminine fit awkwardly with observations about her "moral dualism" and preoccupation with evil in the world.[6] To understand the connecting threads in Hildegard's theological vision, we need to consider how her religious thought developed in response to her situation at Disibodenberg.

Hildegard reveals very little about the evolution of her ideas about God and the world before she finally acceded to Volmar's urging that she record the visions she said she had experienced from childhood. In autobiographical reflections written late in life, she explains that she had experienced visions as a child but stopped speaking about them through fear of ridicule in her fifteenth year.[7] Significantly, she never describes herself as a recluse or recalls the ceremony held on the Feast of All Saints, 1 November 1112, by which she and her mentor Jutta, along with at least one other girl, were formally enclosed in a cell, intended to be their home for life.[8] That Hildegard only recalls being offered to the religious life by her parents in her eighth year leads her biographers Godfrey and Guibert of Gembloux to telescope these two events and imagine her as being formally "buried with Christ" as a young child in 1105, when work had not even begun on the new abbey church on Disibodenberg.[9] In the annals of St. Disibod the events that mattered were the ceremony by which a recluse became dead to the world and the day that recluse passed into eternity. Unlike her biographers, Hildegard never uses this imagery of "dying to the world" but rather remembers only how she started to fall silent out of fear of what other people might think.

There is a strong focus on the anticipation of death in the *Life of Jutta,* a text written after 1139, but before Hildegard had acquired a public reputation, at the request of both Hildegard and Abbot Kuno.[10] This vita presents a very different perspective on the religious life from that offered in Hildegard's own autobiographical reflections. The author reveals that Jutta was in her twentieth year when the women were officially enclosed in 1112 but emphasizes that she chose this way of life against the wishes of her family. It does not record much about any interest of Jutta in the natural world, apart from a remark about her ability to heal the sick "in mind and body" and a story about how a rare waterfowl once came to rest in Jutta's cell when she was refusing to accede to her abbot's demand that she eat meat for the sake of her health.[11] Jutta's biographer also reveals how a certain brother (the writer himself?), struggling with a "temptation of the flesh against the spirit," once exposed his difficulty to her, asking that she heal his wound. Thanks to her prayers, he overcame these temptations.[12] Hildegard may have learned much from these delicate situations of monastic life, as well as from Jutta's response to many visitors and to letters from those who could not visit her in person.[13] The biographer presents Jutta as a glutton for self-mortification whose harsh personal asceticism led to ill health and eventual death in 1136 at the age of forty-four. He reports a vision enjoyed by her "intimate disciple in the flesh" (certainly Hildegard herself) about Jutta's entry into heaven. The biographer is quite possibly Volmar, one of the few people in whom both Jutta and Hildegard confided.[14] Even if Jutta had made herself into a public figure at the abbey, her biographer presented her as a recluse who sublimated sexual desire and an ambition to go on pilgrimage with a life of deliberate mortification, in silent anticipation of her own death and subsequent entry into paradise.

In the opening declaration of *Scivias,* in which she describes her initial realization in 1141 that she had to write down her visions, Hildegard never acknowledges any debt to Jutta. While she rectifies this omission in later autobiographical recollections, her comment that she was subjected to the discipline of a noble woman, "restless in vigils, fasting and other good works," may betray a certain reserve toward the woman in whose shadow she spent almost half her life.[15] By contrast, Hildegard praises Volmar at length in the introduction to *Scivias* as "a faithful man, working like herself on another part of the Work that leads to Me," noting the crucial role Volmar played in encouraging her to accede to that inner command to "say and write what you see and hear."[16] In a flash, she says, she understood the true meaning of the Scriptures. In subsequent recollections of this moment, she added that she also grasped the true meaning of the writings of the saints and of certain philosophers.[17]

The image Hildegard uses in *Scivias* to describe this experience is that of a fiery light (*igneum lumen*) irradiating not just her brain but her whole physical being. Her identification of this light as "a Living Light that illumines what is hidden" (*lux vivens et obscura illuminans*) subtly transforms the familiar image of John 1.9 ("I am the true light that illumines every person coming into the world") by replacing "true" with "living." In doing so, Hildegard shifts attention away from an unchanging truth beyond creation to a light that is alive. While John's Gospel uses images of light and life to refer to the Incarnation, Hildegard employs the phrase *lux vivens*, never used in this way in previous Latin Christian literature, to describe the source of her inspiration.[18]

Hildegard's claim is that the Word of God is the life underpinning creation itself. This *living* light is subtly different from the perpetual light traditionally asked for those who have died. The preface to *Scivias* is effectively a statement that she now defines herself not as a recluse but as someone who concealed her insights in the past (through fear of what others might say, she later admitted) but who has now acceded to a divine commission to speak out. Her realization is that the underlying message of Scripture, traditionally identified as the Word of God, is a *living* force, which can help her come to terms with her physical distress. She now interprets her physical distress not as a cause for complaint but as the means by which this Living Light speaks to her. Her vision of the source of all health and restoration was shaped by her sense of weakness in her own body.

Hildegard's preference for organic imagery to describe the source of her inspiration takes on particular significance when compared to the tendency of classically educated Christian thinkers to employ more static notions of supreme being or goodness rather than supreme life. The only thinker to be discussed at any length in the annals of Disibodenberg, completed before Hildegard achieved prominence at the council of Trier in late 1147, is St. Anselm (1033–1109).[19] The author of the annals is fascinated by the encouragement Anselm gave his monks at Bec to study both secular and sacred subjects. He is very familiar with Anselm's ambition to present Christian teaching not from the basis of Scripture or any written authority but from concepts Anselm considered philosophically self-evident. The chronicler is familiar with all of

Anselm's writings and incorporates otherwise unrecorded conversations between Anselm and a certain young man at Bec (perhaps the source of his information). Thus Hildegard was raised at an abbey familiar with one of the most fertile thinkers of Benedictine tradition.

At first sight, one cannot imagine a greater contrast than that between St. Anselm's emphasis on reason and Hildegard's insistence on her lack of education and her dependence on divine inspiration. Yet both share a desire to present Christian teaching on the basis of self-evident truths rather than any imposed authoritative text. They differ in the starting point of their reflection. Whereas Anselm takes for granted the capacity of reason to come to terms with static philosophical concepts like "being," "substance," and "accident," Hildegard develops her thought from organic concepts like "life" and "greenness" or "viridity" (*viriditas*). Scholastic theological discourse, whether framed in terms of sacrament, as in the writing of Hugh of St. Victor (d. 1141), or in terms of abstractions about form or essence, as in the writing of Peter Abelard (1079–1142) or Gilbert of Poitiers (ca. 1075–1154), developed within sophisticated conceptual categories shaped by a very different philosophical tradition. Even the thought of Bernard of Clairvaux (1090–1153) is structured around the theme of the visitation of the Word in the soul, without relation to the natural world.

Hildegard begins *Scivias* with a vision of a brilliant figure seated on a mountain, from whom many living sparks (*uiuentes scintillae*) stream out, unnoticed by those figures who live securely in the mountain but gaze in different directions (I.1). Whether or not these sparks were provoked by a migraine, she interprets them as manifestations of the *Living* Light. Without dwelling on the divine nature, she first explains the presence of evil in the world through the fall of the angel of light into the pit of darkness and then the consequent deceit Lucifer worked on Adam and Eve, all through a vision (I.2) in which she does not use any of these familiar names from Scripture. She sees a great pit, from which a foul-smelling stench ensnares Adam, from whose rib issues a cloud containing many stars. By presenting her own version of the story of the Fall, Hildegard introduces her own themes into the Genesis account. She blames the fallen state of humanity firmly on the devil, who seduces an innocent woman, rather than on Eve for disobeying God (I.2.10). A consequence of the Fall is that creation, previously calm, became hostile to humanity (I.2.27). Yet paradise still exists as a physical place, "blooming with the freshness (*viriditas*) of flowers and grass and the charms of spices, full of fine odors" (I.2.28).

Hildegard's interest in the physical aspect of the Garden of Eden and in the responsibilities of man and woman within marriage, prefigured by Adam and Eve (I.2.11–21), echoes themes dear to Rupert of Deutz (ca. 1079–1129), a severe critic of those who insisted only on allegorical interpretations of Scripture.[20] His copious and sometimes controversial commentaries on Scripture enjoyed wide popularity in reformed Rhineland abbeys while Hildegard was still at Disibodenberg. Rupert's interest in Scripture as a historical record extended to considering the sexual relationship between husband and wife in the privacy of their chamber as a form of prayer. Although Hildegard never went quite as far as this, her interest in the complementarity of the roles of man and woman was not unprecedented in monastic tradition.[21]

It is impossible to know how far both Hildegard's individual ideas and the final structure of *Scivias* were worked out through discussion with Volmar, who was certainly familiar with the contemporary theological treatises and scriptural commentaries. Her reading of the history of salvation can be compared to that of Hugh of St. Victor in his major synthesis of Christian doctrine, *On the Sacraments of the Christian Faith,* composed in the early 1130s. His unifying theme is the idea of sacrament, evident in creation and the written law as well as in the restoration of humankind, made possible by Christ and his church. For Hildegard, the unifying thread is the notion of life itself.[22] Reflection on Adam and Eve in the second vision leads her to contemplate the nature of marriage not as a sacrament but as a natural condition. She suggests that the relationship of woman to man is like that of soft earth to hard stone (I.2.11). They must be bound together by a pure love. Their interaction is as close as that of the air and the wind (I.2.12). After twelve chapters on the natural relationship of a man and a woman, she has just one (I.2.24) on chastity. The most important virtues, those of humility and charity, apply to all people (I.2.33). Her major concern is not so much with the feminine as with the complementary roles of man and woman in the transmission of life itself.[23]

At the beginning of the second of the three books of *Scivias,* Hildegard returns to the theme that God is a dazzling fire, totally alive (II.1). Just as St. Anselm introduces terms like *God* or *Father, Son* and *Holy Spirit* gradually into his discussions, so Hildegard also introduces these notions only in the course of commentary on her visions. Whereas it was conventional in theology to identify God through the order inherent in creation, Hildegard focuses on fruitfulness, vitality, and above all *viriditas* as attributes of the divine nature (II.1.2–3).[24] Translators sometimes supply a range of terms to capture its meaning, which relates much more than the color green: freshness, vitality, fertility, fecundity, fruitfulness, verdure, growth. She uses the word as a metaphor of health, both physical and spiritual. Thus she understands the Word of God as a flame within the divine fire which became incarnate through the viridity of the Holy Spirit. The Word gives life to humanity by pouring into it "warmth in viridity," "just as a mother gives milk to her children" (II.1.7). Through the incarnate Word, divine viridity is seen (II.1.11). Indeed Creation itself would not have been possible without this viridity (II.2.1).

The search for rational analogies to describe Christian doctrine is a characteristic feature of twelfth-century theology. Peter Abelard had suggested that the relationship between the Father and the Son in the Trinity was like that between genus and species in a bronze seal.[25] He was writing for an audience familiar with philosophical argument. Hildegard's originality is to find metaphors from the natural world to interpret Christian teaching. Her main image in *Scivias* is that of a perfect human being (the Son) bathed in light (the Father) and blazing with fire (the Holy Spirit). Like Abelard, she is aware that Father, Son, and Holy Spirit are names applied by tradition to signify aspects of divinity, but she differs from him in drawing on a number of different images, taken from the natural world rather than from a royal chancery. She is reasoning from nature. A stone combines damp viridity (the Father), solidity of touch (the Son), and sparkling fire (the Holy Spirit) (II.2.5).[26] A flame has brilliant light (the Father), red power (the Son), and fiery heat (the Holy Spirit) (II.2.6). Her preferred imagery is very different from that of Abelard, who only mentions viridity once, in relation to worldly life as being like chaff, "cut from the earth, without the strength of its viridity."[27] The term *viriditas* occurs with great frequency in Gregory the Great's *Moralia in Job* to refer to the spiritual health to which Job aspires. Augustine, by contrast, only uses the word once in his *City of God,* as an image of mutability.[28] Intriguingly, in a collection of over a hundred love letters apparently exchanged in the early twelfth century between a brilliant teacher and the gifted student with whom he was in love, the term *viriditas* occurs three times in letters from the woman but not at all in letters from the man.[29]

Hildegard is more interested in the relationship of God to creation than in the doctrine of the Trinity as such. It is instructive to compare her use of the Pauline text "the invisible things of God are revealed through the created things of the world" (Romans 1.19–20) to that of her contemporaries. While Abelard explicitly uses this Pauline text in his *Theologia* to justify his exploitation of texts like Plato's *Timaeus*, Hildegard alludes to its phraseology to justify her interpretation of different parts of the natural world, which she presents as a cosmic egg (I.3.1).[30] The image of a cosmic egg was not in itself original, having been mentioned in a scientific context by Macrobius and Martianus Capella as well as by Honorius Augustodunensis (ca. 1070–ca. 1140) in the opening chapter of his *Imago mundi*.[31] The earth was often compared to the yolk of an egg, the ether or the air to its white, the surrounding firmament to its shell. Peter Abelard was one of the few twelfth-century authors to suggest a theological significance to the image in his commentary on the Hexaemeron, written at Heloise's request.[32] When observing an alternative translation of Genesis 1.2, "the spirit nourished (*fovebat*) the waters," Abelard suggested that the Holy Spirit, divine goodness, could be understood as nurturing and giving life to the world like a bird warming its egg, from whose different elements life came into being. His interest, however, is in the meaning of the word *fovebat* and the nature of the Holy Spirit as divine goodness, infused into the hearts of the faithful. He never uses this organic image in his *Theologia*, where there is lengthy comparison of the Holy Spirit to the world soul, as described in Plato's *Timaeus*. Hildegard, by contrast, develops in detail the image of the cosmic egg as bathed in a divine fire, which in turn envelops a dark fire where there is disturbance from malign winds. She sees different features of the universe as impregnated with spiritual significance.

Although Hildegard is more concerned in *Scivias* with human behavior than with the structure of creation itself, she still touches on the fundamental connections between the human person and the rest of creation. In vision I.4 she interprets her vision of a woman with a child in her womb, an echo of Revelation 12.1–9, not as an allegory of the church but as part of her vision of the condition of humanity, assailed by storms (*turbines*, depicted by the artist of the Rupertsberg codex as demons). Hildegard's concern is with the inner unity of the soul and the body. The relationship of the soul to the body is like that of sap to a tree, the intellect being the viridity of its branches and leaves (I.4.20). Such an analogy is very different from the more static explanation of the relationship as that between form and matter offered by Aristotelian tradition. Redemption lies in turning to the Son of God, who became incarnate when the Word of God came into "the deep viridity" (in the translator's poetic image, "the high fecundity") of the Virgin (I.4.10).

Hildegard's sensitivity to the dynamism of life leads her to focus more on the incarnation of the Word, born of a woman, than on specific details of the suffering of Christ on the cross. In *Scivias* her attention is drawn to the figure of the Synagogue, as the mother of the incarnation of the Son of God (I.5.1). While belief that redemption has been made possible through the Incarnation permeates the entire work, her account of Christ's life and the redemption wrought by his death and resurrection is relatively brief and unexceptional (II.1.13–17; II.6.22). Much more elaborate is her image of a woman, as large as a city, the true church, bride of Christ and mother of the faithful (II.3). The human race itself issued from woman, whose moisture was like that of the earth (II.3.22). The three different orders who make up the church—clergy, monks and virgins, and laypeople—all have a role within Ecclesia, in making it blossom with viridity (II.5.26). Hildegard reserves some of her strongest words for those who pursue the religious life for the wrong reasons or commit their children to religion without eliciting their consent. Such children will only try to run away. Such parents do not confer dew or moisture ("dampness in viridity") onto a green field, as this has to be the work of the Holy Spirit (II.5.45–46). True commitment to the religious life comes from "the viridity of the virile mind of a human being" (II.5.48).[33]

Redemption is made possible by the incarnation of the Word of God in Christ (III.7.7). The Son exists from the beginning of time, proceeding from the Father "in burning viridity" (III.7.9). In the incarnate Christ all the virtues are fully manifest (III.8.13). He emerges like a branch from the viridity of the Virgin, emblematic of the viridity of women and of the earth itself (III.8.15).[34] Hildegard's interest is in the principle of incarnation rather than in specific devotion to Jesus. In the final vision of *Scivias,* which presents a musical foretaste of the heavenly city, she observes that while words symbolize the humanity of the Son of God, so celestial harmony prefigures his divinity (III.13.12).

There are many other areas of Christian doctrine on which Hildegard has an opinion to express. She discusses sacraments, for example, in the second book of *Scivias.* In the baptism of children, sins are forgiven, even though children are not yet of an age of understanding and the priest might not be blameless (II.3.31–37). While her teaching is basically traditional, she uses images from human experience to make her point. Around the font, the priest, godfather, and godmother symbolize the Father, Holy Spirit, and incarnate Son respectively (II.3.32). Baptism on its own is not sufficient. Just as a baby needs to be nourished by milk from its mother and food ground up for it, so a baptized person needs nurturing instruction from the church (II.3.33). Hildegard's concern is always with internal purity, not necessarily guaranteed by the sacraments of Baptism and Confirmation (II.4.11–14).

Hildegard expresses reverence for priestly office in *Scivias* while at the same time emphasizing the need for priests to lead moral lives. They must give generously to the poor (II.3.3) and live chastely (II.5.3; II.6.62). By performing the sacrament of the altar, the priest re-presents the sacrifice by which Christ offered himself for all humanity, "as if in a mirror" (II.6.17). Hildegard does not allude to any grace conferred by the sacrament, as conventional in so much formal eucharistic debate, or use categories of substance and accident to discuss any formal change that takes place in the consecrated bread; but she sees the divine mystery as present in the bread and wine in the same way as the soul exists within flesh and blood in a human person (II.6.12). She prefers to describe the Eucharist in the same way as she describes the incarnation of the Son of God, who "arose in an unplowed field, a flower so excellent that it will never wither from any accident of mortality, but will last forever in the fullness of viridity" (II.6.24). Bread is offered on the altar because wheat is the strongest of all fruits of the field, yielding no bitter juice, but only dry flour, and wine because the grape is not covered by any hard shell (II.6.26–28). The mixture of water and wine evokes both the divinity and humanity of the Son, present on the altar. To answer doubts about whether the body and blood are truly present on the altar, she explains the process in naturalistic terms: just as a man gives his seed to a woman to create a baby, without establishing its identity, so bread and wine conceal the flesh and blood of Christ not visible to physical eyes (II.6.43). She denies women the right to become priests because she sees their role as to bear children, just as a fertile field must be plowed by another (II.6.76).[35] Hildegard's quite conventional biological assumption that a human being exists in embryo in the human seed received by a woman shapes her understanding of priestly office. This idea may have been reinforced by discussion with Volmar, an ordained priest. She justifies liturgical practice from her understanding of natural process. At the same time she is outspoken about those priests who do not live up to the standards of purity expected of them. If they abuse their authority they are simply ravening wolves, whose crimes are bewailed by all the elements in creation (II.6.94–95). While they have been entrusted with the power of judging and forgiving sinners, they must not use their position to bind an innocent person (II.6.96–99).

Hildegard's emphasis on the importance of correct living rather than on the grace conferred through the sacraments is paralleled by her focus in the third part of *Scivias* on the moral path that the faithful must follow. Her concern is always with life, whether it be the life of creation or the life of humanity, or indeed divinity as the Living Light itself. An individual has to choose between the paths of good and evil. There is no doubt in her mind about the path to life. With the aid of the virtues, a faithful person grows like a palm tree to adorn the city of God (III.2.26). By speaking of the assistance given by the virtues and the inspiration of the Holy Spirit rather than of the work of grace, Hildegard develops her theme that the virtues, engaged in building up the heavenly city, embody life itself (III.4.13).

Hildegard's desire for the restoration of paradise, imagined as a new heaven and a new earth, leads her to an apocalyptic vision of the future. She sees a succession of difficult times and Antichrist deceiving many people before order is finally restored, the physical elements settle into calm, and the righteous are redeemed. The three spheres of vision III.12, symbolizing God, the righteous, and creation, relate to three spheres of life now brought together into harmony. The musical program that underpins the final vision of *Scivias*, expanded more fully in the *Ordo virtutum,* is itself a celebration of organic life.[36] Hildegard here picks up a theme introduced much earlier in *Scivias* (I.4) of the soul who returns to mother Sion. Initially faithful, Anima begins to lose her sense of direction: "Oh, heavy effort and hard load which I must endure while garbed in this life! It is most hard for me to fight against the flesh. . . . Oh I know not what to do or where to flee! Woe is me! I cannot use rightly that which clothes me. I really want to throw it off! . . . God created the world; I do him no wrong, but I want to enjoy it" (III.13.9). Dramatic tension here, as in the *Ordo virtutum,* is created by the contrast between the encouragement offered by the virtues and the depth of despair plumbed by Anima, who only gradually learns the lesson of humility and hope. Rather than use the word "grace" (never employed in the *Ordo*), Hildegard prefers images of fragrance and gentleness (*suauitas*) to describe how the soul is led back to its home. In particular, it is through song that the sluggish soul is wakened to the path of justice. The performance of heavenly music crystallizes her ideal of the fusion of body and spirit. Words symbolize the body, music the spirit, a fusion achieved most fully in the harmony of divinity and humanity in the Son of God (III.13.12). This final vision links up with the original vision of *Scivias* (I.1) in which brilliant light pours down on a young woman representing "the poor in spirit." Now that woman is transformed into the Bride of Christ.

After Hildegard completed *Scivias* in 1151 and had moved from Disibodenberg to Rupertsberg, she never wrote much more about the sacraments. The first major project to which she committed herself at the new community of women was a compilation about the "subtleties of the different natures of created things."[37] Although Hildegard does not present her scientific writing in the form of individual visions, she subsequently states explicitly that it had the same source of inspiration as the rest of her output.[38] Her biographer Theoderic of Echternach certainly believed that her writings about the nature of humanity and the rest of creation were as much indebted to prophetic inspiration as the rest of her writing.[39] While the label "creation spirituality" touches on an important aspect of her thought, it should not conceal her fundamental concern with the source of life itself, with humanity's need to be redeemed from sin, and with its blindness to this fructifying life. The viridity and moisture present to a greater or lesser degree in different parts of creation she sees as manifestations of a life fundamentally divine in origin yet ignored by humanity.

After she had written about the "subtleties" of creation, Hildegard turned in 1158 to human behavior in the *Book of Life's Merits*. Her central vision is of a human being who stretches from earth to heaven, through whom all creation takes sustenance. Only gradually does she explain that this is "the fighting man" foretold in Isaiah 42.13, and thus an image of the Word of God, made known to humanity through the Incarnation (I.21; I.28–29), covered to his knees by the winds, air, and greenness of the earth (III.1). Hildegard uses this figure, whom she sees looking in every direction, to comment on all forms of human behavior which do not live up to those ideals the figure embodies. From a storm cloud sustained by this figure, in which a crowd of the blessed dwell, issue responses to a variety of images of sinful behavior. Hildegard's main theme is the consequences of behavior that has fallen away from the norms embodied by the figure in her vision. The *Book of Life's Merits* takes a different tack from *Scivias* in that its central image is no longer Ecclesia but the Son of Man. By using visually evocative images, she communicates relatively traditional ethical teaching without resorting to the concepts of "sin" and "grace" so conventional in monastic theological writing. Her central message is that humanity needs to give up behavior that leads away from awareness of God, the fire that animates creation (I.25) but becomes everlasting torment for those who reject God (VI.12). While her focus is on the character of life rather than of creation, she represents the relationship between soul and body as like that between water and earth (V.14–15).

In her last major work, the *Book of Divine Works*, Hildegard looks further at that fiery life (*ignea vita*) she identifies as both the heart of creation and the central insight of all Scripture. Again her visions elaborate on her understanding of the Word of God, expounded on in the opening of John's Gospel and in the first chapter of Genesis, as life itself. Her visions are structured around the theme of God's Word resonating through creation and fully manifest in the Son of God, but she does not emphasize the sacraments of the church. When she does comment on Ecclesia, it is to complain about the worldliness of some ecclesiastical prelates and coming challenges that the church will face.

Even more explicitly than in *Scivias*, Hildegard identifies divinity as the fiery life that shines on the waters, in the sun, moon, and stars and all things. This fiery life is rationality itself, through which all things exist, and in which the Word resonates through creation. She considers God not as an omnipotent being above creation but as the life of the universe: "All these things live in their essence, and are not found in death, since I am life" (I.1.2).[40] She explains more briefly at the end of her exposition that the Father, Son, and Holy Spirit refer to eternity, the Word, and the connection between these two. Divinity is omnipresent in all creation, which existed in the mind of God even before the beginning of time (I.1.6). All things are brought into being through this rational light that emanates from God and gives all creatures life (I.1.9). Her doctrine that all things have existed in the mind of God enables her to explain that God was never without potential for creativity. The Son of God tramples on the injustice and dissension sown by Satan, that force of darkness which is overshadowed by the Living Light. Following the fall of Adam and Eve from paradise, they were deprived of that "beautiful viridity of the field, which is the blessing of God" (I.1.15). The only way for humanity to return to its rightful inheritance is through the Son of God.

In the second, third, and fourth visions of the *Book of Divine Works*, Hildegard develops her understanding of the spiritual significance of all parts of creation in far more detail than in *Scivias*. The sun and moon, stars and winds, as well as all the parts of the human organism, have an inner significance. Comparable twelfth-century syntheses of Christian teaching which might begin with an account of the divine nature and the creation of the world never devote such attention to the place of humanity within a wider physical universe. The essence of Hildegard's teaching is that physical disturbance is invariably a sign of deeper imbalance within the soul and that humanity must reject the forces of darkness if it is to be restored to health. The key to physical and spiritual health lies in moderation, so that no humor dominates another. Hildegard is most unusual among her contemporaries in wanting to connect traditional understanding of the humors to a wider cosmology.

Hildegard also develops in much more detail than in *Scivias* her theme of the intimate interconnection of body and soul. Humanity was structured according to the same principles as the universe (I.4.16). The soul is as a living fire within the body, which always has to choose between the path of self-indulgence of the flesh and the direction of the soul (I.4.17). This theme of psychological tension between flesh and spirit is a traditional one in ascetic literature. Less conventional is the way Hildegard integrates this psychological understanding (an important theme of the *Book of Life's Merits*) into her wider perception of both the physical body and the spiritual vocation of the soul. Thus she argues that the soul has two powers by which it tempers its activities, one capacity for rising through its senses to God, the other for delighting in the body "because it is created by God" (I.4.19). By identifying the soul as the life force of the body rather than as its form, she is able to connect these two dimensions of experience. The soul may do things "according to the taste of the flesh" until the blood dries out and the soul becomes exhausted. In the same vision (I.4.24) she then ventures a quite new picture of the relationship of soul and flesh, suggesting that sometimes the soul might give in to the flesh for the sake of some immediate enjoyment, just as a mother knows how to make a weeping child laugh. The soul comes to an agreement with the flesh just as the moon is warmed again by the sun (I.4.24). Her emphasis here on the interaction between flesh and soul, explored much more fully than in *Scivias*, suggests that Hildegard had moved a long way from the rigorous asceticism that Jutta had displayed and that had ultimately led to her early death. Hildegard reinforces her theme of complementarity when she explains that woman could not be called woman without man (*vir*), or man male without woman. Neither could exist without the other. As man (*vir*) signified the divinity of the Son of God, so woman signified his humanity (I.4.100). This is still a hierarchical vision of the world, but it recognizes the necessary interaction between different poles.

The long discussion of creation and the condition of humanity in the first part of the *Book of Divine Works* flows out of the opening explanation that God is "the fiery life" that sustains creation. It serves to explain what Hildegard sees as the true meaning of the great hymn of John's Gospel, explained at length at the end of the fourth vision (I.4.105).[41] The Word of God is indistinguishable from the rationality (*rationalitas*) that animates creation through the sound of its voice (I.4.105, p. 251). Although traditional exegesis did identify the Word of God as divine wisdom, few authors interpret the beginning of John's Gospel as about creation as a whole. The hymn is usually taken as a proof text for the divinity of Christ. By concentrating first on the relationship between flesh and soul in the human body, Hildegard gives a new meaning to the phrase "the Word became flesh." She sees the Incarnation not as an external intervention in the world but as the full manifestation of an inherently natural process.

In the *Book of Divine Works* Hildegard is similarly more concerned to elucidate the implications of the doctrine of the Incarnation than she is with the suffering and death of Christ as an individual. After elucidating the opening hymn of John's Gospel and reflecting on the mystery of how humanity and divinity were so fully joined in Christ, she does not speak about his death and resurrection but moves on to describe different parts of the world, some in darkness, others in light. There are regions in this world of great horror and wickedness, but the whole of creation "is hidden in a fire that penetrates and tests everything" (II.1.15). This observation leads into a detailed commentary on the meaning of the first verses of Genesis about the creation of the world (II.1.17–46). The seventh day prefigured the Incarnation (II.1.48).

The third section of the *Book of Divine Works* is like *Scivias* in focusing on the work of redemption that has still to be realized rather than on any redemptive act in the past. The Incarnation had long been anticipated, however, in human history. Hildegard emphasizes how Christ transformed human actions through the purity of his life (III.2.14). Her visions move to a climax when she turns to the first of three feminine images, the first being Love (*caritas*), "the splendor of the living God" (III.3.2). Through Love, Wisdom has ordered all things for the best. She has also revealed to a poor woman "the natural powers of different things" as well as "certain writings about meritorious behavior" (III.3.2). Hildegard's concern in the final books of *Divine Works* is no longer with creation but with life itself, sustained by Wisdom. A human being is rightly called "a life" because it lives through life and lives forever after the flesh has died (III.4.14).

The final vision brings together the image of a wheel, the dominant image of the first five visions, with that of the rectangular city used in visions six to nine. The circle represents both divinity and creation, while the rectangle symbolizes the City of God. The fusion of these two images provides a metaphor for what Hildegard was trying to achieve throughout the *Book of Divine Works,* integration of her understanding of creation into her vision of the heavenly city. Her central concern is not so much with the Incarnation as with the fundamental unity behind all creation, which existed in the mind of God even before it came into being. As announced in vision 1, God is the living fire that sustains all things. Even when heaven and earth had not yet come into being, viridity preexisted in the mind of God (III.5.2). This living fire has become fully incarnate in Christ, through whom the devil has been defeated (III.5.4). Recapitulating the closing hymn of the *Ordo virtutum,* Hildegard proclaims the appeal of the Son to the Father: "In the beginning all created things were green. In the middle period, flowers bloomed, but later viridity weakened. . . . My body is weakened, my children have become weak. . . . It wearies me that all my limbs have become an object of derision. See, Father, I am showing you my wounds. Therefore, all people, now bend your knees to your Father, so that he might extend his hand to you" (III.5.8). Hildegard's vision of the suffering of Christ is of a suffering that still endures, because of the blindness of humanity as a whole. All things were green in paradise, and after the Flood flowers started to bloom again, but now there is a great dryness and suffering.

This is a fundamentally apocalyptic vision of history, in which the golden age of the early church had given way to a time of darkness and corruption. Hildegard's attack on worldly prelates in III.5.16 of the *Book of Divine Works* forms a natural counterpart to her vision of pristine purity that has now been lost. There will be a time when "the viridity of fruitfulness" will descend on the earth and wisdom be strong among believers (III.5.20). At the same time, there will also be much injustice and corruption, and the authority of the Holy Roman Empire will decline (III.5.25). Some of her strongest denunciation is reserved for those who question the precepts of chastity. They will argue that "your law of continence is against the path of nature. Why should a man not be warm, who has fire in his breath that burns his whole body . . . ? For what reason should any man put aside warming himself on the flesh of another . . . ? Your teacher has not given you correct precepts, wanting you to be like a spirit not clothed with flesh . . ." (III.5.30). Hildegard gives the impression of being very familiar with these arguments against chastity and aware of their force. The irony was that she herself had acknowledged the close interaction between soul and flesh in an earlier part of the *Book of Divine Works*. Ultimately, however, she still defends the way of life she had learned from Jutta. Her preferred form of relationship was spiritual friendship such as she enjoyed with Volmar and those other monks who enjoyed her intimacy.

When Hildegard's community was placed under an interdict in 1178 by the clergy of Mainz cathedral for burying an excommunicated nobleman, Hildegard responded with a letter in which she crystallizes a number of the central features of her thought. Although the community was now deprived of receiving the sacrament of the Eucharist, her principal grievance was that they could no longer celebrate the liturgy with music. She explains that it is through music that humanity can return to the pristine condition of Adam, whose voice originally proclaimed "the sound of every harmony and the sweetness of the whole art of music."[42] Paradise for Hildegard is a place filled with music. Prophets and wise men in the past had devised every kind of melody to express the delight in their soul. This music frightens away the devil. The psalms of David, when set to music, allow humanity to anticipate the vision of the blessed, when paradise will be restored. Hildegard's melodies communicate the image not so much of an eternal peace in the next world as of that "fiery life" she sees at the heart of creation. It is through music that her sense of longing for the union of body and soul finds its fullest expression.

Hildegard's thought may not have that subtlety of reflection on language which characterizes the writing of Peter Abelard, and it does not provide that detailed justification for the Christian sacraments which made Hugh of St. Victor's theoretical writing so useful for preachers. Nonetheless, *Scivias,* the *Book of Life's Merits,* and the *Book of Divine Works* are comparable to other great works of doctrinal synthesis which emerge in the twelfth century. They present Christian doctrine in a way Hildegard considers to be accessible to its readers, answering questions they might raise through the use of images and analogies drawn from experience, rather than through abstractions.

Heir to the ascetic tradition embodied by Jutta, in whose shadow she spent the first half of her life, Hildegard was able to formulate her own distinctive interpretation of the religious life only after Jutta had passed away. It was not easy for her to throw off the image of the silent recluse imposed on her by her situation at Disibodenberg and to think of herself not as a recluse but as a frail human being privileged with insights that went beyond what the ancients had glimpsed. Central to that process was acceptance of her vulnerable physical condition as willed by God. Committed to the religious life, she was a sophisticated thinker who appreciated the necessity of presenting the message of Scripture in a way that conformed to human experience. Underlying her perception was awareness of a Living Light suffusing creation but unrecognized by so many people in society, even by those who claimed official commitment to religion. Hildegard's literary output as a whole can be interpreted as an attempt to come to terms with that realization.

FOUR

Prophet and Reformer

"Smoke in the Vineyard"

KATHRYN KERBY-FULTON

Sometime between 1158 and 1160 Arnold, archbishop of Mainz, sent a transparently supercilious letter to Hildegard, congratulating her on her prophetic gift: "We know that 'the Spirit breatheth where He will' [John 3.8], distributing His gifts to each as He wishes. . . . For if once He made plowmen and harvesters of sycamores into prophets, and caused an ass to speak, how can we be surprised if He teaches *you* with His inspiration?"[1] This was a low blow. The Holy Spirit, he says, can teach anyone to prophesy, even the uneducated prophet Amos, a harvester of sycamores by trade (Amos 7.14), and even less flatteringly Balaam's ass, who was briefly given the gift of speech in order to warn his master of divine vengeance (Numbers 22.28–34). Arnold could afford to be sarcastic, or so he thought. He was one of the "mighty prelates" of whom Barbara Newman speaks in the introductory chapter of this volume; he owed his appointment as archbishop to Emperor Frederick I and so represented the kind of imperial interference in church matters against which reformers like Hildegard raged. But Arnold would live—or, more precisely, *not* live—to regret his arrogance, and Hildegard knew it. In her response she tells him that the Living Light has a message for him: in effect, reform or be cut off from grace. She alludes allegorically to his oppressive tendencies and parodically turns his mockery of agricultural labor menacingly back on him, finishing off the job with a barely veiled prophecy of Arnold's imminent death: "O father, the Living Light has given these words to me for you: Why do you hide your face from me? . . . Why do you not stand firm in your awe of me . . . cast[ing] aside anything that stands in your way, like an overzealous thresher of wheat? . . . Therefore, rise up to God, for your time will come quickly."[2] Whether her prediction was based on divine inspiration or mere political foresight, it was not just a lucky hit: in June 1160 Arnold was murdered. Though Hildegard's most recent editor has suggested that the "your" of the final sentence was added after Arnold's death (this would make it *vaticinia ex eventu* or "prophecy after the event"), it would likely not have been hard for a politically alert contemporary—and Hildegard was certainly that—to foresee that Arnold was indeed running out of time. In return for the emperor's patronage, Arnold had exacted war tribute from the people of Mainz to fund Frederick's Italian campaigns. They revolted and he excommunicated the entire city, a notorious instance of clerical abuse of the power "to bind and unbind" that Christ had given to Peter and an instance that Hildegard apparently never forgot.[3]

This single incident—and one could cite many such from her correspondence—introduces us to the complex world in which Hildegard's gift for prophecy operated. That she had such a gift—what a modern secular society might call "second sight," what a faith community would call divine inspiration—had been apparent ever since as a child she astonished her nurse by correctly predicting the color of an unborn calf (a story too guileless to be fabricated).[4] What needs to be underlined about Hildegard is not then the fact of her prophetic gift but its centrality to her thought. Arnold likely little knew that he was attacking the very essence of Hildegard's self-image, an area in which she brooked no opposition. She had various strategies for handling such attacks. In this case, she starts off by letting Arnold know that her own Patron is mightier even than *his*. You behave, she writes, "as if you are perturbed and angry at the mystical words which I bring forth, not from myself, but as I see them in the Living Light. Indeed, things are shown to me there which my mind does not desire and which my will does not seek, but often I see them under compulsion."[5]

This statement, in the context of what Paul Franche aptly called Hildegard's "business letters [*papiers d'affaires*]," is an unusually personal remark;[6] it is one of Hildegard's more defensive assertions about her experience as prophet, a word used here in the classic sense of one who speaks, willingly or unwillingly, on behalf of God. (The Bible provides many instances of both types.) Hildegard's rather extreme insistence here that she speaks "under compulsion" may have been prompted by a sense of underlying malice in Arnold's otherwise oily letter, but the conviction is close in spirit, if not in tone, to what she wrote on the same subject to Elisabeth of Schönau. Elisabeth was her visionary protégée, and when the credibility of the young woman's prophetic vocation similarly came under attack, Hildegard wrote to her that

> those who desire to perform the works of God . . . should abandon celestial matters to Him Who is celestial . . . only sounding the mysteries of God like a trumpet. A trumpet simply renders the sound and does not produce it unless

> another breathes into it. . . . Let them . . . become mild, gentle, poor and
> lowly, as was the Lamb, of whose trumpet they are only the sound . . . Even I
> lie in the pusillanimity of fear, occasionally resounding a little from the Living
> Light, like the small sound of a trumpet, whence may God help me to remain
> in His ministry.[7]

This belief in her own instrumentality (here rendered unforgettably literal by the image of the trumpet) is the essence of her self-image as
prophet: charismatic, self-effacing, inspirational, evangelical. It is also,
one has to notice, politically foolproof, the perfect defense mechanism
for a reformist thinker who had to speak out against some of the most
powerful leaders of her day, most of whom were male and who had
over her the twin advantages of formal education and gender superiority in a patriarchal society.

How the political Hildegard relates to the prophetic Hildegard is a
complex question, but one comes away from reading her prophetic
writings with the sense that she could not have had the impact she had
without her immense political acumen. Indeed, without this shrewdness
she could not have survived (ecclesiastically) to prophesy as she did, for
even though Hildegard's sacramental theology was comfortably orthodox, her reformist thought was radical. So she used her prophetic
stance largely in the service of that reformist thought (one notices that
the nonreformist uses to which Hildegard put her prophetic gifts are
comparatively few and were nearly all solicited by other people).[8] What
is most remarkable about Hildegard, especially if we compare her
to the monastic reformers of her day—those who people the pages of,
for instance, Giles Constable's encyclopedic new study of the twelfth-
century reformation—is that Hildegard's lasting impact was not in the
area of reformist *spirituality.* That is, she developed no newly influential
view of the "imitation of Christ," the "apostolic life," or the other spiritual reformist preoccupations of her age.[9] Her real impact on her contemporaries and readers right through the sixteenth century was rather
her contribution to the theology of salvation history, especially her
novel views about the church's future and its final end.

Hildegard's reformist thought was then "apocalyptic," by which we
mean, as Marjorie Reeves has eloquently defined the word, "the disclo-
sure of hidden divine purpose in history, to which common usage has
added the dimension of imminent crisis."[10] Hildegard created the most
influential late medieval apocalypticism known to northern Europe.[11]
She was the most high-profile northern European to defy the entrenched and deeply pessimistic Augustinian view that history would

see no spiritual renewal between the ministry of Jesus and the coming of Antichrist. By defying this traditional view, Hildegard became the first internationally known spiritual meliorist,[12] comparable only to Joachim of Fiore (1135–1202)[13] in the scope of her influence and just ahead of Joachim himself in doing so. Although her meliorism was not as highly developed as Joachim's or, indeed, as some of the other alternative apocalyptic thinkers of the twelfth century, it was Hildegard's message that directly reached the largest number of medieval people. And this was largely owing to her prophetic zeal, her polemical pragmatism, and the work of her various disciples. Hildegard "got the message out," as we say today of our politicians and evangelists, by a number of means: her correspondence, her preaching tours, and the frankly promotional editing of her writings for posterity. Most effective of all was a little compilation of her prophecies made after her death and known as the *Mirror of Future Times*. In 1220 the monk Gebeno of Eberbach produced this as a kind of Reader's Digest version of the key apocalyptic passages from her massive visionary works and correspondence, works too large to be fully read or frequently copied.[14]

Although the seeds of Hildegard's radical apocalypticism are present in *Scivias,* their growth is most evident in her correspondence, starting especially with the faltering of the reform movement under Pope Anastasius IV (1153–1154) and the coming of the papal schism in 1159, a schism that would last for the rest of Hildegard's adult life (until 1177). *The Book of Divine Works (Liber divinorum operum)* ends with a detailed "apocalyptic program," a chronicle, so to speak, of the five future ages of the world, representing her life's work in prophecy, her complete vision of the End. But this program was the work of decades. To understand Hildegard's prophetic vocation and her increasingly radical theology of history, one must understand the origins of her reformist apocalypticism (part 1 of this essay) and then trace its growth in her own writings (part 2).

THE ORIGINS OF HILDEGARD'S PROPHECY: GREGORIAN REFORMIST THOUGHT AND THE GERMAN SYMBOLIST SCHOOL

Hildegard's prophetic style can be very difficult to understand. Even her medieval readers complained repeatedly about her obscurity. Gebeno of Eberbach insisted that "many disdain and abhor [or shrink from] the books of Hildegard because she speaks in an obscure or unusual style."[15] What they don't understand, he says, is that this is proof of "the true finger of God [*veri digiti Dei*]." But while we might all wish God's finger had pointed more lucidly, there was a good reason for her obscurity. She prophesied on dangerous issues, issues that caught church and lay leaders alike in vicious webs of intrigue, intimidation, and bloodshed.[16] Given the number of prelates who fled or were forced into exile or worse during Hildegard's lifetime, one can only conclude that being a woman was in some respects to her advantage. Hildegard was also astute enough to know when she could speak openly and when she could not, when to be partisan and when not. Especially when she addresses issues such as simony, imperial interference in ecclesiastical appointments, or papal schism, issues traditionally associated with the Gregorian reform and given a sadly new lease on life by Frederick I's policies, she becomes especially obscure.[17] At such times she makes use of a technique of coded prophetic writing, that is, of *deliberately* obscured wording, carefully calculated so as to communicate with those readers she wishes to understand her writing yet opaque or vaguely threatening to those she does not. A good instance of this obscurity is the short visionary treatise she wrote against the Cathar heretics, the so-called letter to the clergy of Mainz, actually written for Elisabeth of Schönau and a circle of anti-Cathar activists.[18] In this extremely oblique prophecy Hildegard blames the current ecclesiastical corruptions for the rise of heresy among the laity, using a cumbersome metaphor of the winds of "great destruction" which during her lifetime "have blown out of the mouth of the black beast," bringing evil works into

> the West, blasphemy and obliviousness of God among his holy ones, through the notoriety of a calf and through the cult of idols, crucifying the holy sacrifice . . . and into the North, phylacteries of vestments, enlarged according to the crooked serpent . . . But nevertheless sixty years and twenty-four months there are since the old serpent with phylacteries of vestments began to delude the people . . . But, now, the innumerable saints of God lift up their voices from under the altar . . . [causing] a wind to blow which is now working miracles. Still, the one who sits upon the black horse is sending forth the noise of a contrary wind to destroy those miracles. But it will not prevail.[19]

The most generous thing one can say about this sort of prophetic writing is that it must assume a target audience "in the know," that is, readers who have a good understanding of reformist rhetoric, or lots of experience of Hildegard's style, or, preferably, both. What is interesting from a modern perspective is that Hildegard usually indulges *this* degree of obscurity only when she is addressing her most intimate readers, and these seem to have been most often female. For this letter Elisabeth of Schönau, with whom Hildegard shared a zealous campaign against heresy, is the only certainly known recipient, and in another similar instance Hildegard addressed an equally obscure political prophecy (on imperial matters, schism politics, and impending clerical chastisement) to her own nuns at the Rupertsberg.[20] This suggests that Hildegard clearly thought women an important audience for her political and intellectual reformist thought—and this brings us closer both to her active coterie and to a sense of the kind of role women could play in twelfth-century political and ecclesiastical life.

As for what the "Mainz" prophecy might mean, we do know that it draws on the kind of biblical symbolism used by the Gregorian reformers: the "notoriety of a calf" refers to Old Testament idolatry, and thus to simony, that is, to the illicit buying or selling of church appointments or spiritual services (named after Simon Magus, the magician who tried to purchase the secret of the disciples' power in Acts 8.18–19). The "enlarged phylacteries" refer to the hypocrisy of the Pharisees (Jewish priests who wore small scrolls of the Commandments tied to their foreheads to symbolize their meditation on the Law; Christ had accused them in Matthew 23.5 of enlarging these to draw attention to their piety).[21] That much anyone familiar with the tradition of Gregorian biblical rhetoric would have picked up. But one needs to know Hildegard's prophetic typology (which fortunately she makes clearer elsewhere) to understand that the Pharisees are for her the second branch of forerunners of Antichrist, the first being the Old Testament worshippers of Baal (associated with the idolaters or simoniacs alluded to above)[22] and the third branch being the heretics themselves, that is, the long string of heretics who have plagued Christianity from the followers of Arius to those of Hildegard's own day (the Cathars) to an even more dangerous group she prophesied for the future (in the Cologne prophecy).[23]

The specific period of sixty-two years she names takes us back to the final phase of the long and destructive reign of the emperor Henry IV, who, like Frederick in Hildegard's own time, created papal schisms and fought with reformers. Hildegard never directly names Henry but speaks of him often as a "worshipper of Baal" (and worse). The key point here is that, using prophetic license, she symbolically conflates *all* the time periods to suggest apocalyptically the persistence of all three forerunning groups of Antichrist in her own time. She elsewhere called her own time the *tempus muliebre,* the time of effeminate weakness,[24] the beginning of which she dates to the end of Henry's reign; here in a deliberately roundabout way she implies that Frederick ("the one who sits upon the black horse" of Apocalypse 6.5) is perpetuating that time. The voices of the saints under the altar (Apocalypse 6.9–11), now performing miracles, are for Hildegard the only hope in this entire dark prophecy—and, we should note, they figure also in Elisabeth's prophecy against the Cathars (likely written in response to this one), suggesting that she, at least, understood perfectly what Hildegard was writing, even if we do not.

This tendency toward symbolic conflation across the Testaments and into contemporary times is typical of a school of twelfth-century monastic theology known to modern scholars as German Symbolism ("der deutsche Symbolismus"), among whose theologians the best known, after Hildegard herself, are Rupert of Deutz, Gerhoh of Reichersberg, Anselm of Havelberg, and Otto of Freising.[25] Theologically, the Symbolists worked from a conviction that there were inherent correspondences, or "concordances," between the Old and New Testaments, the key to which lay in symbolic similarities that, properly understood, revealed important parallels between pre-Christian and Christian history. Since pre-Christian history was complete, its symbolism could be used, they believed, to predict (by extrapolation) the course of Christian history still to come. This seductive idea eventually found its most elaborate and celebrated expression in the prophetic thought of Joachim of Fiore, the ultimate heir, according to H. D. Rauh, of the German Symbolists, but it was highly developed in Germany first. The essence of *Symbolismus* is poetic, not intellectual; its "three pillars" (and massive ones they are) Rauh identified as symbolism, history, and monasticism itself.[26] German Symbolism, then, was essentially a monastic movement, the product of a leisurely, richly digressive, meditative approach to the Scriptures—the mental world of the cloisters, not the schools. The Symbolists tended to distrust the new dialectical thought concurrently being developed in the fledgling universities of France, and we know that Hildegard had among her readers a strong male following who appreciated this conservatism.[27] Symbolist writing takes on a multitude of genres (ranging from the biblical commentaries of Rupert and Gerhoh, to liturgical drama such as *The Play of Antichrist,* to the *Weltchronik,* or world history, of Otto, to the visionary and dramatic writing of Hildegard), but poetic impetus always characterizes Symbolist work and is fundamental to the methodology of all these thinkers.[28] This was a highly visual way of thinking, entirely suited to and likely even stimulating to a visionary mind.

Hildegard exploited the resources of the Symbolist mentality more creatively than any of her colleagues. She likely learned much from her older Benedictine contemporary Rupert of Deutz, who also had some visionary tendencies[29] and who combined his *Symbolismus* with the strident reformist apocalyptic language the Gregorians reserved for their most hated imperial enemies. Hildegard owes much to the embryonic apocalypticism of Gregorian reformers like Rupert, whose widely influential writings she almost certainly knew. The differences between them are also instructive. While Rupert drew on biblical and classical tradition for all his symbols, Hildegard was much more likely to use original allegory, "homegrown parables" (as Newman aptly calls them),[30] and maverick visionary imagery to elaborate the repertoire of Gregorian and Symbolist language they had both inherited. Both Rupert and Hildegard had been oblates, raised in an essentially conservative Benedictine tradition; they both believed that reform should be accomplished through a return to the pristine state of the early church rather than through the desertion of Benedictinism for one of the newer orders. But, as Charles Czarski has shown in his important, still unpublished study, Hildegard's prophetic thought was radicalized in response to her midcentury disillusionment over the schism—and this seems to have pushed her decidedly beyond the traditions she shared with writers like Rupert.[31]

Rupert wrote his *Songs [or Prophecies] on the Calamities of the Church of Liège (Carmina exulis de calamitatibus ecclesie Leodiensis)* when he was a young monk. The work is a series of dramatic apocalyptic poems written when Rupert's abbot, Berengar, was deposed to make way for an imperial favorite, an event that drove twenty-five monks into exile, inspired the *Carmina*, and made intellectual history.[32] The *Carmina* is the earliest work of German Symbolism; it makes an unprecedented break with the Augustinian tradition by interpreting the figures of the Apocalypse historically—that is, Rupert used the Apocalypse to understand *contemporary* events.[33] Hildegard's break with Augustinian tradition would be even more startling, but Rupert's was pioneering.

In the *Carmina* the Church (Ecclesia) appears as the Bride of Christ, but now sadly disheveled, lamenting before the celestial court that she is being overwhelmed by simoniacs, forerunners of Antichrist: "Woe is

me! . . . Who among those who are afflicted can be healed when Nero
holds Rome and Simon is called Pope?" (I.43–44). We find throughout
the fluidity of typological reference we have seen in Hildegard's Mainz
prophecy: Simon Magus, Nero, Arius, Antichrist are all more or less
conflated and thus made suddenly historically *present*, while the horror
of simony itself provokes from Rupert a cluster of Old Testament images of idolatry (such as Mammon and Baal).[34] Some of the typological
passages are heavily historicized: Henry IV is the beast from the sea;
his antipope, Wibert, is Arius, and so on. The *Carmina* contains all
the elements, then, of Gregorian apocalyptic rhetoric: the images of
trafficking in spiritual goods, of worshiping golden idols, of forerunners of Antichrist, of terrible beasts and embattled exiles holding to the
true faith in a life of penury. It is apocalyptic *drama* in every sense.
There are also other common Gregorian images, such as the wolf in
sheep's clothing (that is, the imperial interloper Otbert [IX.77–80]) who
keeps the true pastor (Berengar) from his flock, and Simon Magus's attempt to fly (XII.17–24)—images we find in Hildegard's prophecies repeatedly and especially in the Cologne letter and the *Book of Divine
Works*. But there are some important differences. In these two works by
Hildegard the secular leadership plays a key role in church reformation;
however, there is no positive role for secular leadership either in the
Carmina or elsewhere in Rupert's thought.[35] Rupert believed that secular power (*regnum*) would perish with the end of the world, unlike the
priesthood (*sacerdotium*), and that the church itself would remain the
bulwark against Antichrist that St. Paul had spoken of so mysteriously
in 2 Thessalonians 2.7–12.[36] By contrast Hildegard, a few decades later,
could speak only of the faithful remnant, not the institutional church itself, as that bulwark. Rupert never envisioned any future reform for the
church; his *Carmina* ends with Ecclesia lamenting just as she had at the
outset, "Woe is me! How many sufferings I have borne! How many
evils I have seen!" (XII.9)—textbook Augustinian pessimism.[37]

We have only to turn to Hildegard's famous Kirchheim prophecy to
see how different her views were. In this letter Hildegard condemns the
corruption of the clergy by using an allegorical image of the church as a
battered woman. This vision is strikingly like Rupert's *Carmina* in its
central conception of Ecclesia in womanly distress and may even have
been influenced by it. In any case, both Rupert and Hildegard drew
upon the same genres (the Passion play of liturgical drama and the
Boethian vision of Lady Philosophy) for their portraits of the disheveled, corruption-torn Ecclesia in full, dramatic lament.[38] But Hilde-

gard does something Rupert would never dream of: she prophesies the confiscation of clerical wealth in order to clean house on the corruption his poem seems only to lament. She relies, in true Symbolist fashion, on a firm sense of the applicability of biblical concords to present history; in the following passage the biblical parallel with her own age is the period of the destruction of Jerusalem. To this she adds a liberal dose of Gregorian rhetoric:

> And I, poor womanly form, saw an extended sword hanging in the air, of which one edge was turned toward heaven, the other toward earth. And that sword was extended over the spiritual people . . . and I saw that sword cut off certain places of the spiritual people in the same way as Jerusalem was cut off after the passion of Christ. But nevertheless I saw that God will watch over for Himself many God-fearing, pure and simple priests in that adversity, just as He responded to Elijah when He said that He would leave to Himself seven thousand men in Israel whose knees have not been bowed before Baal (Vulgate, 3 Reg. 19.18). Now may the inextinguishable fire of the Holy Spirit fill you, so that you may be converted to the better part.[39]

There is always hope at the end of Hildegard's prophecies, and judging by their huge popularity with medieval readers, that hope did not go unappreciated.

In Hildegard it is the clergy who have desecrated Ecclesia through political cowardice and corruption; in Rupert it is the interference of imperial powers. In Rupert's poem the church becomes a powerful symbol of pathos through his conflation of the distressed Ecclesia with the apocalyptic image of the "woman clothed with the sun," laboring to give birth while under attack by the dragon (Apocalypse 12.1–4)—an image that Hildegard would shockingly reverse in *Scivias*. Rupert describes the lamenting woman in some detail in section III of the poem: she is barefoot, and stripped of her jewels and crown, like the chastised daughters of Syon (Isaiah 3.18–24), one of Hildegard's favorite prophetic images. The woman laments her laceration at the hands of simoniacs (IV.1–2) and the fall of the crown from her head (IX.16; see Lamentations 5.16), an image used prominently in Hildegard's prophecies to Cologne and Trier.

In the Trier prophecy Hildegard castigated the bishops for tamely submitting to imperial schism and manipulation.[40] The prophecy as we have it today is a written version of the sermon she delivered at Trier on the feast of Pentecost 1160, warning, once again, of the coming expropriation of clerical properties as a punishment for their laxity. She dwells on the theme of past expulsions God has inflicted for disobedience, and she alludes to the coming of "a certain tyrant" (Henry IV) who is the source of all evils of the current "effeminate" age. Using the same image as Rupert had, Hildegard prophesies:

> O daughter of Sion, the crown of your head will be ruined, and the cloak of the pride of your riches will be diminished, and, constrained to small number, you will be expelled from region to region. Through powerful men many cities and cloisters must be dispersed. And princes will say, "Let us take away from them the iniquity which through them subverts the whole world."[41]

But the prophecy is also about reformist hope. Based loosely, again, on a sense of biblical concordance, Hildegard prophesies a return to the "first dawn of justice" for a purified clergy, which is paralleled with the peace and harmony of the Pentecost period, "because the passion of Christ made all things temperate."[42]

Compared to Hildegard, Rupert was a textbook Gregorian in his reformist thought and use of apocalyptic rhetoric. Generally speaking, while he worried about the recovery of monastic possessions, Hildegard prophesied their confiscation as punishment for laxity; while he idealized the role of the papacy and believed in its primacy over the emperor, Hildegard castigated popes and emperors alike, prophesying the end of *both* seats of power well before the Last Judgment.[43] Rupert defended Cluny and the black monks while Hildegard castigated laxity in all monasteries, reserving what little praise she had for the Cistercian order (which Rupert distrusted heartily). These differences are largely a result of changes that took place in the few decades separating them: Rupert (1070–1129) did not live to see what Hildegard (1098–1179) did, a decline in reformist zeal and encroaching materialism even in reformed abbeys.[44] Desperation was to make Hildegard bolder and bolder.

THE RADICALIZATION OF HILDEGARD'S REFORMIST APOCALYPTICISM

In describing some of the variations in attitudes among Gregorian reformers, John Gilchrist issued a reminder that "it is a grave mistake to see ecclesiastical reform in this period as solely a struggle between opposites, i.e., between laity and clerics, imperialists and papalists. . . . Such harsh divisions ignore the complexity of the situation."[45] There could be no better case in point than Hildegard's; hers is anything but a simplistically pro-papal and anti-imperial stance. We can trace this complexity back to Disibodenberg, the monastery she entered as a young oblate. As the Disibodenberg annalist wrote under the year of

Henry's death, 1106 (by then Hildegard would have been eight years old and possibly already living with Jutta): "It is perfectly clear that Henry was a perverse man and excluded from the church by a just judgment. For he sold all spiritualities, [and] was disobedient to the apostolic see in advancing a usurper."[46] But the annalist also speaks of Henry as merciful, forgiving, and charitable to the poor. Perhaps it is not surprising then that Hildegard's attitude is equally complex. On the one hand, she followed the Gregorian line in castigating Henry for the church's woes and in having no truck with popular apocalyptic hopes for a holy Last World Emperor (such as one finds, for instance, in the *Play of Antichrist*, a contemporary German Symbolist work). But if she never idealized the emperor, nor did she ever idealize the papacy, even apocalyptically; there is no place in her thought for an infallible, all-powerful pope such as one finds in the *Dictatus Papae* of Gregory VII. She castigated Pope Anastasius IV with the same vehemence as she did Frederick I, who provoked her epistolary wrath not, it seems, for creating the schism, but for prolonging it.[47] Her abbey enjoyed privileges granted by Frederick, and her reliance on the aristocracy in many crises (partly a facet of her own aristocratic background) makes Hildegard a different kind of reformer. More pragmatic and even-handed in church/state politics than Rupert, Hildegard would eventually reject both institutions in her apocalyptic program. This is one of the most unusual and radical features of her thought.

The second unusual aspect of Hildegard's apocalyptic stance, given her Benedictine outlook and her fondness for a return to the ideals of the early church, was her willingness to contemplate institutional change. It is perhaps no accident that this willingness is most clearly delineated in one of her letters to a Cistercian convent. Unlike Rupert, who viewed institutional change with suspicion and the Cistercians with antagonism, Hildegard reserves her greatest praise (or better, her fewest criticisms) for this newer order. She writes to the Cistercians of Eberbach:

> You therefore who fear God, hear the Spirit of the Lord saying to you: . . . purge yourselves before the day of those tribulations when the enemies of God and of you will put you to flight and turn you around [*conuertent*] to the right place of humility and poverty . . . Indeed, in the same way God changed the Old Law from its usage into the spiritual life, *when he purged each single prior institution toward greater utility.*[48]

This suggests that her concording mode of thought led her to think the changes of her own times comparable to the upheavals that produced

the New Testament era. Hildegard never formalized this idea the way
Joachim of Fiore did, but its significance should not be overlooked—or
underestimated. It is an important instance of reformist thought and
Symbolist method producing progressive ideology.

Hildegard shares with both Rupert and Joachim an ideology of the
primacy of the contemplative life and its power to salvage and sustain
the Christian mission through the worst times of history. She also
shares, especially with apocalyptic thinkers from the newer orders, like
Gerhoh of Reichersberg, Eberwin of Steinfeld, Anselm of Havelberg,
and Joachim himself, a sense of meliorism about the possibilities of the
spiritual life.[49] This is striking in a Benedictine writer. This departure
from the traditional pessimism of Augustinian eschatology seems to
have arisen for Hildegard, as we have seen, in creative new Symbolist
understandings of the concordances between the Testaments. The one
most fundamental to her prophetic thought seems to have been the belief that just as there had been peace before the first coming of Christ,
there would be peace before the second.[50] Hildegard's mature "apocalyptic program" in fact suggests more than one period of future renewal, but the one she speaks most often and most lyrically about is
"the return to the first dawn of justice." This period she foresees as the
result of a terrible clerical holocaust God would soon rain down on the
corrupt clergy of her day.[51] This chastisement would leave, as she says
in the Kirchheim prophecy, a few simple and devoted clergy living an
eremitical life of pristine purity, but it would represent a heightened
spiritual state and a new zenith of the monastic ideal.

As the chronological study of Hildegard's apocalyptic writings reveals, her long-term optimism grew, ironically, out of an increasing pessimism about the immediate future and growing disillusionment with
the institutional church. Traditional apocalyptic thought in Hildegard's
time was epitomized in a very popular little treatise on Antichrist by
Adso of Moutier-en-Der. Writing in the tenth century, Adso had seen
the Frankish empire as the mysterious, unnamed agent that, according
to 2 Thessalonians 2.7, would hold back Antichrist, so his work was
popular with imperial apocalyptic thinkers.[52] For Rupert it was the
church that would perform this function; for Hildegard it was the faithful (few) themselves.[53] She explicitly named the schism as a cause for
her later disillusionment and the final reason she decided to give up the
preaching tours that taxed her always delicate health.[54] In the few
decades between Rupert's death and Hildegard's publication of *Scivias*,
the targets of reformist apocalypticism were already shifting from the

enemy without to the enemy within. Rupert's central apocalyptic image of the church, the woman in labor fleeing from the dragon (Apocalypse 12.3), illustrates the older mentality succinctly. Attacked from without, Ecclesia nevertheless still labors to give birth to the Word of God, just as Mary gave birth to Christ, the Word Incarnate.[55] But as early as *Scivias* Hildegard shockingly portrayed Ecclesia as giving birth to Antichrist himself. The image is an inversion—whether deliberate or not—of Rupert's.

In this disturbing scene Ecclesia is described as bloody and bruised from many beatings. Hildegard's celebrated interest in gynecological studies may explain the graphic detail of the passage, as may also her interest in exorcism, but neither would explain its savagery:

> From the navel to the groin she had various scaly spots. In her vagina there appeared a monstrous and totally black head . . . Lo, the monstrous head removed itself from its place with so great a crash that the entire image of the woman was shaken in all its members. Something like a great mass of much dung was joined to the head; then, lifting itself upon a mountain, it attempted to ascend to the height of heaven.[56]

This is a striking passage for many reasons. Bernard McGinn has pointed out that this appears to be the earliest direct reference to Antichrist's attempt to mimic Christ's ascension, one of many notable features in Hildegard's often unique treatment of the Antichrist legend—a treatment fraught, in fact, with "overtones of sexual violence."[57] These overtones arise in her account of the corrupt clergy, Antichrist's forerunners, who commit a kind of sexual assault on Ecclesia, a metaphor that would likely have occurred to Hildegard because the Gregorian reformers often rhetorically referred to simony as rape.[58] One can further partially explain the shocking quality of the passage by suggesting that Hildegard treats the birth of Antichrist like an exorcism. We know that some years after she wrote this prophecy, when she was asked to exorcize an evil spirit, she described its emergence as happening "together with a terrible voiding from the woman's private parts."[59] One can also point to the strikingly female interest in the mechanics of childbirth. But all the rhetorical, exorcist, and gynecological resonances in the world (interesting as they are) cannot explain away the fundamental theological point here: for Hildegard, and indeed even for the early Hildegard, the church was not going to be a bulwark against Antichrist but rather his point of origin.

Some other early works of Hildegard's, written before 1159, show a similar sourness of tone with respect to the institutional church. The notion that the secular powers would play a welcome role in the chastisement of the clergy also appears relatively early, sometimes bringing with it a positive view of imperialism. This had not yet appeared in the letter written to Pope Eugene III (1145–1153), which sets out a straightforwardly pro-papal/anti-imperial allegory.[60] At the synod of Trier in 1147–1148 Pope Eugene had approved Hildegard's writings and given her papal license to continue, so it is perhaps no wonder that she was inclined to cast the pope so positively (the emperor, by contrast, is allegorized as a greedy bear). In 1150–1151, however, Hildegard also addressed a letter to King Conrad III, who had written to her for counsel in the wake of his failed efforts in the Second Crusade and the death of his eldest son. Hildegard's response is remarkable for its positive suggestion about the role of the "bear." This is also one of the few instances in which Hildegard's apocalyptic vision contains anything like a secular leader, the warrior, or *vir praeliator.* Although the image is just a simile in this early letter, Hildegard later developed it into a full prophecy. It was perhaps inspired by her desire to make a kindly allusion to Conrad's crusading efforts. These images occur toward the end of the letter, after Hildegard has described vaguely distinctive "times" to come:

> The next time will arouse itself somewhat toward justice, but will afterwards arise like a bear tearing apart *all riches gained wrongfully.* Following this, signs of masculine virility will show, so that all the ointment-handlers [i.e., the bishops] will run back to the first dawn of justice, with fear, modesty and wisdom. Princes will be unanimously in concord with one another, just like a warrior [*vir praeliator*] raising a banner against the time of error, which God will destroy according to what he knows, and as it pleases him. And he who knows all things says to you, "O King, restrain yourself from your will and correct yourself, so that you may come to that time purified rather than embarrassed by your deeds."[61]

The letter's tone is reproving but by Hildegardian standards only mildly so. The real criticism is directed toward the church and makes use of some virulent Gregorian rhetoric, for instance, in the comment that "the spiritual people will be lacerated as if by wolves." Hildegard prophesies severe castigation for "the vineyard of the Lord": "Afterwards, in truth, worse times will come in which the true Israelites will be scourged, and in which the catholic throne will be shaken by error: and therefore the last times will be blasphemous, like a cadaver in death. Whence the vineyard of the Lord smokes with pain."[62] Her contemporaries held this to have been an accurate prophecy of the schism, which occurred some eight years later (it may, of course, have been *vaticinia ex eventu*). Be that as it may, what is beyond doubt is that in this early letter all the tenets of her mature apocalyptic program are present, though in a vague form: a conviction that the papacy would err; that she lived in an "effeminate" time (*velut in muliebri persona*); that religious would have their temporalities confiscated as just punishment for their greed; that they would be expelled from their homes; that a faithful remnant would survive to live humbly in solitude; and that such a purified clergy would effect a return to the ideals of the early church in the "first dawn of justice."

This letter indicates that even by 1151 Hildegard seems to have distrusted both the major institutions of her day. By the time she wrote the *Book of Divine Works* (1163–1174), this distrust had solidified into the prophecy that neither the papacy nor the empire would survive to see the world's final eras.[63] If she ultimately trusts anyone (aside from the faithful remnant, among whom she numbers, with rather endearing partiality, her own convent), it seems to be the aristocracy, from whose ranks she herself sprang and to whom she appealed for help in many of the administrative crises of her abbacy.[64]

Hildegard's prophetic ideas about monastic possessions (and these seem to have been rather distinct from her practical ones!) reflect early and mid-twelfth-century reformist ideology.[65] The older view is well represented by Rupert in his defense of the black monks' endowments and right to "spiritualia" (that is, payment for performance of priestly duties, or ecclesiastical revenues more generally). More radical reformers, however, in a nostalgia for the simplicity of the early church, sought to separate and discourage certain types of revenues for monasteries, a tendency almost counter to the original Gregorian impetus to recover all ecclesiastical property and revenues from lay control. Pope Paschal II's famously idealistic proposal in 1111, that the German churches renounce and return to the empire all the endowment lands and that bishops hitherto become simple pastors without temporal responsibility, revealed a fundamental dichotomy among Gregorian reformers on the question of property.[66] As Brian Tierney has said, Paschal was simply taking the Gregorian notion of the superiority of spiritual leaders to its logical conclusion: if spiritual leaders were superior, then they should not be involved in temporal affairs. The opposite (that is, the Humbertian) view, however, would be that if spiritual power is superior, then temporal possessions and secular power ought to be subject to it.

Paschal's view, "always a minority opinion within the ecclesiastical hierarchy but never quite extinct," according to Tierney, "found its classical formulation towards the middle of the twelfth century in the writings of St. Bernard of Clairvaux"—who was, of course, Hildegard's great mentor.[67] In Bernard's well-known words, "Tell me, which power and office dost thou consider to be the greater, that of forgiving sins, or that of dividing possessions? . . . These vile terrestrial things have their own proper judges, namely, the princes and rulers of this earth . . . For wherefore shouldst thou try to again wield that sword which thou wert commanded of old to replace in its scabbard?" (see John 18.11).[68] It is in this Bernardine tradition that, I believe, we must see Hildegard, in her repeated apocalyptic prophecies of confiscation of clerical temporalities and in her carefully explicit prophecy on the "dividing of possessions" in the *Book of Divine Works*.[69] Via Hildegard, this particular radical Gregorian motif crept into reformist apocalyptic thought and there it stayed, to be given a whole new lease on life in the Franciscan Joachite handling of poverty controversies of the thirteenth century. But Hildegard's idealization of temporal monastic poverty and her persistent prophecies of confiscation (a fantasy perhaps piqued by her extended struggle with Disibodenberg for her nuns' endowments) placed her among the "never quite extinct" minority who, in spite of the charisma of reformers like Bernard, saw their cause going down to defeat by midcentury.[70]

By midcentury another cause for disillusionment was on the horizon. In 1153–1154 Hildegard wrote to Pope Anastasius to prophesy the ruin of Rome, using the same kind of allegory of the church as Bride of Christ and daughter of the king (*filia Regis*) that Rupert had used in the *Carmina*. Here the *filia Regis* is also *Justicia*, a key word in Gregorian polemics, referring originally to the ideal of the church's liberty or freedom to exercise power over all spiritual affairs. But Justicia, or Justice, so hard won during the heady years of Gregorian zeal, is now, Hildegard complains, abused by the papacy itself:

> And you, O Rome, lying as if at the point of death (*in extremis*), will be so perturbed that the strength of your feet on which you have thus far stood will weaken, because you love the daughter of the King, that is, Justice, not with ardent love but as if in the torpor of sleep, so that you expel her from you, whence she wishes to flee from you, if you will not call her back. But nevertheless the great mountains will reach out still to your aid, lifting you upwards, and the great trunks of great trees will support you, so that you will not be wholly destroyed and scattered in your honor as the Bride of Christ. But you will have some wings of your distinction until the snow comes, flinging forth many mockeries and insanities.[71]

The prophecy is written in one of her mildly obscure prophetic styles. In it Hildegard promises the decay of Rome's powers, and, despite the sustaining or revivifying forces available to it, she suggests that it will remain crippled when the End comes ("you will not be *wholly* destroyed and scattered in your honor as Bride of Christ," retaining "some wings of your distinction until the snow comes"). The prophecy ends with a Gregorian warning against "pagan rites" and a mass of undifferentiated, vaguely periodized gloom. It was not until the *Book of Divine Works* that Hildegard developed a clear periodization of future times (a detailed elaboration of the five periods still to come, designated by the five animals of her apocalyptic vision in *Scivias*).[72] In the *Divine Works* she would also say explicitly what she only hints at here: that Rome would dwindle in importance to just another bishopric, a reference no doubt to tensions between Frederick Barbarossa and the pope over jurisdiction. As Tierney explains:

> Pope Hadrian IV once wrote to inform the emperor that the government of Rome belonged to "St. Peter." Barbarossa replied grimly that if the imperial title conveyed no rights in Rome it conveyed no rights anywhere. To the twelfth-century popes it seemed intolerable that the Roman church should be reduced to the status of just one more imperial bishopric, but they could hardly deny that the man they crowned in St. Peter's as emperor of the Romans was in some sense ruler of Rome.[73]

By 1174 Hildegard would have news for both parties: neither was immortal.

This left, for Hildegard, a leadership vacuum, so to speak, on both the secular and the religious fronts—a problem she never fully solved, but her attempts to solve it were typically visionary and charismatic. She proposed, in effect, two candidates: a vaguely realized warrior or crusading hero to oversee secular government, and—characteristically—a corps of prophets to oversee spiritual government. (We should note here that she did not envision a *single* spiritual leader; Hildegard seems to have implicitly distrusted single-figure leadership of the church and might well have approved of fifteenth-century conciliarism, had she lived to see it.) Her letter to the clergy of Trier (ca. 1160) is unusual for its attempt, only hinted at in her early letter to Conrad, to overtly fill the secular leadership void in her apocalyptic program with this crusader, or *vir praeliator.* He will reign during the long period of coming spiritual renewal (the "return to the first dawn of justice"), and his wisdom, supported by the prophets, will prolong that renewal:

Indeed, a warrior [*vir praeliator*] will do this who will consider in the beginning
and end of his works how far he may resist the erring people. He will constitute
prophets at first as the head . . . [with whose help] for the understanding of [the
people] he will explain prophecy. . . . After this, all spiritual things will be
strengthened without taint or defect . . . because the warrior will replenish the
wholesomeness of the air and will bring forth the viridity of virtue.[74]

As this passage indicates, Hildegard saw prophetic leadership as so
wholesome that it actually improved the natural environment. In the
Book of Divine Works she would predict a zenith of prophetic wisdom
and revelation on earth to occur during the second great period of spiritual renewal (which would happen at the end of her third "time," the
time of the Pale Horse), and again the elements and the fruits of the
earth would flourish amid such sweetness.[75]

Hildegard was, finally, most famous in the later Middle Ages for a
prophecy from her mature years which combined all the themes we
have seen so far: her optimism about spiritual renewal, her prophecy of
confiscation of ecclesiastical property and the rise of heresy, Gregorian
reformist rhetoric, and Symbolist concordances. These all appear in her
fabulously influential Cologne letter (ca. 1162) castigating the local
clergy for their laxity, which, she believed, was the root cause of the rise
of the Cathar heresy there and of new heretics still to come. Many,
many medieval and Reformation readers who knew nothing else about
Hildegard of Bingen knew this prophecy. In the early period of Gregorian reform the church had gradually pressured lay lords to hand over
ecclesiastical properties; it seemed logical, then, that, seeing the wealth
abused by the church, the secular lords might force its return. In the
Cologne letter Hildegard attaches a new significance to this old fear.
Here she physically describes the heretics of the future who will incite
the aristocracy to confiscation—a description that would actually cause
the expulsion of the first friars approaching Cologne and that would
form the basis of a whole thirteenth-century antimendicant propaganda.[76] This prophecy was also to carry Hildegard's fame into late-
fourteenth-century England (among other places), where two hundred
years after her death the Wycliffites were preaching the enticements of
clerical confiscation to a cash-strapped king and nobility.[77] Here is
Hildegard's influential description: "But those people . . . sent and seduced by the devil . . . will come with pale faces and compose themselves as if in all holiness and will join themselves with the greater secular princes, to whom they will say concerning you, 'Why do you hold
with these and why do you suffer with them? They pollute the whole

earth with their stained iniquity.' "[78] As in the Trier letter and as in the Kirchheim letter eight years later,[79] the Cologne prophecy leaves it up to the secular powers to save the church from these forerunners of Antichrist:

> But those unfaithful men, seduced by the devil, will be the rod [scopa] of your castigation ... However, those deceivers are not the ones who will come before the Last Day, when the devil will fly on high ... rather, they are a forerunning branch of them. But nevertheless, as soon as they will have been found out in the perversities of Baal and other depraved works, princes and other great ones will attack them and just as rabid wolves they will be killed, wheresoever they are found. ... Then the dawn of justice [will arise], and your last days will be better than your earlier ones ... and you will shine like gold, and so you will remain for long periods to come.[80]

Medieval marginalia tell us that some later readers of Hildegard did notice the visionary hope she offered—amid all the terror.[81] But by the time Hildegard completed the final apocalyptic vision of the *Divine Works* in 1174, her faith in the institutional church was at an all-time low. In a dramatic interlude where she portrays the lamenting Justicia—like Rupert's *Carmina*, almost a closet drama in its own right—she allowed the traditional enemies of the church, the princes, to speak judiciously and even self-searchingly about the need for confiscation of ecclesiastical property. By contrast, and an astonishing contrast it is, she ruthlessly satirizes the shrill voices of the clergy, who protest the confiscations with arrogance, making them the target of a low humor she usually saves for her portrayals of the devil and his minions.[82] It is not a flattering portrait of the clergy, but it is surprisingly flattering of secular powers. As an indication of her mood on ecclesiastical politics near the end of her life, it is sobering: she clearly felt that the only possible reform for the clergy was going to have to come forcibly and from without. To carry it through, she looked to the class she seems most to have trusted, the aristocracy. In this way the *Divine Works* portrays an *enlightened* aristocracy, playing their role in her final apocalyptic drama with dignity and wisdom.

Hildegard's is probably the most detailed apocalyptic program produced by a twelfth-century writer, and the *Book of Divine Works* is its most elaborate explication. Unfortunately, we have not the space here to follow its twists and turns. The last vision of book 3 was her magnum opus as an apocalyptic writer and prophet, and in it she incorporated all the ideas we have traced, in one grand scheme of five coming ages. Across these five ages she prophesied three coming chastisements and three beautiful periods of spiritual renewal: one during the time of the Lion, the second during the time of the Pale Horse, and the final, and most doctrinally controversial, *after* the Antichrist.[83] About this last one she is understandably cautious. Joachim of Fiore would be bolder, but later in the Middle Ages, by the time Joachite ideas had repeatedly met with church condemnation, Hildegard's would remain the safer option for reformers and dreamers for centuries to come.[84]

It would be difficult to overestimate the importance Hildegard placed on prophecy and prophets in human history. Even the coming of Christ, she says in the *Divine Works,* might have gone unnoticed had it not been for prophets.[85] Her own prophetic self-image is likely nowhere more eloquently, poignantly, and defiantly laid out than in the epilogue of this work, where she implicitly compares herself to St. John, charging that no man be so bold as to add or take away anything from this book, lest he be deleted from the book of life (cf. Apocalypse 22. 18–19).[86] John's Revelation is the most political piece of literature in the Bible, the most lavishly visual, the most cryptically allegorical, the most urgent, and the most uncompromising. In these final words of her final apocalyptic work Hildegard revealed, if she did anywhere, the real mentor of her stunning career as prophet.

FIVE

Correspondent

"Blessed Is the Speech of Your Mouth"

JOAN FERRANTE

It is a testament to Hildegard's importance as a public figure both that her letters were preserved, copied, collected, and revised and that the range of her correspondence is so vast. Many men (but very few women) in the twelfth century either preserved their own letters for collection or allowed them to be preserved by secretaries and admirers.[1] But no woman and few men (outside of official archives) had the numbers or the scope of Hildegard's correspondence. Bernard of Clairvaux, one of the few exceptions, had a larger production but he had more than one secretary at a time. The scope and subject matter of Hildegard's correspondence suggest that she served as abbess to the world, a mother superior in every sense to the ecclesiastical, monastic, and secular communities who brought their problems—religious, moral, psychological, and practical—to her for solution and consolation. Hildegard's letters will number 390 when the current edition is complete.[2]

Since letters were collected in the Middle Ages for the same reasons much history was written—either to enhance the writer's image, or to edify the reader, or both—most of the collections we have were edited by the authors or by their secretaries or friends. The new edition of Hildegard's letters (1991, 1993) is based on manuscripts that represent earlier versions than the one used in previous editions. But her most recent editor, Lieven Van Acker, believes that Hildegard agreed to the extensive changes made by her secretaries in the "official" collection (the so-called Riesenkodex) produced at the end of her life.[3] If, as he suggests, the format of this collection was designed by her first secretary, Volmar, it must have had Hildegard's consent and is "authentic" to the extent that she is indeed the author of the letters that appear in her name and approved of the editorial revisions. Even though her last secretary, Guibert of Gembloux, edited the Latin letters in the Riesenkodex more zealously than Volmar had done, the collection still remains a public statement that Hildegard authorized.[4] It is true that some questions about letters addressed *to* the abbess cannot be definitively answered.[5] But these do not cast doubt on the authenticity of Hildegard's own compositions, which were, for the most part, said to be God's words and therefore beyond the range of human tampering. Leaving aside the issue of divine authorship, one can certainly say that Hildegard's letters are as much hers as Bernard of Clairvaux's are his and perhaps even more so, since Bernard often left his secretaries to flesh out his thoughts, sometimes complaining of the liberties they took.[6]

I attempt here to give an overview of this vast correspondence and to show what the letters reveal about Hildegard: as the voice of God, the instrument by which God addressed and admonished mankind and especially the church in her time; as a mediator with the divine, carrying God's message to humankind and individuals' prayers back to God; as a mediator among humans, particularly in the monastic world, between abbesses and their nuns or abbots and their monks; as a source of knowledge and wisdom—theological, prophetic, moral, and practical; as a crusader for what she believed in (and/or believed God wanted); and as a woman who inspired both awe and affection in the women and men who knew and worked with her. In her letters Hildegard deals sternly with those in power and sympathetically with those in distress. She preaches mercy as well as justice, love rather than fear, compassion rather than anger, moderation rather than fanaticism, and always a strong sense of responsibility. Her advice is often practical, though her style is usually rich with parables and striking imagery. Her correspondents range from emperors, kings, queens, and popes through archbishops, abbesses and abbots, to nuns and monks, laywomen and laymen. Her reputation extended as far as Jerusalem: Bishop Amalric of that city, who had heard about her from pilgrims to the Holy Land, wrote "in a storm of anxieties," asking her consolation and prayers (*Epistolarium,* ep. 34).

The letters with few exceptions do not tell us much about Hildegard's own feelings or even about her life. This is not because she was reticent—she seems to have spoken openly to her biographers—but because it is primarily God's advice that is being asked and given. There are, nonetheless, a few details to be gleaned from them. In the first extant letter, to Bernard of Clairvaux, Hildegard adopts the posture of a tabula rasa, a slate blank but for what God writes on it. This position not only enables her to speak with God's voice but also reveals her assurance that God communicated directly with her. She tells the famous mystic and monastic leader about her own visions in a diffident tone, looking presumably for his encouragement to reveal them publicly while nonetheless making it clear that her source ("the Spirit of God taught me") is the same as his ("according to what you are taught by the Holy Spirit," ep. 1).[7] As she did in her later letter responding to Guibert's questions about her visions (ep. 103r), Hildegard here insists on her lack of formal learning, her total dependence on direct revelation for what she knows about Scripture and religion.[8]

In letters to friends Hildegard reveals her deep attachments to the two who worked most closely with her in the composition of her visions. The death of Volmar, her first secretary-colleague (*symmista* is the word he uses), left her bereft like an orphan, as she says in a letter to Ludwig of St. Eucharius (ep. 215r). And in a rare avowal of emotion to its object, she writes to the nun Richardis, whose departure she had fought so hard to prevent: "Woe to me, mother, woe to me, daughter, why did you leave me like an orphan? I loved the nobility of your customs . . . and your soul and all your life so that many said, 'What are you doing?' " (ep. 64, my translation). And perhaps most revealing, in a letter to the nuns of Zwiefalten, Hildegard strongly implies that she preferred the life she lived as a nun married to God to what she might have had in the secular world: "A woman ought to remain as Eve was before God presented her to Adam, when she looked not to Adam but to God. So a woman does who refuses a carnal husband for love of God; she looks to God and not to another man whom previously she did not wish to have" (ep. 250r).[9]

But such glimpses of Hildegard's feelings are rare. The letters function primarily as a means of transmitting God's message, which is often an attack on corruption, correcting the vices of the mighty and the small. Her attacks were accepted, indeed even solicited as salutary warnings, because her prophetic powers had repeatedly been validated. A provost of Koblenz wrote that "you always revived me with your consolations in all my tribulations and everything that you predicted was fulfilled" (ep. 154). The provost and clergy of St. Peter's of Trier asked for her written predictions so that posterity could know of the vengeance and mercy that had come to them as she foretold (ep. 223).[10] Frederick Barbarossa said that what she had predicted in his presence "we now have in hand,"[11] and John of Salisbury reported that Pope Eugene III wanted to consult her prophecies because what she had predicted about his reign had been right.[12] It was therefore just as well to hear what she said, however unflattering it might be. She reminds Frederick that although he may rule on earth, he has to answer to "the highest king" who says: "I

destroy obstinacy and contradiction in those who scorn me . . . hear
this, king, if you wish to live, or my sword will bore through you."[13] She
warns Henry II of England, who "would willingly do good," that he
should not listen to a "black bird" [the devil] that comes from the north
and encourages him to follow his own will rather than justice, adding
that this "thief" who counsels him stripped him of great glory in his first
age.[14] More gently she tells Henry's queen, Eleanor of Aquitaine, that
her mind is like a wall covered with clouds: "You look everywhere but
have no rest. Flee this and attain stability with God and man, and God
will help you in all your tribulations."[15]

Hildegard is equally if not more demanding of ecclesiastical authority, whose responsibility is greater because it is for the salvation of
souls. Sometimes with an elegant parable, sometimes with accusation,
she admonishes popes and bishops to fight corruption and injustice. To
Pope Eugene III she writes that a jewel lies on the road, but when a bear
comes to pick it up with his paw, an eagle sweeps down and snatches
the jewel: "Choose the better part, so that you may be the eagle"
(ep. 3). More fiercely she warns his successor, Pope Anastasius IV: "You
are neglecting the King's daughter who was entrusted to you, that is,
heavenly Justice. You are allowing this King's daughter to be thrown to
the ground, her beautiful crown and tunic torn asunder" (ep. 8).[16]
Hildegard admonishes Philip, archbishop of Cologne, to discipline his
subordinates instead of adopting their foul ways, pointing out that "hog
slop fattens pigs, but if it is mixed in with the fodder given to clean animals that chew the cud, those animals waste away. So it is with you"
(ep. 16r). To Arnold, archbishop of Mainz, who had written to Hildegard with somewhat condescending praise,[17] God speaks sharply: "Why
do you hide your face from me? . . . Why do you not stand firm in your
awe of me? And why do you overcome and cast aside anything that
stands in your way . . . ? Such action goes against my will" (ep. 20r).

With abbesses and abbots, whose powers were less broad than bishops' but whose daily confrontations were probably as frustrating and
anxious, Hildegard balances reminders of responsibility with sympathy
for their problems. Though she usually tells those who, from fatigue or
fear for their souls, want to relinquish their positions and retire to a
quieter life that they must continue to bear the burdens they have accepted, she does try to help them. She not only offers advice about balancing discipline with compassion and never giving in to anger or injustice but she also sometimes writes to the monks or nuns who are
causing difficulties, admonishing them to avoid pride and contradiction

and not to reject their leaders. It is hard, of course, to know when her advice is generic and when it is directed at a specific situation. When, for instance, a prioress says she cannot bear the weight of correcting the twistedness of the sisters, that she is beset by dangers on all sides, Hildegard tells her to carry on but to prohibit sin with reason, to use the scourge of penance but not in excess (ep. 140r). One wonders if she knew that the prioress's problems arose from excessive rigidity and austerity.

Hildegard seems to know Hazzecha, abbess of Krauftal, well enough to tell her directly that the problem is in her and will not be corrected by a change in lifestyle. Hazzecha, who says Hildegard had helped her in her pusillanimity and anxiety (her "tempest") when she visited Krauftal, asks her further about something they had discussed then, apparently her desire to retire to a solitary life (ep. 159). Hildegard's response is unusually direct and suggests some exasperation:

> You have eyes to see and to look around everywhere. Where you see mud, there wash, and what is dry make green. But the spices you have, give them savor. If you did not have eyes, you could excuse yourself. But you do have eyes and why do you not look through them? . . . You frequently judge others in ways you do not wish to be judged. Yet sometimes you speak wisely. Carry your burden, therefore, attentively . . . in the solitary life you will not be able to rest because of the vicissitudes of different customs, so then your end will become worse than your beginning and heavy as a thrown stone. (ep. 159r)

In another letter (ep. 160r) Hildegard tells Hazzecha that we are good soldiers when we conquer wrath and worldly desire and reject hate and envy, when we do not scorn sinners like ourselves, nor make unjust judgments about them, when we do not seek false testimony against the just and innocent. In desert places, she writes, there are large and small and blind mice (impiety, foolishness, the vanity of this world), which gnaw at holy customs. She warns against being like a foolish farmer who rejoices when the plow goes straight by itself but is too weary to turn it when it goes crooked. Hazzecha should think of the needs and problems of those subject to her and protect them.[18] Her remarks to Sophia, abbess of Kitzingen, are similar: "The burden of the labor is good for you, which you accepted to carry in God, if the sheep wish to hear the admonition of God through your teaching. If any spark glow in them, do not leave them, lest the raptor [the devil] seize them" (ep. 150r). Even stronger: "You walk on the narrow road in which you look to the sun, but whirlwinds of vicissitude cover your mind with clouds. And you call out, 'When will God free me?' And he answers, 'I will not let you go, but I want you to hold the net so it does not tear; if you let it go, it will pull in a direction that is unworthy of God' " (ep. 151).

The telling point is that God chose each abbess or abbot for the position because of the needs of the flock, so God alone would decide when she or he might give it up. Once one assumes the responsibility for others, no personal considerations can interfere. Even when someone says she is inexperienced, not sufficient to the task, and should yield to one who could do it better, Hildegard insists that she continue as long as she has doctrine to impart, that she is purging her disciples as they are purging her (ep. 174r). Hildegard makes the same arguments to abbots when they write about their anxieties and their desire to resign: "Divine Love says to you: O faithful friend, we do not wish for you to withdraw from the obligations of your office . . . you say: I wish to flee. But you have a burden to bear into the vineyard, and yet you stand still and will not walk forward. And so totally caught up in your own weariness, you look for another way." Divine Love tells Abbot Adam to work with his people while they love him but promises to help "when the wind roars with the disturbance of war and the instability of men's customs" (ep. 85r/a). To a provost who writes complaining about his physical and moral problems, Hildegard replies that he is tired out because he has borne the staff of correction too heavily: he should raise himself and hasten to help others (ep. 111r). A priest who wants to abandon the tumult of this world and retire to a cloister is told that he should not let his mind be clouded by his own desires but should, like the Samaritan, minister to others, as it pleases God (ep. 164r).

An abbot who asks if he should persevere in his burden or rest and take time to contemplate (meanwhile asking for a copy of Hildegard's book) is told that often what we are not doing seems better than what we are, but he should guide and teach his flock rather than follow his own will and seek a different life. If he concentrated on himself, tedium would overwhelm him and his mind would dry up (ep. 190r). Another abbot is given a parable: a man who labors with plow and ox in dry earth tells himself he cannot go on, so he goes to a place where the flowers grow without his labor, but they are suffocated by useless weeds that have to be pulled out—and what use is that? "See for yourself if it is better to work usefully with a plow or to uproot weeds from flowers" (ep. 196). An abbot who had had a difficult time in one house and was then elected abbot of a second asked Hildegard if it would be wiser and better to give up the honor (ep. 200). She answers that one "who leaves his sheep pen and takes another is called a transgressor of the precepts of God"; a thief can take what he wants and leave the rest, but a shepherd should care for all his disciples, however troublesome (ep. 200r). Judging from his letter to Hildegard, Abbot Adalbert of Ellwangen seemed to be at the end of his rope: "Our conscience accuses us, guilt terrifies, sins reprove us. We are distressed within, endangered without. There is no security, enemies everywhere, on the right a deceptive friend, on the left a truculent enemy" (ep. 91). Adalbert may have thought of a pilgrimage as a restorative journey, but he is told: "Carry your burden firmly on the right road and compel your sheep as best you can. This is better for you than a trip in pilgrim regions, for God has equal power in all places . . . don't let your mind wander like a day that is partly sunny and partly stormy . . . now rise in the purest sun and righteous heat: God wants you" (ep. 92).

It is perhaps not surprising that someone who saw herself as a chosen instrument of God, compelled to carry out the tasks she was given as visionary and as abbess, despite illness and advanced age, should see others in the same light. Once the title of abbot or abbess was bestowed and accepted, once the burden was assumed, it was not to be laid down. Anxiety, depression, even hostility and physical danger, were tribulations to be borne because of the dual responsibility to God as his chosen steward and to the congregation as their spiritual leader, protector, and provider. For this reason Hildegard advises great caution in accepting the burden, not only to her nuns, Richardis and Adelheid, whom she wanted so desperately to keep with her, but also to monks like Manegold of Hirsau (ep. 122) and Gerwin of St. Eucharius. She had told Gerwin's abbot of her vision that he would be a dry tree with little green if he took the offered abbacy (ep. 210), and she warned the monk himself that God did not want him to go into dangerous sin and perdition by following his own will, preferring his sacrifice in simplicity (ep. 211 and 212). But when he became abbot nonetheless and faced vice and disobedience and rebellion, she advised him not to indulge in wrath but to heal and correct as best he could (ep. 213).[19]

If Hildegard does not approve resigning the abbatial function, she is more than willing to give advice about carrying it out, sometimes directly, more often through striking imagery. Though she recognizes the need for discipline and correction of vice, she insists that discipline must be applied without anger and with mercy and discretion. She encourages an abbess to "use discipline to keep your daughters in check, for just as a child fears to be beaten with a rod, so also the master must be feared by everyone. Do not be afraid to punish them" (ep. 61r). But she warns an abbot that "a shepherd who holds the rod of correction without discretion does not please God nor is he loved by his sheep, but rather hated . . . God wants mercy, not burnt-offerings" (ep. 118). Discipline without mercy and justice is both wrong and ineffective: "He who loves justice and afflicts injustice . . . is just, even if he is not heard by his disciples" (ep. 240r).[20] Telling Abbot Bertulf that he must judge whether "an ox is more useful than an ass, green earth than dry, a noun than a pronoun, or a mountain than a valley among enemies," she urges him to be more active in his mastership, to offer light in maternal sweetness and cleanse wounds without tyranny, for a good doctor anoints wounds with mercy. He should place mercy, the beautiful love of the King, in the bedchamber of his mind and clothe himself in holiness with sweetest charity, as if in purple and a diadem (ep. 209r). In a series of effective similes Hildegard tells Adalard, abbot of St. Martin of Cologne, that he is like a potter who casts vessels but does not fire them (ep. 155r). He must learn to use charity and judgment in his works, for just as thorns cannot be eaten as bread, so harsh words do not edify disciples but lead them into error. A master should sift the words of doctrine through maternal (compassionate) sweetness, so that disciples can happily open their mouths and swallow them, and he should hold his obedient disciples in the embrace of charity, not in wrath. They are the kiss of God and should be fed on bread of pure flour, while the disobedient need cruder bread and harsh correction. Those who have abandoned obedience altogether should have bran, which is the food of animals without intelligence.

Moderation is essential to good governance, in the moral as in the physical regimen for men and women. Moderate nourishment of the body encourages happy and gentle habits, while excess festers in vice and immoderate abstinence wastes the body and makes for bad temper. So an abbess should console her daughters when they weep, correct them when they are angry, discipline them when they are out of control, and recall them with stories and Scripture when they are lax or forgetful (ep. 156r). Just as dry sand is useless, overplowed earth does not give good fruit, and dry, rocky earth produces thorns and weeds, so unfitting abstinence prostrates the flesh and dries it up, and the virtues of beautiful flowers like humility and charity perish. Unsuitable abstinence produces wrath, not peace (ep. 234, to Jutta, a lay sister). Rational abstinence, according to the Rule of St. Benedict and the fathers, produces a happy soul and restores the body, while irrational abstinence grows thorny pride and vainglory and depresses the mind (ep. 249, to a male recluse). Indeed, excessive punishment of the body is a temptation of the devil: he attacks those who hope to curb their illicit desires and sins with fasts, prayers, abstinence, and tears by telling them it cannot be done without such distress to the body that it dries up, and then the sinner loses hope and joy and grows sick (ep. 198, to an abbess).

Hildegard, who was experienced in problems of physical and mental health, clearly believed in a healthy soul in a healthy body.[21] Her own regime, at least in old age when Guibert describes it, involved small amounts of food and wine. He in fact describes her as a model of the life she suggested for others, despite her special gifts: no fiction, falsehood, or hypocrisy, all religion, discretion, modesty, edification, and honor. He says she was assiduous in holy meditation, self-controlled, not wandering in her visions, studious in hearing the Holy Scriptures, swift and fearless in elucidating their obscurities; solicitous in observing divine mandates, strenuous in works of mercy, reverent in all things, presumptuous in none; eager in exhorting, effective in persuading and consoling, severe in reprimanding members of her house, temperate in correcting outsiders. She spent sleepless nights singing psalms, closed her ears to slanderers and detractors, with a heart full of charity and a lamp always bright in work. She was circumspect in speech, sparing in her consumption of food.[22] Guibert felt himself "directed by her counsels, supported by her prayers, advanced by her merits, sustained by benefits, and daily restored by talks."[23] And apparently her nuns felt the same way in

> this wondrous competition of virtues, where the mother embraces her daughters with such love and the daughters are subject to their mother with such reverence, that one can scarcely tell which passes the other in zeal. These holy servants of God cultivate God with such devotion, themselves with such care, and each other with such honor and obedience in harmony, that truly in them with the help of Christ the fragile sex is seen to triumph over itself and the world and the devil in happy spectacle.[24]

While this is certainly a rosy picture, the overall sense of harmony may not be exaggerated. Guibert, who felt the need to justify his presence among the nuns, might well have been tempted to emphasize any problems he saw. There had, after all, been trouble in the past, when Hildegard removed the community to a much harder life at Rupertsberg than they had known in Disibodenberg, and some of the nuns had rebelled and left. It is likely that later in her life she was successful by practicing what she preached and preaching what she practiced.

In her role as abbess and mother to a larger world Hildegard was asked to provide not only advice on monastic life but information on all manner of subjects. Of course, she was consulted in part because of her experience in governing, mediating, and preaching but especially because she had direct access to God for the answers. While many wanted to know what the future held for them or their church, she was also asked to provide a life of St. Disibod by abbots of her old monastery (ep. 74 and 77), an explication of Benedict's Rule by an unidentified monastery,[25] and answers to two series of questions about Scripture and doctrinal issues from Guibert of Gembloux and the monks of Villers.[26] Among the queries addressed to Hildegard there are ticklish theological questions from a bishop about the attributes of the Trinity (ep. 31); from a master of the University of Paris about paternity and divinity in God (ep. 40); from an abbot and a monk about the Eucharist (ep. 46 and 89); and from a convent of monks about the Cathar heresy (ep. 169). She was asked for the texts of sermons she had preached on ecclesiastical negligence and corruption by clergy who heard her in Cologne (ep. 15), in Trier (ep. 223), and in Kirchheim (ep. 149).[27] Requests for her books of visions came from an archbishop (ep. 14), an abbot (ep. 190), and a priest who wanted to transcribe a copy (ep. 187). A bishop who despaired because of his sins wanted not only prayers but also comfort or any "admonition necessary for our salvation" (ep. 32). The abbot of Brauweiler asked Hildegard how to exorcize a woman possessed by a demon who himself had revealed that only she could do it (ep. 68).[28] She was asked to cure a noblewoman's sterility by five abbots (ep. 70) and perhaps by a sixth (ep. 118). A priest wanted to know how to cure his nightmares,[29] a laywoman how to treat hemorrhaging.[30] A countess asked about handling a legal claim to an estate,[31] a matron about revenge for her kidnapped daughter,[32] and another about getting away from her adulterous husband.[33]

Some of Hildegard's advice to these petitioners is quite practical: speak to the emperor about your legal claim; for nightmares, read yourself to sleep with the Gospel of John; your husband's disease cannot be cured, so pray and admonish him for his soul.[34] Some of it seems superstitious or bizarre: the ritual of exorcism (ep. 68r), and a charm putting words about the blood of Adam and the blood of Christ on the patient's body to treat the hemorrhage.[35] Sometimes Hildegard answers with parables, sometimes with language so symbolic it is hard to understand and must have been even harder for those who were not versed in her writings. One abbot laments, "Though I am often made

happier by the consolations of your words, yet by their obscurities, because they do not lie fully open to my intellect, I am made sadder." He
begs her for a message he can understand: "Wherefore, through this
messenger I beat at your ears with tearful and miserable petitions, that
you send some solace to me through letters fit for the capacity of my little wit" (ep. 244). I offer one example of such obscurity in my own pur-
posely literal translation:

> Under their feet I saw another crowd of men, surrounded by a white cloud
> and having beautiful faces and looking at heaven, who yet approached petu-
> lance with awakening of many uselessnesses, like fat bulls, so that when they
> looked at heaven, tending their bows against heaven, they loosed their ar-
> rows, and struck against heaven with leaden cudgels and so set their mouth
> in heaven and their tongue crossed over on earth [Psalms 72.9]. Whence
> thunders came over them and hail fell over them and many clouds covered
> them. (ep. 78r)

As with any famous personality who receives a lot of mail, Hildegard
had trouble keeping up with it. Sometimes God did not send the revelation with the requested answer, or Hildegard was busy with other things.
In the last years of her life Guibert and the monks of Villers wrote again
and again, asking for the answers to their questions; they finally got the
first set but never the second.[36] While she was working on the answers,
Hildegard wrote twice explaining how tired and how busy she was, particularly since Volmar, her main support, was gone (ep. 106r, 109r).
Other correspondents complain that they have written letters and never
received an answer. Some are tactful: "I don't know if my letter reached
you, so I keep writing" (ep. 112); "I sent you a letter by messenger but
got no response; in case it was the messenger's negligence, I shall repeat
the contents" (ep. 176). Some are more aggressive: "I have never got a
letter, despite my many letters and requests in person . . . it would be sinful to believe it is because of my low birth or abject person" (ep. 139).[37]
Or perhaps they are more desperate: "I've had no response to my letters
. . . at least send an answer to my two questions through the messenger"
(ep. 186). Some seem to chastise Hildegard for negligence: "With what
special affection of charity we have chosen you as our spiritual mother
. . . your love could have observed from the frequent messengers we sent
to you. But you never showed the reciprocal affection of a mother; the
commonitory letters, which you ought to have sent as a mother to her
sons, even to those not wishing for them, you did not offer to those de-
siring them" (ep. 206). One abbess sent a letter asking only a brief response but reminding Hildegard both of the parchment she sent for the

purpose and of the Canaanite woman who told Christ that "even the dogs eat of the crumbs which fall from their masters' tables" (ep. 156; cf. Matthew 15.27).

Hildegard did find time to write a number of unsolicited letters, particularly when she was fighting for something she strongly believed in or believed was God's will. The will of God often seems to be suspiciously in harmony with Hildegard's desires, but I have no doubt she was sincere in her belief in the divine message, however much we might think her own will exerted an influence over what she saw and heard in the visions. When she was engaged in such a battle, whether over a matter of principle, as in her right to bury a man who had died in grace, or over a personal need, like a provost for her convent, she carried her cause to the highest authorities, archbishops and popes. Implicit and sometimes explicit in her stand was the assertion that she was speaking for an authority higher than any on earth, one she had to obey no matter what the human hierarchy determined and one they would do well to obey themselves. In the struggle over the once-excommunicated nobleman buried in convent ground, Hildegard wrote to no effect to the prelates of Mainz, who had ordered him to be disinterred and had laid an interdict on the convent when they were not heeded.[38] Her letter explains very briefly that he was buried with his own priest officiating and that the "true light" threatened a terrible harm if she let him be disinterred. Hildegard then concentrates on the importance of music for the salvation of souls, in a letter deservedly famous for its discussion of music which is also, however, a ploy to ascribe moral responsibility for the prelates' actions (ep. 23).[39] When they proved obstinate, she wrote to the archbishop in whose name they had acted, who had apparently accepted the authority of her visions in the past: "You have never, I remind you, given me trouble about my visions before" (ep. 24). Hildegard takes care to give him a more detailed account of the deceased man's spiritual state ("fortified with all the sacraments . . . one whom God instructed me He had received from the bosom of the church into the glory of salvation"), along with reports of witnesses who testified to his prior absolution. The archbishop did eventually lift the interdict, though not without some comment on the seriousness of her action (ep. 24r).

There are no letters I know of dating from Hildegard's much earlier struggle with the abbots and monks of her old house at Disibodenberg over her move to the monastery she founded at Rupertsberg. But bad feelings continued and a number of letters testify to them. She had the right to a provost of her convent's choice from Disibodenberg to function as priest for the nuns and (coincidentally) as her secretary.[40] When her lifelong friend and secretary, Volmar, died, she requested the appointment of another monk, Godfrey, but his abbot refused to release him, so Hildegard appealed to the pope, Alexander III (ep. 10). The pope put the matter in the hands of the provost of St. Andreas in Cologne, Wezelin, who happened to be a nephew of Hildegard's, which suggests that Alexander intended the matter to be resolved in Hildegard's favor, as indeed it was. There were occasional attempts to improve relations between the two houses, including a letter from Abbot Kuno acknowledging unspecified sins on his part and asking her for revelations about their patron, St. Disibod (ep. 74), which Hildegard answered with liturgical songs and admonitions about the abbot's spiritual state (ep. 74r).[41] Kuno's successor Helengar wrote later to ask for consolation (ep. 76) and more material about Disibod (ep. 77), a request Hildegard answered with remarks very critical of the abbot: "Sometimes you are like a bear which growls under its breath, but sometimes like an ass, not prudent in your duties . . . Indeed, in some matters you are altogether useless" (ep. 76r). She also sent the monks a sermon she had apparently already preached to them about their dangerous spiritual state (ep. 77r).[42] When Hildegard went to negotiate with them over disputed property, she was not well received, as she reminds the abbot: "A mob of some of your monks rose up and gnashed their teeth at me, as if I were a bird of gloom or a horrid beast, and they bent their bows against me in order to drive me away. But I know for a fact that God moved me from that place" (ep. 75). To reinforce the property agreements that were finally made, Hildegard wrote a letter to the nuns of her own congregation, a "paper trail" that would serve as her witness if counterclaims were made after her death. This letter specifies that after she left Disibodenberg, the monks granted her petition to ensure that the convent or any new holdings given to it would not be bound to the old house but free, a right they confirmed in writing in the presence of the greater and lesser members, with great good will (that is, there was no dispute to be reopened later). Her rather legalistic account of the transaction ends with a legal formula, "Let all who adhere to God hear and learn these things, and affirm, carry out, and defend this case with benevolence" (ep. 195r).

The battle Hildegard fought most fiercely through her letters was one she lost, the battle to keep Richardis of Stade and her niece Adelheid at Bingen.[43] Since this affair is well known, I will simply list the relevant extant letters: to Hildegard from Pope Eugene III (ep. 4); to

Hartwig, archbishop of Bremen and Richardis's brother (ep. 11, 12); to Richardis, marchioness of Stade, mother of the nun Richardis and an early supporter of Rupertsberg;[44] a stinging exchange with Henry, archbishop of Mainz (ep. 18–18r); and a report of Richardis's death from Hartwig to Hildegard (ep. 13) with her response (ep. 13r). There are also letters from Hildegard to Richardis (ep. 64) and to Adelheid (ep. 99, 101), and from Adelheid to Hildegard (ep. 100). Despite the conflict, the affection of the two younger women for Hildegard endured. Richardis, according to her brother, wept in longing for her old cloister before she died, and Adelheid wrote, "Do not let the flower of ancient nurture dry up in your heart, which once flourished between you and me when you sweetly brought me up."

The affection that other monastics, particularly but not only women, felt for Hildegard pervades the letters. She is a cherished friend or surrogate mother to many of them, to some a role model, a mentor.[45] Elisabeth of Schönau wrote to her for support when she felt impelled to publish her visions, and Hildegard responded with empathy and encouragement in a typical mode: a vision explaining why their services were needed by God, the persecutions they could expect from the devil, and their role as earthen vessels to be filled, trumpets to be blown. At the end she also acknowledged the fear they shared: "I too lie in the cowardice of fear, sounding a little, at times, like the small sound of a trumpet from the Living Light" (ep. 201r). Elisabeth seems to have gained confidence from Hildegard and is able to speak with assurance by her second [extant] letter about the mission she by now shares: "Rejoice with me, that the finger of God writes in you . . . your words enflamed me as if fire touched my heart . . . carry out the work of the Lord as you have done, for the Lord placed you in his vineyard to work it; for the Lord sought workers in his vineyard and found them all lazy."[46] Hildegard was a model to Elisabeth not only in her life as visionary and monastic leader but also in her writings: her *Scivias* was a precursor of Elisabeth's *Liber viarum Dei*.[47] And Hildegard took that responsibility seriously, not only encouraging Elisabeth directly but writing to her superior about the younger woman: "Hold God's daughter Elisabeth with ardent love in your heart, so that you always nourish her with the milk of consolation" (ep. 95).

Hildegard's letters also show solicitude for the needs of another nun, one who had formerly been a generous patron of Rupertsberg—Gertrude of Stahleck, countess palatine and aunt of emperor Frederick. The countess had first entered a Cistercian monastery, which was not appropriate for her, and Hildegard wrote to the bishop of Bamberg to help her transfer (ep. 30). Gertrude wrote later of her affection for Hildegard: "I have become drunk on the wine of sorrow of your absence . . . I could almost believe it would have been better for me never to have seen you at all, never to have known your kindness and maternal feeling, for now . . . I grieve over you without ceasing" (ep. 62). Hildegard responded with her own joy that Gertrude had given up the world for God and that the Holy Spirit dwelt in her heart (ep. 62r).

Abbesses, many of whom met Hildegard during her preaching tours, seem to have taken comfort in her advice and sympathy as well as pride in her fame and the respect accorded her by the world. They wrote to her for advice about changing their lives, but also for moral and spiritual support in the life they shared and to express and ask for love.[48] The abbess of Altena, anxious for some of Hildegard's time but not daring to hope for another meeting, laments that it has been so long since she wrote and suggests that Hildegard give a little less time to her heavenly husband and a little more to her friend(s) on earth and send some news of herself for consolation (ep. 49). The abbess of Erfurt, who begins with high praise—"glorious things are said of thee" (Psalms 86.4)—asks Hildegard to pray to "your husband and mine" for her (ep. 94). An abbess of Regensburg, who calls Hildegard her special friend and injects a *carissima* into her assertion that "my heart is joined to you in perfect faith and love," has developed her own relationship with God. She hopes that Hildegard will not feel she has abused their friendship if she too has been called to confer with God more familiarly (ep. 185).

The abbess of Bamberg, who asks not only for letters but also to be taken into Hildegard's community, takes pride in another woman's special gifts: "Christ gave us special joy in this, that he not only foresaw and predestined you for this from the female sex but illumined many through your teaching" (ep. 61, my translation). The abbess of Wechterswinkel commends herself and her daughters to Hildegard, rejoicing in her honor, her high position in the world (ep. 231). Another abbess asserts her love ("I will always see you in my soul, I will always love you") and blesses God who through Hildegard declares "wondrously in our time the mysteries of his secrets never before heard in the world, and confirms our faith and illumines his holy Church through you . . . Who ever heard these things? Who has seen such?" (ep. 117). Sophia of Kitzingen asks, "Who is not delighted in the dwelling of Mother Wisdom [*sophie,* both a compliment to Hildegard and a link with herself]? Who does not willingly give ear to heavenly harmony? Who does not wish to hear the organ of the Holy Spirit ringing with so many virtues, mystically sealed with the marks of so many miracles? This sound goes out through the whole earth" (ep. 150). An abbess of Cologne writes: "How much I rejoice in your beatitude I cannot express in words. Though physically separate, yet I am bound to you with the deepest affection of charity. I want to see you and tell you the grief I bear in my heart without any human consolation. I want to have you, who are filled with all charity, in the place of my mother" (ep. 157).

Though many men wrote to praise Hildegard and to ask for her help or her writings, only a few seem bound to her by such deep affection. Her colleagues Volmar and Ludwig, who helped her prepare her manuscripts,[49] were among these, and Manegold of Hirsau, whom she shores up in a series of letters, was probably another. Her other secretaries—Godfrey, her nephew Wezelin, and Guibert of Gembloux—may have won her trust and even affection, but there is nothing to indicate they were friends in the same way. Volmar, the monk of Disibodenberg who worked with her throughout her writing life until he died in 1173, is remembered in the prefaces to her three books of visions as "that man whom I had secretly sought and found." His one extant letter to Hildegard, occasioned probably by a serious illness of hers, is a litany of impending loss for himself and the nuns of Rupertsberg. Speaking of her absence that must some day fall on them, he asks,

> Where then will be the answer to those asking about all their affairs? Where the new interpretation of Scriptures? . . . Where the new and unheard-of sermons on the feasts of saints? Where the revelations about souls of the dead, the unveiling of past, present, and future? Where the exposition of the natures of different creatures? . . . and the maternal affection to all from the overflowing compassion we have known in you? (ep. 195)[50]

Volmar's death left Hildegard with the unfinished manuscript of her third major book, the *Book of Divine Works*, but another old friend, Ludwig of St. Eucharius, who "knew me and the visions well . . . was moved with great mercy for my grief, so that through himself and other learned men, he faithfully offered me help with unfailing constancy."[51] Between Hildegard and Ludwig there are five extant letters, four of them from her. In one she makes a reference to his early "cloudy" life but applauds and encourages his work as an abbot, a "farmer who with great solicitude looks about everywhere and puts the plow rightly in the earth" (ep. 214). Nonetheless, she advises him not to accept a new position or honor, which might endanger the stability of his good intention, even as she thanks him for his help (ep. 215r). In a discussion of the four modes of human behavior, she tells him that he is one of the airy kind, wavering in behavior but fearful of God; the other types that make up his congregation give him trouble, but God loves him and purges his soul through his suffering (ep. 216). In the letter that apparently accompanied the manuscript of her book, she reminds Ludwig that he was foolish in his childhood and assured in his youth, but now he has "embarked on an adventure of the unicorn—unknown to you in your youth—and this indeed was my writing, which often carries echoes of the mortal dress of the son of God." She asks him to correct the book lovingly, "that your name too may be written in the book of life" (ep. 217).[52] Ludwig's enormous respect for Hildegard is manifest in his surviving letter to her, which begins with perhaps the most appealing of all humility topoi: "It would seem ridiculous enough if butterflies greeted eagles, if fleas greeted stags, if worms greeted lions with their letters. So it is more than wondrous, indeed laughable, that a sinner worth little or nothing in divine or human arts should presume to write to one whom God has magnified so high" (ep. 215).

Hildegard's correspondence includes an unusual number of letters to Abbot Manegold of Hirsau (fifteen, of which two are uncertain, with only one from him to her). Although some are very brief, there is enough to suggest that she felt affection as well as concern for the abbot. In his letter to her he says he has long wanted to love, honor, admire, and serve her in word and deed, and he asks her to remember him in her prayers and write to him (ep. 121). And she does. She knows he is a good man who is easily discouraged, even depressed: he looks to God, but a black cloud tires him (ep. 122). So again and again she offers him exhortation combined with reassurance. When he is first offered a gift (probably the abbacy) but is obstructed in taking it by the malice of those who gnash their teeth like bears, she foretells a great whirlwind followed by light (ep. 122). As abbot, he must contend with people who act like bears, panthers, and asps, but she tells him to be an upright soldier, to control his disciples and chastise the wicked (ep. 123), to pasture his sheep so the Lord will not ask why he abandoned them (ep. 124). The peace he had expected is not possible in this world: even the chosen of God, like David and the Jews who were promised milk and honey, were made to suffer.[53] God has sent Manegold beautiful girls (virtues) who knock at the door of his mind, but he is so oppressed by his thoughts and worries that he tells them he cannot stay with them (ep. 125). Hildegard tells him to cleanse his unquiet mind, to cut off despair from himself and his flock; it is a time of war in human customs. If he suffers, so did Christ (ep. 126). If a column is cut down, the house falls; the abbot must keep watch at the seven windows so that no hawk will come and seize him (ep. 127). "I see that you do not burn a strong fire in your soul or among your flock; you say 'I can't resist'—you let your mind sleep . . . but God will help you" (ep. 128). During a time of rebellion in the cloister, which Hildegard attributes to outside instigators (prelates and common people), she advises Mane-gold to take a recess from his sons, who will welcome their father back when they recover from their obstinacy, but he is not to resign (ep. 129). She uses parables of towers (ep. 130) and gardens, trees that have solid roots but no leaves in winter (ep. 131), a tree that is green with one dry branch (ep. 135), storms and shipwrecks (ep. 132), and storms in the mind (ep. 133), but the message is always the same: do not give up, endure with patience, for God is with you.[54]

It is possible to deduce from these repeated reassurances to a man so lacking in confidence or strength of will, yet wanting to do good, why so many monastics who knew Hildegard relied so much on her. She understood what troubled them and knew what to say to keep them going. She offered moral support, practical wisdom (however disguised in parables), and compassion—gifts less striking perhaps than her divine revelations of the future or her stirring attacks on corruption but far more valuable for their lives. To men and women alike she was a cherished counselor just as she was a revered prophet. "God made you wondrously venerable to men and women equally," said an abbot of Kempten (ep. 148).

It seems fitting to end this survey of Hildegard's correspondence with the words of her admirers, a few examples of the praise that pervades the letters she received. A monk writes, "I would walk barefoot just to hear your words" (ep. 48); the dean and clergy of Cologne come to her "in admiration as if to the living temple of God . . . the very oracle of God" (ep. 15); an abbot of Ellwangen, noting that she is to be doubly honored for the divine gifts of sanctity and prophecy, exclaims, "You are to be wondered at and venerated by the people of this time" (ep. 91). Monks of Haina call her "a lantern burning for the illumination of the church" (ep. 113). She is the "chosen and beloved spouse of the highest king" (ep. 138), one who "can get whatever you ask from God" (ep. 155), a person by whom God has adorned the church wondrously (ep. 183), a "beautiful olive tree and precious pearl" (ep. 173).

To her last secretary, Guibert of Gembloux, she is a new Mary who, like the Virgin Mother, brings forth the Word of God: "Hail, after Mary full of grace, the Lord is with you! Blessed are you among women, and blessed is the speech of your mouth."[55] Yet she is also a chosen vessel, a *vas electionis* like St. Paul (Acts 9.15), who said women should not teach in public (1 Timothy 2.12). But God had chosen Hildegard to carry his word, and no man, not even Paul, could stop her.

SIX

Artist

"To See, Hear, and Know All at Once"

MADELINE CAVINESS

How we assess Hildegard's achievements as a pictorial artist depends on the credibility of my assertion that she designed the unique sets of pictures that go with two of her texts, the *Scivias* and the *Book of Divine Works,* although we know these graphic designs only in photographs and later copies.[1] The figure drawing and colors of these illuminations localize their production satisfactorily in the Rhineland, but a number of the compositional and iconographic features are quite eccentric. Whereas clarity and orderliness are period features, the pictures in the *Scivias* have irregular frames, with immense figures too large to fit juxtaposed with clusters of tiny ones, some turned sideways or even upside down along with their architectural settings. Jagged, flamelike areas of brilliant gold or silver light, or of torrid darkness, irregular stars, clouds, and mountains all contribute to the kinetic effect. Here and in the later *Book of Divine Works,* magisterial figures—the Almighty, the Trinity, Holy Church, Wisdom—are strange composites, part abstract, part figural, even part beast. I regard these pictorial expressions as counterparts of Hildegard's idiosyncratic writing style, forming the perfect complement to her texts.

A role as the designer of these pictures seems to be the last area of Hildegard's multimedia outpouring that has been denied to her by recent scholars, even though most posited her supervisory intervention in the process of "illustration."[2] Barbara Newman, in the first chapter of this volume, "Sibyl of the Rhine," has referred to the reluctance of nineteenth-century scholars to acknowledge Hildegard's full authorship of her theological and scientific works, their resistance stemming most probably from disbelief that a woman could have written such works. The denial of her role as a pictorial designer, however, is a more complex case and it is worthwhile touching on some of the reasons for this denial.

First, with the rise of the professional artist in the Renaissance, the universities excluded from the curriculum the "mechanical arts" (that is, the practices of making art, as opposed to the study of the "fine arts" as a branch of history) and gave primacy to verbal skills and textual study. Since then, the authorship of texts has been understood in Western culture very differently from that of images, even though some modern thinkers have urged recognition of "visual thinking," that is, of "visual perception as a cognitive activity."[3] I will have more to say about visual thinking in the twelfth century. Given the logocentricity of our discursive practices, it is not surprising to find that even an art historian like Otto Pächt, who had a sharp eye for individual styles and a high appreciation of artistic talent, suggested that Hildegard's visions (as optic experience) had to pass through verbalization (the cognitive phase), only to be retranslated into images under Hildegard's supervision![4]

The second major problem in recognizing Hildegard's role as a designer is a canon of sequential styles that modern art historians regard as a development, much as Hegel had posited an overall development of the human spirit throughout history.[5] And although German scholars initially included the production of the Rhineland in their canon, after World War II even they agreed that the most important developments in the second half of the twelfth century occurred further west, with the "birth" of Gothic in France.[6] Innovation and change were regarded as the hallmarks of artistic creativity, in line with a critical assessment in capitalist countries that applauded the twentieth-century "avant-garde."[7] The style of the only manuscript that can be directly associated with Hildegard, the Rupertsberg *Scivias,* in no way responds to the innovative trends of its contemporary from the south of England, the Winchester Bible, to cite just one example from the canon.[8] Indeed, relatively few German works were included in the 1970 New York exhibition that definitively presented the scholarly construction of a "style 1200," and the exhibition catalog, organized by medium, placed all the German pieces in a derivative position, after the French, English, and Mosan works.[9]

The third problem is that, tragically, the Rupertsberg *Scivias* disappeared from Dresden during World War II, leaving us with black-and-white photographs and a handmade replica in full color from which to judge the qualities of the original.[10] I find it of some comfort that the last scholars to claim Hildegard's participation in the design of these pictures were German graduate students who had access to the original manuscript.[11] Modern art historians have attached great importance to having access to the original work of art, a desideratum that carried increasing weight even as the means of mechanical reproduction were being improved.[12] Connoisseurship, the branch of the discipline largely concerned with authenticity and attributions, insisted on the irreplaceable value of the unique object that bore the mark of the artist.[13] Hence any relation between Hildegard's "style" and the Lucca manuscript of the *Book of Divine Works* had been consistently overlooked by connoisseurs, because this deluxe recension is so evidently later than her lifetime; in fact it is plausibly associated with the bid for her canonization made by the archbishop of Mainz in 1227.[14] My argument is that some core of the images is based on lost designs that Hildegard devised as she composed the text. This is a kind of connoisseurship that is not much in vogue now, although my early mentor, Francis Wormald, talked about the "bones" of Ottonian images structuring English Romanesque illuminations.[15]

The lost Rupertsberg *Scivias* illuminations deserve our attention at the outset. The manuscript contained thirty-five pictures, including one placed between the subject headings and the text of each of the twenty-six visions. Five of these were full-page compositions and thus of majestic size (figures 6, 10, 11).[16] Most illuminations, however, were variably framed to fill all or part of the equivalent of one column of text or to extend into the other column to form an L-shape (figures 1, 2, 3, 8, 12); a few are narrow bands extending across two columns (figure 5). The layout of these pages demonstrates such a symbiotic relationship between writing and painting that they were clearly devised for this manuscript (or one identical in layout). Other illustrations in the text include the famous (self-)portrait, which precedes the preface in which Hildegard describes the voice that instructed her, "dic et scribe quod vides et audis" (proclaim and jot down what you see and hear).[17]

Like all the works associated with Hildegard, the manuscript illuminations need to be considered in a local and an international context. My analysis makes it apparent that they share certain features, such as the palette, the delineation of clinging drapery, the use of inscribed scrolls within the frame to report speech, some of the architectonic forms, and the repertory of plain or ornamented frames, with a number of manuscripts of the second half of the twelfth century from a wide region encompassing the Rhineland and modern Austria (figure 4). Pächt placed the *Scivias* illuminations with conservative "didactic works" of the kind produced in the abbeys for internal use, though he found them "closer to 'art' " than the mnemonic pictograms that accompanied a contemporary work of Honorius Augustodunensis.[18] Indeed, for the most part, the actual compositions of the *Scivias* pictures are very particular and highly original, serving Hildegard's claim that they did not stem from "human invention" (though she also denies the role of "the requirements of human composition").[19] A similar blend of conservatism in the theology, exegesis, and spirituality that inform her text and a uniquely personal way of writing has been observed by Newman.[20] Whereas it is reasonable to suppose that medieval artists confronted with new subject matter (such as the life of a newly deceased saint to illustrate) could depend on adapting compositions that had served elsewhere for similar events, there is no hint in the Rupertsberg *Scivias* that any standard images were appropriated piecemeal; in this feature it is quite unlike the later illustrated recension from the Cistercian abbey of Salem, which clearly made use of biblical illustrations as a base.[21] That set of pictures seems to have been created as "illustration," that is, their genesis was secondary to the text, and they are a good demonstration of standard invention and adaptation.

Perhaps the strongest argument for Hildegard's direct involvement in the designs that appeared in finished form in the Rupertsberg *Scivias* manuscript is based on features that have long been recognized as reflections of the visual disturbances typically associated with migraine attacks.[22] These include irregular, jagged-edged forms that spread aggressively over the framed surface—whether an ellipse edged in flame that signified the universe, a great threatening black cloud like a wing, a monstrous black demon shooting forth flames, or a colossal, blindingly bright figure with outstretched wings and arms (figures 1, 2, 10). The genesis of such forms is recognizable to clinicians who treat these headaches (and to those of us who have them): with visual field deficit, a black hole, or occasionally a blindingly bright one, grows across one's view, its jagged edges shimmering with points of white or steel-grey light (though some patients see colors too). Examining the *Scivias* illustrations again, the "colors"—black, gold, silver, color of iron, and steel grey—accord with such auras (and are not always supplied by the text), and even the finish of the paintings, with a very unusual use of tiny light points that make the contours shimmer, could stem from someone who knew these auras firsthand. The effect is very disturbing to someone who does suffer from migraine, since attacks can be brought on by flickering lights.[23] To be sure, such dots are not Hildegard's invention, but she uses them with a greater intensity than do any manuscript illuminators whose work she could have seen.[24]

Then, too, there are many stars in the illuminations, but they are not static stars like the ones found in earlier or contemporary astronomical or Apocalypse manuscript illustrations (or like those on the American flag).[25] Their irregular forms and placement on the dark field and sometimes their varied sizes give them a dynamic quality; some even turn black and fall into an abyss (figures 1, 6). These stars behave like the phosphenes or scintillating scotoma (shimmering spots in the visual field) of migraine auras, which appear in the direct line of vision, moving with the eye, and are briefly retained (though reversed to steel-grey or black) with the eyes closed. Responding to eye movements, phosphenes can seem to move more or less rapidly, like comets or shooting stars, and they interfere with the normal perception of colors and forms in one's surroundings. Streaming light that seems to volatilize forms also makes an appearance in the *Scivias* pictures (figure 3).[26] One form of scotoma is known to neurologists as fortification spectra because of the architectonic shapes that impinge on the vision; crenellated forms, with walls and towers laid at odd angles, are particularly insistent in the pictures of *Scivias* III (figures 5, 10, 11, 12).[27] In this context, it is significant that Hildegard insisted that her new abbey be built at Rupertsberg because it had appeared to her in a vision, after which she fell very ill.[28]

There is reasonable evidence that some of Hildegard's physical ailments were caused by migraine. She herself associated the visions with pain: "I have never fallen prey to ecstasy in the visions, but I see them wide awake, day and night. And I am constantly fettered by sickness, and often in the grip of pain so intense that it threatens to kill me."[29] An increased incidence at menopause is common and would explain the escalation of attacks in her forties (while she worked on the *Scivias*) and fifties (when she worked on the *Book of Life's Merits*); stress is an additional factor in the timing of attacks, and her anxieties were at a maximum during the years that she struggled to found Rupertsberg and move there.[30] The authentic rendition of these visual auras is therefore best attributed to Hildegard herself—even if she did not mix the paints or apply the brush for this deluxe illuminated copy—unless we suppose that an illuminator was found to work on the Rupertsberg *Scivias* who also had migraine.[31] I prefer to believe Hildegard was as much the author of these paintings as she was of the fair copy of the text that accompanies them. The same precepts would have governed her sense of authorship in both media, whether or not they were fully respected. When she completed the *Liber vite meritorum* (1158–1163), she was adamant that not an iota of the matter revealed to her be changed by editors or copyists, and at the time she was probably still involved in organizing the pictures for the Rupertsberg *Scivias*.[32] The tendency of modern translators to understand

Hildegard's problematic use of *scribere* (normally to write as a copyist) to mean her own authorship of the text has overemphasized the textual component of the work. What is needed—as she uses *scribere* in several instances—is a single verb to connote her setting down, or drafting, or sketching, the words and pictures.[33] The interdependence of these words and pictures was similar, I believe, to the "mutually influential" relationship between words and music that Barbara Newman noted in Hildegard's musical compositions of the 1150s.[34]

The process of artistic creation I envisage is this: Hildegard would have sketched the outlines of her auras, with color annotations, at the time of their occurrence. She probably did the sketches on wax tablets, of the kind she drew in her self-portrait at the opening of the book. She could have dictated part of the text more or less simultaneously—as she shows herself dictating to Volmar in this frontispiece. The subsequent layers of picture and text—the figures that people the compositions, the allegories and exegesis of the text—would take considerably more work. The pictorial compositions were most probably worked up on single parchment leaves that were easily rotated, like the ones we know from the slightly later "Sketchbook" of Villard de Honnecourt.[35] In several cases the rectilinear module of the wax tablet seems to be repeated within a full-page or L-shaped composition (figures 2, 6); in others its tall narrow format is readily adapted to fill one column of the page (figures 1, 3, 8, 12). Geometric forms are not regularized by the use of compass and ruler in the process of redrawing, in adherence to Hildegard's instruction not to use "human invention" or follow "the requirements of human composition."[36] But to produce a fully painted set of pictures, standard colors had to be added to the austere repertory: the text mentions blue, green, purple, and red as well as "subdued colors" and color of iron, but soft pinks and beige, orange, and ochre were also added.[37] The resulting palette is that of other manuscripts from the area, differing only in the balance of hues (and it varies greatly from one picture to another in *Scivias*).[38] The most unusual feature of *Scivias* is the quantity of silver used, in addition to burnished gold, a risky choice because silver tarnishes, whereas Hildegard intended the silver to represent blinding light. The overall richness matches the more sumptuous productions of the time and harks back to imperial books of the eleventh and early twelfth centuries.[39]

The compositions vary greatly in complexity. Some combine several different phases of a vision sequence in a single frame and some anticipate the allegorical meanings that Hildegard applies to the forms and

figures. Gaps in the text are audaciously filled in by the pictures, in a
way one could hardly expect of anyone restrained to making literal illustrations. The opening vision of book 2, for instance, is a retelling of
Creation which sees human life emanating from a flame, but the picture
inserts God amidst gold flames and shows the six stages of Creation in
the sphere above him, in anticipation of Hildegard's allusions later in
the text.[40] In this case, the pictorial rendering adds a kind of normalcy
to a text that begins in a highly unorthodox way. The most probable
scenario is that Hildegard herself provided the pictorial as well as the
textual gloss to her vision since they are so complementary.

Whatever the basis of some of the compositions in migraine auras, a
preponderance of the detailing and finish draws on a standard repertory of figure types and gestures, drapery styles and folds. Even unusual
figures such as the personification of Fear of the Lord covered with
eyes, as she appears in *Scivias* I.1 and III.8, and the Life Force "ensouling" the full-formed child in the womb, have some visual ancestry, as
evidenced in the St.-Sever Apocalypse manuscript (figures 6, 7).[41] Medieval artists collected such motifs in model books, to draw upon at
need.[42] Rhenish painting, as we know it from manuscripts, wall paintings, and stained glass, adhered to Romanesque representational codes
into the second half of the twelfth century. Somewhat stiff, majestic
figures are silhouetted on solid-colored grounds of blue, red, or gold;
landscape elements such as hills and rivers extend up the picture surface
and are recognizable by boulders or a wave pattern; trees also spread
fantastic scroll-like branches or exotic foliage over the surface. Comparisons reveal that these features of the *Scivias* illuminations are quite
standard and the execution is not particularly refined.[43]

Yet the Rupertsberg *Scivias* pictures, if they were painted as late as
1160–1179 (the date preferred for the manuscript by the text scholars),
are extremely conservative. I suggest that this archaism is deliberate,
stemming from a resistance to depicting the visionary world in corporeal terms. Before Hildegard's death a changed attitude to naturalism
had begun to transform the art of the region, as elsewhere in northern
Europe. Often ascribed to Byzantine influence, draperies began to cling
to limbs that were modeled to look three-dimensional, and the movement of figures as well as their interactions looked more natural. These
are traits that can be readily seen in another great manuscript from a
Rhenish monastic house for women, the *Hortus deliciarum* made for
Herrad of Landsberg, abbess of Hohenburg (1167–1195), which was
fortunately copied before its destruction in the bombardment of Stras-

bourg in the Franco-Prussian War of 1870.[44] A perusal of the Rhenish
and Mosan works in a variety of media reveals this widespread trend,
and a few exceptions to it.[45] It is perhaps significant that the closest
comparison I am able to suggest for the *Scivias* figure types and drapery
is a sacramentary made for another Rhenish Benedictine abbey for
women, at Maria Laach, about 1160 (figure 4).[46] Another instructive
comparison is with two manuscripts containing the Life of St. Amand
from his cult center near Tournai, dating from 1124–1145 and
1160–1180. The abbess Aldegonde's vision of the apotheosis of St.
Amand is similar in composition to the second picture in *Scivias* II.6,
though the Tournai page is more tightly ordered by the use of frames
(figures 8, 9). The stiff, flat rendering of the figures in the earlier of these
two books (illustrated here) is far closer to Hildegard's style than is the
slick modeling of the later copy; Barbara Abou-El-Haj has suggested
that the restraint of the earlier mode resulted from the influence of St.
Bernard.[47] By 1200 the great Rhenish metalworker Nicholas of Verdun
had worked out another system, wrapping bulky drapery around his
figures, whether sculpted or executed in flat enamels; the series of parallel troughs in this drapery suggested the term *muldenfaltenstil* to earlier art historians.[48] A late version of this style is seen in the *Book of Divine Works* (figure 16).

In both sets of pictures Hildegard adapted standard forms to her purposes. When traditional motifs reappear in her pictures, sometimes
dwarfed by immense figures that burst out of the frame, sometimes trun-
cated by it, they are transformed in her unique way. She even builds up
composite figures, such as the church invaded by Antichrist, in *Scivias*
III.11, in which the upper part of a crowned *orans* woman (the Ecclesia
that had appeared in II.3, as Hildegard notes) is fused with a scaly torso,
a monstrous genital mask "with fiery eyes, and ears like an ass, and nos-
trils and mouth like a lion's," and bare legs that are bruised and bleeding
(figure 10).[49] Even the Almighty in the upper frame of this composition
has an imbricated midpart. These kinds of hybrids or grotesques have a
considerable legacy in the margins of thirteenth- and fourteenth-century
manuscripts from northern Europe, but Hildegard's are unlikely to have
served as prototypes. Rather, she altered existing iconographic codes so
radically that meaning was threatened.[50] It was quite common to represent the devil as a hybrid, with bestial hind parts, a genital (and/or anal)
mask, distorted facial features, and horns.[51] Here she interprets this
shocking hybrid as the church beset by "fornication and murder and
rapine" and penetrated by "strong vices and mordant madness."[52] The

subversive role of Antichrist is arrestingly portrayed by this bestial rapist, but the hyperbole did not "take" because the iconographic norm was to separate ideal from monstrous beings, so that the hybrid was by nature evil. Yet we will see the grotesque emerge again in an even stranger context in the *Book of Divine Works*. And across the centuries Hildegard's grotesque finds a resonance with numerous self-images of contemporary feminist artists, who fragment and mask their bodies to repel the male gaze.[53]

Hildegard also developed her own perspectival codes in the treatment of architectural forms, which she employed a great deal in book 3 of *Scivias*. Some of these pictures present a kind of ground plan, with walls indicated by lines or by crenellations (figures 5, 10). When compass directions are mentioned in the text, they are not consistently oriented; east may be to the top, as in III.1, or to the bottom, as in II.2. Towers or crenellated walls may be represented clapped out (extending outward from the ground plan) in all directions, and major architectural forms are often on an oblique angle to the frame, with walls continuing beyond it; figures associated with these structures may be upside down to the final orientation of the picture. There are no coherent buildings except in the "real" setting of the frontispiece, where Hildegard is in a central vaulted space, like the nave of a church, between two towers that are conflated with aisles; the compression and sectioning are typical conventions of the period. A fondness for domical roofs goes back to Carolingian prototypes, but these are greatly emphasized when they signify Ecclesia (III.3; cf. II.4 and III.9, figure 5); here, as a kind of aureole for the figure, they resonate with descriptions and built representations of the Holy Sepulchre.[54] Overall, these architectonic forms are more symbolic than actual.

Yet the depictions of buildings also show a concern for regular stone cutting and coursing, which give a stability to even the most tilted tower (figures 11, 12). This, and the textual description, with phrases such as "miraculously even and without roughnesses," show a considerable attention to structure, including for instance the importance of sturdy junctures between angled walls. I have elsewhere made a particular examination of one of these original compositions for the way the text mediates the visionary image, particularly in relation to its authority in matters of the highest theological import. The illustration for book 3, vision 7, depicts the Trinity (figure 12).[55] The composition is of additional interest because it demonstrates the nonfigural mode of Hildegard's visions. As noted above, in most other cases, although the

1. The Fall, *Scivias*, book 1, vision 2: Hildegard sees the creation of Eve as "a white cloud that had come forth from a beautiful human form . . . bearing in her body the whole multitude of the human race." At the Fall, a black pit opens and casts them out of paradise. She did not think in terms of the traditional temptation of Adam by Eve.

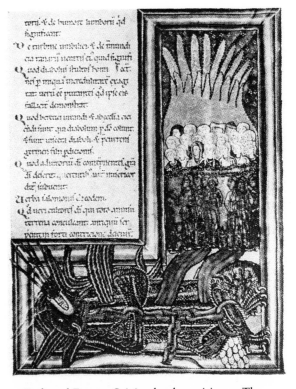

2. Defeated Enemy, *Scivias*, book 2, vision 7: The form of the black pit from figure 1 is reversed here into "a burning light, as large and high as a mountain," the heaven that crowds try to reach. They are threatened by a monstrous devil, which, though chained, continues to spew forth flames.

Decima visio tercie partis:

T post
hec ihmira
ce orientali
anguli pre
monstrati
edificii. ubi
pdicte due
partes muri ipsi. illa lucida et lapi
dea videlicet ouuelt crat. uidi
qsi septe gradus candidissim lapi
dis. qui ad lapide illu magnu sup
que psatus lucidus sedens ithrono
apparuit. inmodu testudinis ad
uoluti uidebant. et sup eolde gra
dus sedes posita erat. sup qua rune
sui quida sedens. uirilem et nobilem
uultu. palludi tam coloris. et capillo
subnigros usq; ad scapulas ipsi descen
dentes habebat. purpurea tunica
induitur. Qui a cipite suo usq; ad um
bilicu in apparuit. s; ab umbilico
deorsu obumbrat in ad uidendum
fuerat. et ipse respiciens in mundu.
maxima fortitudine uociferabat
ad hominet qui in eo erat dicens:

Verba filii hominis:
Stulti hominet qui tepide et
turpit marcetis iuobismetipsis.
nolentes uel oculu unu aprire ad in
tuendu qd i bonitate spe uri sitis. s;

.xxv.

3. Son of Humanity, *Scivias*, book 3, vision 10: Hildegard sees "the Shining One" (the youthful Christ) seated at the eastern corner of a building but hidden from her from the waist down. Below him appear Constancy (the stag connotes transience), Celestial Desire, and Compunction of Heart, then a bodiless Contempt of the World and winged Concord, whose face is so bright Hildegard "could not look fully at her."

4. Male and female saints, Sacramentary from Maria Laach, ca. 1160.

5. Virtues in the Tower of the Will of God, *Scivias*, book 3, vision 3: The tower, drawn as a crenellated circle, signifies the foundations of virtue in the Old Testament; in its turrets are the Christian virtues of Heavenly Love, Discipline, Modesty, Mercy, and Victory, "each dressed in silk garments." Longing, carrying a crucifix, and Patience appear in the lower right corner.

7. The Lamb opening the seals and the beasts taking John's hand (detail of left half), Saint-Sever Apocalypse, ca. 1075.

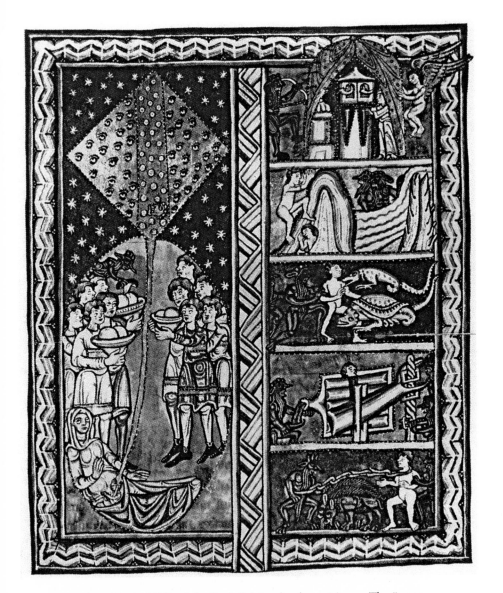

6. Soul and Body, Walk of the Soul, *Scivias*, book 1, vision 4: The "great and severe splendor, flaming with many eyes," appearing like a kite, is the "Supernal Creator" ensouling a "perfect human form" in the womb of a reclining woman, who is about to give birth. The small scenes on the right show the trials of the soul.

t post
hec uidi.
cu filiuf
di metu
ce pepen
dir.quod
pdicta
muliebri
imago ueluc lucidul splendor ex an
tiquo confilio ppere pgrediens.p di
uinam potentiam ad ipfu adducta
e.⁊ fanguine qui de latere ei flux
it se fursu eleuante pfusa. ipfi p uo
luntatem fupra patris felici despon
fatione associata e.atq carne ⁊ san
guine ei nobilit dotata. Et audiui
uocem de celo illi dicentem. Hec fili
sit tibi sponfa in restauratione po
puli mei. cu ipfa mater sit animas
p faluationem spiritus ⁊ aque rege
nerans. Et cum eadem imago tam
hoc in muneris sui pficeret. uidi qñ
quodda altare ad quod ipfa frequent
accedebat. ⁊ ibi dotem fua denote
reuisens eam fupno patri ⁊ anglis
ei humilit oftendebat. Unde etia
cu facerdos facris uestib induit. ad
celebranda diuina facramta ad ide
altare accederet. uidi qd fubito
magna ferenitas lucis cu obfequio

8. Giving of Life: Communion, *Scivias*, book 2, vision 6: Two pictures at the opening of this chapter show a crowned woman (Ecclesia) receiving the blood of the Eucharist from Christ on the cross, and (reproduced here) a priest saying Mass at an altar with a great light (drawn as angels) coming down at the moment of transubstantiation when "the offering is made true flesh and blood." The members of the congregation vary in readiness, but all will be received if they repent.

9. Abbess Aldegonde's vision of the Apotheosis of St. Amand,
ca. 1125–1145.

10. The Day of the Great Revelation, *Scivias*, book 3, vision 11: Hildegard
sees five beasts in the north, like a dog, a lion, a horse, a pig, and a wolf, pre-
saging "five ferocious epochs of temporal rule" toward the end of time. In
the west the youthful Christ of her previous vision (figure 3) appears again;
below, Hildegard recognizes the crowned woman of book 2, vision 6, but
with "scaly blemishes" on her hips and a monstrous head at her genitals,
which leaves her violently and is destroyed by a thunderbolt (lower right).
The church is invaded by Antichrist and betrayed "because those who should
love her will violently persecute her."

11. Tower of Church, *Scivias*, book 3, vision 9: The tower of the church rises out of sight from foundation walls that are still under construction, and is filled with people, some of whom are "very dirty and black and act insane." A female figure Hildegard identifies with Knowledge of God (with a scroll) encourages people to keep the garment they have been given (Christian faith and God's law), while Wisdom rises from her pavilion with seven pillars, her face too bright to see. Justice tramples a dragon and three-headed Sanctity brandishes a sword. All pay homage to Christ, who however is not seen; the female Virtues appear very powerful.

aut acutas aures inaiores intellect' viniD edifferentia c intitate trim pfon.g.
habet. hic i ardente amore speculi x. De trib' similitudmib' ad trinitate.
mei aduerba hec anbeder. cea in xi. Verba de libro regn id eande ven.
ofcientia animi sui conscribat.

Explicit sexta insio terne par
tis. Capitula septime insi
onis terne partis:

I Qd ineffabilis trinitas istinc tepg.
declarata. simplici c humili
afidelib' credenda c colenda
cne qs plus inuestigans qua
oportet. qa ophendi n potest.
indeteri cadat.

II Qd ilanigne xpi mundus sal
uatus e. c cultus sce trinitatis
manifestissime declaratus c. ipsa
tam nulli intellectui patet.

III Qd ineffabilis trinitas oim creatu
re aptissime impio c potestate
apparet. excepti icreduli cor
dib. cuncta tam uelut i ciden
gladius penetrat. S fuerdit.

IIII. Qd i xpiano pplo catholice fidi
i ariditate infidelitatis aduer
saute hosti dimitas i ofusione

V Qd dimitas uac'antia malicie
ppli deterr.

VI Qd diabolici serisina gentili ppli
ado absi sui uadit ipdicione.

VII Parabola ad eande re.

VIII Verba iohis ad eande re.

12. Column of the Trinity, *Scivias,* book 3, vision 7: This very unusual
image of the Trinity, as a compound pier forming the corner of a building,
is explained on pp. 118–119. The Christ in Majesty in figure 3 merges with
the steps to his throne, but here the Godhead has no human features. Like
many images in book 3, this one demonstrates the very high symbolic value
Hildegard placed on architecture.

247

cubitū xp̄ q̄nq̄. Jungant̄ ista x̄
q̄nq̄ suptariby; c̄ q̄nadraginta
habent. Hiſ omniby adhuc ſu-
pra rectum ipſius porte quaſi
appugnacula facienda q̄nq̄
cubitoſ adicium. c̄ ſic quadra-
ginta q̄nq̄ cubitoſ altitudi-
abinteriori parte implentur.

ſarratū ū ſup̄ dicē ē. xlv. cubitis
demiſſior in pciō lat̄. zf̄ ħ tota
ti altitudo abyctiou parte uidē
in nouaginta cubitoſ oſurgı̄. Vi
detr̄ ū abyctiou parte duo cenacla.
inui aui ab ſctiou parte habē. 7 dcino
z̄ īuio thalamo dicē ē. Criuſtuſ eſt
porū. ā recto thalami uſq̄ ad rectū eſt.

13. Richard of Saint Victor, Temple gatehouse, illustration for Ezekiel's vision; probably before 1173.

14. Rupertsberg Abbey, engraved after a drawing by Daniel Meissner, before 1625.

15. Heavenly Jerusalem with Saints, *Book of Divine Works,* part 3, vision 2: People of all ages huddle in a mountain that is brilliantly illuminated. Two hybrids hover above, combining human features with those of a leopard and a bear or a hawk. Hildegard glosses them as the era before the Flood, when men mated with animals, and the era after the Flood, or under the law. Above the heavenly city a crowd plays music which "resounds like a delightful resonance in the clouds." These are the saved. Hildegard's text mentions the Virgin Mary several times, but she never appears in the images.

16. The Trinity, *Book of Divine Works*, part 1, vision 1: This time the Trinity appears to Hildegard in human form, trampling underfoot the satanic serpent (compare figure 2). The beautiful young man with a face too brilliant to look at, and with four wings, is the Holy Spirit, while the older face of God the Father rises from the first head and the Son is figured by the "Lamb or Light of God." This brilliant red and gold image explains itself to Hildegard as the "fiery life of the divine essence."

17. The Heavenly Jerusalem with Wisdom and God, *Book of Divine Works*, part 3, vision 4: Hildegard recognizes the richly dressed woman on the left, in white and green, as Wisdom. The resplendent hybrid in the center, with mirrors in his wings, is Almighty God; the face is too bright to look on, but it is a human face because mankind was created in God's image. The second face in the stomach of this figure connotes the salvation of mankind that was foreseen from the beginning, but the darkness swirling next to heaven is a "place of punishment."

18. Tree of Jesse, *Speculum virginum*, mid-twelfth century.

primary visual experience she describes is nonfigural, these dynamic schemata incorporated figures at a later stage in the development of text and image as part of her explanation of their metaphorical meanings. In this case, a vast seamless column at one corner of a building has three sharp metallic ridges, and she explains the configuration as the Trinity: "Thus the Father, the Son and the Holy Spirit testify that they are in no way disunited in power, even though they are distinguished in Persons, because they work together in the unity of the simple and immutable substance."[56]

Thus Hildegard did not portray the Trinity in any of the standard twelfth-century ways, including the identical bearded pair with a dove that Christina of Markyate had seen in a vision some twenty-five years earlier, even though Hildegard here refers several times to Christ's becoming human and once to the Holy Ghost as a dove.[57] She construed her vision as having a particular relationship to non-Christians: The straw scattered to the southwest (our right) represents heretics, the severed wings (or feathers as drawn) to the northwest (left) are Jews, and the excised dead branches in the west (center) are pagans (figure 12). She finishes with a long passage describing the punishment of one who "obstinately sought out what he should not have sought out," indicating her awareness of heretical beliefs concerning the Trinity, probably including those of the famous theologian Abelard. She had submitted her own writing to St. Bernard of Clairvaux, who was well known to have judged Abelard. This rare nonfigural rendering of the Godhead might have met with the approval of the Cistercians. Lest we doubt her authority (and her text provides the usual humility topoi), a reference here to the Holy Spirit coming to the Apostles "openly in tongues of fire" recalls the author portrait at the beginning of the work, in which Hildegard herself is shown receiving tongues of flame from heaven and making a record on tablets like those of Moses.

A strong intervisuality operates throughout the work, so that later texts (or images) may recall earlier images and build meanings with their help. Thus even a nonfigural symbol is overlaid with figural reference. An instructive comparison can be made with the "pure" architectural drawings produced in Paris by Richard of St.-Victor, probably between 1159 and 1173, as pointed out to me by Walter Cahn, who noted that "Hildegard, in contrast to Richard, is concerned to represent her visions in such a way as to seem at once very concrete, yet unmistakably personal and removed from ordinary reality" (figure 13).[58] The Victorine was extremely interested in seeing with the mind's eye, and in these drawings he attempted to follow Ezekiel's Temple vision literally in order to recreate its likeness.

During the last three years of her work on the *Scivias* Hildegard was also preoccupied with the rebuilding of Rupertsberg, which had long been a ruin. The several drawings and prints that portray it in the six-teenth century, before its destruction, show a substantial walled hilltop monastery, dominated by a large church whose apse is flanked by tow-ers (figure 14). It appears to be a spectacular example of Rhenish Ro-manesque architecture.[59] Yet begun in 1148, probably completed in 1150, and consecrated in 1151, it was already outmoded in comparison with the Abbot Suger's abbey at Saint-Denis, north of Paris, which had been partially rebuilt almost a decade earlier in the new French Gothic style. By German standards, however, Rupertsberg appears a reason-able precursor of the cathedral of Bamberg as it was rebuilt later in the century. And there is no reason to give Hildegard less credit for the new buildings than the twelfth-century priors of Christ Church, Canterbury, for their Romanesque choir or Suger himself for the Gothic choir at Saint-Denis (though Suger laid claim to his role in a justificatory piece). The architectural elements and metaphors in book 3 of the *Scivias* speak to a preoccupation with building and an understanding of struc-ture at just the time Hildegard would have been supervising her builders at Rupertsberg (figures 5, 11, 12).

Another composition of these years is the extraordinary Sequence for Saint Rupert, *O Ierusalem*, that Hildegard probably composed for the 1151 consecration of this church.[60] It celebrates both the visionary celestial city and the spiritual perfection of the youthful patron saint, transforming both into radiant gems. Yet one can also read in the se-quence a eulogy of the new church (which had first appeared in a vision to Hildegard), resplendent with polychromy and stained glass. The saint's life gleams forth from the windows, responding to changing light, uniting its splendor with that of "Jerusalem." And even the prose life that could have served as a source for a glass designer was supplied by Hildegard.[61] The colored gems are those of Ezekiel's vision, also called into play in Suger's famous passage on the anagogical function of his church furnishings, and they are the colors of twelfth-century stained glass: purple, blue (sapphire), deep yellow (topaz), rose, green (sweet green of the fruit), blood-red and scarlet, as well as colorless (lily-white, shining white) and translucent (without pith).[62] In excerpts from Newman's poetic translation, look for the reading I am suggesting that conjures this church, its windows filled with the lives of the saints:

Jerusalem! royal city,
walls of gold and purple banners,

building of utmost bounty,
light never darkened,

lovely at dawn,
ablaze at noon.

Blessed be your childhood
that glimmers at dawn,
praised be your vigor
that burns in the sun.

O Rupert! Pearl
in the morning, diamond
at noon, ever sparkling!
Fools cannot hide you, nor the vale the mountain.

Jerusalem! In the frames
of your windows glisten your gems,
lapis lazuli with topaz,

Rupert among them,
a light never quenched.
Indifference cannot hide you,
nor the vale the mountain—
rose-crowned, purple-mantled,
lily-veiled,[63]
the mount of vision.

O delicate
bloom of the field, green
as of fruit before harvest, sheath
without pith: your ripeness
weighs lightly, burdens no hearts.

. . . .

Blood-red beacons
of martyrs flash there, candor
of virgins, splendor
of saints without number,
flashing forever—
in your turrets, Jerusalem.[64]

Rupertsberg also seems to make an appearance in the later picture cycle of the manuscript of the *Divine Works* in Lucca (Biblioteca Governativa MS 1942).[65] Its sumptuous quality, as well as the delineation of drapery folds, accord well with the hypothesis that this manuscript was produced to help make the case for Hildegard's canonization in Rome in 1227, as Rita Otto has argued.[66] Among the neatly rendered

buildings of various types which cluster within the walls of the heavenly
Jerusalem, as represented in five of the ten pictures, is a church; it has
the double-ended plan typical of Ottonian and Romanesque churches
in the region and which seems visible in drawings of Hildegard's
monastery before its destruction (figures 14, 15, 17). Twin towers flank
both the western apse and the eastern choir and apse, although some
confusion is caused by the thirteenth-century copyist who could not always decide between a flat and an apsidal end.[67]

There are other indications that the copyist revised some aspects of
an original set of pictures, particularly in the use of ruler and compasses
to regularize the compositions. It is likely also that the insistent presence of Hildegard as witness to her visions, as if she were constantly
gazing at the heavens, is a rhetorical gesture to persuade the viewer of
her sanctity; and this effect was even improved upon as the work pro-
gressed by the addition of scrolls, serving to connect her to heaven au-
rally as well as visually.[68] The first three instances (in visions I.1, 2, and
3) were clearly painted over finished pictures, but in visions I.4, II.1,
and III.2 scrolls—in two instances held in the hand of God—were
planned from the beginning (figures 15, 16).

What then is left of Hildegard's own compositions for the *Book of
Divine Works?* Several of the most original aspects of the Rupertsberg
Scivias designs are in fact recognizable in these later paintings, notably
an immense, frontal composite figure (I.1), baffling hybrids (III.2, III.4,
figures 15, 16, 17), diminutive figures clapped out (I.4), irregular-
shaped compartments and voids (II.1), and elements piled up vertically,
such as a mountain with rays descending on it (III.1, III.2).[69] Nor is the
field within the regularized geometric frames ordered in the normal
manner (as represented here by the Apotheosis of St. Amand, figure 9).
The underlying concept that the surface of the parchment is a map, so
that its edges represent the four cardinal compass directions, is common to both sets of illuminations.[70] And, as in the *Scivias* pictures,
there are occasionally leaps of imagination that fill a gap in the text,
such as when Love, Humility, and Peace are given diadems to wear on
their long loose hair (III.3). Novel ideas, such as the winds blown by
beasts rather than by men, are effortlessly executed by the artist.[71] It is
scarcely probable that the thirteenth-century illuminator could have entered into the mode of composition of the *Scivias* pictures to design the
Divine Works set in the manner of Hildegard, yet employ a contemporary style for the execution that gives pronounced corporeality to the
figures.

I will touch on just one more aspect of the *Book of Divine Works* designs: the ways the Almighty is depicted. In the Rupertsberg *Scivias* the several representations have little in common; the Trinity was at one time nonfigural, at another a divine person was surrounded by two halos, or God in Majesty might be seated (never enthroned) and bearded (figures 3, 6, 10, 12). So too aspects of God's nature appeared as a winged head in *Scivias* III.5 (Jealousy) and as two pairs of wings in *Divine Works* II.1 (Justice and Providence). As if to complete this strong impression of corporeal instability, the Trinity appears with two pairs of wings and two heads (holding the Lamb) at the opening of *Divine Works* and as a scaly creature with six wings, bestial feet, and a bright red head in vision III.4 (figures 16 and 17). In specific details this hybrid coincides with the text, but its composite nature and outstretched arms as well as an abdominal mask recall the terrifying image of Ecclesia invaded by Antichrist of the earlier book (figure 10). These images appear to have been generated through the same cognitive processes.

To claim Hildegard as a creative artist, as I am doing, needs to be placed in a historical context. She was not known as such in her lifetime, even though there were a few famous craftsmen in the twelfth century whose names and praises appear in texts. The best known were seculars, and several were Rhenish or Mosan goldsmiths. Spanning the century were Roger of Helmarshausen, who made an altarpiece for Henry of Werl, bishop of Paderborn, before 1100; Rainer of Huy, whose work on the baptismal font in Liège is documented between 1107 and 1118; canon Godefroid "de Claire" of Huy, who worked at midcentury for Abbot Wibald of Stavelot; and Nicholas of Verdun, who signed the Klosterneuburg Ambo in 1181 and the Shrine of the Virgin in Tournai in 1205.[72] More versatile, according to the texts, was Master Hugo, who painted and sculpted at Bury St. Edmunds in the first half of the century.[73] But fame did not necessarily serve such craftsmen well; a Nicholas who was burned as a heretic at Braine in 1205 was described as the most famous painter in all of France.[74] And none of these men were also known as writers.

In a monastic context humility was always called for. One German monk who acquired an enormous theoretical and possibly empirical knowledge of the materials and processes for making art in the early twelfth century hid his identity under the pseudonym Theophilus.[75] His book was widely disseminated and would have been read by ecclesiastical patrons as well as by learned practitioners. A century before him,

Bishop Bernward of Hildesheim had profited from his travels to learn the techniques of bronze casting and to set up an "art school" on his return north, where he became known as a patron. As Hanns Swarzenski pointed out, the distinction between making art and having it made was less clear in the Middle Ages than it now is.[76] It is generally assumed that abbots or priors directed monastic building enterprises, so the role I propose for Hildegard at Rupertsberg is a standard one, comparable to that of Suger. Closer to her mentality, however, were monastics like Lambert of St.-Omer, Honorius Augustodunensis, and Herrad of Landsberg, who engaged in visual thinking such that their texts virtually require images.[77] Hugh of St.-Victor's writings have a similar vivid quality, even though there is no evidence for actual pictures.[78] Sometimes the line between the concrete image and the image in the mind's eye was a fine one, but the purists preferred not to cross it. Crediting Hildegard with designing pictures might not have furthered the cause of her canonization.[79] In any case, she slipped into oblivion.

Yet from a modern viewpoint the question remains: Is Hildegard an unsung genius, comparable to Leonardo da Vinci in the range of her endeavors and the height of her achievements? In 1971 Linda Nochlin raised the question "Why were there no great women artists?" alerting art historians to the need for a particularly supportive environment to achieve the reputation of a genius.[80] Whereas the postmedieval women invoked by Nochlin were largely deprived of these support systems, it might be argued that Hildegard was more fortunate. She had contact with others of her stature, indeed she was held in awe by her peers and patrons, and she traveled, which gave her access to libraries with illuminated books and to other churches. Yet the claim that she was a genius is problematic in that no twelfth-century person would have recognized its terms, particularly for a monastic. Hildegard's unique talents would have been viewed as part of her prophetic gift, and even artists of the highest reputation were not honored as "geniuses," in the sense of being regarded as having their own private source of inspiration.[81] Nonetheless, I believe that Hildegard can be credited with the quintessential part of creativity that Renaissance theorists regarded as the highest level of artistic creativity, that is, *idea* or concept. To claim such a role for her is compatible with the fact that none of her original works survive.

SEVEN

Medical Writer

"Behold the Human Creature"

FLORENCE ELIZA GLAZE

In the medical books, she records with a subtle exposition the
many wonders and secrets of nature in such a mystical sense,
that only from the Holy Spirit could a woman know such
things.

— *Johannes Trithemius*

With these words the Renaissance humanist and bibliophile Johannes
Trithemius (1462–1516) registered his admiration of Hildegard of Bingen's medical writings, known today as the *Physica* and the *Causes and
Cures.*[1] Trithemius's evaluation of the books, which he viewed at the
Rupertsberg while on a visit from his nearby abbey of Sponheim, also
betrays his sense of Hildegard's status as a medical author: her writings
about the human body, disease, and medicines seemed so perceptive
that, to his mind, they must have been the product of supernatural inspiration. Trithemius's assumptions about Hildegard's medical writings
largely reflect the medical culture of his own era, when medical learning
and literature were the jealously guarded prerogatives of university-
educated and publicly licensed male physicians or of strictly regulated
medical guilds.[2] In Trithemius's day women did not produce medical
literature of expansive scope in a bookish, Latin presentation, and he
could scarcely conceive of a time when such a marvel might have lain
within a woman's capabilities. But in fact Hildegard's medical writings
display precisely the sort of inspiration Trithemius rejected (but perhaps suspected): namely, that she was familiar with medical literature,
that she read, absorbed, and interpreted Latin medical writings with a
high degree of individuality, and that evidently she felt entirely un-
apologetic about her right to expound at length on medical subjects.

When the convent on St. Rupert's Mount was constructed and Hildegard and her community of nuns moved into the new establishment in 1150, some provision for their health care would have been made, in keeping with general Benedictine practices. The Rule of St. Benedict, written before the middle of the sixth century in southern Italy and widely adopted across Europe from Carolingian times, explicitly dictated the construction of a monastic infirmary as a separate installation dedicated to caring for sick members of the professed community. Although Benedict's rule says little about the actual practice of medicine, in general the tone of moderation concerning the consumption of food and drink, with special dietary indulgence for the sick, indicates a regimen for living conducive to health and not intolerant of bodily illness.[3] In her *Explanation of the Rule of Benedict,* Hildegard advocates a similar dietary license, explaining that the sick members of the community should be permitted to eat the flesh of quadrupeds (such as cattle, sheep, or swine), while the elderly and children should be allowed to eat more frequently and to consume more delicate foods than the rest of the community.[4]

As a place for the recovery of the sick, the infirmary at the Rupertsberg would have been outfitted with furniture and implements necessary to the fulfillment of its mission. These would include several beds, one or more tubs for medicinal baths, an *armarium pigmentorum,* or medicine cupboard, to house the more expensive imported medicinal ingredients, possibly a fire for the preparation of nourishing food for the sick, as well as mortars for grinding drugs, bowls, wooden spatulas, bandages, and phlebotomes, or lancets, for bloodletting. Books kept in the infirmary would be intended to support the spiritual life of the patients and would probably consist of missals, breviaries, and psalters; the infirmary would either possess its own small chapel or would be located close enough to the abbey church for the nuns to maintain at least partial participation in the exercise of the Divine Office.[5] Medical literature kept in the infirmary would probably have been limited to simple lists of recipes, arranged according to the needs of practical utility.[6] One of the members of the community would preside over the whole infirmary and might have one or more assistants, either lay assistants or perhaps novices, to help with the wide variety of nursing tasks.

While all enclosed communities would have access to simple nursing care in the infirmary, the degree of medical care available to a monastic populace would vary widely from house to house, depending on each house's material, financial, intellectual, and human resources. The skill of the sister infirmarian would be largely contingent on the availability of a person trained in the practice of phlebotomy (therapeutic bloodletting) and the preparation of medicines. In his prescriptive letter to Heloise, Peter Abelard (1079–1142) detailed idealistically the responsibilities of the infirmarian at the Paraclete, noting,

> The Infirmarian shall take care of the sick, and shall protect them from sin as well as from want. . . . Medicaments too must be provided, according to the resources of the convent, and this can more easily be done if the sister in charge of the sick has some knowledge of medicine. . . . And there should be someone with experience of blood-letting, or it would be necessary for a man to come in amongst the women for this purpose.[7]

Certainly, many monastic communities in the early medieval period depended on the skills of outside practitioners, and numerous letters survive from the ninth through twelfth centuries in which regular and secular clergy suffering from some illness importuned the assistance of distant clerical friends or ecclesiastical superiors skilled in medicine.[8]

The ambitious plan for the abbey of St. Gall, produced on the island of Reichenau early in the ninth century, proposes an ideal medical establishment that was never realized and assuredly cannot be seen as representative of the medical experience of most monastics. It is, nonetheless, suggestive of monastic inclinations to provide for the care of the community's residents. In its plan St. Gall boasts an entire sector of the monastic enclosure dedicated to the care of the sick. There is not only a "physician's residence" replete with pharmacy but also a building devoted solely to bloodletting, a separate kitchen and bathhouse for the sick, a sizable medicinal herb garden, an infirmary with several rooms, and both a cloister and a separate chapel to serve the infirmary patients.[9] In this respect the plan of St. Gall advocated solving the dilemma of medical care by formally incorporating the physician's activity into the monastic life. Yet the presence of trained, professional physicians in monastic communities was almost certainly the exception rather than the rule, a situation that only began to change in the final decades of the twelfth century, when scholastic training at Salerno and Montpellier began to churn out higher numbers of medical scholars in search of ecclesiastical positions.[10] And even in these cases the physicians in question would have been male, as women were barred from all higher education because of their nonclerical status.[11]

Within Hildegard's lifetime, moreover, attitudes toward monastic involvement in professional medicine were undergoing something of a
crisis, occasioned primarily by a sharp increase in the popularity of
scholastic medical studies and the promise of significant financial gain
through medical practice. Starting in 1139 with the Second Lateran
Council, the church issued several decrees forbidding the departure of
monks from their communities either to pursue medical studies or to
practice medicine for profit.[12] At about the same time Bernard of Clairvaux became involved in a dispute over a renegade monk of considerable medical skill who had fled his monastery in order to escape the pe-
cuniary exploitation of his talents; coming to Clairvaux, the monk
received asylum when Bernard refused to force his return to his home
institution.[13] In general, the main concern seems to have been not that
professed monastics were engaged in the practice of medicine but rather
that immoderate practice might divert them from their primary vocation, living the spiritual life. In this sense, the care of the body was only
problematic when it prevented the appropriate care of the soul.

The practice of medicine by regular monastics was given implicit approval in 1163 when Pope Alexander III issued a more moderate decree
at the council of Tours, which merely prohibited the departure of professed monks from their institutions for the sake of pursuing medical
studies and said nothing negative about medical practice within the
monastery. Bernard himself expressed a preference for simple monastic
medicine over complex professional remedies when, in a tone of Cistercian austerity, he rebuked the wayward self-indulgence of monks who
had sought expensive remedies from outside practitioners in order to
combat recurrent fevers: "The use of common herbs, such as are used
by the poor, can sometimes be tolerated . . . But to buy special kinds of
medicines, to seek out doctors and swallow their nostrums, this does
not become religious."[14] Ironically, Bernard's attitude here parallels
that of his enemy Peter Abelard, who similarly advocated the medical
self-sufficiency of the nuns at the Paraclete. Whether Hildegard was
motivated by these contemporary trends to provide medical literature
for her nuns at the Rupertsberg cannot now be determined, but it is certainly possible that more than a few of the many medicinal recipes
recorded in her writings would have been practicable if needed.

The possibility of self-reliance in medical care for monastic communities was facilitated by medical literature copied in monastic scriptoria, preserved in their libraries, and available to interested audiences
throughout Europe. While most monastic houses had no medical books

at all in their collections, surviving manuscripts as well as patterns of medical book ownership indicate that monastic communities interested in medical literature had little difficulty locating texts, provided their interests were not too narrowly specialized.[15] This textual tradition dates from at least the sixth century, when Cassiodorus directed his monks to a number of important medical books deposited in the library at the newly founded Vivarium. In subsequent centuries European monasteries, and especially the Benedictines, played a pivotal role in the preservation and proliferation of these and other medical treatises, just as they did with all varieties of literature.[16]

It is frequently assumed that in the early medieval period and until the rise of the schools in the twelfth century, medical knowledge was limited to a few readings gleaned from Pliny's *Natural History* and the more widely popular *Etymologies* of Isidore of Seville. Moreover, this fragmentary learning was supposedly supplemented by popular practice or folk medicine that had nothing to do with literate traditions.[17] Yet the material evidence that survives in over 145 volumes of medical literature copied from the ninth through eleventh centuries reveals a far more complex tale in which monastic scriptoria functioned as the primary transmitters of a diffuse medical literature derived from classical scientific traditions.[18]

In general, the content of early medieval medical books, which provide the intellectual context for Hildegard's own medical writings, preserved practical traditions and small portions of theory adapted and reduced from the voluminous medical literature of classical antiquity. Because most medical writings in the ancient world were composed in Greek, transmission necessitated not only the reduction of material but also its transformation into Latin, a language ill suited to convey the nuances of meaning indicated by Greek phraseology and vocabulary. As a result, early medieval medical treatises frequently presented condensed information studded with a transposed Greek terminology that occasionally challenged the comprehension of monastic readers. The same problematic medical terminology also stimulated the production of sometimes lengthy glossaries that not only defined Greek terms but also equated the names for Greek medicinal ingredients with their Latin, and, more rarely, vernacular equivalents.[19] In the process of transmitting medical thought to the West, late ancient translators tended to favor the more approachable writings of the Hippocratics over the writings of Galen, whose verbosity, polemic, and abstruse theory made his texts both less appealing and less practical to an audience interested in "just the facts." The portions of Galenic texts and ideas which *were* transmitted to the West prior to the late eleventh century (when they were reintroduced at much greater length by the translations of the Benedictine monk Constantine the African) were reduced to snippets of theory or compressed into the Latinized encyclopedias of Greek Byzantine authors like Oribasius (ca. 325–400) and Alexander of Tralles (525–605).[20]

So what might the medical literature available to Hildegard have looked like? One good example is a ninth-century manuscript formerly preserved by the abbey of Echternach, which contains the following: the Hippocratic *Aphorisms;* various treatises about the effects of the four seasons on health; treatises on the four humors of the body (blood, phlegm, yellow bile, and black bile), attributed to Hippocrates and Galen; the *Medical Questions* derived from Soranus of Ephesus; a catalog of diseases and their anatomical sites of origin; numerous treatises on phlebotomy, or therapeutic bloodletting; some prognostics guides; a long compilation derived from ancient scholia (or formal scholastic commentary) on Galen's *On the Medical Sects* and Cassius Felix's *De medicina,* among others; a *Hermeneumata,* or glossary, "on the ten species of medicines taken from animals of land and sea, herbs and seeds, trees and stones, flowers and gums, saps and metals, translated from the Greek into Latin"; an herbal; the so-called *Gynaecia* of Vindician (a treatise on anatomy and embryology); and a version of the Hippocratic *Diseases of Women*—in all, more than two hundred folios of medical literature derived from ancient sources.[21] The manuscript was augmented in the eleventh and thirteenth centuries with Old High and Middle German glosses of medicinal ingredients.[22] This sort of collection was by no means exceptional; numerous similar examples were copied and owned by monastic houses along the Rhine and its tributaries, and their existence reveals much about the interests of copyists as well as the practical utility of the manuscripts in successive generations.

But the medical literature available to interested monastic thinkers like Hildegard was significantly increased in the twelfth century. Around the beginning of the century Europe witnessed a "bloom" in the production of manuscripts in general, a trend that also saw the rapid proliferation of medical literature. Not only were more of the older treatises being copied but newly available literature found an eager audience across Europe, from Italy to England and France to Germany. For medical literature, in particular, this intellectual flowering had significant consequences. Throughout the early medieval period the study of *physica,* or the natural sciences, had often attracted the attention of scholars who viewed medicine as one component of liberal studies. In the twelfth century this tendency was dramatically amplified by the introduction of a new medical corpus that conceptualized, articulated, and promoted medicine as a philosophical art.[23]

Of the new medical literature rapidly acquired by Benedictine communities and cathedral libraries in the twelfth century, the treatises rendered into Latin by the monk Constantine the African (died before 1098/1099) at the abbey of Monte Cassino enjoyed particular favor. Along with his corpus, particularly the *Pantegni, Viaticum,* and *Isagoge,* a range of other medical literature from Salerno spread northward across Europe, where it was readily glossed and assimilated by cathedral scholars at Chartres and Benedictines at Hildesheim.[24] The chief aspect of the new medicine which most attracted the interest of scholars was the radically expanded treatment of medical theory which the texts publicized. The eleventh-century translations placed new emphasis on expounding the causes of disease rather than simply listing practical remedies.[25] Although this literature did not immediately supplant earlier textual traditions, it certainly provided a more intellectually complex view of the human body, the natural world, and disease. This rich mixture of new medical literature and scholarly activity provides the appropriate backdrop against which we must measure Hildegard's own activities as a medical thinker and writer.

Such were the institutional and intellectual contexts in which Hildegard composed her medical writings. What now can we say about her activities as a medical writer as well as her medical perspective, theoretical conventionality, and subject matter? The first and most noticeable characteristic of Hildegard's medical writing is the clear sense of organization she imposed on her material. The *Causes and Cures* begins with an account of the creation of the universe and moves on to the creation of the human being, which Hildegard characteristically presents as the apex of divine creativity. As a medical writer Hildegard defines the human creature as one subject to diseases, which she then sets about detailing one by one in a highly descriptive narrative. This portion, book 2, comprises almost three hundred chapters that explore the etiology, or causes, of disease as well as human sexuality, psychology, and physiology. After extensively outlining the causes of disease in a roughly head-to-foot arrangement, she turns in books 3 and 4 to an account of the cures and concludes with book 5 on prognostics and book 6 on a lunar horoscope.[26] For Hildegard the latter two topics involved not only foreknowing the outcome of a patient's illness through standard clinical examination but also foreknowing the outcome of conception. In this sense Hildegard's work follows a temporal and linear chronology, beginning with the Divinity, Creation, the Fall, and the Flood, arriving at the human creature's present state of disease, and then looking into the future to predict as fully as possible the bodily outcomes of human activity.

The complementary *Physica,* Hildegard's extensive pharmacopoeia, was arranged in nine books, cataloging the medicinal qualities and uses of plants, elements, trees, stones, fish, birds, quadrupeds, reptiles, and metals.[27] Here Hildegard clearly utilized the organizational principle of delineating categories in her account of the natural world, much as had other encyclopedic naturalists before her.[28] By detailing each category according to its medicinal properties, Hildegard explicitly conveyed her sense that the created things of the world were to be used to benefit humans, the most complex and subtle creatures on earth.[29] In both phases of her work Hildegard generally observes the same hierarchical schema found elsewhere in her writings, as in the *Unknown Language.*[30] In that mysterious glossary Hildegard carefully structures her own materials: she begins with God, proceeds through heavenly creatures (good and bad angels), the human creature (including terms of anatomy and some diseases) and human activities, and closes with an account of the non-human creatures (including trees, plants, birds, and insects).

As a medical writer crafting her material, Hildegard did not simply reproduce a randomly arranged collection of shorter treatises, such as those described above in the manuscript from Echternach, where pieces on prognostics and phlebotomy were copied with little sense of their appropriate delivery within a larger textual unit. Such copying would have been customary work for a monastic scribe, whether male or female; but Hildegard never settled for the ordinary.[31] Her sense of textual order was more sophisticated than that of her early medieval monastic predecessors and more ambitious than that in most of the practical manuals composed by her contemporaries. Yet not surprisingly Hildegard's work was considerably less sophisticated than scholastically arranged philosophical medicine, exemplified by Constantine's *Isagoge* and *Pantegni* (although the latter text too began with an analysis of the universe and was divided into the two broad components of medical theory—the causes of the body's function in health and sickness—and medical practice—the means of curing therapeutically).[32] Neither do the *Physica* and the *Causes and Cures* betray the same degree of disorderly randomness exhibited by the practical manuals of some of her contemporaries. It especially bears noting that Hildegard's medical interest was not devoted solely to practical remedies suitable to the care of her nuns or to recording her own pathological experiences of migraine and paralysis. She was, as a medical thinker, clearly interested in the broader universal context through which she might understand and explain the reasons for diseases, both cosmic and microcosmic, as well as revealing the means by which diseases might be vanquished. In this respect Hildegard's ambition as a medical writer attempting to produce a synthetic, largely encyclopedic overview of the human creature, the reasons for disease, and the means and methods for curing all manner of complaints places her squarely in the company of the most advanced thinkers of her day.[33]

When we look at the subject matter covered by Hildegard in the *Physica* and the *Causes and Cures,* two points immediately become obvious. The first is that in terms of content Hildegard's medical topics are completely congruent with contemporary medical literature, which regularly addressed issues from headache to gout, from menstrual retention to the consistency of semen, all of which are addressed in the *Causes and Cures.* Similarly, the encyclopedic listing of medicinal ingredients and their active properties, which we find in the *Physica,* was also part of a long literary tradition dating from Greek antiquity.[34] The second point is that Hildegard's composition of medical literature (rather than simple mechanical reproduction of preexisting texts) represents a significant departure from the dominant traditions in medical writing which predominated in the monastic environment of the twelfth century. First, Hildegard was a nun writing about medicine, which in itself was unprecedented.[35] In this sense, she provides us with a rare opportunity for gauging the ways in which medieval women participated in medical discourse.[36] This opportunity is especially vital, for women's voices are surprisingly underrepresented in the history of the medical enterprise, both as practitioners and as medical writers. Although the identities of many female practitioners of medicine have been gleaned from medieval records, only one other female medical writer, Trota of Salerno, Hildegard's contemporary, has been verified for the entire medieval period.[37] No other community of religious women, moreover, has been documented as owning medical literature until at least the thirteenth century. This dearth of information may, of course, merely reflect the many lacunae surrounding early medieval women and book ownership in general. Nonetheless, in this respect, as in so many others, Hildegard was crossing traditional, albeit tacit, gender boundaries.

But, second, Hildegard's medical writing is remarkable not only for what she was but also, and this is especially important, for how she viewed the natural world and the operation of the human body in health and in sickness. In the first two books of the *Causes and Cures* Hildegard articulates a vision of the created universe and of the human creature unprecedented in early medieval medical literature. She begins with the creation of the world, produced from nothing by divine will, with raw unformed matter fashioned into the orderly cosmos. With considerable skill, she presents a hierarchical and largely chronological image of the created universe, prefiguring in many respects her deeper cosmological perceptions recorded in the *Book of Divine Works*.[38] Sun, stars, planets, the moon, winds, weather, and vegetative matter are all described through colorful analogies and in highly imaginative terms. In many cases Hildegard seems to employ combinations of metaphors to express deeper truths about her topics than would otherwise be possible through simple narrative.[39]

After relating the creation of the cosmos, with its diverse components that moderate one another for the best possible arrangement and operation, Hildegard introduces in book 2 the ultimate purpose for all this divine creativity: the human being. As elsewhere in her writings and visionary illustrations, Hildegard depicts the human creature as integrally connected with the universe, both reflecting it and yet having dominion over it. After the first human was created, "he was a prophet of the heavens, and he had knowledge of the powers in all creatures and in all activity. And God gave all creatures to him so that in virile power he might arrange them, because he knew them and recognized them."[40] The image of the human reflecting the cosmos is also common in Hildegard's other writings and appears here in her depiction of the created world: "O man, behold the human creature! For man holds heaven and earth and other created things within himself, he is one form, and within him all things are concealed."[41] Her analogies of the macrocosm and microcosm, the universe and the human being, poetically express her sense of their mutual relations. In describing the cosmos she argues that "the firmament is like the head of man, the sun, moon, and stars are like his eyes, the air like his sense of hearing, the winds like his sense of smell, the dew like his sense of taste, the sides of the world like his arms and his sense of touch. And the other creatures, which are in the world, are like his belly, the earth moreover is like his heart."[42] As we shall see later, this perspective that the human creature both reflects the cosmos and has dominion over the rest of creation will have special significance for Hildegard's philosophy of medicine.

Hildegard's intermittent exposition on the "interrelated fours"—the four elements (fire, air, water, and earth), the four seasons, the four humors, the four zones of the earth, and the four major winds—displays her ready familiarity with the "doctrine of the fours," a favored and fluid subject in early medieval medical art and literature.[43] She asserts and reiterates that the four elements, although distinguished and named as individual entities, are inherently interconnected and incapable of being separated from one another, in the sense that each material substance, such as "fire" or "water," has something of more than one element within it. Thus fire is not absent from air, nor air absent from water, nor water absent from earth.[44] In much the same way, the human body is made up of these four elements, which literally "bind it together" and provide it with elemental components and qualities. From fire the body has heat, from air breath, from water blood, and from earth flesh. Just as the earth benefits from the proper function of the elements, receiving warmth and rain in proper measure, so the human body also benefits from the proper proportion of the elements in it. The four humors, analogous to the four elements, maintain human health when they exist in a tranquil state and with a "right temperament" in the human body.[45]

Although Hildegard's doctrine that there are four bodily humors is fundamentally consistent with certain trains of ancient and contemporary medical thought, in articulating the processes of *eucrasia* and *dyscrasia*, or humoral balance and imbalance, she develops an entirely original conceptualization.[46] Hildegard, ever hierarchical, divides the humors, like the elements, into dominant and subordinate pairs; of the elements the "higher" are celestial and immaterial, while the lower are terrestrial and material. Similarly, the humors within each person are divided into two classes, the dominant *flegmata* and the subordinate, occasionally obstreperous *livores*. When the humors maintain their respective dominant and subordinate relationships, the body exists in a state of health. But when the subordinate humors overcome the designated dominant ones, the body and mind of the person are adversely affected; the greater the degree of disharmony, the graver the illness that befalls the sufferer.[47]

Hildegard's account of the created world and the presence of disease in the human creature has as its focus one pivotal event: the original fall from grace of the two progenitors of the human race, Adam and Eve. For Hildegard that catastrophe had a devastating effect on both human history and the nature of human existence. By choosing to sin, and thereby ignoring the commands of the Creator, the original pair upset the harmony of the material world as well as their own harmonious and uninterrupted enjoyment of health. One chapter's account of this process is so intricate as to deserve quoting in full:

> It happens that certain men suffer diverse illnesses. This comes from the phlegm which is superabundant within them. For if man had remained in paradise, he would not have had the *flegmata* within his body, from which many evils proceed, but his flesh would have been whole and without dark humor [*livor*]. However, because he consented to evil and relinquished good, he was made into a likeness of the earth, which produces good and useful herbs, as well as bad and useless ones, and which has in itself both good and evil moistures. From tasting evil, the blood of the sons of Adam was turned into the poison of semen, out of which the sons of man are begotten. And therefore their flesh is ulcerated and permeable [to disease]. These sores and openings create a certain storm and smoky moisture in men, from which the *flegmata* arise and coagulate, which then introduce diverse infirmities to the human body. All this arose from the first evil, which man began at the start, because if Adam had remained in paradise, he would have had the sweetest health, and the best dwelling-place, just as the strongest balsam emits the best odor; but on the contrary, man now has within himself poison and phlegm and diverse illnesses.[48]

With this explanation Hildegard eloquently asserts that the Fall altered history and changed the state of the body and the enjoyment of health for all humanity by introducing illness into the realm of human experience.

Yet this theological reading of the history of disease does not inspire Hildegard to offer a spiritually simplistic, orthodox course of action; on the contrary, her "solution" is confidently materialistic and naturalistic. Most important, her answer to the problem of illness dignifies the art and the tools of medicine in a remarkable way. For rather than advocate that humanity suffer through illness as a trial visited by a justifiably vengeful Divinity, Hildegard ignores the example of the patient and long-suffering Job. Neither does she reduce humanity to sole reliance on the merciful intercession of *Christus medicus*, Christ the Physician, who heals all ills and erases all suffering.[49] Certainly she would not have denied the efficacy of faith and prayer, but she does not advocate them as the first course of action.[50] Instead, Hildegard privileges the practice of medicine, based on the knowledge of the powers of created things, a knowledge granted by God but deserving careful attention. Thus, "the good and useful herbs," and the "bad and useless ones" just discussed, can only be known through informed discernment, part of the knowledge of the powers or "virtues" of created things which God had granted to Adam at his creation. In this sense, Hildegard's catalog of the *virtutes* or medicinal "virtues" of created objects, which she details meticulously in her *Physica,* stands as a sort of naturalistic parallel to the catalog of spiritually healing penances listed in the *Book of Life's Merits.*

By articulating the ideas that disease entered the world as a consequence of the Fall and that humanity was granted knowledge of the natures of creatures as well as dominion over them, Hildegard indicates a philosophy of medicine in which medical knowledge and practice can be used to ameliorate the bodily consequences of the Fall, much as theology and right faith ameliorate the spiritual ones. Hildegard's effort to dignify medicine is unprecedented in monastic medical literature, which, as we have seen, was itself not intolerant of bodily healing. A positive outlook on medical knowledge was certainly not unknown in literate medical traditions, but it was never described with the degree or extent of philosophical articulation attempted by Hildegard. In a few cases monastic advocacy of medicine even survives in the form of illustrations, such as in a manuscript copied at the abbey of Fleury in the ninth century. At the beginning of the *Practica* ("On Medical Practice") by the sixth-century Byzantine medical author Alexander of Tralles, there stands a carefully prepared illustration in which an arcade of decorated columns frames two scenes. On the left a man sits enthroned as in a bishop's chair; he is tonsured like a monk and haloed like a saint. Around him a caption reads: "Alexander the wise physician set forth this little book of the art of medicine." The scene on the right depicts a large decorated cross with the caption "Holy Cross, save us, because through you Christ redeemed us through his holy blood." The text of Alexander's handbook on medicine begins on the next page: "In the name of our Lord Jesus Christ, here begins book one of the therapeutics of Alexander the Iatrosophist."[51] While such favorable depictions, where bodily medicine quite graphically parallels spiritual medicine, were not by any means the rule in Hildegard's day, neither were they so unknown that they might not have had some influence on the development of her medical philosophy in which the practice of medicine, the employment of God's material creation to relieve human suffering, takes on an almost sacramental status.[52]

Evaluating Hildegard's medical orthodoxy, that is to say, the extent to which her descriptions of diseases correspond to known contemporary traditions, reveals both her debts and her originality. What she writes about disease and healing is fundamentally in agreement with contemporary medical literature, but in no case does she take information from any one source and reproduce it unchanged. In every case where we have determined Hildegard's textual sources, she interprets in her own unique and highly visual way the processes at work. In borrowing several ideas, for instance, from the complex philosophical treatise *De semine,* "On Seed," Hildegard fixed on certain medical and physiological theories—that semen is the foam of the blood, that blood is changed to the whiteness of semen in men and to breast milk in women, that sexual maturity and the appropriate time for sexual activity are signaled by beard growth in men and menstruation in women—but in each case Hildegard assimilated these theories to her own viewpoint, or *visio,* of the human body.[53] She also adopted specific analogies and questions from *De semine,* such as the image of the medicinal cupping glass to explain the mechanics of conception or the philosophical question "Why do animals walk soon after their birth but humans do not?" But in neither case did Hildegard allow her source to dictate either the form or the content of her presentation.[54] It seems, in fact, that Hildegard may well have fixed on certain medical, cosmological, or physiological ideas precisely *because* they grabbed her attention by stimulating her own highly imaginative, visually oriented intellect. If this speculation truly approaches in some way the process of Hildegard's creative dynamism, then she may have experienced discrete portions of medical (and other) literature in a manner akin to, or at least informed by, her visionary experiences. In this view Hildegard's visionary reception was integrally involved in her cognitive processes. It remains possible, therefore, that when she borrowed specific ideas from medical literature, she may have done so chiefly because she "pictured" the structures and events in her own mind, absorbing them, assimilating them, and verbally reproducing them in an entirely unique and creative manner.[55]

At times Hildegard's assimilation of discrete ideas encountered in her medical sources permits us to perceive her teleological reasoning at work. When Hildegard explores the physiological differences between the male and the female, which she does frequently in the *Causes and Cures,* she finds that different gender roles are determined by different physiological constructs. Consequently, the different temperaments of men and women—four for each—are determined by their physiologically different profiles, which in turn broadly influence the diverse personality traits of each as well as their health, sexuality, and longevity.[56] Hildegard further read the Genesis story of the creation of Adam from the earth and of Eve from Adam's rib as signifying various differences in male and female flesh, and even in appropriately gendered occupations. In much the same way, Hildegard read a particular anatomical treatise in a comparably teleological fashion. The widely popular anatomical and embryological treatise composed by Vindician (fl. 400), St. Augustine's friend and mentor, provided Hildegard with several medical ideas and phrases. Deriving his materials from the ancient Greek traditions of human and animal dissection, which were no longer allowed in late antiquity, Vindician opened his text with an account of the human skull, noting its major sutures and their different arrangement in men and women.[57] To Hildegard, presuming that differences exist for a reason, this different division of the skull in women was interpreted as serving a specific physiological purpose unique to women, that of menstruation. As a result, Hildegard paints a highly visualistic image of the woman's skull opening up to allow the blood to flow out; in this case interpretively reading her source's literal meaning inspired her to create a unique, almost pictorial explanation for a basic physiological function.

Although in most cases Hildegard maintains her own interpretation and her own textual arrangement, in some areas her topical structure is adapted from her medical sources, as in her description of the organs within the human body, especially the lower abdomen. Human dissection for promoting scientific and medical purposes had been abandoned during Roman times and would only begin to be practiced again in the later Middle Ages.[58] Consequently, anatomical knowledge, like most learned medical traditions, was conveyed over the intervening centuries by the condensed medical writings of authorities like Vindician. In the late eleventh century the translator Constantine the African introduced a whole new series of authoritative texts that provided a more expansive account of the human body and disease. And it was from this newer, widely popular tradition that Hildegard adapted her accounts of the abdominal organs and their pathological conditions. In her characteristic and largely descriptive phraseology, Hildegard recounts in chapter after chapter the functions, appearances, and diseases of the internal organs in greater, more theoretical detail than ever appears in early medieval medical literature.

In several instances Hildegard was not only inspired by the content of Constantine the African's *Pantegni* but even followed that text's basic arrangement and presentation.[59] For instance, Hildegard opens the discussion of hernia in her chapter "De sifac extensione aut ruptura" (on protrusion and rupture of the peritoneum). This issue is raised within the context of digestive pathologies brought on by the consumption of indigestible foods; subsequent chapters detail the operation and malfunction of the male reproductive system, gout, and the activities of the uterus in health and sickness. Hildegard's topical arrangement echoes Constantine's *Pantegni, Theorica,* book 9, where "De passionibus siphac" (on diseases of the peritoneum) falls amid chapters on urinary disorders and diseases of the male and female reproductive organs.[60] Hildegard also borrows some of Constantine's more evocative verbal forms, using *rumpitur, scinditur, rupta est,* and *scissuram* to describe the rupturing and tearing of the peritoneal tissue. No other medieval author working prior to Hildegard presents a similar analysis of hernia, except for Constantine.

Hildegard's analysis of the causes of hernia, while borrowing from the *Pantegni,* is nonetheless presented almost visually, with a less complex scholastic structure and a selective etiology. Where Constantine details several varieties of hernia, applying to each its technical name, Hildegard describes mainly one.

> Certain people, regardless of whether they are thin or fat, have soft tissues in their bodies, and this little interior skin, which binds up the intestines, is fatty and thin, so that either on account of certain illnesses, or through work, or through a fall, or from the extension of the belly when it is filled with foods, it is easily ruptured. But still this same little skin is thicker in women and more durable than in men, on account of women's role in childbearing, and therefore it is torn more often in men than in women.[61]

Her account, although simplified and largely transformed into her own words, agrees etiologically and philologically with that of her esteemed predecessor and fellow Benedictine, the monk who introduced to the Latin West the more advanced, complex medical thought of the Arab world. The new translations from southern Italy had become in the early twelfth century the basis for medical instruction in the new educational centers at Salerno and Montpellier. And although women were barred from attending the schools, Hildegard's borrowings from the *Pantegni* betray the intellectual possibilities open to literate monastics who were willing to plumb the depths of the isolated text in search of broader knowledge. That her readings proved idiosyncratic and untutored should not surprise us; how could she possibly have written like a scholastic when she had had no training in the methods and structures of scholastic discourse? The *Pantegni,* with its sophisticated structure and Greco-Arabic terminology, proved daunting enough even for those men who studied formally at Salerno. That Hildegard was willing to wade into so dense a text and extract what passages she could from it, in what may have been a short window of accessibility, stands as no small achievement.[62]

While access to a diverse but selective body of medical literature certainly provided Hildegard with numerous ideas, phrases, and structural guidelines for articulating the body's operation in health and illness, these sources never overwhelmed her own interests or determined the full structure or content of her discourse. Unlike other medical compilers working from late antiquity through the eleventh century, Hildegard did not simply produce a work that was an accumulation of textual bits and pieces, rearranged and partially integrated at best.[63] In this sense Hildegard's method of recomposing and in most cases reconceptualizing the ideas of her written sources marks her as fundamentally different from other monastic writers, whose cut-and-paste approach to compilation produced patchwork medical texts of little vision or originality. It is likely, in fact, that Hildegard's modus operandi was essentially the opposite of that of other monastic compilers. Where these other medical composers allowed the textuality of medical authority to dominate and overwhelm their own scarcely perceptible agendas, Hildegard allowed her own overriding vision of the universe and the natural creation to determine the content of her medical writings, which were informed and bolstered by her forays into extant medical literature.

We might even be able to gain a sense of Hildegard's struggle with the often difficult language, structure, and content found in many of her sources as well as her confidence in the integrity of her own medical perspective. In the chapter "On Knowledge" from the *Causes and Cures* Hildegard presents an explanation of the learning process which echoes a similar but more autobiographical passage of her *Vita.*[64] In "On Knowledge" she writes:

When the birth of a human is about to begin, so that the divine power opens the closed womb of the mother, then the infant senses the power of God, and knowledge then arises in its soul for learning and grasping whatever it wishes, since it is inspired to this by its own wish and its own desire. For when a human wills to know any work, or any art, through its own wish and desire, then the Holy Spirit fills it with the greenness of its knowledge, whence the human learns and grasps whatever it wishes to learn. Just as the father and mother answer the child when it asks something of them, so also the Holy Spirit aids human knowledge of whatever art the human seeks to learn through its own choice, desire, and labor.[65]

As in the autobiographical passage in the *Vita,* this blanket definition of learning articulates Hildegard's own sense that, although formally untrained in scholastic literary analysis, she was nonetheless able, through work, effort, and desire, to gain deep and worthwhile insights into the meaning of the literature before her and to explain those insights in writing. And although Hildegard acknowledges that understanding (like everything) is granted ultimately by the Holy Spirit, she emphasizes the essential importance of the individual's role in pursuing willfully and laboriously the desired goal. This passage not only reflects the painfully ambitious course she so diligently followed in all aspects of her life but it also expresses Hildegard's essential trust in the goodness of the Divinity.

But did Hildegard's lengthy forays into medical literature, her carefully constructed interpretations of humanity's physical state and experience of disease, have no practical application? It is almost impossible to imagine that Hildegard's extensive cataloging of the causes of disease in physiological and anatomical terms or her lengthy explanation of the many medicinal properties of the created world's natural components did not inspire her to look favorably on the practice of medicine. As we have seen, her basic philosophy of medicine dignified the ideas of medical activity and the medical art to a considerable degree. Given her positive depiction of the medical enterprise, would either Hildegard herself or her nuns at the Rupertsberg, confronted with illness and suffering in their own community, have been able to ignore the painstaking accounts of widely recognized healing herbs or the detailed recipes for the preparation of medically orthodox confections? It certainly seems unlikely, especially since, as noblewomen, Hildegard's nuns would have come from the kinds of elite families that were accustomed to consulting professional medical practitioners when necessary. Hildegard's evident determination to relieve her community of dependence on the monks of Disibodenberg may well have provided additional motivation for accumulating the practical elements featured in her medical writings.[66] The details of health care at the Rupertsberg and at Eibingen remain shrouded in the same silence that circumscribes so much of our knowledge of the actual practice of monastic medicine. It does seem likely, however, that Hildegard's foundations shared with other monasteries the tendency to own two sets of related medical literature: the books of treatises kept in the library, treasury, or cloister bookpresses and the shorter, more practical extracts of these same works, mainly recipes and brief instructions, kept on hand in the infirmary.

In the centuries following Hildegard's death her medical writings enjoyed no great popularity, but a few medical thinkers and practitioners found her accounts of medicines sufficiently valuable to warrant copying them as condensed practical handbooks or as extracts to be incorporated into their own texts and translations. During the fourteenth and fifteenth centuries Hildegard's *Physica* found a particularly ready audience in two broad groups of the German populace: vernacular or bilingual readers and educated medical practitioners. Producers of *Fachliteratur,* practical technical manuals on specialized topics like dietetics, simple medicines, veterinary cures, and agricultural practices, found in Hildegard's *Physica* a wealth of information on common plants, fish, birds, and trees. Consequently, extracts from the *Physica* were incorporated into the *Cookbook of Master Eberhard* and into the *Medical Book* accompanying it, with some portions left in Latin and others rendered into German by the anonymous compiler.[67] Another more sophisticated adaptation appears in the *Speyerer Kräuterbuch,* where Hildegard's book on plants was broken up and translated into German, then arranged alphabetically with accounts from other sources into a well-orchestrated vernacular herbal.[68]

In the fourteenth and fifteenth centuries a few highly educated Latin readers, including university-trained professors of medicine and educated medical practitioners, similarly found Hildegard's medical writings attractive enough to own, copy, and excerpt. Two rectors at the university of Heidelberg, for example, included short extracts from Hildegard's recipes in their own medical manuals, while a copy of her *Causes and Cures* was donated to a Heidelberg library at approximately the same time.[69] Farther south a Doctor Barbatus of Bern owned an abbreviated version of Hildegard's *Physica,* along with many other Latin medical treatises that he had acquired while traveling through Germany. Nearly all of his practically oriented medical books were arranged to facilitate use in medical practice.[70]

Generally speaking, there is overwhelming evidence that Hildegard's medical writings were adapted by later copyists and redactors to exploit and maximize their utility in practical situations. Even the earlier Latin manuscripts of the *Physica,* those preserved in Florence and

Wolfenbüttel, show signs that they were augmented with users' aids, to make them more universally meaningful as well as textually usable. To this end German-Latin glossaries were added to make Hildegard's medicinal ingredients more uniformly identifiable; Latin indications were also added, either in the margins or prominently at the openings of chapters.[71] Such indications would point to the ailments for which particular recipes were useful, such as "contra dolorem capitis" (against headache). Thumbing through such an annotated text in search of a cure would have proved far easier in locating particular remedies for specific ailments, especially because none of the owners of these copies of the *Physica* had access to the *Causes and Cures,* where therapies were laid out in a more approachable fashion.[72]

Such patterns of adaptation and use, and especially the overwhelming evidence that later readers found her recipes efficacious, bring us back to the question of whether Hildegard herself intended the medical writings to be used. Her own testimony does not help us reach any firm conclusion on this subject. The only time she refers to her own medical writing, she uses the most general and formulaic of terms. At the opening to the *Book of Life's Merits,* composed between 1158 and 1163, Hildegard details the numerous activities and undertakings that had preoccupied her after she completed the *Scivias* in 1151. Among several other literary projects, Hildegard's *visio* had shown her that she should explain the "subtleties of the different natures of created things." This passing reference, something of a blanket title, is her only surviving characterization of her own medical work; there are no explicit references in her letters and she does not seem to have circulated the medical writings among her network of admirers as she did several of her other books.[73] Ironically, Hildegard's biographer Theoderic of Echternach gives a somewhat more descriptive account, perhaps because of his objectivity. In book 2 of the *Vita* he writes that Hildegard had shown "something of the nature of man, and of the elements, and of diverse creatures, and of how man ought to be helped by these."[74] Not only does this description provide a fuller representation of the various topics addressed in Hildegard's medical writings but the final phrase emphasizes her proactive medical philosophy, implicit throughout the first two books of the *Causes and Cures* and echoed in parts of the *Physica.*

Is it possible that Hildegard herself was unwilling to publicize the practical applications of her medical writings? There is some circumstantial evidence supporting this suggestion. As I mentioned above when framing the context for Hildegard's medical compositions, there was more than a little uncertainty in the twelfth century regarding the issue of appropriate medical practice by professed monastics. With church councils issuing canons on the matter and formulating prohibitions that in their most extreme forms threatened violators with excommunication, and with revered monastic leaders like Bernard of Clairvaux cautioning against excesses inconsistent with monastic austerity, such as the use of exotic and expensive medicines (which figure prominently in Hildegard's pharmacopoeia), we should not be surprised that Hildegard maintained a cautious silence on the subject.[75] Moreover, there had been other, even grimmer developments for those who embraced medical practice too openly or who endorsed too enthusiastically ideas found in the new medical writings translated by Constantine the African. Earlier in the twelfth century the favored candidate for elevation to the post of archbishop of Canterbury, the abbot Faritius of Abingdon, was rejected on the explicit grounds that he had practiced medicine and especially that he had treated female patients.[76] In addition, in the 1140s the immensely popular teacher at the cathedral school of Chartres, William of Conches, was forced by conservative critics to withdraw from teaching because of his eager assimilation and dissemination of ideas found in newly available treatises on natural philosophy. During his exile William skillfully revised his early book, the *Philosophia mundi*, into the more circumspect *Dragmaticon*, or "Dialogue about Physical Substances," one of whose sources was Constantine's *Pantegni*.[77] In this light we might argue that Hildegard may have felt uneasy broadcasting her own naturalistic medical treatises, particularly as they would not have been so immune to criticism as her great visionary writings.

But additional and more serious doubts have been raised about Hildegard's intentions as a medical writer as well as about the chronology of her activity in producing medical literature. At the core of the problem is the rather vague statement in the *Book of Life's Merits* which has been interpreted as signifying her authorship of one united medical book, already completed by 1158.[78] But the earliest extant manuscripts date only from the thirteenth century and clearly present two distinct but complementary treatises. Moreover, her medical work is not represented in any fashion in the Riesenkodex; it thereby stands out as the only part of Hildegard's corpus omitted from that compendium, which was begun either in the final years of her life or shortly after her death.[79] These difficulties invited Charles Singer in 1917 to reject both the *Physica* and the *Causes and Cures* as inauthentic works unworthy of Hildegard's "virile intellect." Singer's opinion has since been refuted through careful comparative analysis of Hildegard's ideas in general, but the medical writings, more than any other of her many productions and activities, have been dogged by suspicions of inauthenticity, fragmentation, and interpolation.[80] I suspect that these doubts have arisen more from our modern assumptions about female medical authorship, as well as general ignorance of early medieval medical literature, than from substantial evidence.

More recently objection has been made that significant portions of books 3 and 4 of the *Causes and Cures* duplicate recipes and remedies given in the *Physica* and that these books can consequently be rejected as rearrangements produced by an owner of the texts following Hildegard's death.[81] Such objections have received no irrefutable proof and the proponents' conclusions are neither necessary nor inevitable. No one has yet shown any portion of either treatise to be the work of another author or even to be derived from the ideas of later authorities not available during Hildegard's lifetime. Nor has any plausible arrangement been proposed to suggest what the original, unified "subtleties" that Hildegard mentioned in the *Book of Life's Merits* would have looked like. Would books 1 and 2 of the *Causes and Cures,* depicting the cosmos and the human creature, have preceded the protracted descriptions of the rest of the created world given in the *Physica?* And where in such an arrangement would the medical therapeutics and prognostics most suitably have belonged? And if, in fact, the therapeutic remedies of books 3 and 4 of the *Causes and Cures* are not in the position that Hildegard originally planned but instead were scattered among the chapters of the pharmacopoeia, then how could they possibly have been located for practical medical use? The answer, of course, is "not at all, or only with the greatest difficulty and delay." Yet as an interpretive compiler assembling a lengthy text from numerous sources over a period of several years, Hildegard must at some point have had these same recipes written down in some format other than their final one. And that rough draft, exhibiting patterns of oral dictation, vernacular terms, and literary revision, is what I think we find peeking through the "textual rifts" and the recipe duplications of the *Causes and Cures* and the *Physica.*[82] This interpretation offers the additional prospect that we might be able to determine, through careful analysis of the practical chapters, the actual nature and content of the medicine practiced at the Rupertsberg.

I think it quite possible, in fact, that the medical texts as we have them in the earliest manuscripts are fundamentally in the state and form they enjoyed at the time of Hildegard's death: they never existed in a finished format and may in fact have been ongoing projects still in draft, with portions either on wax tablets or loosely bound scraps of parchment. This hypothesis might best explain the medical works' omission from the Riesenkodex as well as Trithemius's eyewitness opinion that the Rupertsberg pharmacopoeia was the "more beautifully edited" text, with tables of contents and a preface (features normally added by Hildegard as she completed the final editing of her texts).[83] The duplication of textual portions in the *Physica* and the *Causes and Cures*, which has been employed to cast doubt on the authenticity of the structure of these writings, has elsewhere proven an authentic feature of Hildegard's habitual patterns of activity as a writer. In the *Scivias*, for instance, she introduced an early version of the work she later revised and expanded into the *Ordo virtutum*. And portions of her song texts survive in different forms, showing greater and lesser degrees of editorial correction.[84]

But even if we were to leave the issue of the treatises' format unresolved, the breadth and depth of Hildegard's accomplishment as a medical thinker and writer would in no way be compromised. Her exploration of disease in both its universal, cosmological sense and its individual pathological sense, which she melded synthetically to her greater *visio* of the universe, the human creature, and the created world, sets Hildegard's medical perspective apart from all but the most revered philosophers of her day. That her achievement and the dynamics of her labor as a reader, thinker, and writer perplexed and confounded men like Trithemius (and ourselves, in large measure) should not surprise us. Hildegard was exceptional precisely because she refused to be satisfied with the ordinary and conventional. She managed in her medical writings, as in most of her enterprises, to achieve so much because she confidently pushed the limits that in the twelfth century were still flexible enough to accommodate her unique talents and contributions. As a medical thinker, she was indeed a wonder, an ardent laborer in the field of medical study and philosophy. The questions that remain regarding her activities and achievements are surely innumerable. What we might wish to contemplate at this point is not "How did she do it?" but "Why did so few women accomplish as much?"

MANUSCRIPTS OF HILDEGARD'S MEDICAL WRITINGS

CAUSAE ET CURAE

Copenhagen, Det Kongelige Bibliotek, Ny. kgl. saml., 90 b. Copied in the Rhineland in the mid-thirteenth century, ca. 1250–1260. Folios 1–93.

PHYSICA

Florence, Biblioteca Medicea Laurenziana, cod. Ashburnham 1323. Copied in the Rhineland ca. 1300. 104 folios.

Wolfenbüttel, Herzog August Bibliothek, cod. Guelf. 56. 2, Aug. quarto. Copied very early fourteenth century. Folios 1–174.

Paris, Bibliothèque nationale, cod. lat. 6952. Copied ca. 1425–1450. Folios 156–232.

Brussels, Bibliothèque royale, cod. 2551 (formerly 1494). Copied mid-fifteenth century. 130 folios.

Vatican, Biblioteca Apostolica Vaticana, cod. Ferraioli 921. Fifteenth century. 163 folios.

CAUSAE ET CURAE: EXCERPTS

Berlin, Staatsbibliothek Preussischer Kulturbesitz, cod. lat. quarto 674. Excerpts mixed with others from Hildegard's writings. First half of the thirteenth century. Folios 103r–116r.

PHYSICA: FRAGMENTS AND EXCERPTS

Vatican, Biblioteca Apostolica Vaticana, ms. pal. lat. 1207. Copied late fourteenth or early fifteenth century. Excerpts at folios 64r–64v.

Vatican, Biblioteca Apostolica Vaticana, ms. pal. lat. 1216. Copied late fourteenth or early fifteenth century. Excerpts at folios 91v–95r.

Freiburg, Universitätsbibliothek, cod. 178a. Copied ca. 1390–1400. Fragment constitutes Hildegard's "Book of Stones," here attributed to Isidore of Seville. Folios 1–15.

Augsburg, Universitätsbibliothek, cod. III 1, 2. Copied early fifteenth century. Excerpts scattered through the "Arzneibuch" and "Kochbuch Meister Eberhards," folios 2r–58v and 59r–70r, respectively.

Paris, Bibliothèque nationale, cod. lat. 6952. Fifteenth-century excerpts. Folios 232v–238v.

Vatican, Biblioteca Apostolica Vaticana, ms. pal. lat. 1144. Copied after the middle of the fifteenth century. Excerpts at folios 128v–129r.

Bern, Bürgerbibliothek, cod. 525. Copied after ca. 1450. Excerpts appear at folios 18r–23r.

Berlin, Staatsbibliothek Preussischer Kulturbesitz, ms. germ. fol. 817. Dated 1456. Excerpts appear at folios 2r–61v.

EIGHT

Composer and Dramatist

*"Melodious Singing
and the Freshness of Remorse"*

MARGOT FASSLER

One of Hildegard of Bingen's most famous letters laments the injustice of an interdict imposed on the Rupertsberg community for the burial of a formerly excommunicated man on monastery grounds. Forbidden the singing of the Divine Office and denied their monthly Communion at Mass, the nuns "were greatly distressed and saddened." In defense of liturgical chant, Hildegard wrote:

> Just as the body of Jesus Christ was born of the purity of the Virgin Mary through the operation of the Holy Spirit so, too, the canticle of praise, reflecting celestial harmony, is rooted in the Church through the Holy Spirit. The body is the vestment of the spirit, which has a living voice, and so it is proper for the body, in harmony with the soul, to use its voice to sing praises to God.[1]

In a subsequent letter Hildegard charged that the silencing of their song—they were allowed to continue to *read* the Office—threatened not only the stability and purpose of the nuns' lives but also the souls of the archbishop and his prelates because of their unjust actions. The incident offers striking proof of the central importance singing had for monastic communities in the Middle Ages and for the Rupertsberg nuns in particular.[2] In executing this work of God (*opus Dei*), the women offered up hundreds of chants familiar to religious throughout Europe as well as a significant array of pieces written by their own abbess to strengthen the efficacy of communal prayer and praise. As the quotation above indicates, Hildegard defined the rendering of communal song as an incarnational act, basic to the creative regeneration of life which takes place within the monastic community. Singing was central to her definition of what it meant to be a nun.

MUSIC IN THE MONASTIC COMMUNITY

The emphasis that Hildegard placed on the act of singing within the monastic community has made her unique in the history of Western music. No other twelfth-century composer has left such a large corpus of varied and securely attributable compositions as Hildegard of Bingen. She is quite simply the most prolific composer of monophonic chants known to us, not only from the twelfth century but from the entire Middle Ages.[3] Even with her rivals, men such as Notker of St. Gall in the ninth century or Adam of St. Victor and his school in the twelfth, there are problems, either with specific attribution or with recovery of texts or music.[4] Scholars also believe that Hildegard herself first collected her works, the texts as well as the music, and supervised their initial circulation outside her own community. Her sacred songs fall into two large categories, both designed by her own hands: the *Symphonia armonie celestium revelationum* (*Symphony of the Harmony of Celestial Revelations*), her cycle of all the extant liturgical pieces she wrote (except her play); and the texts and music making up the play itself, the *Ordo virtutum* (*Play of the Virtues*).[5] Even in the earliest extant sources Hildegard divides her liturgical songs from the play; yet the songs and the play, although separate, are interrelated in ideas and function together within the framework of Hildegard's theological scheme and educational purposes. Thus in both the large number of pieces and in their modes of organization Hildegard is distinctive, and her activities demonstrate the great importance that she, and through her, her community, placed on the musical dimensions of their lives. Her music cannot be fully understood apart from the monasticism that inspired her to compose in the first place and then to create the particular kinds of music she produced.

As can be seen from table 1, the bulk of Hildegard's songs were composed for the Divine Office and fall into the two most common genres of office chants: antiphons (usually relatively short chants, sung by the choir in conjunction with the intonation of psalms and canticles) and responsories (long and elaborate chants made up of two major sections, a choral response and a verse sung by a soloist). As can be seen in table 3, responsories served as music to follow the simply intoned readings of the night office (matins). The play also may well have been associated with the office, as it was most common in the twelfth century for large-scale musical dramas to be performed at the close of matins or vespers services (see table 2 for the most standard location of these plays). At the Mass, however, nuns, although permitted to sing

TABLE I.   HILDEGARD'S MUSIC

1. The Songs: *Symphonia armonie celestium revelationum*
   For the Mass: 1 Alleluia; 1 Kyrie; 7 sequences
   For the Divine Office: 43 antiphons (14 of which are votive); 18 great
   responsories; 3 hymns; 4 devotional songs

2. The Play: *Ordo virtutum*
   Opening and closing processions; over eighty songs and segments of songs,
   many in the style of simple Psalter antiphons.

the chants in most communities, could not officiate or serve as priests and were thus always in the presence of male clergy who did the actual celebrating.[6] In addition, the heyday of trope composition for the Mass was long past by the twelfth century, and the only new monophonic pieces commonly being written for the Mass in Hildegard's region during her lifetime were sequences, long chants sung after the Alleluia and before the reading of the gospel.[7] The office, by contrast, belonged exclusively to the nuns, as it would to any particular monastic community. More new music was written for the office throughout the central Middle Ages than for any other part of the liturgy. Whereas the chants of the Mass (with the exception of sequences) were fairly standardized by Hildegard's lifetime and could be adapted for recently elevated saints, these same saints each had to have a unique vita and office readings and sometimes chants, based on the vita. Thus it was in the office that every monastic community heard chants and readings celebrating the lives not only of the standard saints known throughout a given region but also of the particular saints distinctive to their own church.[8] When Hildegard's community moved to the Rupertsberg, for example, she composed a new vita and office for Rupert, the saint to whom the restored church was dedicated.

The importance of the Divine Office in monastic life affected not only the kinds of pieces Hildegard wrote but also, to a degree at least, their musical style. The style of her songs was most strongly influenced by music composed in the eleventh century, especially new responsories and antiphons for the office. Great responsories in the Carolingian period had often been composed by adaptation of a series of formulae, one set for each of the eight church modes, the kinds of scales used by composers in Hildegard's time.[9] New responsories composed from the eleventh century on more often broke from the tradition and became wildly ornate, with magnificent leaps and long melismas (musical

TABLE 2.   THE DAILY ROUND: HOURS
OF THE DIVINE OFFICE IN BENEDICTINE
MONASTICISM OF HILDEGARD'S TIME

Hour	Approximate Time of Day
Matins	Before sunrise
Lauds	At dawn
Prime	Around 6 A.M.
Terce*	Around 9 A.M.
Sext	Around noon
None	Around 3 P.M.
Vespers	At sunset
Compline	Directly before bed

*The main Mass of the day followed terce.

TABLE 3.   BRIEF SKETCH OF MATINS FOR SUNDAYS AND MAJOR
FEAST DAYS IN THE LATER MEDIEVAL BENEDICTINE OFFICE

1. Introductory call to prayer and a hymn
2. First nocturn:
   Six psalms, each sung with an antiphon
   Four readings from Scripture, each followed by a responsory
3. Second nocturn:
   Six psalms, each sung with an antiphon
   Four readings from patristic or hagiographic literature, each followed
      by a responsory
4. Third nocturn:
   Three canticles with one antiphon
   Four readings from a church father or pope, each followed by a respon-
   sory. (The final responsory of each nocturn, and especially of the last noc-
   turn, was the most elaborate. Hildegard's responsories for major feasts
   would have been sung in this final position.)
5. Closing:
   Play (on rare occasions)
   Te Deum laudamus
   Gospel reading
   Te decet laus
   Prayer

Introductory explanations of subjects presented in tables 2 and 3 are available in John Harper,
*The Forms and Orders of Western Liturgy: From the Tenth to the Eighteenth Century: A Historical
Introduction and Guide for Students and Musicians* (Oxford, 1991).

phrases sung on a single vowel sound) to decorate ends of lines or important words in the texts.[10] Divine Offices composed in this period
were frequently rhymed, but sometimes not, as in the case of Hildegard's office texts. Responsories are mighty works, with the final section of the initial respond serving in many traditions as a kind of refrain

for the soloistic verse and for the doxology.[11] Thus the chants as performed are even more extensive than they appear on the page. The final responsories of a particular liturgical unit, be it a matins nocturn or the entire service, were traditionally the most elaborate. Hildegard's responsories were almost surely sung in final position and could perhaps have been used in vespers services as well, where a single great responsory was sometimes rendered. Thus, in her responsories Hildegard created the music that would have been the stunning summation of the matins service, the crowning jewel of the entire liturgical day. In addition, it was customary for the abbot or abbess to intone the final responsory. Hildegard's music would therefore have served to emphasize her own liturgical role as head of the monastic community.

Features of this developing musical style affected antiphons as well as responsories. As David Hiley says, "There are more pieces called antiphons than anything else in the chant repertory."[12] The shortest and simplest of these chants, the Psalter antiphons, were the workhorses of the Divine Office, used to introduce and close the intoned psalms throughout the week. Antiphons were also written for singing with intoned canticles at lauds and vespers, and these pieces tend to be slightly more ornate than Psalter antiphons.[13] The most elaborate of all antiphons were those sung for processions (elaborate chants, even in the Carolingian period), and votive antiphons, chants that might serve as independent pieces to honor a saint, particularly the Virgin Mary. Two great votive antiphons for the Blessed Virgin, "Alma redemptoris mater" and "Ave regina celorum," were in use by the time Hildegard was a girl, shaping Marian piety within the monastic liturgy.[14] The popularity these pieces experienced during Hildegard's lifetime arose from the intensification of Marian devotion then asserting itself in several areas of Europe, a devotion that would find a major spokesperson in Hildegard's contemporary and patron, Bernard of Clairvaux.[15]

The style of these newer Marian antiphons displays characteristics not usually predominating in so-called Gregorian chant, the repertories of which were set by the close of the ninth century. "Ave regina celorum" (example 1, below) is forcefully centered tonally, with repeated and direct emphases on the main and final pitch C, a pitch not offered this sort of prominence in the scales of the church modes, which are organized around the tonal areas of D, E, F, and G.[16] The intervallic leaps are more frequent and dramatic in "Ave regina celorum" than is characteristic of earlier antiphons in the Gregorian tradition. Most important, there is a dependence on repetition of pairs of phrases, a feature that shapes the fabric of the song.[17] I have bracketed these repeating sections in the example that they might be readily appreciated, even by those who do not sing or read music.[18]

Hildegard's songs join her primary interest in the Divine Office with an apparent love of the most ornate kinds of music for the office. Her Psalter antiphons, for example, are more in the style of complicated votive antiphons; her votive antiphons are much more elaborate than is customary. Her great responsories are long and ornate, with extensive melismas exceeding by far the norms even of later medieval office repertories. The composer herself suggests the reasons this style may have seemed appropriate. Hildegard conceptualized "songs" not as text or as music but as the connected whole made by both dimensions, and she gave this understanding theological underpinnings: "And so the words symbolize the body, and the jubilant music indicates the spirit; and the celestial harmony shows the Divinity, and the words the Humanity of the Son of God."[19] Jubilation was frequently expressed in the medieval liturgy by an abundance of notes on a single syllable, a melisma. The most melismatic of all Gregorian chants are the Alleluias sung at Mass, which were thought to represent the music of the angelic hosts.

At least some of Hildegard's chant texts, although richly imagistic, are within the range of what is typical for liturgical poetry of the period. The unleashed torrents of her melodies, however, push the texts forth with an abundant life that supersedes conventional expectations. In fact, she probably composed her liturgical texts as she sang, in the way the twentieth-century composer Igor Stravinsky wrote music at the piano or Charlie Parker improvised compositions on his saxophone. There is every reason to believe that Hildegard herself was a capable singer: as the leader of a monastic community, she would have had to sing many of the complex intonations in responsories herself.[20] Look, for example, at the opening of "O nobilissima viriditas," printed below in example 4. The many notes on the initial word O form a single long melisma. Whoever was responsible for intoning this responsory, that is, for giving the pitch by singing the opening word or words, may have rendered this entire melisma. In the Mass singing the intonation was customarily the work of the major singer, the cantor, or of his assistant, the precentor; but in the office, especially on major feast days, the abbot or abbess was involved in intoning the great responsories, as were other monastic officials.

The liturgical context of Hildegard's compositions goes far to explain a paradox frequently noted in her music. Her style has sometimes been viewed by modern scholars as old-fashioned: why, they wonder, wasn't

Example 1. Ave regina celorum.
Hail, Queen of heaven! / Hail, Lady of the angels! / Hail, root and gate / from
which the light of the world was born! / Rejoice, glorious Virgin, / fairest of
all! / Farewell, most beautiful, / and pray for us to Christ!

Hildegard, a creative force in so many ways, writing rhythmic sequences
in the new style popularized by Adam of St. Victor (d. ca. 1146)? But as
a Benedictine nun she could not have been expected to know well or to
take great interest in the vogue for rhythmic sequences championed in
her lifetime by Augustinians, first apparently by canons of St. Victor
in Paris. Moreover, there were *no* large repertories of such late-style
("rhythmic") sequences in any Benedictine liturgy known to us from the
first three-quarters of the twelfth century, Hildegard's lifetime.[21] A
"modern" sequence to Hildegard would have been a work such as
the late-eleventh-century Easter sequence, "Victimae paschali laudes,"
which is very different in style from the Victorine corpus.[22] The rhythmic
sequences were first written and adopted in great numbers by canons
regular to celebrate the priestly office as they conceived of it, with references to the Rule of St. Augustine.[23] The Mariology of the earliest layers
of Victorine sequences was secondary, although certainly important. For
Hildegard, in contrast, the Virgin Mary and the Incarnation were central
to liturgical composition.[24] Hildegard's music, we will see, was part of
an elaborate program of education she designed for the nuns of her community and arises from a Benedictine understanding of religious life.[25]

Singing was to play a major role in promoting *conversio,* the turning from sin to God, the ongoing process of change and betterment which is the vocation of monastic life.

HILDEGARD'S MUSIC AND SYSTEMS OF MEANING: THE JESSE TREE

Singing the Divine Office was the defining action of monastic life for Hildegard of Bingen. Her attention to office music, apparent in the out-line of works found in table 1 above, was part of her intention to lead the nuns entrusted to her care more fully into Benedictine life. The in-tensity with which she set about the work of education has made her the only composer from the entire Middle Ages whose works include all of the following: an ensemble of liturgical chants (both poetry and music), art works to accompany them (planned by the composer), a full-length music drama (the most sophisticated of the genre from the twelfth century), and a theological text explaining the significance of the songs and the drama for spiritual life. What is more, we know when Hildegard created the works upon which this claim for the uniqueness of her compositions is based, that is, in the fifth decade of her life.

It was quite a decade! Having decided it was God's will that she write, Hildegard composed the first of her major visionary books—the mammoth *Scivias,* a summa resembling in scope the *De sacramentis christianae fidei* (*On the Sacraments of the Christian Faith*) of Hugh of St. Victor. She also completed and organized her first run of songs; wrote the *Ordo virtutum* (at least in an early form); fought and won the battle to detach her convent from the monastery of Disibodenberg; began building a new church and rebuilding community amid the dis-ruption of moving; and faced the torment of losing her most beloved nun, Richardis, first through the young woman's departure to become an abbess herself and subsequently through Richardis's death.[26]

I now wish to concentrate on musical works we know were formed during this time, that is, from about 1141 to 1151, for they are the foundation of all Hildegard's other compositions.[27] The composer sig-nals to us how we should work with these songs, for *Scivias* closes with the texts of fourteen of them, the so-called "*Scivias* songs," as well as with a sketch of the play *Ordo virtutum*. All three then—theological text, songs, and play—are part of a whole, and our work is to under-stand them together, using the *Scivias* as the framework for music and drama. We are extraordinarily lucky to have a body of works falling in the same period from such a prolific composer and writer, and it is most unusual to be able to work with a medieval composer with such a degree of historical precision and knowledge of repertorial layers.[28] We are also fortunate to have copies of Hildegard's music which can be transcribed. The common practice in her region and time was to notate without indicating precise intervals; the music was learned orally, with the manuscript notation serving as a guide to memory. But Hildegard's music was newly composed and would have had no earlier tradition to help the singer. Hence it had to be written more precisely if it was to be preserved or transmitted elsewhere.

Hildegard's productivity under the fragmented conditions of her life at the time surely depended to some degree on the concentrated way in which she thought; she was able to be such a prolific and original composer because of masterful control and use of systems of thought to underlie all she did. Her work from that turbulent decade—*Scivias,* songs, and play—is dominated by powerful images that become complexes of thought and provide organizational frameworks not only for her theology but also for her art works in various media.[29] Using the force of any of the handful of images she particularly favored allowed Hildegard to translate freely from theological writing to drama, to songs, to visual arts. An image clearly beloved by the seer is the Jesse tree, and I will use it, as did she, to organize discussion of her music and its meanings.[30]

The visual power of the Jesse tree image as it evolved in the twelfth century is well known to students of stained glass, of sculpture and church furniture, and of illuminated manuscripts.[31] As she was very much a woman of her times, it should come as no surprise that Hildegard of Bingen was attracted to the complexity and power of the Jesse tree as a vehicle for explanation. In the first half of the twelfth century the region in which she lived gave birth to the *Speculum virginum* (*Mirror of Virgins*), a dialogue written for the education of nuns. The manuscripts are frequently illuminated for pedagogical purposes, and Jesse tree images are of central importance in the program; some of the sources also contain music, written in a style not unlike that of Hildegard.[32] The composer, who was constructing her own educational paradigm, may have been directly influenced by this work, as was her contemporary Herrad of Landsberg, whose *Hortus deliciarum* (*Garden of Delights*), also a work for the education of nuns, featured the Jesse tree as well. The standard scriptural source underlying the Jesse tree is Isaiah 11.1-2, and Isaiah was the book of the Bible read during the Advent liturgy in the office. Isaiah 11.1-2 was used as the source for several chant texts as well, works that would have been known to Hildegard and absorbed into her memory through long years of singing the office.[33]

The extraordinary fecundity of Jesse tree imagery doubtless appealed to theologian/teachers such as Hildegard who sought to bring ideals of regeneration and birth to chaste females, women who had willingly traded in one form of sexuality for another, a spiritual ideal of reproduction. A manuscript leaf now in Bonn survives from a twelfth-century *Speculum virginum* and depicts the lush growth associated with this image (figure 18; see plates section). As the leaf once belonged to the church of Rheinbrohl near the town of Neuwied, located on the Rhine some forty miles from Bingen, it takes us very close to Hildegard's region. Arthur Watson says the image forms "a sort of encyclopaedic collection of ideas associated with three leading words in Isaiah's prophecy: *radix* [root], *virga* [branch], and *spiritus* [spirit]."[34] At the heart of the meaning of the Jesse tree is the mystery of the Incarnation, with prophets (chief among them Isaiah) pointing to Christ's coming in the fullness of time: the main stock of Jesse's root depicts the lineage of Christ from the house of David, through the flesh of his Mother, the Virgin Mary. Above all, the Holy Spirit guides, usually depicted in the form of a dove or of flower petals representing its seven attributes.

It is clear that Hildegard's own Jesse tree, designed as it was to promote the teaching of the patron of her monastic order, sprang up in the groves of the Rule of St. Benedict. This particular plan for personal and conventual life had been central to the customs and spirituality of the black monks and their affiliated houses of nuns ever since the monastic reforms of the early ninth century.[35] Hildegard's nuns were charged through her liturgical music to put on new kinds of garments, garments of renewed flesh, which were represented by the elaborate robes the well-born women in her community were known to wear during religious services.[36] In the summary of her views concerning the Incarnation and monasticism in *Scivias,* St. Benedict is brought forth as a second Moses who taught his followers to honor the Incarnation in the garment of his way of life, that is, the Rule.[37] During Hildegard's own lifetime the Cistercian reforms championed by Bernard of Clairvaux inspired a resurgence of commentaries on the Rule and a desire to renew monastic life through better implementation of its ideals.[38] Hildegard was clearly struck by the challenge posed in the prologue to the Rule, calling each person who chose the monastic life to battle for his or her soul.[39] She was also inspired by the great organizing image of chapter 7,

Jacob's ladder, which is important for the *Speculum virginum* as well.[40] Descriptions of Jacob's ladder and the Jesse tree are found near each other in *Scivias* III.8, the "Pillar of the Humanity of the Savior" vision. It is the fusion of these two ideas—the traditional Jesse tree with its fecundity and the virtues of the Holy Spirit, and Jacob's ladder with its idea of struggle and change—which impart to Hildegard's vision and to her songs and musical play their unique character.

For Hildegard the pillar sustaining the church has many aspects. In it "there is an ascent like a ladder from bottom to top." This ladder is the Son of God in whom "all the virtues work fully."[41] The Virtues come and go, and their queen, reflecting the emphasis of the Rule of St. Benedict, is Humility. Among these Virtues are seven in particular who designate the seven fiery gifts of the Holy Spirit, and these lead to Hildegard's description of the Jesse tree.[42] The flowering branch is Mary who rises from the "royal race," and the sweet fragrance of her intact fecundity is inundated by the Holy Spirit so that a tender flower is born from her. "And in the branch that came forth from Jesse, the virtues of this Flower put forth buds." Hildegard's Jesse tree is dynamic: it shows the comings and goings of the Virtues from the incarnational heart as they battle for the souls not only of nuns but of every person. The plans of Hildegard's *Scivias* songs and of the *Ordo virtutum* are sustained, in different ways, by her particular working out of the Jesse tree. I will treat each of these musical works in turn in the two sections to follow.

THE *SCIVIAS* SONGS AS SONIC ICONS

The *Scivias* songs are paired by subject and by genre and arranged hierarchically (see table 4). Most of these fall into the categories by which general liturgical pieces were grouped at the end of Mass and Divine Office books in the later Middle Ages. In the case of many saints it was typical for the office of the day to draw on a common fund of such pieces; in fact, such chants are known as belonging to "the common for Apostles" or "the common for the Blessed Virgin," and so forth. Thus, in her first cycle of liturgical songs Hildegard wrote serviceable chants that would have been appropriate for many occasions throughout the church year. These chants would have suited the liturgy of the Disibodenberg, a monastery of men and women, if Hildegard composed some of them during her years there, as is certainly the case. But we can be even more precise in our understanding of the liturgical purposes for which Hildegard composed this cycle of songs. The liturgy of All Saints'

TABLE 4.   THE CONTENTS OF THE FIRST LAYER OF SONGS
(IN ORDER IN *SCIVIAS*)

Numbers in *Symphonia*	Pages in *Lieder*	Genres	Subject
10/21	28/44	Antiphon and responsory	Virgin Mary
29/30	57/59	Antiphon and responsory	Angels
31/32	62/64	Antiphon and responsory	Patriarchs and prophets
33/34	66/69	Antiphon and responsory	Apostles
37/38	82/83	Antiphon and responsory	Martyrs
40/39	87/85	Antiphon and responsory	Confessors (bishops)
55/56	97/99	Antiphon and responsory	Virgins

The numbers mean that the antiphon for Mary is no. 10 in the *Symphonia* (text edition) and p. 28 in *Lieder* (music edition). The responsory for Mary is no. 21 in the *Symphonia* and p. 44 in *Lieder*, and so forth.

Day, November 1, required a complex of such works to celebrate the saints, category by category, including special readings and chants for the Trinity, for Mary, for angels, for patriarchs and prophets, for apostles, for martyrs, and for virgins. Hildegard's *Scivias* songs would have served for this feast also. The use of the songs for commons throughout the year, and for All Saints' as well, would have created a profound liturgical undergirding for the meanings of the works as explained in *Scivias* itself.[43] Hildegard doubtless worked under the influence of the Holy Spirit when she composed, but the Spirit as it guided her had a side sensitive to the needs of liturgical practice.

Most of the persons represented in the *Scivias* songs are placed in relationship to the Jesse tree, and with some consistency it is the responsories that "ingraft" them.[44] The first responsory for the Virgin Mary, "O tu suavissima virga," depicts the sweetest branch, Mary, who, glistening like the sun she will bear, catches the eye of the supernal father (*Symphonia*, no. 21). Her mind, filled with light, brings forth the first great flower. The angels, one of whom brought the message of the Incarnation to the Virgin, gaze in hierarchical order on the mystery of God's regeneration within Mary (nos. 29 and 30). The patriarchs and prophets are celebrated in the responsory Hildegard wrote for them as the "happy roots, with whom the work of miracles was planted" (no. 32). The apostles are part of the tree through the antiphon "O cohors milicie" (no. 33). Members of the army of the "flower of the branch," they preach throughout the world, where they, like gardeners, sink roots in the hearts of the churches. The responsory for martyrs, "Vos flores rosarum" (no. 38), shows the secondary flowers of the Lamb, who is the great central bloom of the tree. The bishops or confessors are those who bind and loose in the great drama of salvation. With the bishops we stray from the tree imagery, only to be brought back with the responsory for virgins, "O nobilissima viriditas." In this piece, the music of which is discussed below in example 4, the most noble *viriditas,* the greenness that stands for the regenerative powers of the church, belongs to the virgins (no. 56).[45]

As will be seen, the songs are musically ornate, like the fronds of the Jesse tree; they are difficult and long and could sustain a lifetime of contemplation, lifetimes of singing, as the composer intended for her nuns. They are sounding icons for study and meditation on the words and phrases of their luxuriant imagery, meant to conjure up pictures in the mind of the vibrant colors and verdure they depict, each singer/listener mentally painting as she can, each being taught and transformed through the process. The analysis below attempts to offer the untrained listener some practical lessons on how to approach Hildegard's *Scivias* songs, thinking of them as liturgical music for the Divine Office.

The subjects of Hildegard's songs and their relationships to monastic life as she conceived of it form a necessary preface for understanding how the notes were ordered and designed to serve meaning. The music of Hildegard's songs functions on several levels, a select few of which I will describe as "soundposts" for the listener. On the page this music may seem impossibly difficult, with its high passages and melismatic runs down the scale; perhaps it appears scattered and formless as well. But it is music built from a select range of idiomatic phrases and it has a constant sense of direction and of modal character which provides cohesion. The singer who knows even a few of Hildegard's songs in representative modes has a tool kit for singing all of them and becomes sensitive to truly dramatic shifts (which may sometimes warn of mistranscribing!) when they do occur.[46] Hildegard's use of stock phrases is the only feature of her style which has been much studied; but exploration of this aspect of her compositional practice requires the ability to read music and some understanding of medieval modes and theory.[47] I will turn instead to other topics, not less important, but more readily accessible to a general audience. I emphasize, however, that repetitions of particular modal gestures do not prevent each individual song from having its own melodic character. These are all distinct and recognizable pieces of music and not mere collections of idioms.

There are basically three ways in which music interacted with text in the twelfth-century world of Hildegard of Bingen's new liturgical compositions. First of all, music served to proclaim the sounds of the words and sentences and often to underscore various structural levels, from phrases to sentences to larger units. Second, it worked by genre, every class of liturgical piece having a particular style and historical sense growing out of the style. And third, music was capable of bearing symbolic meanings, both because of its association with genre and style and also because of the power generated by particular famous melodies, which, charged with the sense of their texts and positions in the liturgy, could be reused with new texts and offer symbolic meanings to new words through past associations.

The most important idea to keep in mind when listening to Hildegard's songs is the concept of *ruminatio*, the "chewing on the cud" of text, which was a process central to monastic learning and to learning within the liturgy. Almost all of Hildegard's songs, certainly all of the *Scivias* songs, are connected with the intoning of a text for meditation, either a psalm or some other reading from Scripture or the church fathers. In addition, all of the songs have as their own texts Hildegard's heavily imagistic poetry. Hence the music provides the opportunity to think, both about the texts that are being intoned and about the words of the song itself. The music is a vehicle for the text, offering time to connect one word or phrase to another and to build up a stockpile of interrelated images in the mind. This kind of singing and listening is ideal for the style of Latin poetry Hildegard wrote.

In Latin the meaning of a sentence is based more on the inflections of individual words than on the ordering of the words themselves. Thus the music of Hildegard's songs is designed for different linguistic procedures than those common in modern English poetry and prose, where sentence structure is often of primary importance. Also a different time sense operates in Hildegard's songs from that experienced in much modern music. The expectation of forward motion and the sense of an ongoing, driving pulse or beat are both missing here.[48] All of these features give Hildegard's songs a different orientation toward sound and time, a sense that may initially make the modern listener impatient with the repertory. Unfortunately, we know almost nothing about rhythmic practice in Hildegard's songs; her idea of tempo, the speed of the music, is also terra incognita. Those who wish to enter this composer's world, so different from our own, must be willing to take time to learn new ways of listening to music.

Let us begin with the first of the *Scivias* responsories, "O tu suavissima virga."[49] Read the textual excerpt in English in the extract below. Then look at how the text, in Latin and in the word-for-word English

Example 2. From "O tu suavissima virga."

O tu suavissima virga
frondens de stirpe Iesse,
o quam magna virtus est
quod divinitas
in pulcherrimam filiam aspexit,
sicut aquila in solem
oculum suum ponit:

O sweetest branch
budding from the stock of Jesse,
what a mighty work this is!
God gazed
on his fairest daughter
as an eagle
sets its eye upon the sun:

Cum supernus Pater claritatem Virginis
adtendit
ubi Verbum suum
in ipsa incarnari voluit.

When the supernal Father
saw the Virgin's splendor
and wished his Word
to take flesh in her.[50]

translation in the score (example 2), is transformed by the music. First of all, the words now function almost as individual units, giving us time to ruminate on, to savor slowly, every image of importance. Second, Hildegard uses melismas to create structure and sense: through them she stretches important words; through them she also outlines structure. You can see right away that the final word of this entire section of music (*voluit*, "wanted") receives the longest melisma. We listen to the *vo-* for a very long time before our sense of expectation is fulfilled by the brief *-luit*. He loved her indeed.

Relative pitch also plays an important role in Hildegard's songs.[51] She is very sensitive to highs and lows in music and underscores meanings of words by contrasts in this dimension of sound. Hildegard usually begins a song through brief reference to the lower part of the tonal range explored in the piece, as here on the word *frondens* (budding). She delights in moving rapidly, sometimes with large leaps from one pitch to another, to the upper range soon after this gesture toward the low part of the scale. It is her love of this particular device of quickly changing registers which gives her music its rhapsodic quality. The words receiving the leap are often key in the poetry. In "O tu suavissima virga," "stock of Jesse" (*stirpe Iesse*) gets the first sound leap, as we travel quickly from *de,* which begins on g below c', all the way to g' above c', or the space of an octave, on the first syllable of "Jesse." This upward motion, which any listener can hear, though dramatic and rapid, is typical of Hildegard's style.[52] But then farther into the song, on the word *solem* (sun), comes an even greater leap in sound, here to the highest point in the range for this particular work.

Mary, the beloved, is the sun attracting the eagle's eye; her beauty transfixes God the Father. After the heights of *solem,* the contour of the melody tumbles rapidly downward by the opening syllable of the next word, bottoming out on the fourth below c', a journey of an octave and a half. The verb *ponit,* meaning "sets," growls down in the lowest part of the range and emphasizes the end of this sense unit. I have mentioned already the long and dramatic melisma used to mark the end of the entire section of the responsory before the verse, a melody almost fifty notes long, covering a range of an octave and a fourth. This melisma leads us to another aspect of Hildegard's music: the use of repetition. Here, in the melisma used as the setting for the verb *voluit,* at the high point of this melisma of God's desire, the shorter melisma for *solem* is repeated.[53] Thus the sonic representation of Mary in this particular song is engulfed in the embrace of God's love, and the climactic ending

O splen - di - dis-si - ma gem - ma et se

re - num de - cus so - lis,

Example 3.   From "O splendidissima gemma."

takes our ears and eyes back through the power of memory to the opening of the song. This passage in example 2 is bracketed within the
longer melisma so it can be easily seen.

Repetition forms an essential feature of Hildegard's style, and the technique works on a large-scale level, as above, but also on the small scale.[54]
"O tu suavissima virga" is centered on the tonal area C, one of Hildegard's three favored tonal complexes. The first *Scivias* song, "O splendidissima gemma" (*Symphonia*, no. 10), is centered on E, the wailing or
lamenting mode in chant, and this mode gives the song an entirely different character because the note just above the E is only a half-step away.[55]
In this brief analysis of part of this first song, I must begin by mentioning
how important the main pitch is in a Hildegard song. Departures and returns to it are here, as in all monophonic chant of the Middle Ages, what
makes the music dramatic and beautiful to those accustomed to singing
and listening to the repertory. Thus the main pitch E, which is also the
first and last note of the song, forms a strong sonic pillar around which
many musical phrases are shaped. The droning on stringed instruments,
such as one hears in recordings by Sequentia, for example, is centered on
the major pitch of the mode in which the song, or section of a song, is
composed. It is a good exercise to try to hear the main pitch and then
make oneself increasingly aware of the motion to and away from it.

Notice that the first word, *O*, is but a decorated e′. *Splendidissima*
(resplendent) breaks down syllable by syllable as follows: *splen-:* a decorated e′; *di-:* motion surrounding e′; *dis-:* e′; and *si-* and *ma,* each set
to a phrase emphasizing pitch a, the fifth below e′. The next word
gemma (jewel) returns to e′; *et* is a connecting word, which is set to the
pitch d′ just below the main pitch e′. And then follows the setting of
serenum (unclouded), which demonstrates several common features of
Hildegard's style. As the brackets demonstrate, there is a repeated phrase,
and this makes the word undulate with sound, the rhyming *se-* and
re- creating a musical rhyme as well. Hildegard's songs are filled with

such tricks as well as with frequent small-scale repetitions to charm the ear and underscore sounds of words, or meanings, or both. Notice too that E is here, as in Gregorian chant, a rather unstable pitch, even when it is the tonal center of the mode and the song. Hildegard continues to emphasize the d'-to-a' leap and the notes filling it in, only then to surround the e', and finally to pull back to it. Music for *decus* (beauty) is another example of this motion from and return to e', and *sol-* of *solis* (sun) moves even farther afield, with a gliding return at the end.

These simple analytical observations serve as keys to the kinds of motion and text-music relationship governing the formal aspects of Hildegard's songs. Yet she also worked in another important fashion to make her music meaningful, choosing well-known pieces that offered a powerful symbolic sense related to her newly composed works and either weaving their notes into the fabric of her songs or using them as models on which to hang her own music.[56] One of her favored preexisting chants was that mentioned above as example 1, "Ave regina celorum," a votive antiphon for the Blessed Virgin Mary. Here we will observe what happens when Hildegard models a new chant on a beloved older melody. It is especially important that she chose this technique of composition for the piece closing the cycle of *Scivias* songs (*Symphonia*, no. 56).

"O nobilissima viriditas," whose text describes the virtues as virgins in the heart of the Jesse tree, is an imaginative reworking of "Ave regina celorum," and this modeling of a new piece on an older one provides a sense of Hildegard's improvisatory powers as a singing composer.[57] Her technique demands that we recall the text of the chant on which she modeled "O nobilissima viriditas." By reusing the notes of the famous "Ave regina," she could bring to the mind of singers and listeners its text as well, making sound and sense resonate simultaneously within her own song. In "Ave regina," Mary is Queen of Heaven and Ruler of the Angels. She is hailed as "root," and Hildegard, we will see, especially played upon this reference to the Jesse tree as she understood it. Mary is the person from whom light arose for the world: here is the sun imagery that predominates in Hildegard's Marian texts, especially in the idea of rising, of dawn. The dawn is the greatest time for monastic song, the early morning hours when monks or nuns, called in darkness from their beds, served longest in their acts of prayer and praise during the services of matins and lauds and witnessed in community the coming of the light. A chant such as "O nobilissima viriditas" brings the singing and the Incarnation together with constant emphasis on the new light blooming forth from Mary's womb.[58]

Example 4. Opening lines of "O nobilissima viriditas" and "Ave regina celorum."

As can be seen in example 4, Hildegard models "O nobilissima viriditas" fairly strictly on "Ave regina" in the beginning, but the music becomes increasingly free as the song develops.[59] The music of the first phrase in "Ave regina" repeats, and Hildegard therefore repeats her use of the model as well. The setting for O is one long melismatic reworking of the opening of "Ave regina," and this is the section of Hildegard's song which depends most directly on the model. Clearly Hildegard wanted to cement the reference early on, and any twelfth-century monastic would have heard the allusion immediately and understood its symbolic power to evoke the Virgin Mary. The virgins in their hailing O are hailed with the *Ave,* the "hail" of Gabriel to Mary and the "hail" of all the saints and angels over whom she is queen. The virgins (like the virtues) are manifestations of Mary, her own minions. The repeat of the phrase emphasizes the key word in Hildegard's understanding of Mary, the church, renewal, and regeneration—*viriditas* or living green. Mary and the virgins are the new life possible through the new flesh of the

Incarnation. Music and text together create a multifaceted complex of ideas in the listener's or singer's mind which neither could offer alone.[60]

As the second system in example 4 shows, the second phrase of the model, on the words "salve radix, salve porta," is set twice by Hildegard, continuing her favored mode of composing through pairs of interconnected phrases. From the example we can see that Hildegard moved in and out of the connection between the two phrases. Thus at first the ascent to f' and descent back to c' is present in both of Hildegard's reworkings of the model, but the second reworking on "et que in candida" is more highly decorated. The second in the pair (see the long melisma on *di-* of *candida*), explores the upper range of the mode, reaching its peak on c'', decorated with the upper neighbor d'', whereas, in approximately the same place, the first in the pair, on *in sole*, moves downward to the low part of the range, with a leap of a fourth down to f. The two phrases are very close again at their cadence on c'.

Hildegard was thinking of her model "Ave regina" both in its text and in its music as she composed the song "O nobilissima viriditas." Just as she interweaves the model chant set to the word *radix* (root), she turns her own poem to roots, making a deep text/word association that would have resounded in the minds of the singers and listeners on many levels. It is in such moments that Hildegard's art as a songwriter reaches its pinnacle. Both in the text and now in the sound, the virgins are models of the Blessed Virgin Mary, extensions of her goodness reigning in heaven, reaching to a troubled church on earth. Hildegard's depiction of that sin-sick world itself is found in the *Ordo virtutum*.

ORDO VIRTUTUM: THE SOUND OF STRUGGLE

The *Ordo virtutum* provides a different view of the themes found in the song cycle, with which it was early connected by the composer. The songs are the celebration of jubilant souls in their hierarchies resounding through the cosmos. The play depicts the microcosmic struggle of a human soul in the process of falling into sin and its subsequent conversion to virtuous life.[61] Hildegard has imagined a new artistic form in her play, taking models of dramatic works then in existence as her starting point. Her title is suggestive: the *Ordo virtutum* is a new *Ordo prophetarum,* the way of representing the prophets.[62] Prophets' plays were celebrated at Christmas time throughout northern Europe in simple and more elaborate forms, their origin in a dramatic reading commonly found at matins.[63] In these works Old Testament patriarchs and prophets offer evidence that Christ-to-come is the Messiah, the incarnate Divinity. In the prologue to her play Hildegard collapses the groups found in the first layer of songs discussed above to two: the prophets, who both foreknew and are the roots of the Jesse tree, and the Virtues, who are described in terms of the songs written for virgins and who continue the salvific action initiated by the church in ancient times.[64] In their opening speech the Virtues make immediate connection to the virgins depicted in "O nobilissima viriditas" as flowers with roots in the sun:

> You holy ones of old, why do you marvel at us?
> The Word of God grows bright in the shape of man,
> and thus we shine with him,
> building up the limbs of his beautiful body.[65]

The action of Hildegard's play begins in the heights of the Jesse tree, in the incarnational eye of intersection between Word and Flesh, where the Sun burns through Mary's body and where the virtuous are called to dwell.[66] The newness of this creation, gazed upon by all the hierarchy, is tended especially by the Virtues, who call lamenting souls into the heart of the tree. In the opening of the play Virtues run into the flower of their beloved, like bees drawn to nectar, making the structure at once a garden and a royal bedchamber of the Song of Songs, sustained within the tree.[67] *Thalamus*, the bedchamber, had a host of connotations in the Middle Ages, including associations with bees, believed to be models of chastity. Most important for Hildegard and the *Ordo virtutum* is the chamber of Psalms 18.6: "He has set his tabernacle in the sun; and like a bridegroom coming out of his bridal chamber, he has rejoiced as a giant to run his way." The marriage of the Lord is to the faithful servant, who has been converted through the "unspotted" law, and the psalm ends with a plea for cleansing from sins. The *Ordo virtutum* presents this bride as the soul, who struggles against the Devil with the powers of the Virtues to put on the new garment of renewed flesh.[68]

On one level Hildegard's play is a defense of monastic life and an expression of the importance of chastity to that life. It creates an "antimarriage," wherein she who does *not* marry a man is, after the model of Mary, offered prelapsarian flesh in the divine embrace.[69] The heat of the sun is a different kind of sexual heat, one that protects rather than withers the flower of chastity.[70] But on another level the play presents the challenges of sin faced by Everysoul on its perilous journey toward the eye of the Jesse tree. The Virtues are its guides as well, and repentance and purity of heart matter in everyone, not just in nuns. Hildegard's long challenge to all humanity, found in *Scivias* I.4, mirrors the action of the play and the end of Anima's journey.[71] Thus the time given individual Virtues in the play, which allowed a role for every nun in the convent, is not mere display, nor need it be dramatically static. The guides needed in the fight against vices are many, and the Virtues line up appropriately against the Devil's particular appeals. The Virtues answer to the complexity of sin, although the Devil in this play offers no panoply of matching vices.

The action of the play is concentrated on Anima's robe, her flesh, and its nature and signification; the Virtues fight for her wholeness while the Devil attempts her subversion. The Devil's arguments all focus on his desire for her flesh, his lustful ability to "devour greedily, with the gullet of the serpent of old."[72] Eve was seduced through her desire to know, so the first Virtue to speak is Knowledge of God, who tries to call the ignorant fallen back to true understanding. In this second assault the Devil tries the trick that worked on Eve, appealing again to the desire for knowledge; he tells the Virtues and their Queen: "You do not even know what you are!" This threat, through its root *scio*, to know, takes the participant back to *Scivias* and to the kind of knowledge that prevents the Devil from working his wiles.[73] In direct and powerful contrast to Eve, Humility (Mary) *knows* the Devil for what he is, and the Virtues *know* that they dwell in the heights from which he plummeted.[74]

The Devil's third challenge is offered amidst hoarse croaks of false praise, *Euge!* (Well done!) (perhaps ironically used as an antithesis to *Ave!*), and once again refers to lack of knowledge. Not only do they not know themselves, he taunts, but these Virtues do not know God either. Neither fear of him nor love of him can help: God is a phantom of their imaginations. For nuns who were being encouraged to take Christ as a bridegroom, this challenge surely had a harsh ring. The Virtues of Obedience and Faith are the first to answer, and those who follow confirm that what is needed in the life of the convent is the Rule of St. Benedict.[75] The knowledge needed for salvation is understanding of human weakness and fault and recognition of the remedies for these lacks. Anima's desire for the wrong kind of knowledge, worldly knowledge, and her wish not to perfect her "robe" but rather to throw it off, lie at the root of her personal fall.

Midway through the play, the Virtues lose Anima: "Our master's sheep has fled from life!" Gunilla Iversen has interpreted the play as Hildegard's way of working through the painful loss of the nun Richardis, who first left the community to take a position of leadership in another convent and then died, but not before expressing her desire to return to Hildegard.[76] Anima, perhaps in an echo of Richardis's deathbed confession of a wish for stability, yearns for the beauty of home. Home exists on two levels, the royal chamber of the Bridegroom (praised in the opening of the play) to which all souls are called and the home of the convent, where each nun was encouraged to become a living allegory of the virtuous life, hard at work attempting to become better. In any case Anima has fallen, through the Devil's devices, but she comes back, both penitent and fetid with wounds caused by the serpent's contamination. Her flesh, once shining with light, is now "riddled with sores." Like all humankind, she can only be saved by the blood of the cross. From this point, the play's implicit emphasis on the Passion and the medicine of the cross dominates. Every sinner falls again, joining with Eve in desire for the wrong kinds of knowledge, and then must be healed.

The Devil tries to regain Anima by fighting with the Virtues, who bind him. Even tied, he continues to challenge them: as females they are virgins and empty-wombed, denying God's commandment to be fruitful. He repeats himself, branding the Virtues again as unknowing: "unde nescis quid sis! (whence you know not what you are)." Using the common understanding that "to know" means "to have sex with," the Devil claims intercourse will produce offspring and is therefore positive: to be so engaged follows God's commandments. The chaste do not "know" and cannot counsel this sinner, but Chastity has the rebuttal: the Virgin, whom she represents, brought forth a Man. Knowledge of the virgin birth strengthens and empowers both Virtues and virgins, breaking the ancient curse on females and on all humans. This knowledge is the antidote to the damning revelations of the Fall. The point in the play when the Devil is finally vanquished is the climax of all the action in the drama. During this section Victory sings in the tonal area of C, a region represented primarily in this part of the play. The model for the music is a phrase from "Ave regina celorum," the phrase which reads "Rejoice, Virgin, fairest of all."

Here, as with "O nobilissima viriditas" studied above, Hildegard has Victory parallel the model textually as well as musically: the *gaude* (rejoice), a singular imperative, has changed to the plural form of the verb, *gaudete*. Mary is one, while the Virtues are many in her image. Many forces, textual and musical, are brought to bear on this dramatic moment: the original Marian significance of "Ave regina celorum," its use in Hildegard's song repertory, which reworks and deepens its meaning,

Example 5.   Victory over the Devil, from *Ordo virtutum*.

and the "everyperson" struggle of the play, where the song of triumph echoes throughout the length of the Jesse tree, which has now become the church universal. Through the educational program embodied in songs and play, nuns in Hildegard's convent were assured not only of the importance of their individual struggles but also of the ways in which their model of life served to explain and sustain the central meanings of the faith.

The closing procession is a lamenting plea for the final fruition of the Jesse tree, as garden and as church. The tree bloomed with flowers in the beginning, but its greenness (*viriditas*) had faded as Christ awaited the golden number for his incarnation in the fullness of time. At that defining moment the Mirror of the Father, Christ in the flesh, came forth to suffer and die. Now he displays his body, which must flower and be filled with jewels or buds, each of which is another virtue-filled soul, converted to follow him.[77] He tires, longing for the end of time, like the church which is his body. The plea at the end is a prayer that God may reach out and touch the penitent as He did Anima, reinforced by Mary and the Virtues. As in *Scivias* book 1, we are left with the Lord's outstretched hand, with the welcoming call to salvation from a weary Lord. The call to bend the knee before the wounded Christ at the end may refer to an actual cross with the corpus, or body of Christ. If this is true, the play functioned to help define the community's relationship to its own sacred art.[78]

The musical style of the *Ordo virtutum* is very different from that of the *Scivias* songs, although still fully dependent on outlines of the melodic idioms Hildegard favored. Part of this difference may have derived simply from performance forces: whereas the songs would have been rendered by soloists and a select group of choir nuns, the play, like the hymns and sequences, would have been sung by the entire community. Thus the hymns, sequences, and especially the play are musically much simpler than the lavish antiphons and responsories discussed above. But there is more to the play's relatively simple musical style than this. Hildegard herself, in the introduction to the final vision of *Scivias,* describes three types of music, all relating to their sacred purpose: "Then I saw the lucent sky, in which I heard different kinds of music, marvelously embodying all the meanings I had heard before. I heard the praises of the joyous citizens of Heaven, steadfastly persevering in the ways of Truth; and laments calling people back to those praises and joys; and the exhortations of the virtues, spurring one another on to secure the salvation of the peoples ensnared by the Devil."[79]

In the songs the hierarchies of angels, Mary, and the saints are creating the symphony that is the body of Christ. In fact, in all of Hildegard's liturgical songs, there is no music for Christ specifically: He is the Music that the members of his body make together in heaven, the music of the City of God. But there is another music for those who are trapped in the snares of sin, and this *symphonia* is Christ as well. Just as the body of Christ reigns in heaven and battles on earth, so too does the music, which is itself his body, as Hildegard conceived of it. Thus the play depicts the wounded body. Its music mirrors that of the *Symphonia* but with the melismas of joy broken down for the sake of words, for explanation and exhortation. Indeed, if one were to remove the texts and "jubilate," or sing wordless melismas, to the music of the play, the heavenly sound of the *Scivias* songs would be recaptured at once. In the play the most melismatic sections are often the most jubilant and dramatic, and, as in the songs, Hildegard uses melismas to heighten texts and mark off sections. The Devil, by contrast, has no song in him at all and no hope for salvation.

On another level the music is used to join particular scenes and to develop character.[80] But the styles of the music and the choice of modes set up a polarity between sorrowing for sin and rejoicing in victory which is basic to the work as a whole. For the sake of time and space, I offer a single example to demonstrate the ways Hildegard uses the music to underscore both continuity and change in the dramatic action. The opening melodies move from a D tonality, in the interaction of patriarchs and prophets with Virtues, to a modulation to the lamenting E sound on the prophets' second speech. Thus, the complaint of the souls begins on e' and is unified through a constant return to the phrase quoted below as example 6.1. Even in the midst of this woe, the entrapped souls think on the Living Sun, and when they do the music changes to a proclamation of hope, with a shift to a', part of the C complex of pitches Hildegard seems especially to associate with victory, as seen above in example 5.

sed in   um - bram   pec   -   ca - to - rum ce - ci - di- mus.
but into   the shadow   of sin   we fell.

Example 6.1. A Unifying Phrase from the First Lament.

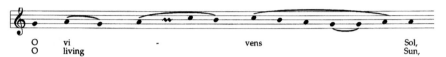

O   vi   vens   Sol,
O   living   Sun,

Example 6.2.   Reference to the Sun.

With an emphasis on lament established, Hildegard continues to build on the force of this sorrowful pleading sound. There is a kind of climax in the laments just after the Devil makes his first speech and the Virtues moan out against him. This mournful sound prepares us for the return of the torn and bleeding soul later in the play, after the Virtues have proclaimed their various strengths. The soul, finally acquiring understanding of its sickness, cries out for help. It is at this point that salvation becomes possible and the Devil can be defeated. The *societas*, the social group, welcomes and encourages the soul back onto the paths of victory. This play depends on group dynamics, on wars against sin within the community itself. The Devil is bound by all the Virtues, just as nuns and monks in community are bound by the Rule and their mode of life to work for each other's fortitude.

All of Hildegard's music, but especially the play, takes us back in time, setting us in the midst of a particular religious and worshiping community.[81] The play offers a small slice of actual communal life. Here is how nuns in a particular region reenacted and celebrated who they were and proclaimed their relationships not only to God but also to one another. We need to remember, as we study this great work, that the parts were designed for real people, with personalities and interactive lives. Who would have played the Queen of Virtues, Humility? Perhaps Hildegard herself? Which nuns were chosen for the other roles: those who lacked most keenly the particular virtues they were chosen to represent? Or would a nun have played the virtue she most especially seemed to embody? Did the only man in the convent, Hildegard's secretary Volmar, play the Devil and end up bound, virginal heels crushing his head? This reversal of hierarchical norms would have seemed humorous on one level; on another, the play would have warned nuns who lusted after men, perhaps even after Volmar, to control themselves. The play, which may have been enacted more than once in the church year, embodying as it does a powerful call to penance and confession of sin, would have shifted in meaning and emphasis as the personalities of the players and relationships between them changed. It would always have been a play within a play, a mousetrap for conventual souls.

My discussion of Hildegard's songs and dramatic work has tried to show the interconnectedness of the *Scivias,* the fourteen songs it includes, and the play. I believe that Hildegard designed all three together to support a particular educational program for her nuns. If this understanding is correct, Hildegard's is the only such program that survives in its entirety from the Middle Ages, with the texts, the music, and the explanation of meanings intact, and all organized by the creator's own hands.

NINE

Poet

*"Where the Living Majesty
Utters Mysteries"*

BARBARA NEWMAN

More than fifty years after Hildegard's death, when the legates of Pope Gregory IX had gathered at the Rupertsberg to hear witnesses testify about her "life, behavior, reputation, merits, and miracles," a nun named Hedwig of Alzey offered the inquisitors her own small tidbit. Hedwig must have been a very young novice when the old seer died. But she vividly recalled how the abbess on her sickbed always seemed *perlustrata*—"shining with light"—and not only then, she added, but also "when she walked through the cloister and chanted, at the Holy Spirit's prompting, the sequence that begins 'O virga ac diadema.' "[1]

This was not the usual stuff of canonization hearings. Hildegard's *Acta* are filled with miracles more spectacular but also more conventional: sick people healed, sight restored to the blind, mothers helped in childbirth, demons expelled from the possessed. Yet Hedwig's affectionate memory tells us far more about Hildegard. As we envision the composer swathed in her "Living Light," visible for once to an observer, we might wonder if her aging voice could still sustain the demands of her virtuosic melody as she sang the Virgin's glory:

Unde, o Salvatrix,	O saving Lady,
que novum lumen	you brought forth new light
humano generi protulisti:	for humankind:
collige membra Filii tui	gather the limbs of your Son
ad celestem armoniam.[2]	into the harmony of heaven.

The theme of this strophe echoes Hedwig's epiphany: light and song inextricably fused, each issuing in and from the other, at the juncture where God and the body meet. Hildegard, like Mary in her vision, brings into the world a new light that is also a new song, the *canticum novum* of the Psalter. Here she calls the Virgin *Salvatrix,* literally "fe-

male Savior." In another lyric she proclaims Mary as mother not of
God's Word but of his Song, setting her own prayer on the Virgin's lips:

O Fili dilectissime,	O beloved Son,
quem genui in visceribus meis	whom I bore in my womb
de vi circueuntis rote	by the might of the circling
sancte divinitatis,	wheel of the holy
que me creavit	God who created me
et omnia membra mea ordinavit	and formed all my limbs
et in visceribus meis	and laid in my womb
omne genus musicorum	all manner of music
in omnibus floribus tonorum	in all the flowers of sound . . .
constituit . . . [3]	

Such an understanding of the union between soul and body, song and
speech, God and humanity, underlies all of Hildegard's teaching and al-
lows us to read the *Symphonia* as an epitome of her message in distilled
and concentrated form. As she famously wrote near the end of her
Scivias, in God's praises "the word designates the body, but music manifests the spirit. For the harmony of heaven proclaims the Divinity, and
the word reveals the humanity of God's Son."[4]

Though this essay treats Hildegard as a poet, I begin with her music
as a reminder that any purely textual study of the *Symphonia* remains
incomplete. If we refer to the abbess as a "poet" at all—as indeed we
must—it is important to remember that her lyrics were not meant as art
for art's sake but were designed for the liturgical use of her nuns and, in
some cases, neighboring monks.[5] Her chants for the Divine Office and
the Mass are first of all prayers and must therefore address the dual audience of all public prayer, at the same time offering praise to God and
his saints in heaven, wisdom and inspiration to his saints on earth.[6] The
lyrical mode precludes the use of allegory, so pervasive in Hildegard's
prose writings, for it would not do to explain the meaning of sacred
symbols to the ears of heaven itself. Nevertheless, the lyrics aim in their
own way to teach as well as delight, for the mind must be edified even
as the spirit sings. So even the most rhapsodic poems are also subtly didactic, conveying each spiritual truth as new cause for celebration. But
where Hildegard's visions teach explicitly, her lyrics do so covertly, letting their condensed and often startling images bear the full weight that
would elsewhere be carried by expository prose. The images themselves
are largely inherited, each freighted with its own cargo of meaning derived from biblical commentaries and older liturgical texts. But as

Hildegard combines and recombines them, they take on new resonance: fresh motifs are invented, familiar ones reimagined.[7]

In the history of English verse, those poets moved by the most profoundly original religious visions have often been remarkable innovators in the technical realm as well—and for both reasons they were largely unappreciated by their contemporaries. Richard Crashaw introduced the luscious, grotesque sensibilities of Italian baroque piety to seventeenth-century English ears, reaping centuries of neglect and condescension as his reward. Gerard Manley Hopkins (d. 1889), one of the most brilliant metrical pioneers in the language, invented "sprung rhythm" and experimented with long alliterative lines on the Old English model; but the few who read him thought his verse precious and incomprehensible. Emily Dickinson, though confining herself to the familiar stanzaic forms of mid-nineteenth-century American hymnody, mastered a supremely expressive diction and could say more with a punctuation mark than lesser poets could with a lexicon. Yet she too was dismissed as a quirky, ill-taught eccentric. Hildegard of Bingen stands to the twelfth century somewhat as Crashaw does to the seventeenth or Hopkins and Dickinson to the nineteenth. To compare her with her most famous and successful contemporaries, like Hildebert of Lavardin (1056–1133)[8] and Adam of St. Victor (fl. ca. 1107–1147),[9] is a little like comparing Hopkins to Tennyson or Dickinson to Longfellow. Yet such comparisons are useful, for they show precisely where this remarkable poet, though very much a daughter of her age, diverged from its conventions to forge means of expression that were uniquely hers.

The dominant form in twelfth-century liturgical poetry is the rhymed metrical sequence, a lyric constructed (in Patrick Diehl's words) of "a series of trimly rhymed trochaic stanzas . . . that are all perfectly identical in form."[10] Highly regular and (at best) tightly constructed, such poems could be sung to flowing and at times highly irregular melodies, creating a pleasant asymmetry between textual and musical structure. Since the relationship between text and melody was so loose, but also since so many sequences used identical stanzaic forms, any number of them could be sung to variants of the same tune, or conversely the same text might be sung to several different melodies. (The musically unsophisticated can grasp this idea by reflecting that one can set virtually any Dickinson poem to the tune of "The Yellow Rose of Texas.")[11] This mix-and-match practice, known as *contrafactura,* dominated the performance of lyric poetry in both the vernaculars and Latin.[12] As a result, only a small proportion of the thousands of extant sequence texts are linked to unique melodies. One of these is the well-known "Golden Sequence" for Pentecost by the English poet Stephen Langton (1151–1228), a much younger contemporary of Hildegard's. The first two strophes will give an idea of its form:

Veni, Sancte Spiritus,	Holy Spirit, come to us:
et emitte caelitus	let your light shine down on us
lucis tuae radium.	from heaven's height.
Veni, pater pauperum;	Father of the poor, now come;
veni, dator munerum;	Giver of all bounty, come;
veni, lumen cordium.[13]	Come, our hearts' light.

Such two- and even three-syllable rhymes are typical in twelfth-century verse. Though many rhyme schemes exist, one of the most familiar is the *aabccb* stanza, used in "Veni, Sancte Spiritus" and in this Nativity sequence ascribed to Adam of St. Victor:

Lux est orta gentibus	Light has dawned on the nation
In umbra sedentibus	That lay in desperation
Et mortis caligine;	And death's blind shade;
Gaudet miser populus,	Wretched people shout for joy:
Quia mundo parvulus	Unto the world a little boy
Nascitur de virgine.[14]	Is born of a Maid.

While the trochaic rhyming stanza had gained the most recent and widespread popularity, it did not entirely oust older forms. Gifted poets like Peter Abelard and Hildebert of Lavardin could achieve fine effects with classical quantitative meters, such as elegiacs and hexameters. Abelard, a tireless innovator, used no fewer than twenty-one different stanza forms in his hymns for Heloise and her nuns,[15] including one to St. Benedict in sapphics:

Vīctĭmām nōstrāe	tĭbĭ, Chrīstĕ, laūdĭs
Sānctĭtās ēiūs	fácĭat plăcēntĕm,
Cūĭus hānc lūcēm	fácĭt ēssĕ lūcĭs
Lūcĭdă vītă.[16]	

Christ, let our praise be	an oblation worthy,
Pleasing to you, Lord,	through your saint's great virtue:
Benedict, lighting	with his lucent merits,
Luminous feast days.	

Yet another option, more versatile than the regular sequence perfected by Adam, was the elegant "filigree stanza," a variable form that combined internal rhyme with the syllabic parallelism characteristic of the classical sequence.[17] A fine early example is Hildebert's composition, once again on the theme of the Holy Spirit:

> Tu nostra salus,   tu nostrum decus;
> Vita et praemium,   finis et gaudium.
>   Vis reatum   cogens agnoscere,
>   Jus paratum   libens ignoscere.
>   Te praevio fugit   nox et interitus;
>   Nam dextrae Altissimi   tu digitus.
> Subtilis et docilis,   sublimis   et humilis,
> Tu mitis et hilaris,   amabilis,   laudabilis;
>   Vanitatis mundator,   munditiae amator;
> Sanctitudinis,   rectitudinis,   beatae plenitudinis
>   Et plenae beatitudinis   donator.[18]
>
> You our salvation,   soul's decoration,
>   our life and our prize,   our end and our bliss.
>   Force compelling   the sinner to shame,
>   Law most willing   to forgive the blame.
>   Night flees in terror   as you draw nigh—
>   you are the finger   of God Most High.
> Subtle and peaceful,   lofty   and humble,
> Gentle and cheerful,   lovely   and noble,
>   You purge all vanity,   lover of purity:
> Of holiness,   righteousness,   blessed fulfillment,
> And fullness of bliss,   you are the source.

In English the delicacy of such verse slides inescapably toward doggerel, for the subtleties allowed by inflected Latin syntax do not survive translation.[19] But if these fine twelfth-century poets are more difficult to appreciate now than they were a century ago, the main reason is surely the shift in English poetic taste. Ever since *The Waste Land,* the dominant mode has shifted so far toward free verse that rhymed stanzas on the Victorine (or Victorian) model sound more apt for greeting cards than for serious poetry. By virtue of the same shift, however, Hildegard's lyrics have at last come into their own. Ignored or belittled in the standard histories of medieval Latin poetry,[20] they now appear strikingly original and avant-garde. For Hildegard used neither accentual nor quantitative verse, neither rhyme nor regular stanzas. Her medium has been variously described as "free verse" and *Kunstprosa,* or "art prose," but it would be a serious mistake to read her as a twelfth-century modernist precociously "rebelling" against the "constraints of form." If she was at all self-conscious about her artistic choices—a possibility she could not admit, given her commitment to the claim of divine inspiration—Hildegard was decidedly conservative rather than "cutting-edge." Whether or not she was acquainted with the regular sequence and other rhyming forms,[21] she modeled her own compositions on the received repertoire of liturgical chant, chiefly antiphons and responsories, meant to be sung in connection with the unrhymed, unmetrical Latin psalms. Her innovation lay in using the irregular lines typical of these texts not only for her own antiphons and responsories (the shorter liturgical genres) but also for the longer and normally regular genres (hymns and sequences).

We might hypothesize several reasons for this choice: a girlhood steeped in Benedictine psalmody; a preference for unpredictable and free-flowing (though certainly not formless) poetic and melodic movement; and, not least, the absence of formal study. Hildegard's oft-repeated admission that she had never studied "grammar" (that is, Latin literature, as well as the rules of the language) in childhood, as almost all monks did, goes a long way to explain her extraordinary creative freedom. It is not so much that she could not have written regular stanzas had she tried but that she had absolutely no reason for trying and was therefore at liberty to invent forms more suited to her visionary gift. Even more pertinent is her approach to music. Unlike many twelfth-century hymnodists, who were first of all poets and secondarily (if at all) composers,[22] Hildegard was first a musician who, as we have seen, thought words and melody as inseparable as the human and the divine in Christ. Hence, just as she eschewed metrical form, she shunned the precise repetition of melodies. Her practice of *contrafactura,* as Margot Fassler has shown, is allusive and improvisatory rather than exact:[23] it does not defile the monogamous union of text and tune with promiscuous couplings. Not only is each of her poems wedded uniquely to its music but several of her long pieces are through-composed—that is, instead of using the same melody for all stanzas or strophes, she gives each its own.[24] Even when she does repeat a tune from one stanza to the next, some variation always disrupts the expected regularity. It is no wonder that contemporaries called her songs *nova et inaudita*—"novel and unheard-of"—and some like Hedwig considered the music itself a luminous miracle.

This apparent spontaneity does not mean that the pieces necessarily sprang full-blown from Hildegard's mind like Athena from the head of Zeus. Much like the romantic poets whose aesthetics also relied on inspiration, Hildegard's respect for her creative afflatus—the "heavenly voice" that spoke and sang to her—did not keep her from returning to her original drafts at a later stage to revise and refine. In the case of her

Book of Divine Works, we are fortunate to have a contemporary manuscript with countless authorial revisions, allowing us to study her
working methods in detail.[25] For the *Symphonia,* too, successive manuscripts make it possible to trace the stages of her poetic composition in
at least a tentative way. A manuscript now in Vienna contains a jum-
bled miscellany of prophecies, poems (without their music), dramatic
sketches, and homiletic fragments.[26] As I have argued elsewhere, most
of these texts appear to date from the middle and late 1150s, and the
miscellany itself represents an impromptu record of Hildegard as litur-
gist, including lyrics she composed for particular feast days, homilies
she preached, and possible dramatic performances by her nuns (similar
to the *Ordo virtutum* but on a much smaller scale, and surviving in
fragmentary form). A comparison of the song texts in this collection
with the later and more finished versions in the *Symphonia* manuscripts
indicates considerable polishing. The *Symphonia* versions are more elegant and less "prosy," more obviously suited for worship (using, for example, the prayerful "we" rather than neutral third-person forms), and
more clearly designated as belonging to specific liturgical genres.
Hymns are supplied with their "amen" and responsories with their
doxology.[27] A similar process of revision appears when we compare the
sketch of the *Ordo virtutum* that closes the *Scivias* with the fully developed play in the Riesenkodex.

It is also possible to distinguish roughly between Hildegard's earlier
and later pieces, and here we note a distinct change in her poetic style.
The earliest pieces—fourteen songs composed before 1151 and included in the final "vision" of the *Scivias*—are all antiphons and responsories, indicating that Hildegard started small and only later tack-
led the larger, poetically more ambitious (though musically simpler)
forms. More important, many of these early lyrics are written in a cryptic, almost indecipherable style, recalling the *trobar clus,* or "hermetic
poetry," of contemporary troubadours. In some of her later work the
poet would develop her own version of a *trobar leu,* or "easy style,"
more accessible to an audience not initiated into the arcana of her visions (although, in Hildegard's case, "ease" is always relative!).

The fourteen *Scivias* lyrics are already arranged in a hierarchical
order, with two for the Virgin Mary and two for the angels, followed by
two each for five categories of saints: patriarchs and prophets, apostles,
martyrs, confessors, and virgins. In 1158, when she prepared the first
version of her *Symphonia* as a poetic cycle, Hildegard would preserve
this arrangement but expand it to include poems in praise of God (at

the beginning, of course),[28] along with many more Marian lyrics and compositions honoring particular saints, especially Rupert and Ursula. A similar typology of saints is used to structure the third book of Abelard's *Hymnarius Paraclitensis,* although other cycles—Notker's ninth-century *Liber ymnorum,* Abelard's second book, the Victorine sequences—are arranged according to the feasts of the liturgical year. Hildegard's structural principle indicates that she did not aim at comprehensiveness as did Abelard, who provided Heloise and her nuns with hymnody to sing throughout the church year. Rather, the abbess wrote her songs as occasion or inspiration demanded, then ordered them as she believed that heaven itself was ordered, deploying her lyrics in festive ranks around the throne of God like the spheres of Dante's *Paradiso.* But this preliminary recension of the *Symphonia* did not end her poetic career. Hildegard apparently continued to write new lyrics throughout her life, both on commission and as the Spirit moved her, as evidenced by the much longer version of the *Symphonia* in the Riesenkodex, assembled after her death.

Typical of Hildegard's "early period" is the little-known "O spectabiles viri," an antiphon for the patriarchs and prophets. It begins thus:

O spectabiles viri	Clear-sighted men! seeing
qui pertransistis occulta,	with the spirit's eyes,
aspicientes per oculos spiritus	you have pierced the mystery.
et annuntiantes	
in lucida umbra	In a luminous shade you proclaim
acutam et viventem lucem	a sharp living brightness
in virga germinantem,	that buds from a branch
que sola floruit	that blossomed alone
de introitu radicantis luminis.[29]	when the radical light took root.

These remarkable lines show how far Hildegard's own charism influenced her understanding of biblical prophecy. She calls the prophets *spectabiles,* a word whose root meaning is simply "visible," thus "distinguished" or "spectacular." But it comes from the verb *spectare,* to gaze or contemplate, and Hildegard plays as she often does with the ambivalence of active and passive, seeing and being seen. Her prophets are indeed contemplatives, spectators of God's mysteries who see (as she does) "with the spirit's eyes." Gazing on and with them, she beholds the prophets beholding their vision—"in a luminous shade" that recalls "the shadow of the Living Light" characteristic of her own visions. But what the Old Testament prophets see is also light: the divine Brightness to be born of Mary, the virgin branch that "blossomed" on the ancient tree of Jesse (here the poet gestures toward a traditional play on *virgo* and *virga*). Hildegard's mystic tree is at the same time a human lineage (the family tree of King David) and the Tree of Life, whose root and flower are alike divine—the "radical light." This tree is planted at the center of her cosmos and springs up everywhere: it is like a noble evergreen "with roots in the sun,"[30] "planted in a cascade of translucent shadow,"[31] branching "in the windy blast of the quest of the saints."[32] Hildegard continues her tribute to the prophets:

Vos antiqui sancti,	Holy ones of old! you foretold
predixistis salvationem	deliverance for the souls
exulum animarum	of exiles, plunged in death.
que inmerse fuerant morti,	Like wheels you
qui circuisti ut rote,	spun round in wonder as you spoke
mirabiliter loquentes mistica montis	the mysteries of that mountain
qui celum tangit,	that touches heaven
pertransiens ungendo multas aquas,	and soothes many waters, crossing over the seas.
cum etiam inter vos	And a shining lamp
surrexit lucida lucerna,	rose in the midst of you!
que ipsum montem precurrens	Racing beforehand,
ostendit.	he points to that mountain.

These lines in Latin constitute a single sentence, its verbs erratically veering between past and present, its four relative clauses modifying four different subjects. The cascade of images is not merely cryptic but surreal. Linked together as loosely as the grammatical units, they rely on the performer's knowledge both of Scripture and its glosses and of Hildegard's prior visions. To begin at the simplest level, the "exiled souls" are the righteous who died before the coming of Christ and awaited him in limbo, to be gloriously rescued at the Harrowing of Hell. It is this deliverance that the prophets foretold. The "shining lamp" that illumined their darkness is John the Baptist, the final prophet and precursor, whom Jesus called "a burning and a shining lamp" (John 5.35). So far we are on well-trodden ground. But it was not customary to represent Christ as a mountain—for that image we must recall the first vision of the *Scivias*, featuring a radiant winged figure enthroned on an iron-colored peak. And to imagine such a mountain "crossing over many waters" and at the same time calming or anointing (*ungendo*) them, we must abandon the visual altogether and move to a purely conceptual level. The prophet Moses, as a figure of Christ, parted the Red Sea for the crossing of Israel; Christ himself walked upon the Sea of Galilee and stilled a storm. To these allusions we might add the waters of baptism and the voice of the Lord "thundering upon many waters" (Vulgate, Psalms 28.3, echoed in Revelation 1.15 and in Hildegard's "O Ecclesia"). But this is no allegory, for the layered image finally resists decoding and remains obscure like the prophets themselves, *mirabiliter loquentes mistica*—speaking "in wonder" of what is known yet never fully knowable.

Complicating Hildegard's rapid shifts from the sensual to the symbolic or typological is her strong tendency toward synaesthesia, the blurring (or fusion) of sense experiences that are ordinarily distinct. In "Vos flores rosarum," for example, Hildegard blends visual and olfactory perceptions with a highly abstract idea. The martyrs appear as bleeding roses whose blood streams forth like a perfume, exuding from their bodily wounds as it was first distilled from the heart of God:

Vos flores rosarum,	
qui in effusione sanguinis vestri	Blessed are you roses
beati estis,	in the streaming of your blood,
in maximis gaudiis redolentibus	fragrant with supreme delight,
et sudantibus in emptione	distilling the purchase
que fluxit	that flowed from the inmost
de interiori mente consilii	heart of the purpose
manentis ante evum.[33]	of Him who abides before time.

Even more compressed and synaesthetic is "O orzchis Ecclesia," the one song in which Hildegard incorporated words from her secret language (*Lingua ignota*). Here, in only eight short lines, she presents the church as at once "city of knowledge," "fragrance of the wounds of nations," "sparkling jewel," and warrior maid "anointed in lofty music."[34] Images of glittering light, sound, and flowing or circling movement pervade these lyrics, suggesting their genesis in a world of inner experience where blood cries aloud, light swirls and pulses, and flowers gleam with preternatural radiance.

In one of the most celebrated modernist religious poems, "Sailing to Byzantium," W. B. Yeats bewailed the age-old plight of the dualist, "caught in that sensual music" of birth, sexuality, and death even as his soul pines for "the artifice of eternity." His gnostic persona resolves the crisis by imagining beatitude as a mimicry of nature in a state of changeless, inorganic perfection:

> Once out of nature I shall never take
> My bodily form from any natural thing,
> But such a form as Grecian goldsmiths make
> Of hammered gold and gold enamelling . . .

Unlike the Yeatsian persona, Hildegard resolves her own dualistic tendencies in a vision where the sensual music and the eternal artifice are one. Blending the two biblical types of ideal community—the paradisal garden of Genesis, the new Jerusalem of Revelation—she conceives of a heaven that is supremely organic and alive yet also consummately crafted. Her beloved *viriditas,* or living green, with its affiliated images of leaf and flower, root and branches, most often evokes the childbearing of Mary or the bliss of virgins, while the glistening, jewel-encrusted city "built of living stones" denotes the Church Triumphant and the glory of saints. But the two spheres interpenetrate. The child saint Rupert is a "delicate bloom of the field, sweet green of the apple," yet he flourishes in that "golden city decked with royal purple," its windows glinting with topaz and sapphires.[35] Mary is the miraculous blossoming branch, but also the "resplendent jewel and unclouded brightness of the sun,"[36] the "golden matrix" of God's Word.[37] Nature and art converge to evoke the promise of ultimate fulfillment because, in Hildegard's view, sainthood is always synergy, a collaboration of divine bounty and human moral striving.[38] Even more to the point, her God is not "supernatural" (a word she never uses) but "arch-natural"—not merely the creator but the innate, inexhaustible vitality of nature.[39] This quintessentially Hildegardian idea emerges most clearly in her sequence to the Holy Spirit, the *vivificans vita,* or "life-giving life," within and beyond all creatures.[40]

In "O ignis Spiritus Paracliti" we see Hildegard at her most accessible, using apostrophes, occasional rhyme, grammatically parallel clauses, and petitionary prayer to structure a piece less difficult, if not more conventional than "O spectabiles viri" or "Vos flores rosarum."[41] She begins with a trope (or explanatory comment) on the triple "Sanctus" of the Mass, underlining the unity of the Holy Spirit in creation and redemption:

1a. O ignis Spiritus Paracliti,	O fire of the Spirit, the Comforter,
vita vite omnis creature,	life of the life of all creation,
sanctus es vivificando formas.	Holy are You, giving life to the forms.[42]
1b. Sanctus es ungendo	Holy are You, anointing
periculose fractos,	the mortally broken;
sanctus es tergendo	Holy are You, cleansing
fetida vulnera.	the fetid wounds.

In the next five strophes there follow seven "O" apostrophes, a structural device recalling the seven great "O" antiphons of Advent as well as the seven gifts of the Holy Spirit. The paired strophes 2a–2b, 3a–3b deploy careful antithesis to represent the Spirit as source of beatitude and virtue for the saints but healer and deliverer for the lost. In 3a–3b Hildegard offers a threefold litany with petitions for the "blessed," the "imprisoned," and the "bound." Although the latter groups are probably souls in purgatory and those fettered on earth by their sins, the chivalric images of 3a–3b hint that she was praying more immediately for prisoners of war, a group that may at any given time have included a few brothers, cousins, and nephews of her nuns.

2a. O spiraculum sanctitatis,
   o ignis caritatis,
   o dulcis gustus in pectoribus
   et infusio cordium
   in bono odore virtutum.

O breath of sanctity,
O fire of charity,
O sweet savor in the breast
and balm flooding hearts
with the fragrance of virtues:

2b. O fons purissime,
   in quo consideratur
   quod Deus alienos colligit
   et perditos requirit.

O limpid fountain,
in which we can see
how God gathers the strays
and seeks out the lost:

3a. O lorica vite
   et spes compaginis membrorum
      omnium
   et o cingulum honestatis:
   salva beatos.

O breastplate of life
and hope of the integral body,

O sword-belt of honor:
save the blessed!

3b. Custodi eos qui carcerati sunt
   ab inimico,
   et solve ligatos
   quos divina vis salvare vult.

Guard those the foe holds
imprisoned,
free those in fetters
whom divine force wishes to save.

Her petition concluded, Hildegard returns to praise, calling on the Holy Spirit in the guise of *anima mundi* or World Soul, as Abelard and William of Conches had done before her.

4a. O iter fortissimum,
   quod penetravit omnia
   in altissimis et in terrenis
   et in omnibus abyssis,
   tu omnes componis et colligis.

O current of power permeating all—
in the heights, upon the earth,
and in all deeps:
you bind and gather
all people together.

4b. De te nubes fluunt, ether volat,
   lapides humorem habent,
   aque rivulos educunt,
   et terra viriditatem sudat.

From you clouds overflow, winds
take wing, stones store up moisture,
waters well forth in streams—
and earth swells with living green.

This conception of the Holy Spirit is inspired by the portrayal of Wisdom in Ecclesiasticus 24, a text well known to Hildegard: "I have circled the vault of heaven alone, and pierced the depth of the abyss; I have walked amid the waves of the sea, and stood upon all the earth" (24:8–9).[43] But distinctive to this sequence are Hildegard's subtle pairing of *omnia* and *omnes*—the Spirit animates all creation and unites all people—and her celebration of the life-creating waters, obliquely recalling the primal scene of Genesis. Peter Dronke suggested long ago that the composer may have known Notker's sequence "Sancti Spiritus,"[44] where she would have found these strophes:

Quando machinam	When by his Word God
per verbum suum	fashioned the cosmos—
fecit deus caeli terrae marium,	founded sky and earth and sea—
Tu super aquas	You, Spirit, brooded
foturus eas	over the waters,
numen tuum expandisti, spiritus.	unfolded your deity.
Tu animabus	You make waters
vivificandis	fruitful to give
aquas foecundas:	life to creatures:
Tu aspirando	You breathe on men
das spiritales	to make mortals
esse homines.[45]	living spirits.

Hildegard ends her sequence with another allusion to Wisdom, now virtually identified with the Holy Spirit, and an atypical doxology:

5a. Tu etiam semper educis doctos per inspirationem Sapientie letificatos.	You are ever teaching the learned, made joyful by the breath of Wisdom.
5b. Unde laus tibi sit, qui es sonus laudis et gaudium vite, spes et honor fortissimus, dans premia lucis.	Praise then be yours! You are the song of praise, the delight of life, a hope and a potent honor granting garlands of light.

The relatively public or exoteric character of Hildegard's sequences, in contrast to her antiphons and responsories, may be explained by their genre. Alone among her compositions, they were meant to be sung at Mass, a service likely to be attended by pilgrims and guests, whereas in the monastic services of matins and vespers, only "initiated" members of the community would be present and the abbess could afford to use more esoteric texts. Her hymn "O ignee Spiritus" thus offers a more inwardly directed complement to the communal and cosmic orientation of her sequence.[46] Although it too is artfully structured, it presents a private approach to the Spirit's working, a subtle psychology of

desire, temptation, and repentance comparable to the psychodrama of
the *Ordo virtutum*. In the first movement, parallel to Anima's joyous
approach to the Virtues, all is going well for the soul: the Holy Spirit
kindles a burning desire for God, and all the faculties—will, intellect or
moral judgment, and reason—work together in harmony.

1. O ignee Spiritus, laus tibi sit, qui in timpanis et citharis operaris.	Praise to you, Spirit of fire! to you who sound the timbrel and the lyre.
2. Mentes hominum de te flagrant et tabernacula animarum eorum vires ipsarum continent.	From you the minds of mortals catch fire, and the tents of their souls contain their forces.[47]
3. Inde voluntas ascendit et gustum anime tribuit, et eius lucerna est desiderium.	Thence the will mounts up and gives the soul a savor: desire is its lantern.
4. Intellectus te in dulcissimo sono advocat ac edificia tibi cum racionalitate parat, que in aureis operibus sudat.	The intellect invokes you in a cry full of sweetness, and builds you temples with the work of reason, who labors at her golden crafts.

But just as Anima in the play rejects the patient struggle of the Virtues
and yields to the Devil's seduction, so here "will and desire" are overshadowed by a cloud—the poisonous *nebula* that we see overspreading
Eve in *Scivias* I.2—and the soul finds herself helplessly adrift. In this crisis the rational mind must intervene, firmly binding the errant will just as
the Virtues bind Satan in the *Ordo*. But if reason too forgets its duty, the
Holy Spirit exerts a divine violence on the soul, bending it back toward
God through what the poet calls "a flood of experiences" (*per infusionem experimentorum*). The phrase is remarkable and not altogether
clear, though it suggests a very practical psychology in keeping with
Hildegard's pastoral counsels. It is through the ordinary trials and afflic-
tions of life that the Holy Spirit exposes sin, as the abbess herself had to
confess in repenting her possessive attachment to Richardis.[48]

5. Tu autem semper gladium habes illud abscidere quod noxiale pomum per nigerrimum homicidium profert,	But you always hold a sword ready to slash the shoots of the poisoned apple, scions of the blackest murder,
6. Quando nebula voluntatem et desideria tegit, in quibus anima volat et undique circuit.	when a cloud shadows the will and its desires. Adrift in them, the soul flutters and spins about everywhere.

| 7. Sed mens est ligatura | But the mind is a bond |
| voluntatis et desiderii. | to bind will and desire. |

8. Cum vero animus se ita erigit,
quod requirit pupillam mali videre
et maxillam nequicie,
tu eum citius in igne comburis
cum volueris.

But when the spirit exalts itself so
that it yearns to look Evil in the eye,
to stare down the jaws of iniquity,
swiftly you burn it in consuming
fire. Such is your wish.

9. Sed et cum racionalitas
se per mala opera
ad prona declinat,
tu eam, cum vis,
stringis et constringis[49] et reducis
per infusionem experimentorum.

Yet when reason
because of evil works
falls prostrate, you restrain
and constrain her as you will
and lead her back
through a flood of experiences.

Notable in this hymn are the many stanzas beginning with adversative conjunctions: *Tu autem, Sed, Cum vero, Sed et cum, Quando autem.*[50] Despite their "unpoetic" quality, these links indicate the strongly dialectical nature of Hildegard's moral thought. The Christian life is for her a constant struggle between virtues and vices, the Holy Spirit and the Devil, each responding to the other's initiatives. In the closing stanzas she characteristically widens her focus outward to salvation history, showing that the same forces now battling within each soul were already at work in the fall of Lucifer and the primitive church. Like the "publicans and sinners" who followed Christ, a now penitent Anima returns to the fold, her "fetid wounds" to be transformed by the Spirit's alchemy into glistening gems—in a reprise of the initial image from "O ignis Spiritus Paracliti."

10. Quando autem malum
ad te gladium suum educit,
tu illud in cor illius refringis
sicut in primo perdito angelo fecisti,
ubi turrim superbie illius
in infernum deiecisti.

But when the Evil One brandishes
his sword against you,
you break it in his own heart,
as you did to the first lost angel,
when you tumbled the tower
of his arrogance to hell.

11. Et ibi aliam turrim
in publicanis et peccatoribus
elevasti,
qui tibi peccata sua
cum operibus suis confitentur.

And there you raised a second
tower, among publicans and
sinners
who confess their sins to you
with their crafts.

12. Unde omnes creature
que de te vivunt, te laudant,
quia tu preciosissimum
ungentum es
fractis et fetidis vulneribus,

So all creatures
that live by you, praise you,
for you are a priceless salve

for the fractured,

ubi illa in preciosissimas gemmas convertis.	for fetid wounds: you convert them into priceless gems!

No survey can do more than hint at the variety of Hildegard's songs, which range from the rapturous lyricism of "O Fili dilectissime" to the sober realism of "O ignee Spiritus." In "Mathias sanctus" (no. 50) and "Cum vox sanguinis" (no. 65), she displays her immersion in biblical typology. "O dulcissime amator" (no. 57) and "O Pater omnium" (no. 58), composed for the Rupertsberg virgins and widows respectively, come closer to twelfth-century bridal mysticism than anything else in Hildegard's oeuvre, while "O pastor animarum" (no. 4) and "O eterne Deus" (no. 7) express a simple but fervent piety in the midst of pain. "O vos imitatores" (no. 39) is remarkable for its theatricality: Hildegard the dramatist portrays saintly bishops as actors, performing the role of Christ *in preciosissima et gloriosissima significatione*—"in the most precious and glorious symbolic action" (or play?) of the Mass. Not the least inspired of the songs are the seer's brief, almost epigrammatic antiphons. In visionary cameos like "O virtus Sapientie" (no. 2), "Hodie aperuit" (no. 11), "Karitas habundat" (no. 25), and "O rubor sanguinis" (no. 61), a single indelible image is etched on the mind. To this group also belongs the antiphon "O mirum admirandum" (no. 41), written in honor of Hildegard's first patron, St. Disibod.[51]

"O mirum admirandum" is one of three pieces Hildegard composed at the request of her superior and erstwhile adversary, Abbot Kuno, shortly before his death in 1155. Fifteen years later she would write St. Disibod's biography at the petition of Kuno's successor, Abbot Helengar.[52] Aside from Hildegard's writings, virtually nothing is known about this seventh-century hermit, and one may suspect that along with oral tradition not a little of her own history found its way into his vita.[53] According to her narrative, Disibod, exiled from his episcopal see in Ireland, traveled to Germany and built himself a hermitage on the slope of a mountain where the river Glan meets the Nahe. Later he founded a monastery at the summit—the same "Disibodenberg" that would be rebuilt by Archbishop Ruthard of Mainz when Hildegard was ten years old and where she would live until her fifties. St. Disibod is said to have possessed the gifts of healing and counsel and lived a life of stern asceticism (like Hildegard's mentor Jutta) but never entered the community he had established. After his death at eighty-one (the same age, by coincidence, that his biographer would attain), his reputation went into eclipse for centuries until the twelfth-century monks, with

Hildegard's aid, revived his cult. In this context "O mirum admirandum," with its haunting beauty and mysterious apocalyptic close, reads almost as an epitaph for the seer herself.

O mirum admirandum
quod absconsa forma precellit,
ardua in honesta statura,
ubi vivens altitudo
profert mistica.
Unde, o Disibode,
surges in fine,
succurrente flore
omnium ramorum
    mundi,[54]
ut primum surrexisti.

O wonder! the one
who was hidden towers high,
steep on the summit of honor
where the living Majesty
utters mysteries.
So you, Disibod,
shall arise in the end
as you rose in the beginning
when the blossom that sustains you
    blooms
on all the boughs in the world.

Notes

ABBREVIATIONS

Acta   *Acta inquisitionis de virtutibus et miraculis
                        Sanctae Hildegardis* (canonization protocol).
                        PL 197:131–139.

Causae et curae   Hildegard. *Causae et curae.* Ed. Paul Kaiser.
                        Leipzig: Teubner, 1903.

CCCM   *Corpus christianorum: Continuatio mediaevalis.*
                        Turnhout, Belgium: Brepols, 1966–.

CCSL   *Corpus christianorum: Series latina.* Turnhout,
                        Belgium: Brepols, 1953–.

Epistolarium   Hildegard. *Epistolarium.* Ed. Lieven Van Acker.
                        CCCM 91–91a. Turnhout, Belgium: Brepols,
                        1991, 1993.

LDO   Hildegard. *Liber divinorum operum.* Ed. Albert
                        Derolez and Peter Dronke. CCCM 92. Turn-
                        hout, Belgium: Brepols, 1996.

Letters   *Letters of Hildegard of Bingen.* Vol. 1. Trans.
                        Joseph Baird and Radd Ehrman. Oxford, 1994.

Lieder   *Hildegard von Bingen: Lieder.* Ed. Pudentiana
                        Barth, M.-I. Ritscher, and Joseph Schmidt-Görg.
                        Musical edition. Salzburg: Otto Müller, 1969.

LVM   Hildegard. *Liber vite meritorum.* Ed. Angela
                        Carlevaris. CCCM 90. Turnhout, Belgium: Bre-
                        pols, 1995.

MGH.LdL   *Monumenta Germaniae historica. Libelli de lite
                        imperatorum et pontificum saeculis XI et XII
                        conscripti.* 3 vols. Hannover: Hahnsche Buch-
                        handlung, 1891–1897.

MGH.SS	*Monumenta Germaniae historica. Scriptores rerum germanicarum.* Hannover: Hahnsche Buchhandlung, 1826–.
Ordo virtutum	Hildegard. *Ordo virtutum.* Ed. and trans. Peter Dronke. In *Nine Medieval Latin Plays* 147–184. Cambridge, 1994.
Physica	Hildegard. *Physica (Subtilitatum diversarum naturarum creaturarum libri novem).* Ed. Charles Daremberg and F. A. Reuss. PL 197:1117–1352.
Pitra	*Analecta Sanctae Hildegardis.* Ed. Jean-Baptiste Pitra. *Analecta Sacra,* vol. 8. Monte Cassino, 1882.
PL	*Patrologiae cursus completus: Series latina.* Ed. J.-P. Migne. 221 vols. Paris: Migne, 1841–1864.
Scivias	Hildegard. *Scivias.* Ed. Adelgundis Führkötter and Angela Carlevaris. CCCM 43–43a. Turnhout, Belgium: Brepols, 1978.
Scivias, trans. Hart and Bishop	Hildegard. *Scivias.* Trans. Columba Hart and Jane Bishop. Introduction by Barbara Newman. New York: Paulist, 1990.
Symphonia	Hildegard. *Symphonia armonie celestium revelationum.* Ed. and trans. Barbara Newman. Ithaca, N.Y.: Cornell University Press, 1988; rev. ed., 1998.
Vita	Gottfried of St. Disibod and Theoderic of Echternach. *Vita Sanctae Hildegardis.* Ed. Monika Klaes. CCCM 126. Turnhout, Belgium: Brepols, 1993.
Vita Juttae	*Vita domnae Juttae inclusae.* Ed. Franz Staab. In Stefan Weinfurter, ed., *Reformidee und Reformpolitik im spätsalisch-frühstaufischen Reich,* 172–187. Mainz, 1992.

CHAPTER 1: "SIBYL OF THE RHINE"

1. The epithet "Sibyl of the Rhine" apparently derives from a remark of the churchman Henry of Langenstein, who in 1383 in a letter to his friend Eckard

von Dresch referred to Hildegard as *Theotonicorum Sibilla*. See G. Sommerfeld, "Die Prophetien der hl. Hildegard in einem Schreiben des Meisters Heinrich von Langenstein," *Historisches Jahrbuch* 30 (1909): 43–61, 297–307, and Sylvain Gouguenheim, *La Sibylle du Rhin: Hildegarde de Bingen, abbesse et prophétesse rhénane* (Paris, 1996), 182.

2. Wilhelm Preger, *Geschichte der deutschen Mystik im Mittelalter* (Leipzig, 1874), 1:20–21. See also Bernhard Schmeidler, "Bemerkungen zum Corpus der Briefe der hl. Hildegard von Bingen," in *Corona Quernea: Festgabe Karl Strecker* (Leipzig, 1941), 335–366.

3. J. P. Schmelzeis, *Das Leben und Wirken der heiligen Hildegardis* (Freiburg, 1879). For the authentication and foundational manuscript studies of Hildegard's writings, see Marianna Schrader and Adelgundis Führkötter, *Die Echtheit des Schrifttums der hl. Hildegard von Bingen* (Cologne, 1956).

4. This impression is fostered by the publications of Bear and Company, e.g., Gabriele Uhlein, *Meditations with Hildegard of Bingen* (Santa Fe, N.M., 1982); Matthew Fox, *Illuminations of Hildegard of Bingen* (Santa Fe, N.M., 1985); Wighard Strehlow and Gottfried Hertzka, *Hildegard of Bingen's Medicine*, trans. Karin Strehlow (Santa Fe, N.M., 1988).

5. On other preaching by women, see Beverly Mayne Kienzle and Pamela J. Walker, eds., *Women Preachers and Prophets through Two Millennia of Christianity* (Berkeley, 1998).

6. See Robert Potter, "The *Ordo Virtutum*: Ancestor of the English Moralities?" in Audrey Ekdahl Davidson, ed., *The* Ordo Virtutum *of Hildegard of Bingen: Critical Studies* (Kalamazoo, 1992), 31–41. Unlike the well-known vernacular plays, Hildegard's was composed in Latin and sung.

7. The early twelfth-century physician Trota preceded Hildegard, but there is some doubt about the authenticity of the writings ascribed to her. See "Trotula," *The Diseases of Women*, trans. Elizabeth Mason-Hohl (Los Angeles, 1940); John Benton, "Trotula, Women's Problems, and the Professionalization of Medicine in the Middle Ages," *Bulletin of the History of Medicine* 59 (1985): 30–53; Monica Green, "The Development of the *Trotula*," *Revue d'histoire des textes* 26 (1996): 119–203.

8. Recent biographical accounts of Hildegard include Adelgundis Führkötter, *Hildegard von Bingen* (Salzburg, 1972); Peter Dronke, "Hildegard of Bingen," in his *Women Writers of the Middle Ages: A Critical Study of Texts from Perpetua (d. 203) to Marguerite Porete (d. 1310)* (Cambridge, 1984), 144–201; Eduard Gronau, *Hildegard von Bingen, 1098–1179: Prophetische Lehrerin der Kirche an der Schwelle und am Ende der Neuzeit* (Stein-am-Rhein, 1985); Sabina Flanagan, *Hildegard of Bingen, 1098–1179: A Visionary Life* (London, 1989); Elizabeth Dreyer, *Passionate Women: Two Medieval Mystics* (New York, 1989); Heinrich Schipperges, *Hildegard of Bingen*, trans. Eva Jauntzems (New York, 1989); Régine Pernoud, *Hildegarde de Bingen: Conscience inspirée du XIIe siècle* (Monaco, 1994); and Edward Peter Nolan, "Hildegard of Bingen and the *Via Affirmativa*," in his *Cry Out and Write: A Feminine Poetics of Revelation* (New York, 1994), 46–135.

9. For Hildegard's complex attitudes about gender, see Barbara Newman, *Sister of Wisdom: St. Hildegard's Theology of the Feminine* (Berkeley, 1987).

10. On the increasing persecution of heretics and other dissenters in the twelfth century, see R. I. Moore, *The Formation of a Persecuting Society: Power and Deviance in Western Europe, 950–1250* (Oxford, 1987).

11. Godfrey of St. Disibod and Theoderic of Echternach, *Vita Sanctae Hildegardis*, ed. Monika Klaes, CCCM 126 (Turnhout, 1993). The best of several English translations is that of Hugh Feiss, *The Life of the Saintly Hildegard* (Toronto, 1996). For detailed studies of the *Vita* see Barbara Newman, "Three-Part Invention: The Making of the *Vita S. Hildegardis*," in Charles Burnett and Peter Dronke, eds., *Hildegard of Bingen: The Context of Her Thought and Art* (London, 1998), 183–203, and Newman, "Hildegard and Her Hagiographers: The Remaking of Female Sainthood," in Catherine M. Mooney, ed., *Gendered Voices: Medieval Saints and Their Interpreters* (University of Pennsylvania Press, forthcoming).

12. See Klaes, introduction to *Vita*, 77*–78* and 142*–145*. In this edition, page numbers with asterisks refer to Klaes's introduction and numbers without asterisks refer to the text.

13. This unfinished vita by Guibert of Gembloux is printed as part of his letter to the monk Bovo: Guibert of Gembloux, *Epistolae* 38, ed. Albert Derolez, CCCM 66–66a (Turnhout; 1988, 1989), 369–379.

14. As of this writing, two of the three projected volumes have appeared in the critical edition of Hildegard's letters: *Epistolarium*, ed. Lieven Van Acker, CCCM 91–91a (Turnhout, 1991, 1993). Because of the untimely death of Professor Van Acker, the remaining volume will be edited by Monika Klaes. The two published volumes include all of Hildegard's letters to popes, prelates, and monastics. An English version, *The Letters of Hildegard of Bingen*, trans. Joseph Baird and Radd Ehrman, vol. 1 (Oxford, 1994), translates the letters in CCCM 91; three further volumes will follow. For Hildegard's letters to rulers, nobles, and other laity one must still consult the collections in J.-P. Migne, ed., PL 197 (Paris, 1855), and J.-B. Pitra, ed., *Analecta S. Hildegardis* (Monte Cassino, 1882), which do not overlap. Twelve previously unedited letters can be found in Dronke, *Women Writers*, 256–264. Also helpful is the selective German translation by Adelgundis Führkötter, *Hildegard von Bingen: Briefwechsel*, rev. ed. (Salzburg, 1990). For a study of the complex manuscript problems in the transmission of Hildegard's letters, see Lieven Van Acker, "Der Briefwechsel der heiligen Hildegard von Bingen: Vorbemerkungen zu einer kritischen Edition," *Revue bénédictine* 98 (1988): 141–168 and 99 (1989): 118–154.

15. *Mainzer Urkundenbuch*, vol. 2, ed. Peter Acht (Darmstadt, 1968), for the years 1137–1184.

16. *Acta inquisitionis* (1233), in PL 197:131–140.

17. *Vita domnae Juttae* (ca. 1140). The author, a monk of St. Disibod, is anonymous but may have been Volmar, later Hildegard's secretary. A forthcoming translation has been announced by Anna Silvas, *Jutta and Hildegard: The Biographical Sources*.

18. On Hildegard's relationship with Jutta see Miriam Schmitt, "Blessed Jutta of Disibodenberg: Hildegard of Bingen's Magistra and Abbess," *American Benedictine Review* 40 (1989): 170–189; Sabina Flanagan, "Oblation or Enclosure: Reflections on Hildegard of Bingen's Entry into Religion," in Audrey Ekdahl

Davidson, ed., *Wisdom Which Encircles Circles: Papers on Hildegard of Bingen* (Kalamazoo, 1996), 1–14; Julie Hotchin, "Enclosure and Containment: Jutta and Hildegard at the Abbey of St. Disibod," *Magistra* 2 (1996): 103–123; Constant Mews, "Seeing Is Believing: Hildegard of Bingen and the *Life of Jutta, Scivias,* and the *Commentary on the Rule of Benedict,*" *Tjurunga* 51 (1996): 9–40.

19. Marianna Schrader, *Die Herkunft der heiligen Hildegard,* rev. ed. (Mainz, 1981). Of Hildegard's siblings, the eldest brother, Drutwin, was his father's principal heir; Hugh was cantor and precentor at Mainz cathedral and Roric a canon in Tholey; Clementia became a nun at the Rupertsberg. Other sisters were named Irmengard, Odilia, and Jutta. Two siblings unknown to us may have died in childhood. For Hildegard as the tenth (and therefore the "tithe" to be offered to God), see the unfinished vita by Guibert in *Epistolae* 38, p. 370. Among her nephews were two more churchmen, the brothers Wezelin (provost of St. Andreas, Cologne) and Arnold, archbishop of Trier (1169–1183).

20. Henrietta Leyser, *Hermits and the New Monasticism: A Study of Religious Communities in Western Europe, 1000–1150* (London, 1984); Giles Constable, "Renewal and Reform in Religious Life: Concepts and Realities," in *Renaissance and Renewal in the Twelfth Century,* ed. Robert Benson and Giles Constable (Cambridge, Mass., 1982), 37–67. For Hildegard's view of this movement see Kathryn Kerby-Fulton, "A Return to 'the First Dawn of Justice': Hildegard's Visions of Clerical Reform and the Eremitical Life," *American Benedictine Review* 40 (1989): 383–407.

21. *Life of Christina of Markyate,* ed. and trans. C. H. Talbot (Oxford, 1959).

22. At this point there is a discrepancy between the *Vita domnae Juttae* and the *Vita S. Hildegardis.* Godfrey says that "when she was about eight years old, [Hildegard] was enclosed at Mount St. Disibod with Jutta, a pious woman consecrated to God, to be buried with Christ in order to rise with him to immortal glory" (*Vita* 1.1, p. 6). This assertion is extrapolated from Hildegard's briefer remark that she was "offered to God in [her] eighth year" (*Vita* II.2, p. 23). But when Hildegard was eight years old (1105/1106), the Disibodenberg had not yet been rebuilt. The *Vita Juttae* resolves the discrepancy, explaining that Jutta spent three years with the widow Uda and settled at St. Disibod when she was twenty (*Vita Juttae* 3, pp. 175–176). For a longer but thirdhand account of Jutta's religious life see Guibert's vita: *Epistolae* 38, pp. 370–375. John Van Engen in "Abbess," p. 32 in this volume, argues that in spite of her parents' vow of oblation, Hildegard remained at her family home and did not enter religious life until she joined Jutta at the age of fourteen.

23. Yet another discrepancy occurs here. According to the *Vita Juttae,* Jutta was enclosed "with two sisters" (p. 176), but according to the *Annales S. Disibodi,* "this holy woman was enclosed on November 1 along with three others: Hildegard and two girls of her own name [Jutta], whom she strove zealously to train in holy virtues as long as she lived." MGH.SS 17, ed. Georgius Waitz (Hannover, 1861), 25. Guibert of Gembloux mentions only one other girl named Jutta, the niece of the recluse: *Epistolae* 38, p. 372.

24. Hotchin, "Enclosure and Containment," 108n; *Vita Juttae* 3, p. 176. This information is confirmed in *Octo Lectiones* (a set of liturgical readings for Hildegard's feast day), ed. Klaes, in *Vita,* p. 76.

25. Julie Hotchin, "Images and Their Places: Hildegard of Bingen and Her Communities," *Tjurunga* 49 (1996): 23–38; Wolfgang Seibrich, "Geschichte des Klosters Disibodenberg," in Anton Brück, ed., *Hildegard von Bingen, 1179–1979: Festschrift zum 800. Todestag der Heiligen* (Mainz, 1979), 55–76. On recent excavations at the site, see Günther Stanzl, *Die Klosterruine Disibodenberg: Neue baugeschichtliche und archäologische Untersuchungen* (Worms, 1992).

26. Führkötter, *Hildegard von Bingen* (1972), 11.

27. Franz Felten, "Frauenklöster und -stifte im Rheinland im 12. Jahrhundert: Ein Beitrag zur Geschichte der Frauen in der religiösen Bewegung des hohen Mittelalters," in Stefan Weinfurter, ed., *Reformidee und Reformpolitik im spätsalisch-frühstaufischen Reich* (Mainz, 1992), 270–275.

28. Hotchin, "Enclosure and Containment," 109–113.

29. *Vita* II.2, p. 24. Godfrey says that "beyond simple knowledge of the Psalms, [Hildegard] received no human instruction in the art of literature or music, although her extant writings are not few, and her volumes not meager": *Vita* I.1, p. 6.

30. *Vita Juttae*, pp. 174, 175, 179, 183.

31. Hildegard used self-descriptions like *indocta* and *paupercula* ("a poor little woman") frequently. In the *Scivias* preface she says that by divine inspiration she understood the meaning of the Scriptures but not their grammar ("non autem interpretationem uerborum textus eorum nec diuisionem syllabarum nec cognitionem casuum aut temporum"). *Scivias*, p. 4; cf. note 29 above, this chapter.

32. Some adventurous girls disguised themselves as boys in order to get an education. Hildegard herself is said to have met one such girl, Gertrude; she saw through her disguise and warned the girl to repent and resume her female clothing since she had not long to live. Gertrude consented but disfigured her pretty face to avoid being harrassed by men. *Acta* 3, PL 197:133ab. See also Valerie Hotchkiss, *Clothes Make the Man: Female Cross Dressing in Medieval Europe* (New York, 1996).

33. *The Letters of Abelard and Heloise,* trans. Betty Radice (Harmondsworth, 1974).

34. Herrad of Hohenbourg, *Hortus deliciarum*, reconstructed by Rosalie Green, Michael Evans, et al., 2 vols. (London, 1979). The original manuscript of this priceless work was destroyed in the Franco-Prussian War of 1870.

35. On Hildegard's Latin see Peter Dronke, "Hildegard of Bingen as Poetess and Dramatist," in *Poetic Individuality in the Middle Ages: New Departures in Poetry, 1000–1150* (Oxford, 1970), 150–179, and Newman, *Sister of Wisdom,* 22–27.

36. On the extent of Hildegard's reading see Hans Liebeschütz, *Das allegorische Weltbild der heiligen Hildegard von Bingen* (Leipzig, 1930); Bertha Widmer, *Heilsordnung und Zeitgeschehen in der Mystik Hildegards von Bingen* (Basel, 1955); Christel Meier, *"Scientia Divinorum Operum:* Zu Hildegards von Bingen visionär-künstlerischer Rezeption Eriugenas," in Werner Beierwaltes, ed., *Eriugena Redivivus* (Heidelberg, 1987), 89–141; and Peter Dronke, introduction to LDO, xiii–xxxv.

37. On the prophetic-visionary style as a literary mode, see Barbara Newman, "Hildegard of Bingen: Visions and Validation," *Church History* 54 (1985): 163–175; Kathryn Kerby–Fulton, "The Visionary Prophecy of Hildegard of Bingen," in *Reformist Apocalypticism and Piers Plowman* (Cambridge, 1990), 26–75; Christel Meier, "Prophetentum als literarische Existenz: Hildegard von Bingen (1098–1179), Ein Portrait," in Gisela Brinker-Gabler, ed., *Deutsche Literatur von Frauen* (Munich, 1988), 76–87.

38. "Not only did everyone living in that region devoutly obey her salutary warnings and advice, but pilgrims and guests arriving from all parts, people of every station—noble and nonnoble, rich and poor—sought Lady Jutta the recluse alone, hearkened to her alone as a heavenly oracle." *Vita Juttae* 5, p. 178.

39. *Vita* II.2, pp. 22–23.

40. *Acta* 7, PL 197:136b.

41. *Vita Juttae* 9, pp. 185–186.

42. *Vita Juttae* 8–9, pp. 183, 186.

43. *Vita Juttae*, prologue, p. 174.

44. *Vita* II.2, p. 24, and *Scivias*, preface, pp. 3–6.

45. Elizabeth Petroff, ed., *Medieval Women's Visionary Literature* (Oxford, 1986), 42–44.

46. The *Scivias* author portrait, reproduced in the CCCM edition and elsewhere, shows only Hildegard and Volmar. The initial author portrait in the LDO includes a nun with Hildegard, although Richardis had died long before this book was written. See the essay "Artist" by Madeline Caviness, chap. 6 in this volume.

47. Petroff, *Medieval Women's Visionary Literature;* Ernst Benz, *Die Vision: Erfahrungsformen und Bilderwelt* (Stuttgart, 1969); Peter Dinzelbacher, *Vision und Visionsliteratur im Mittelalter* (Stuttgart, 1981).

48. Hildegard to Guibert, *Epistolarium* 103r, pp. 258–265; for partial translations see Dronke, *Women Writers,* 168–169, and Newman, *Sister of Wisdom,* 6–7 (cited here).

49. Dronke, *Women Writers,* 146. Jeffrey Hamburger points out the male bias inherent in these hierarchies, since both the devalued forms of visionary experience and artistic images were associated with the piety of women: *The Rothschild Canticles: Art and Mysticism in Flanders and the Rhineland circa 1300* (New Haven, 1990), 3–5.

50. David Baumgardt, "The Concept of Mysticism: Analysis of a Letter Written by Hildegard of Bingen to Guibert of Gembloux," *Review of Religion* 12 (1948): 277–286.

51. Kent Kraft, "The Eye Sees More Than the Heart Knows: The Visionary Cosmology of Hildegard of Bingen" (Ph.D. diss., University of Wisconsin, 1977), chap. 2.

52. Charles Singer, "The Scientific Views and Visions of Saint Hildegard," *Studies in the History and Method of Science* (Oxford, 1917), 1:1–55. For more recent exponents of the migraine theory, see Oliver Sacks, *Migraine: Understanding a Common Disorder* (Berkeley, 1985), 106–108; Flanagan, *A Visionary Life,* 199–211 (a very strong version of the thesis); and the essay "Artist" by Madeline Caviness, chapter 6 in this volume.

53. Cf. Kerby-Fulton, *Reformist Apocalypticism*, 56–57.

54. See Michael Gervers, ed., *The Second Crusade and the Cistercians* (New York, 1992).

55. *Epistolarium* 1–1r, pp. 3–7; *Letters*, pp. 27–32.

56. Dronke, *Women Writers*, 148–149. Eugene approved both Hildegard's *Scivias* and Bernard Silvestris's *Cosmographia* in 1147–1148. Theologians judged heretical in the same decade included Peter Abelard, William of Conches, and Gilbert of Poitiers, all vigorously opposed by Bernard of Clairvaux. On papal review of controversial books, see Herbert Grundmann, "Zur Vita S. Gerlaci Eremitae," reprinted in *Ausgewählte Aufsätze*, vol. 1 (Stuttgart, 1976), 187–194.

57. *Vita* I.4 and II.2, pp. 9, 24; cf. Newman, "Hildegard and Her Hagiographers." For a contemporary account of the council of Trier (with no mention of Hildegard), see Balderic, *Gesta Alberonis Archiepiscopi* c. 23, MGH.SS 8 (Hannover, 1848), 254–255.

58. Jacques de Vitry, *The Life of Marie d'Oignies*, trans. Margot King, rev. ed. (Toronto, 1993). For Hildegard's influence on holy women of the Low Countries, see Ernest McDonnell, *The Beguines and Beghards in Medieval Culture* (New Brunswick, N.J., 1954), 281–298.

59. Compare *Vita* II.5, pp. 27–28 (Hildegard's account) with I.5, pp. 10–11 (Godfrey's version). The monks' lingering animosity is indicated by the failure of the *Annals of St. Disibod* to mention Hildegard at all except in the notice of Jutta's death.

60. Hotchin, "Images and Their Places," 29.

61. The accusation may have had some force in that another member of the von Stade family then at the Rupertsberg, Adelheid (granddaughter of the marchioness and niece of the nun Richardis), was at the same time elected abbess of the even more prestigious foundation of Gandersheim, although she was still a child.

62. The sole document that refers to Hildegard as *abbatissa* is a charter of privileges granted by Frederick Barbarossa in 1163. Acht, *Mainzer Urkundenbuch*, no. 274 (vol. 2, part 1, pp. 484–486); Felten, "Frauenklöster," 273–275.

63. For detailed and differently nuanced accounts of the "Richardis affair," see Dronke, *Women Writers*, 154–159; Flanagan, *A Visionary Life*, 180–184; Nolan, *Cry Out and Write*, 73–94. Nolan translates all the numerous letters relating to this affair, but the version above is from Dronke, 156–157.

64. Rosemary Curb and Nancy Manahan, eds., *Lesbian Nuns: Breaking Silence* (Tallahassee, 1985); Judith Brown, *Immodest Acts: The Life of a Lesbian Nun in Renaissance Italy* (New York, 1986); E. Ann Matter, "Discourses of Desire: Sexuality and Christian Women's Visionary Narratives," *Journal of Homosexuality* 18 (1989): 119–131.

65. *Ordo virtutum*, 147–184. See Newman, *Sister of Wisdom*, 222–224, for the translation given here and the connection of this passage with Richardis.

66. See Hildegard's letters 5 and 7 (oblique intercessions for Henry) and 19 (a scathing rebuke to him after his downfall), in *Letters*, pp. 36–37, 39–41, 71.

67. *Epistolarium* 75 (to the abbot), pp. 162–163, and 195r (to her nuns), pp. 445–447; trans. in *Letters*, pp. 162–163, and Dronke, *Women Writers*, 153.

68. "Arriving at [St. Disibod's] Mountain, she explained why she had been compelled to come and secured the freedom of her dwelling place, with the lands belonging to it, from the brothers of that monastery—leaving them the larger portion of the possessions that had been given to the house with the reception of sisters, along with a substantial sum of money, lest any just cause for complaint should remain": *Vita* I.7, pp. 13–14.

69. In addition to Dronke's bilingual edition of the *Ordo virtutum* in *Nine Medieval Latin Plays*, there is a performance edition with music, ed. Audrey Ekdahl Davidson, *The "Ordo virtutum" of Hildegard of Bingen* (Kalamazoo, 1985). See also Pamela Sheingorn, "The Virtues of Hildegard's *Ordo Virtutum;* or, It *Was* a Woman's World," in Davidson, ed., *The* Ordo Virtutum . . . *Critical Studies*, 43–62, and the essay "Composer and Dramatist" by Margot Fassler, chapter 8 in this volume.

70. *Vita S. Ruperti*, PL 197:1081–1094; excerpts translated in Sabina Flanagan, *Secrets of God: Writings of Hildegard of Bingen* (Boston, 1996), 141–145. Aside from Hildegard's work, there are no other early sources on St. Rupert of Bingen, who should not be confused with the better-known St. Rupert, bishop of Salzburg.

71. *Symphonia*. The songs to St. Rupert are nos. 46–49. For the music, see Pudentiana Barth, Maria-Immaculata Ritscher, and Joseph Schmidt-Görg, eds., *Hildegard von Bingen: Lieder* (Salzburg, 1969), and Christopher Page, ed., *Abbess Hildegard of Bingen: Sequences and Hymns* (Newton Abbot, Devon, 1983).

72. Peter Abelard, *Hymnarius Paraclitensis*, ed. Joseph Szövérffy, 2 vols. (Albany, 1975); Adam of St. Victor, *Sämtliche Sequenzen: Lateinisch und deutsch*, trans. Franz Wellner (Munich, 1955).

73. Newman, introduction to *Symphonia;* Marianne Richert Pfau, "Music and Text in Hildegard's Antiphons," in *Symphonia*, pp. 74–94; Peter Dronke, "The Composition of Hildegard of Bingen's *Symphonia*," *Sacris Erudiri* 19 (1969–1970): 381–393; Dronke, "Hildegard of Bingen as Poetess and Dramatist"; and the essay "Composer and Dramatist" by Margot Fassler in this volume.

74. Darrel Amundsen, *Medicine, Society, and Faith in the Ancient and Medieval Worlds* (Baltimore, 1996).

75. Schrader and Führkötter, *Echtheit*, 54; Irmgard Müller, "Zur Verfasserfrage der medizinisch-naturkundlichen Schriften Hildegards von Bingen," in Margot Schmidt, ed., *Tiefe des Gotteswissens—Schönheit der Sprachgestalt bei Hildegard von Bingen* (Stuttgart, 1995), 1–17; Laurence Moulinier, *Le Manuscrit perdu à Strasbourg: Enquête sur l'oeuvre scientifique de Hildegarde* (Paris, 1995); and the essay "Medical Writer" by Florence Eliza Glaze in this volume.

76. The existing editions of Hildegard's scientific works, though unsatisfactory, may remain standard for the foreseeable future, as critical editions are under way but not expected soon. In the meantime see Charles Daremberg and F. A. Reuss, eds., *Subtilitatum diversarum naturarum creaturarum libri novem [Physica]*, in PL 197:1118–1352; Paul Kaiser, ed., *Causae et curae* (Leipzig, 1903). A German translation of *Causae et curae* by Manfred Pawlik, entitled *Heilwissen* (Augsburg, 1989), is the basis of Hildegard of Bingen, *Holistic*

Healing, trans. Patrick Madigan (Collegeville, Minn., 1994)—a translation that cannot be recommended. For more trustworthy English selections see Flanagan, trans., *Secrets of God*, 89–118, and Dronke, *Women Writers*, 171–183.

77. This view has been advanced by Müller, "Zur Verfasserfrage." For an alternative explanation see Florence Eliza Glaze, "Medical Writer," chapter 7 in this volume, 146–147.

78. Laurence Moulinier, "Les Merveilles de la nature vues par Hildegarde de Bingen (XIIe siècle)," in *Miracles, prodiges, et merveilles au Moyen Âge*, XXVe Congrès de la Société des Historiens Médiévistes de l'Enseignement Supérieur (Paris, 1995), 115–131.

79. Joan Cadden, "It Takes All Kinds: Sexuality and Gender Differences in Hildegard of Bingen's 'Book of Compound Medicine,' " *Traditio* 40 (1984): 149–174; Bernhard Scholz, "Hildegard von Bingen on the Nature of Woman," *American Benedictine Review* 31 (1980): 361–383; Dronke, *Women Writers*, 180–183; Sabina Flanagan, "Hildegard and the Humors: Medieval Theories of Illness and Personality," in Andrew Weiner and Leonard Kaplan, eds., *Madness, Melancholy, and the Limits of the Self* (Madison, Wisc., 1996), 14–23.

80. Melitta Weiss-Amer, "Die Physica Hildegards von Bingen als Quelle für das Kochbuch Meister Eberhards," *Sudhoffs Archiv* 76 (1992): 87–96; Barbara Fehringer, ed., *Das Speyerer Kräuterbuch mit den Heilpflanzen Hildegards von Bingen* (Würzburg, 1994).

81. *Lingua ignota (Wörterbuch der Unbekannten Sprache)*, ed. Marie-Louise Portmann and Alois Odermatt (Basel, 1986). A fragment of this text can be found in Pitra, 496–502. See also *Symphonia* 68, pp. 252–253, 316–317; Gouguenheim, *La Sibylle du Rhin*, 91–92, 159; and Jeffrey Schnapp, "Virgin Words: Hildegard of Bingen's *Lingua ignota* and the Development of Imaginary Languages Ancient to Modern," *Exemplaria* 3 (1991): 267–298.

82. John Van Engen, "Letters, Schools, and Written Culture in the Eleventh and Twelfth Centuries," in Johannes Fried, ed., *Dialektik und Rhetorik im früheren und hohen Mittelalter* (Munich, 1996), 97–132.

83. Cf. Honorius Augustodunensis, *De vita claustrali*, PL 172:1247–1248.

84. For a good discussion of the familial and personal motives that might bear on a woman's entry into monastic life see Penelope Johnson, *Equal in Monastic Profession: Religious Women in Medieval France* (Chicago, 1991), 18–34.

85. Newman, *Sister of Wisdom*, 16–17, 58–61; Sheingorn, "The Virtues." The most exhaustive treatment of Hildegard's ethics to date is Gabriele Lautenschläger, *Hildegard von Bingen: Die theologische Grundlegung ihrer Ethik und Spiritualität* (Stuttgart, 1993).

86. LVM; *Book of the Rewards of Life*, trans. Bruce Hozeski (New York, 1994).

87. See Lautenschläger, *Hildegard von Bingen*, 154–173, 352–364, and Elisabeth Gössmann, "*Scientia Boni et Mali*: Science and Faith in Hildegard of Bingen," in *Hildegard of Bingen: Four Papers* (Toronto, 1995), 38–46.

88. "With a feeling of due reverence we have received the *Book of Life's Merits*, composed by your holy mother and sent to us by your charity, and we deem it worthy of the highest admiration. First the monks of Villers feasted

richly on its marvelous doctrine at their table, and now we drink of it with delight at the reading of Conferences": Letter of Guibert to the Rupertsberg nuns, *Epistolae* 23, p. 253.

89. John T. McNeill and Helena Gamer, trans., *Medieval Handbooks of Penance* (New York, 1938; reprint, 1990).

90. Jacques Le Goff, *The Birth of Purgatory*, trans. Arthur Goldhammer (Chicago, 1984).

91. Barbara Newman, "Hildegard of Bingen and the 'Birth of Purgatory,' " *Mystics Quarterly* 19 (1993): 90–97.

92. *Letters* 77r, p. 169; *Epistolarium* 223r, p. 491; *Vita* II.2, p. 22; Heinrich Schipperges, ed., "Ein unveröffentlichtes Hildegard-Fragment," chap. 4, para. 28, *Sudhoffs Archiv für Geschichte der Medizin* 40 (1956): 71.

93. Uta-Renate Blumenthal, *The Investiture Controversy: Church and Monarchy from the Ninth to the Twelfth Century* (Philadelphia, 1988).

94. Peter Munz, *Frederick Barbarossa: A Study in Medieval Politics* (Ithaca, N.Y., 1969); Marshall Baldwin, *Alexander III and the Twelfth Century* (Glen Rock, N.J., 1968).

95. "We make known to Your Holiness that the things you predicted to us, when we asked you to come before our presence at Ingelheim, we now have in hand." Letter from Frederick to Hildegard, epistle 27 in PL 197:186bc.

96. Letter to Werner of Kirchheim, *Epistolarium* 149r, pp. 333–337; trans. in Newman, *Sister of Wisdom*, 241–242. See also the essay "Prophet and Reformer" by Kathryn Kerby-Fulton, chapter 4 in this volume.

97. Jean Duvernoy, *La Religion des Cathares* (Toulouse, 1976); Bernard Hamilton, *Monastic Reform, Catharism, and the Crusades (900–1300)* (London, 1979).

98. Hildegard, "De Catharis," in Pitra, 348–351; Raoul Manselli, "Amicizia spirituale ed azione pastorale nella Germania del sècolo XII: Ildegarda di Bingen, Elisabetta ed Ecberto di Schönau contro l'eresia catara," *Studi e materiali di storia delle religioni* 38 (1967), fasc. 1–2:302–313; Anne Clark, *Elisabeth of Schönau: A Twelfth-Century Visionary* (Philadelphia, 1992), 22–25; Beverly Kienzle, "*Operatrix in vinea Domini*: Hildegard's Public Preaching and Polemics against the Cathars," *Heresis* 26–27 (1996): 43–56.

99. For the Cologne sermon see *Letters* 15r, pp. 54–65; the Trier sermon is *Epistolarium* 223r, pp. 490–496. See the essay "Prophet and Reformer" by Kathryn Kerby-Fulton in this volume.

100. Charles Czarski, "The Prophecies of St. Hildegard of Bingen" (Ph.D. diss., University of Kentucky, 1982); Kerby-Fulton, *Reformist Apocalypticism*.

101. 1 Tim. 2.12. Most biblical scholars now ascribe this letter to a disciple of St. Paul, but its authenticity was unchallenged in the Middle Ages and it was frequently cited as a justification for the silencing of women. See A. J. Minnis, "*De impedimento sexus*: Women's Bodies and Medieval Impediments to Female Ordination," in Peter Biller and A. J. Minnis, eds., *Medieval Theology and the Natural Body* (Rochester N.Y., 1997): 109–139.

102. See Gouguenheim, *La Sibylle du Rhin*, 174–175; Konrad Bund, "Die Prophetin, ein Dichter und die Niederlassung der Bettelorden in Köln," *Mittellateinisches Jahrbuch* 23 (1988): 169–260; Flanagan, *A Visionary Life*, 175.

103. Bernard of Clairvaux, sermon 65, *On the Song of Songs, Vol. III,* trans. Kilian Walsh and Irene Edmonds (Kalamazoo, 1979), 184. On relationships between monks and nuns in the High Middle Ages, see John Nichols and Lillian T. Shank, eds., *Distant Echoes: Medieval Religious Women,* vol. 1 (Kalamazoo, 1984), and Jo Ann McNamara, *Sisters in Arms: Catholic Nuns through Two Millennia* (Cambridge, Mass., 1996), 233–323.

104. M.-D. Chenu, "Monks, Canons, and Laymen in Search of the Apostolic Life" and "The Evangelical Awakening," in *Nature, Man, and Society in the Twelfth Century,* trans. Jerome Taylor and Lester K. Little (Chicago, 1968), 202–269.

105. *Letters* 52–52r, pp. 127–130; Alfred Haverkamp, "Tenxwind von Andernach und Hildegard von Bingen: Zwei 'Weltanschauungen' in der Mitte des 12. Jahrhunderts," in Lutz Fenske, Werner Rösener, and Thomas Zotz, eds., *Institutionen, Kultur und Gesellschaft im Mittelalter: Festschrift für Joseph Fleckenstein* (Sigmaringen, 1984), 515–548; and the essay "Abbess" by John Van Engen, pp. 36–37 in this volume.

106. Adelgundis Führkötter, trans., *Das Leben der heiligen Hildegard* (Düsseldorf, 1968), 132–134.

107. On the history of these communities, see Agape Menne, "Vom geistlichen Leben in Kloster der hl. Hildegard zu St. Rupertsberg-Eibingen," *Erbe und Auftrag* 41 (1965): 305–316; Maria Brede, "Die Klöster der hl. Hildegard Rupertsberg und Eibingen," in Anton Brück, ed., *Hildegard von Bingen, 1179–1979: Festschrift zum 800. Todestag der Heiligen* (Mainz, 1979), 77–94.

108. *Vita* III.20–22, pp. 55–65; Flanagan, *A Visionary Life,* 166–170; Newman, "Three-Part Invention."

109. For the ceremony see Peter Dronke, "Problemata Hildegardiana," *Mittellateinisches Jahrbuch* 16 (1981): 119–122, 127–129.

110. On the phenomenon of "demon preachers," of whom Sigewize is the first on record, see Barbara Newman, "Possessed by the Spirit: Devout Women, Demoniacs, and the Apostolic Life in the Thirteenth Century," *Speculum* 73 (July 1998).

111. The English version by Robert Cunningham in *Hildegard of Bingen's Book of Divine Works, with Letters and Songs,* ed. Matthew Fox (Santa Fe, N.M., 1987), is an abridged translation made from a prior German translation, itself abridged; and the English text has been further modified in accord with its editor's theological views. It is to be hoped that since the long-awaited critical edition has now appeared, a complete and accurate English translation will follow.

112. Monika Klaes, "Zur Schau und Deutung des Kosmos bei Hildegard von Bingen," in Adelgundis Führkötter, ed., *Kosmos und Mensch aus der Sicht Hildegards von Bingen* (Mainz, 1987), 37–115; Elisabeth Gössmann, "Hildegard of Bingen's Male-Female Divinity and Macro-Microcosmic Anthropology," in *Hildegard of Bingen: Four Papers,* 17–28.

113. LDO I.1.2, pp. 47–49; translation from Newman, *Sister of Wisdom,* 69–70. "Caritas" is grammatically feminine and appears as a distinctly female

figure elsewhere in Hildegard's works, including later visions of the LDO. In this case, however, the image is less strongly gendered (*quasi hominis formam*) and represents not a Virtue but the Trinity or Godhead as such (*divinitas*). See figure 16. On the meaning of "fiery life," see the essay "Religious Thinker" by Constant Mews, chapter 3 in this volume.

114. For provocative comments on Hildegard's literary method, see Nolan, *Cry Out and Write*, 111–119; on her biblical exegesis, see Angela Carlevaris, "*Scripturas subtiliter inspicere subtiliterque excribrare*," in Schmidt, ed., *Tiefe des Gotteswissens*, 29–48.

115. LDO III.5.38, pp. 462–463.

116. The anthology of Hildegard's prophecies is the *Pentachronon* or *Speculum futurorum temporum* by Gebeno of Eberbach. The text, which survives in several hundred manuscripts, remains unedited except for fragments in Pitra, 483–488. See the essay "Prophet and Reformer" by Kathryn Kerby-Fulton, chapter 4 in this volume.

117. On her working methods, see Albert Derolez, "Die Bedeutung der neuen Edition von Hildegards *Liber divinorum operum*," in Schmidt, ed., *Tiefe des Gotteswissens*, 19–28.

118. Guibert of Gembloux, *Epistolae* 18, 26, and 38, pp. 225–234, 270–294, 367–369.

119. Wiesbaden, Landesbibliothek, Hs.2. On this thirty-three-pound, twelve-by-eighteen-inch manuscript, admired by Goethe among others, see Schrader and Führkötter, *Echtheit*, 154–179, and the introductions to the CCCM editions of Hildegard's works.

120. For the questions, Hildegard's answers, and related correspondence, see PL 197:1037–1054; *Epistolarium* 109r, pp. 269–271; Guibert, *Epistolae* 19–26, pp. 235–257, 264–269, 291–294; and Anne Clark Bartlett, "Commentary, Polemic, and Prophecy in Hildegard of Bingen's *Solutiones triginta octo quaestionum*," *Viator* 23 (1992):153–165.

121. *Letters* 23–24r, pp. 76–83; *Acta* 6, PL 197:135b; Dronke, *Women Writers*, 196–199; Flanagan, *A Visionary Life*, 184–190; Nolan, *Cry Out and Write*, 94–110.

122. Edward Krehbiel, *The Interdict: Its History and Its Operation* (Washington, D.C., 1909).

123. *Epistolarium* 23, pp. 61–66; *Letters*, pp. 76–80. On Hildegard's theology of music, see *Symphonia*, introduction, 17–27.

124. *Vita* III.27, pp. 69–70.

125. Aviad Kleinberg, *Prophets in Their Own Country: Living Saints and the Making of Sainthood in the Later Middle Ages* (Chicago, 1992), 21–39.

126. Newman, "Hildegard and Her Hagiographers."

127. André Vauchez, *La Sainteté en Occident aux derniers siècles du moyen âge d'après les procès de canonisation et les documents hagiographiques* (Rome, 1981), 295–300, 308, 316.

128. Stephan Hilpisch, "Der Kult der heiligen Hildegard," *Pastor bonus* 45 (1934): 118–133; Helmut Hinkel, "St. Hildegards Verehrung im Bistum Mainz," in Brück, ed., *Hildegard von Bingen*, 385–411.

CHAPTER 2: "ABBESS"

1. *Epistolarium* 195, pp. 443–445.

2. *Epistolarium* 195r, pp. 445–447.

3. Especially in *visiones* 2, 3, 4: *Vita* II.5, II.7, II.12, pp. 27–30, 31–32, 37–38.

4. For women's houses between 850 and 1050, an understudied topic, see the useful summary remarks by Michel Parisse, "Der Anteil der lothringischen Benediktinerinnen an der monastischen Bewegung des 10. und 11. Jahrhunderts," in *Religiöse Frauenbewegung und mystische Frömmigkeit im Mittelalter*, ed. Peter Dinzelbacher and Dieter Bauer (Cologne, 1988), 83–97.

5. *Vita* II.2, pp. 22–23; Guibert of Gembloux, *Epistolae*, ed. Albert Derolez et al., CCCM 66–66a (Turnhout, 1988, 1989), no. 38, p. 372.

6. For this crucial date, see now *Vita Juttae* 3, p. 176, esp. n. 156.

7. For the most recent effort to sort out the contradictions, see Constant J. Mews, "Seeing Is Believing: Hildegard of Bingen and the *Life of Jutta, Scivias,* and the *Commentary on the Rule of Benedict*," *Tjurunga* 51 (1996): 12–17. For other views see Miriam Schmitt, "Blessed Jutta of Disibodenberg: Hildegard of Bingen's Magistra and Abbess," *American Benedictine Review* 40 (1989): 170–189; Sabina Flanagan, *Hildegard of Bingen, 1098–1179: A Visionary Life* (London, 1989), 22–31; and Julie Hotchin, "Enclosure and Containment: Jutta and Hildegard at St. Disibod," *Magistra* 2 (1996): 103–123.

8. Guibert speaks of a "locum prouisum" (place provided) by God when the family at Bermersheim learned what the count of Sponheim had arranged for his sister.

9. *Vita Juttae* 2–3, pp. 175–177.

10. *Scivias* II.5.46, p. 215.

11. *Scivias* II.5.45, p. 214.

12. *Scivias* II.5.10, pp. 184–185.

13. Heinrich Büttner, "Studien zur Geschichte von Disibodenberg," *Studien und Mitteilungen zur Geschichte des Benediktinerordens und seiner Zweige* 52 (1934): 1–46; Wolfgang Seibrich, "Geschichte des Klosters Disibodenberg," in *Hildegard von Bingen, 1179–1979*, ed. Anton Brück (Mainz, 1979), 55–75.

14. *Annales sancti Disibodi*, anno 1138, anno 1143: MGH.SS 17, pp. 25, 26.

15. J. May, *Die Heilige Hildegard von Bingen* (Kempten, 1911), 18.

16. "carcerem in quo recluderetur sibi construi fecit . . ." Thus Guibert, *Epistolae* 38, pp. 371–374, who was never there but may have discussed the site with Hildegard.

17. *Vita Juttae* 4, 8, pp. 177–178, 184.

18. *Vita Juttae* 5, pp. 178–179.

19. Guibert, *Epistolae* 38, p. 374.

20. *Vita Juttae* 8, pp. 183–184.

21. *Vita Juttae* 8, p. 185.

22. *Epistolarium* 78, p. 175.

23. *Vita Juttae*, prologue, p. 174.

24. *Vita Juttae*, prologue, epilogue, pp. 174, 187.

25. *Vita* II.2, p. 24.

26. Guibert, *Epistolae* 38, p. 375.

27. Guibert, *Epistolae* 38, p. 375.

28. *Epistolarium* 52, pp. 126, 129–130. See Alfred Haverkamp, "Tenxwind von Andernach und Hildegard von Bingen: Zwei 'Weltanschauungen' in der Mitte des 12. Jahrhunderts," in *Institutionen, Kultur und Gesellschaft im Mittelalter* (Sigmaringen, 1984), 515–548.

29. *Symphonia* 33, p. 162.

30. *Symphonia* 55, p. 218.

31. *Symphonia* 40, p. 176.

32. *Epistolarium* 52, 52r, pp. 126, 128–129.

33. *Vita* I.5, p. 10.

34. *Vita* II.5, pp. 27–28.

35. *Epistolarium* 195r, p. 445; compare *Vita* II.5, p. 27.

36. See Maria Laetitia Brede, "Die Klöster der heiligen Hildegard Rupertsberg und Eibingen," in Brück, ed., *Hildegard*, 77–94, with literature in notes 13 and 16 above, this chapter.

37. *Vita* II.5, p. 28; on the marchioness Richardis of Stade, see Marianna Schrader and Adelgundis Führkötter, *Die Echtheit des Schrifttums der hl. Hildegard von Bingen* (Cologne, 1956), 131 ff.

38. *Urkundenbuch zur Geschichte der mittelrheinischen Territorien*, vol. 2 (Koblenz, 1865), no. 14, p. 366. On this document, see Schrader and Führkötter, *Die Echtheit*, 28–32.

39. *Mainzer Urkundenbuch*, ed. Peter Acht (Darmstadt, 1968), vol. 2, no. 230.

40. *Vita* II.5, pp. 28–29.

41. *Urkundenbuch zur Geschichte*, 366, about their first acquisitions: "Ea vero quae modo possidemus aliqua emimus, aliqua pro animabus fidelium collata sunt."

42. *Mainzer Urkundenbuch* no. 175, pp. 232–234. On the date, see the commentary in *Vita* 103* n. 179.

43. *Vita* II.5, pp. 28–29.

44. Guibert, *Epistolae*, 38, pp. 368–369.

45. *Vita* II.5, p. 30.

46. *Vita* II.5, pp. 29–30.

47. Schrader and Führkötter, *Die Echtheit*, 135.

48. *Epistolarium* 12, p. 28.

49. *Epistolarium* 18r, p. 54.

50. *Epistolarium* 5, p. 13.

51. *Vita* II.7, p. 31.

52. PL 197:1065–1066. The exact shape of this letter, the preface to her *Explanatio symboli sancti Athanasii*, is unclear since it reproduces in part the letter (*Epistolarium* 195r) with which this essay began. This may simply reinforce the importance to her of its language about the house and spiritual care since medieval authors often repeated parts of letters on different occasions.

53. *Epistolarium* 75, pp. 162–163.

54. *Vita* I.7, pp. 13–14.

55. *Mainzer Urkundenbuch*, nn. 230, 231.

56. MGH: Diplomata Frederici I 398.

57. Guibert, *Epistolae* 38, pp. 368–369.

58. Brede, "Die Klöster der hl. Hildegard," 82.

59. *Acta* 8, PL 197:136.

60. Compare the essay "Poet" by Barbara Newman, p. 191 in this volume.

61. *Vita S. Disibodi* 25, PL 197:1105.

62. *Vita S. Disibodi* 22–24, PL 197:1103–1104. See n. 79 below, this chapter, for similar passages describing life in Hildegard's own community.

63. Ibid. 5–6, 10, 14–15: PL 197:1097–1098, 1099, 1101.

64. Ibid. 23, PL 197:1104.

65. Ibid. 30–31, PL 197:1106–1107.

66. Guibert, *Epistolae* 38, p. 368.

67. For Hildegard's role as "abbess to the world" see the essay "Correspondent" by Joan Ferrante, pp. 91 and 100 in this volume.

68. *Epistolarium* 76, 76r, pp. 163–166.

69. *Epistolarium* 77r, pp. 168–175.

70. Scivias II.5.41, p. 209.

71. *Epistolarium* 216, p. 475.

72. *Epistolarium* 15r, pp. 37–38.

73. *Epistolarium* 50r, p. 123 (to an abbess thinking about resigning her charge).

74. *Epistolarium* 3, 5, pp. 9, 12.

75. *Epistolarium* 156r, p. 350. See the essay "Correspondent" by Joan Ferrante, p. 98 in this volume.

76. *Epistolarium* 214, p. 472.

77. *Epistolarium* 22r, p. 60.

78. *Epistolarium* 118, p. 291.

79. *Vita* II.12, pp. 37–38.

80. *Epistolarium* 106r, pp. 266–267, where she assimilates the religious to angels and then to knights.

81. *Epistolarium* 94r, pp. 249–250.

82. *Epistolarium* 110r, p. 273.

83. *Epistolarium* 71, p. 156.

84. *Epistolarium* 192, pp. 436–437.

85. *Epistolarium* 59, pp. 139–140.

86. *Epistolarium* 77r, p. 171.

87. *Epistolarium* 106r, pp. 266–267.

88. *Scivias* II.5.20, p. 193.

89. *Regulae S. Benedicti Explanatio*, PL 197:1055.

90. *Epistolarium* 95, pp. 250–251.

91. *Epistolarium* 77r, p. 173.

92. PL 197:1055.

93. See Kassius Hallinger, *Gorze-Kluny* (1950–1951), 257–263, who was inclined to associate Hildegard more with new Cluniac impulses (especially Hirsau) rather than traditional imperial monasticism but regarded her foundation and observances finally as sui generis.

94. PL 197:1055; *Scivias* II.5.20, p. 193.

95. PL 197:1063.

96. PL 197:1061.

97. See the essay "Composer and Dramatist" by Margot Fassler, p. 149 in this volume.

98. *Epistolarium* 23, pp. 62–65.

99. Barbara Newman, *Sister of Wisdom: St. Hildegard's Theology of the Feminine* (Berkeley, 1987), is good throughout on the nature of these virtues.

100. Thus *Epistolarium* 85r/b, pp. 206–208, and often.

101. *Epistolarium* 32r, p. 90.

102. *Epistolarium* 174r, pp. 396–398.

103. *Epistolarium* 249, p. 528.

104. *Epistolarium* 146r, p. 350.

105. *Epistolarium* 234, pp. 509–510.

106. *Epistolarium* 140r, p. 315.

107. LVM I.28, 52, pp. 29, 33.

108. LVM III.65–66, pp. 162–163.

109. *Epistolarium* 76r, pp. 165–166.

110. *Epistolarium* 66r, p. 150.

111. *Scivias* II.5.23, p. 195; and in many other places, for instance, her general letter to lay people, epistle 7 in Pitra, p. 341.

112. *Scivias* II.5.28, 32, pp. 200, 202–203.

113. *Scivias* II.5.13, 15, pp. 187, 188.

114. *Epistolarium* 84r, p. 193.

115. *Epistolarium* 250r, pp. 530–531.

116. *Epistolarium* 150r, p. 339.

117. *Epistolarium* 177r, p. 403.

118. *Epistolarium* 117r, p. 290.

119. *Epistolarium* 77r, p. 174.

120. *Vita* II.2, p. 22.

121. Letter/sermon to the clergy of Trier in 1160: *Epistolarium* 223r, pp. 490–496.

122. This point about the demand of women for a place in religious life was first made in the 1930s by Herbert Grundmann, *Religious Movements in the Middle Ages,* trans. Steven Rowan (Notre Dame, 1995). For an exemplary follow-up study of the lower Rhine region, see Franz J. Felten, "Frauenklöster und -stifte im Rheinland im 12. Jahrhundert," in *Reformidee und Reformpolitik im spätsalisch-frühstaufischen Reich,* ed. Stefan Weinfurter (Mainz, 1992), 189–300. And in general see now Giles Constable, *The Reformation of the Twelfth Century* (Cambridge, 1996).

123. *Epistolarium* 37, 37r, pp. 95–97.

124. *Epistolarium* 8, pp. 19–21.

CHAPTER 3: "RELIGIOUS THINKER"

1. *Scivias,* Protestificatio, 4. My translation is slightly more literal than that of Columba Hart and Jane Bishop, who render *obscura* and *secreta* as "the

darkness" and "secrets" respectively, obscuring the parallelism between these two images: *Scivias*, trans. Hart and Bishop, 150–151.

2. Sabina Flanagan, *Hildegard of Bingen, 1098–1179: A Visionary Life* (London, 1989), 199–211, in discussion of ideas put forward by Charles Singer, in "Scientific Views and Visions of St Hildegard (1098–1180)," *Studies in the History and Method of Science* (Oxford, 1917), 1:1–55, and Oliver Sacks, *Migraine: Understanding a Common Disorder*, 2d ed. (Berkeley, 1985), 106–108, and *The Man Who Mistook His Wife for a Hat and Other Clinical Tales* (New York, 1970), 166–170.

3. Hans Liebeschütz, *Das allegorische Weltbild der hl. Hildegard von Bingen* (Leipzig, 1930). His contribution to Hildegard studies is sympathetically analyzed by Peter Dronke in a paper delivered to the Warburg Institute symposium: see *Hildegard of Bingen: The Context of Her Thought and Art*, ed. Charles Burnett and Peter Dronke (London, 1998).

4. These views have been widely disseminated through various publications of Bear and Co., Santa Fe, N.M., notably Matthew Fox, *Illuminations of Hildegard of Bingen* (Santa Fe, N.M., 1985), and Fox's introductions to abridged translations of *Scivias* by Bruce Hozeski (1986) and *Hildegard of Bingen's Book of Divine Works with Letters and Songs* (1987), based not on the Latin text but on the 1965 German translation by Heinrich Schipperges.

5. Barbara Newman, *Sister of Wisdom: St. Hildegard's Theology of the Feminine* (Berkeley, 1987).

6. Newman, *Sister of Wisdom*, 251–252.

7. *Vita* II.4, p. 23.

8. *Annales S. Disibodi*, ed. G. Pertz, MGH.SS 17 (Hannover, 1861), 25. While the chronicle mentions that Hildegard and two other girls "of the same name" took the veil twenty-four years before Jutta's death in 1136, only one other girl is mentioned in the *Life of Jutta* (see n. 9 below, this chapter), which confirms the testimony of the chronicle that the act of enclosure took place in 1112. Guibert of Gembloux, *Epistolae*, ed. Albert Derolez, CCCM 66a (Turnhout, 1989), no. 38, p. 372, also mentions only one other girl being enclosed with Jutta and Hildegard.

9. *Vita* I.1, p. 6, and Guibert of Gembloux, *Epistolae* 38, p. 372. Without knowledge of the *Life of Jutta*, Sabina Flanagan suggested that the 1112 date for the act of enclosure in the chronicle (implied by its assertion that Jutta lived as a recluse for twenty-four years) might have been a scribal error: "Oblation or Enclosure: Reflections on Hildegard of Bingen's Entry into Religion," in *Wisdom Which Encircles Circles: Papers on Hildegard of Bingen*, ed. Audrey Ekdahl Davidson (Kalamazoo, 1996), 4. See my "Seeing Is Believing: Hildegard of Bingen and the *Life of Jutta*, *Scivias*, and the *Commentary on the Rule of Benedict*," *Tjurunga* 51 (1996): 16.

10. Jutta's *Vita* is edited by Franz Staab from two fifteenth-century manuscripts in an appendix to "Reform und Reformgruppen im Erzbistum Mainz: Vom 'Libellus de Willigisi consuetudinibus' zur 'Uita domnae Juttae inclusae,' " in Stefan Weinfurter, ed., *Reformidee und Reformpolitik im spätsalisch-frühstaufischen Reich* (Mainz, 1992), 172–187. Otto of Bamberg, described as "of blessed memory" in *Vita Juttae* 3.8, p. 176, died in 1140 according to the *An-*

nales S. Disibodi, 26, implying that the *Life* cannot have been written in 1136–1137 as suggested by Staab: see Mews, "Seeing Is Believing": 15 n. 17. See also Julie Hotchin, "Enclosure and Containment: Jutta and Hildegard at the Abbey of St. Disibod," *Magistra* 2 (1996): 103–123.

11. *Vita Juttae* 4 and 6, pp. 178 and 180.

12. *Vita Juttae* 6, p. 180.

13. *Vita Juttae* 6 and 5, pp. 181 and 178–179.

14. *Vita Juttae* 9, pp. 185–186.

15. *Vita* II.2, pp. 23–24; Flanagan, A *Visionary Life*, 42–43.

16. *Scivias*, Protestificatio, 3–4, *Vita* II.2, p. 24.

17. *Scivias*, Protestificatio, 4, and *Vita* II.2, p. 24.

18. While Scripture never speaks of "the Living Light" as such, Hildegard may have been influenced by Job 33.28 (*Liberavit animam suam ne pergeret in interitum, sed vivens lucem videret*). See also Job 33.30 and Ps. 57.13 (*luce viventium*). The phrase *lux vivens* does not occur prior to Hildegard in the CD-ROM databases of the *Patrologia latina*, issued by Chadwyck-Healey, and of *Corpus christianorum*, the CETEDOC Library of Christian Latin Texts, issued by Brepols.

19. *Annales Sancti Disibodi*, 24.

20. John Van Engen, *Rupert of Deutz* (Berkeley, 1983), 84–85.

21. *De gloria et honore Filii hominis super Matthaeum* VI.9, ed. Rhaban Haacke, CCCM 7 (Turnhout, 1967), 158; see Mews, "Hildegard of Bingen: The Virgin, the Apocalypse and the Exegetical Tradition," in Davidson, "*Wisdom Which Encircles Circles*," 31–33. On the theme of gender complementarity, see Mews, "Hildegard of Bingen: Gender, Nature, and Visionary Experience," in Julie S. Barton and Constant J. Mews, ed., *Hildegard of Bingen and Gendered Theology in Judaeo-Christian Tradition* (Clayton, Victoria, 1995), 63–80.

22. *On the Sacraments of the Christian Faith [De Sacramentis]*, trans. Roy Deferrari (Cambridge, Mass., 1951). For a brief comparison of Hildegard and Hugh of St. Victor, see Newman, *Sister of Wisdom*, 16, and her introduction to *Scivias*, trans. Hart and Bishop, 23.

23. On male-female complementarity in her medical writing, see Joan Cadden, "It Takes All Kinds: Sexuality and Gender Differences in Hildegard of Bingen's 'Book of Compound Medicine,' " *Traditio* 40 (1984): 149–174.

24. The archaic *viridity* perhaps deserves to be restored in translations of Hildegard. Hart and Bishop prefer English fluency to emphasis on its conceptual importance. Thus they translate *viriditas* as both plants and fertility in *Scivias* II.1.2 (pp. 150–151): "The sky holds light, light air, and air the birds; the earth nourishes plants [viridity], plants [viridity] fruit and fruit animals, which all testify that they were put there by a strong hand . . . And he has a receptacle containing humidity, germination and birth, as the earth contains fertility [viridity], fruition and animals. . . ." (II.1.3) "Which in course of time was to become incarnate . . . by the Holy Spirit's sweet freshness [viridity of the sweetness] in the dawn of blessed virginity . . ." They translate *viriditas* as freshness (pp. 86, 103, 151, 177, 212, 252, 402, 405), but also use vitality (113, 161), fertility (113, 177, 251, 461), greenery (124), fecundity (129, 220,

440), fruitfulness (154, 226, 404, 439), verdure (216, 528), growth (258), green (300), greenness (442, 475, 478, 503). They omit *viriditas* completely in "virtues are beginning to show themselves" (115) (literally: show their viridity) and prefer elegant phrases to clumsy literal translations, supplied here in square brackets: (152) fresh warmth [warmth in viridity]; (153) fresh fruitfulness [damp viridity of fruitfulness]; (163–164) cool dampness [damp viridity]; (228) fresh moisture [dampness in viridity]; (229) from the manly strength [from the viridity of the virile mind]; (231) in renewal of soul [in viridity of soul]; (242) fresh beatitude [all viridity of beatitude]; (243) the fresh and living breath [with the viridity of the living breath]; (253) fresh purity [in the viridity of her wholeness]; (377) manly virility [virile viridity]; (438) great virtue [great viridity].

25. *Theologia 'Scholarium,'* II.112–118, ed. Eligius M. Buytaert and Constant J. Mews, in *Petri Abaelardi Opera Theologica III*, CCCM 13 (Turnhout, 1987), 462–464; see also my comments on 207–209.

26. Hart and Bishop translate *umida viriditas* (pp. 163–164) as cool dampness. The belief that stones possessed viridity is a traditional one, defined for example by Rabanus Maurus, *De universo* 17.5 and 19.8, PL 111:463d, 530b, and Isidore of Seville, *Etymologiae* VI.11 and XVI.5, 7, 12, ed. W. M. Lindsay 2 vols. (Oxford, 1911).

27. Peter Abelard, *Sermo* 32, PL 178:584d.

28. The term occurs forty-three times in Gregory the Great's *Moralia in Job*. He defines viridity as the life of grass and trees in VI.16, ed. Marc Adriaen, CCSL 143–143b (Turnhout, 1979–1981), p. 298. See also: IV.4, p. 161; VI.15, p. 297; VII.12, p. 344; VIII.42, pp. 433–435; XI.44, p. 620; XI.50, p. 624; XII.4, p. 631; XII.5, pp. 632–633; XII.53, p. 665; XIV.20, p. 712; XIV.55, p. 742; XVII.15, p. 864; XIX.27, p. 995; XX.27, p. 1044; XXI.1, p. 1063; XXII.7, pp. 1104–1105; cf. Augustine, *De ciuitate dei* XXII.1, ed. B. Dombart and A. Kalb, CCSL 48 (Turnhout, 1955), 806; see Mews, "The Virgin, the Apocalypse, and the Exegetical Tradition," in Davidson, "*Wisdom Which Encircles Circles,*" 34. On Gregory's sense of the continuum between God and creation as stronger than that of Augustine, see Carole Straw, *Gregory the Great: Perfection in Imperfection* (Berkeley, 1988), 32–33.

29. *Epistolae duorum amantium: Briefe Abaelards und Heloises?* ed. Ewald Könsgen (Leiden, 1974), nos. 1, 25, 48, pp. 3, 16, 25.

30. Romans 1.19–21 plays a key role in Abelard's argument in the *Theologia christiana* I.58 and IV.85, ed. Eligius Buytaert, CCCM 12 (Turnhout, 1969), 95 and 305.

31. Peter Dronke comments on medieval authors who use the image of the cosmic egg and he lists these writers in an appendix in *Fabula: Explorations in the Uses of Myth in Medieval Platonism* (Leiden, 1985), 79–99 and 154–166.

32. *Expositio in Hexaemeron*, PL 178:735d–736a, reprinted by Dronke, *Fabula*, 159.

33. "de uiriditate uirilis animi hominis," translated as "manly strength" by Hart and Bishop, *Scivias*, 229.

34. On Hildegard's Mariology, see the essay "Composer and Dramatist" by Margot Fassler, chapter 8 in this volume.

35. Augustine Thompson, "Hildegard of Bingen on Gender and Priesthood," *Church History* 63 (1994): 349–364.

36. On the *Ordo virtutum*, see Audrey Ekdahl Davidson, ed., *Hildegard von Bingen: Ordo Virtutum* (Kalamazoo, 1984), and the essay "Composer and Dramatist" by Margot Fassler in this volume.

37. Laurence Moulinier argues that the *Physica* (PL 197:1125–1352) and *Causae et Curae* are part of a single *Liber subtilitatum de diversis creaturis*: see her *Le Manuscrit perdu à Strasbourg: Enquête sur l'oeuvre scientifique de Hildegarde* (Paris, 1995). For a different view, see the essay "Medical Writer" by Florence Eliza Glaze, chapter 7 in this volume.

38. Hildegard comments at the outset of the *Book of Life's Merits* that "the same vision showed me the subtleties of the different natures of created things" as well as various other writings, in the prologue to LVM I.1, p. 8: "postquam eadem uisio subtilitates diuersarum naturarum creaturarum, ac responsa et admonitiones tam minorum quam maiorum plurimarum . . . mihi ad explanandum ostenderat." We may need to distinguish between the "true vision" that revealed all these writings and the individual "true visions" discussed in *Scivias* but not used as a framework for her exposition in the scientific writing.

39. *Vita* II.1, p. 20.

40. These parenthetical citations for the *Book of Divine Works* refer to the edition by Albert Derolez and Peter Dronke (CCCM 92), whose vision numbers do not coincide with those in the older edition (PL 197) or the abridged English translation. The CCCM edition renumbers the visions in each part to begin with 1, so that Vision II.5 in PL 197 becomes II.1 in CCCM 92, and Visions III.6–10 become III.1–5.

41. Peter Dronke comments on one of Hildegard's Gospel expositions in which she discusses John's Gospel in "Platonic-Christian Allegories in the Homilies of Hildegard of Bingen": in Haijo Jan Westra, ed., *From Athens to Chartres: Neoplatonism and Medieval Thought* (Leiden, 1992), 388–389.

42. *Epistolarium* 23r, p. 64.

CHAPTER 4: "PROPHET AND REFORMER"

I would like to thank Margot Fassler and the other members of Giles Constable's Medieval Seminar at the Institute for Advanced Study for their energetic and enthusiastic engagement with my work on Hildegard and ecclesiastical politics. I am also very grateful to E. Randolph Daniel for sharing with me his entire forthcoming book, *Bound for the Promised Land: A History of Reformist Apocalypticism,* and for his advice on this article. Grover Zinn, Bernard McGinn, and the other University of California Press readers also made helpful comments. Most of all I am grateful to Barbara Newman for her judicious editorial work and her cheerful patience during every step of this book's production.

1. *Epistolarium* 20, p. 56, emphasis added; translations not otherwise attributed are my own. The Vulgate translations throughout this essay are cited from *The Holy Bible, Douay Version* (London, 1956).

2. *Letters* 20r, pp. 72–73; for Latin text, *Epistolarium* 20r, p. 57. Note here that in *Letters* Baird and Ehrman have silently emended Van Acker's text of the final words, "quia tempus cito ueniet," to readopt the PL reading "quia tempus tuum cito ueniet" (PL 197:158a). The reinstated reading is found in both manuscripts R and Wr (see Van Acker's variants, *Epistolarium*, p. 57). Baird and Ehrman apparently reject Van Acker's view that the reading "tuum" is "vaticinia ex eventu," that is, inserted after Arnold's death in 1160 and therefore not in Hildegard's *Grundtext*. See Lieven Van Acker, "Der Briefwechsel der heiligen Hildegard von Bingen: Vorbemerkungen zu einer kritischen Edition," *Revue bénédictine* 99 (1989): 139.

3. LDO III.5.16, p. 433. Baird and Ehrman provide further details on Arnold's murder: *Letters*, p. 72.

4. See Barbara Newman, "Sibyl of the Rhine," chapter 1, p. 7.

5. *Letters* 20r, p. 72; *Epistolarium* 20r, p. 57.

6. Paul Franche, *Sainte Hildegarde* (Paris, 1903), 114.

7. *Epistolarium* 201r, p. 457.

8. The monks of Villers asked her to answer their thirty-eight theological cruxes, many of which required prophetic or divine insight: see Barbara Newman, "Sibyl of the Rhine," pp. 26–27 in this volume, and Anne Clark Bartlett, "Commentary, Polemic, and Prophecy in Hildegard of Bingen's *Solutiones triginta octo quaestionum*," *Viator* 23 (1992): 153–165. Hildegard was also asked to exorcize a demon from a possessed woman, Sigewize, but, as Newman rightly suggests (chapter 1, p. 23), she certainly did not seek out this kind of use of her spiritual gifts.

9. On these and other reformist concepts, see Giles Constable, *The Reformation of the Twelfth Century* (Cambridge, 1996), 125, and chapter 4 especially. Heloise is, of course, another welcome instance of a female writer on issues of monastic reform; see Constable, ibid., 163.

10. Marjorie Reeves, "The Development of Apocalyptic Thought: Medieval Attitudes," in *The Apocalypse in English Renaissance Thought and Literature*, ed. C. A. Patrides and J. Wittreich (Ithaca, N.Y., 1984), 40.

11. See Kathryn Kerby-Fulton, *Reformist Apocalypticism and* Piers Plowman (Cambridge, 1990), chap. 2; and for evidence of widespread pseudonymous fame, Kerby-Fulton, "Hildegard of Bingen and Antimendicant Propaganda," *Traditio* 43 (1987): 386–399; Emil Donckel, "Visio seu prophetia fratris Johannis: Eine süditalienische Prophezeiung aus dem Anfang des 14. Jahrhunderts," *Romanische Quartalschrift* 40 (1932): 361–379; and Stuart Jenks, "Die Prophezeiung von Ps.-Hildegard von Bingen: Eine vernachlässigte Quelle über die Geisslerzüge von 1348-9," *Mainfränkisches Jahrbuch für Geschichte und Kunst* 29 (1977): 9–38.

12. "Meliorism" is the view that the world will improve or is capable of improving in the remaining course of salvation history. On the meliorist apocalypticism of Hildegard's immediate German contemporaries, especially Gerhoh of Reichersberg, Eberwin of Steinfeld, and Anselm of Havelberg, see Guntram Bischoff, "Early Premonstratensian Eschatology," in *The Spirituality of Western Christendom*, ed. Rozanne Elder (Kalamazoo, 1976), 41–71, and E. Randolph Daniel's forthcoming *Bound for the Promised Land: A History of Reformist Apocalypticism*.

13. Joachim of Fiore, monastic thinker and biblical commentator, developed an elaborate prophetic scheme explaining the future course of salvation history. He is today the best-known apocalyptic thinker of the Middle Ages, his influence extending even to ideological movements in our own century, but his genuine works were not widely known in the medieval period. On Joachim see Marjorie Reeves, *The Influence of Prophecy: A Study in Joachimism* (Oxford, 1969).

14. *Speculum futurorum temporum sive Pentachronon*, also called simply the *Pentachronon* (in reference to Hildegard's five future ages of the world), abridged ed. in Pitra, 484–488. See Kerby-Fulton, *Reformist Apocalypticism*, 29–31, and Kerby-Fulton, "Hildegard and the Male Reader," in *Prophets Abroad: The Reception of Continental Holy Women in Late-Medieval England*, ed. Rosalynn Voaden (Cambridge, 1996), 1–18.

15. Pitra, 485; for further discussion of this passage, see Kerby-Fulton, "Hildegard and the Male Reader."

16. For a good, brief introduction to the horrors of schism politics, see *Letters*, pp. 10–13.

17. There is no scholarly agreement on what to call issues traditionally associated with the Gregorian reform in reference to mid-twelfth-century history. For a general but inconclusive discussion, see Gerd Tellenbach, *The Church in Western Europe from the Tenth to the Early Twelfth Century*, trans. T. Reuter (Cambridge, 1993), 157–158.

18. Both manuscript evidence and internal evidence show that Elisabeth was prominent in the initial audience for the prophecy. See Anne Clark, *Elisabeth of Schönau* (Philadelphia, 1992), 22–23 and note 73: "Although it was not composed as a letter to Elisabeth, Elisabeth seems to have received a copy of the text. In addition to its transmission with other Hildegard letters, it is also found in MSS of Redaction D of Elisabeth's visionary collection." F. W. E. Roth argued in *Die Visionen der hl. Elisabeth* (Brno, 1884) that it was originally written for Elisabeth, and Van Acker's comment that it was addressed to a larger audience only suggests that the text (at least as we now have it) was not written solely as a *letter* to Elisabeth (*Epistolarium*, pp. 238–239, and "Vorbemerkungen" [1989], 150). But the likeliest explanation of the textual evidence is that Hildegard sent her a copy since she was involved in the antiheretical ministry for which the two women visionaries are known. Moreover, Clark also points out (p. 23) that the treatise and Elisabeth's apparent response to it both use Apoc. 6.9–11.

19. *Epistolarium* 169r, p. 379.

20. *Epistolarium* 193, pp. 437–438; for a discussion of the textual problems, see Barbara Newman, *Symphonia*, pp. 69–70.

21. On the biblical rhetoric of the prophecy and the question of typology, see Kerby-Fulton, *Reformist Apocalypticism*, 61, and "Hildegard and Antimendicant Propaganda," 390–391, n. 16.

22. Horst D. Rauh, *Das Bild des Antichrist*, Beiträge zur Geschichte der Philosophie und Theologie des Mittelalters, n.s. 9 (Münster, 1979), 490.

23. *Epistolarium* 15r, especially pp. 39–43; on the Cologne prophecy (the interpolated version, that is, which Gebeno's text made famous), see Kerby-Fulton,

Reformist Apocalypticism, 39–40, and "Hildegard and Antimendicant Propaganda," 391–393.

24. As Emily Bayley has pointed out in an unpublished paper, the source of this image is probably Isaiah 3.4, "et effeminati dominabuntur eis."

25. First formulated by Alois Dempf, *Sacrum Imperium: Geschichts- und Staatsphilosophie des Mittelalters und der politischen Renaissance* (Munich, 1962), 261–268; more recently in Rauh, *Das Bild des Antichrist,* 177.

26. Rauh, *Das Bild des Antichrist,* 177.

27. See Bartlett, "Commentary, Polemic, and Prophecy."

28. Rauh, *Das Bild des Antichrist,* 174.

29. See John Van Engen's superb study *Rupert of Deutz* (Berkeley, 1983), 346–347. On Rupert's visionary tendencies, see Kathryn Kerby-Fulton, "Langland and the Bibliographic Ego," in *Written Work: Langland, Labor, and Authorship* (Philadelphia, 1997), 91–95, and Barbara Newman, "Hildegard of Bingen: Visions and Validation," *Church History* 54 (1985): 172–173.

30. Newman, "Sibyl of the Rhine," chap. 1 above, p. 22.

31. Charles Czarski, "The Prophecies of Hildegard of Bingen" (Ph.D. diss., University of Kentucky, 1983).

32. See Van Engen, *Rupert,* 26. Otbert, who was appointed by the emperor Henry IV in 1091 as bishop of the important diocese of Liège, was instrumental in installing simoniac abbots in, among other places in the diocese, the abbey of St. Lawrence, where he replaced Rupert's abbot, Berengar, with the simoniac Wolbodo.

33. As Van Engen explains, "The leading reformers, including Humbert, Pope Gregory and Pope Urban, . . . applied apocalyptic images specifically to persons and events in their own times; and Rupert's poem did so more concretely and extensively than any other eleventh-century text" (*Rupert,* 32). See also Rauh, *Das Bild des Antichrist,* 185; Bernard McGinn, *Visions of the End: Apocalyptic Traditions in the Middle Ages* (New York, 1978), 96; and Daniel, *Bound for the Promised Land.* As Rauh notes, it is here that the eschatological horizon emerges out of which Rupert would later design an original theology of history (p. 186).

34. " 'Ei michil! dixit, Symon atque Nero / Nunc revixerunt . . . / Nemo tam sevus fuit antichristus / Arrius quamvis fuerit malignus . . . / In Dei Templo sedet, aureumque— / Ei michi matri!—populus fidelis / Mammon adorat. / Israel quis rex Baal invocarit, / Qui sacerdotes Baalim sacrarint, / Qui super montes statuas locarint, / Tu bene nosti." Rupert of Deutz, *Carmina* III.29–48, MGH. LdL 3.625. Rupert's obsession with forerunners of Antichrist is Humbertian; see Rauh, *Das Bild des Antichrist,* 194.

35. Rupert distrusts *regnum* in any form and refers to Cain as the first founder of a state. *Carmina* XIII.8–12; see Rauh, *Das Bild des Antichrist,* 196.

36. Rauh, *Das Bild des Antichrist,* 217.

37. See Daniel's analysis, *Bound for the Promised Land.*

38. Rupert's Eccelesia (III.3–20) is portrayed as disheveled, like Boethius's Philosophia in *The Consolation of Philosophy* and Ecclesia in *The Shepherd of Hermas;* Hildegard very likely knew both works. Maria Arduini has recently

drawn attention to the *Carmina*'s resemblance to liturgical drama; see her *Non fabula sed res: Politische Dichtung und dramatische Gestalt in den Carmina Ruperts von Deutz* (Rome, 1985), 115–137; see also, though not in connection with the *Carmina*, her "Der Einfluss Ruperts auf die Werke Hildegards von Bingen," in *Rupert von Deutz und der "Status christianitatis" seiner Zeit* (Cologne, 1987), 314.

39. *Epistolarium* 149r, pp. 336–337. Cf. PL 197:271bc.

40. Barbara Newman, *Sister of Wisdom: St. Hildegard's Theology of the Feminine* (Berkeley, 1987), 28.

41. *Epistolarium* 223r, pp. 493–494; cf. PL 197:256c.

42. *Epistolarium* 223r, p. 493. See Kathryn Kerby-Fulton, "A Return to 'the First Dawn of Justice': Hildegard's Visions of Clerical Reform and the Eremitical Life," *American Benedictine Review* 40 (1989): 383–407.

43. On the primacy of the papacy over the emperor, see Rauh, *Des Bild des Antichrist*, 216.

44. See Giles Constable, "Monastic Possession of Churches and *Spiritualia* in the Age of Reform," in *Religious Life and Thought, Eleventh-Twelfth Centuries* (London, 1979), 304–331.

45. John Gilchrist, *The Collection in Seventy-Four Titles: A Canon Law Manual of the Gregorian Reform* (Toronto, 1980), 4.

46. Quoted from Sabina Flanagan, *Hildegard of Bingen: A Visionary Life* (London, 1989), 20.

47. See Newman's analysis in *Sister of Wisdom*, 13.

48. *Epistolarium* 84r, p. 195, emphasis added; cf. PL 197:264a.

49. On meliorism see note 12 above, this chapter.

50. LDO III.5.17, p. 437.

51. For a chart of Hildegard's entire apocalyptic program as it is laid out in the LDO, see my *Reformist Apocalypticism*, 49–50; see also Kerby-Fulton, "A Return to 'the First Dawn of Justice.' "

52. See the appendix "Adso's Essay on Antichrist" in *The Play of Antichrist*, trans. John Wright (Toronto, 1967), 100–110.

53. LDO III.5.29, pp. 450–451.

54. *Epistolarium* 15r, p. 44: "Sed quia Ecclesia diuisa erat, uocem hanc subtraxi."

55. Van Engen, *Rupert*, 285 n. 74.

56. See McGinn, *Visions of the End*, 101, for this translation, plus a helpful introductory analysis of the apocalyptic themes in the notes (p. 309).

57. Bernard McGinn, *Antichrist: Two Thousand Years of the Human Fascination with Evil* (San Francisco, 1994), 131; the quoted phrase is from an unpublished article by Ray Clemens cited by McGinn, 131.

58. See McGinn, *Antichrist*, 320 n. 67, and Gerd Tellenbach, *Church, State, and Christian Society at the Time of the Investiture Controversy* (New York, 1970), 131–132.

59. See Flanagan, *A Visionary Life*, 170, for a translation of the full passage; see also Newman, "Sibyl of the Rhine," chapter 1, p. 23.

60. Beginning "Gemma iacet in uia . . ." *Epistolarium* 3, p. 9.

61. PL 197:185c–186a, emphasis added.

62. PL 197:185c.

63. LDO III.5.25, p. 446.

64. On Hildegard's partiality to her sisters: "Yet your home, O my daughters, God will not destroy ..." *Epistolarium* 193, p. 438: "Locum autem uestrum, o filie mee, Deus non destruet."

65. Constable, *Reformation of the Twelfth Century,* 317.

66. Brian Tierney, *The Crisis of Church and State, 1050–1300* (Englewood Cliffs, N.J., 1964), 85–87.

67. Tierney, *Crisis of Church and State,* 87–88.

68. Tierney, *Crisis of Church and State,* 92–93, citing Bernard's *De consideratione.*

69. LDO III.5.16, pp. 434–435.

70. Constable, *Reformation of the Twelfth Century,* 329–330.

71. *Epistolarium* 8, p. 21.

72. A fiery hound, a tawny lion, a pale horse, a black pig, and a gray wolf; see Kerby-Fulton, *Reformist Apocalypticism,* 49–50, for a chart detailing the major events of each of the five ages.

73. Tierney, *Crisis of Church and State,* 99.

74. PL 197:257ab.

75. LDO III.5.26, p. 447.

76. See Kerby-Fulton, "Antimendicant Propaganda."

77. On the Wycliffite disendowment program and its fiscal enticements, see Steven Justice's chapter on "Lollardy" in the *Cambridge History of Medieval English Literature* (forthcoming).

78. *Epistolarium* 15r, p. 40.

79. The Kirchheim letter is Hildegard's most politically sensitive treatment of the issue of disendowment before the LDO. Here she sees the kings of the earth participating with princes in the takeover of clerical wealth, but with a difference: the kings will do so out of greed (*inhiabunt*) while the princes will "wish to show themselves obedient to God" (*et in hoc facto obsequium Deo se exhibuisse volunt*). Although she registers ambivalence here about the motives of the seculars, she is never ambivalent about the necessity of what they will do. *Epistolarium* 149r, p. 336.

80. *Epistolarium* 15r, pp. 42–43.

81. See, for instance, the marginalia in Bodleian Library, Oxford, Digby 32, or in Corpus Christi College, Cambridge, 404, discussed in Kerby-Fulton, "Prophecy and Suspicion: Closet Radicalism, Censorship, and the Vogue for Hildegardiana in Ricardian England," forthcoming; provisionally, see "Hildegard and the Male Reader" on some of the marginalia in Digby 32.

82. For a detailed analysis of this passage see Kerby-Fulton, *Reformist Apocalypticism,* 36–39.

83. Kerby-Fulton, *Reformist Apocalypticism,* 50.

84. See Kerby-Fulton, "Prophecy and Suspicion."

85. LDO III.5.20, p. 441.

86. LDO III.5.38, pp. 462–463.

CHAPTER 5: "CORRESPONDENT"

1. On letter collections in the Middle Ages, see Giles Constable, *Letters and Letter-Collections* (Turnhout, 1976). Constable points out that revisions could be made to letters already sent either by the sender or by the recipient (or a secretary) and that letters were usually preserved in copies rather than in their original form. Among women, the letters of queens and other noble women of importance are usually preserved with the letters of the men they corresponded with. But Ekbert, the brother and secretary of Elisabeth of Schönau, preserved twenty-two of her letters among her own writings.

2. Responses are sometimes counted separately, sometimes not, in the new edition by Lieven Van Acker, *Epistolarium*, which so far covers 250 letters in two volumes; Monika Klaes will complete this edition. I use Van Acker's edition for those 250 letters where I can and supplement it with texts from Peter Dronke, *Women Writers of the Middle Ages* (Cambridge, 1984); Marianna Schrader and Adelgundis Führkötter, *Die Echtheit des Schrifttums der hl. Hildegard von Bingen* (Cologne, 1956); PL 197; and Pitra. When I cite only the letter number in the text, I am following Van Acker's numbering; "R" denotes a response. The editions are arranged by category and rank of addressee, not by year, so the numbers do not indicate chronology. The first volume of letters has been translated by Joseph Baird and Radd Ehrman (*Letters*). I draw on this version with some modifications up to letter 90. Translations of other letters are my own. Peter Dronke has discussed as well as edited a number of letters, and Sabina Flanagan discusses many of them in chapter 8 of *Hildegard of Bingen: A Visionary Life* (London, 1989).

3. The Riesenkodex, a manuscript produced at Rupertsberg shortly after Hildegard's death, is the primary source for the PL and Pitra editions of her letters. Van Acker's edition draws on a wider range of sources, including manuscripts that represent an older tradition and a manuscript (Vienna, Österreichische Nationalbibliothek, cod. 963) that he argues was probably prepared by Volmar before his death and used by Guibert as the basis for the Riesenkodex. Constable notes that if a letter is considered a conscious literary product, as it usually was in the Middle Ages, the final version may be the most authentic; but if it is a spontaneous expression of the author's ideas or feelings, the earliest version may be (*Letters and Letter-Collections*, 64). For details about the manuscripts, see Lieven Van Acker, "Der Briefwechsel der heiligen Hildegard von Bingen: Vorbemerkungen zu einer kritischen Edition," *Revue bénédictine* 98 (1988): 141–168 and 99 (1989): 118–154; the introductions to the two volumes of his edition (*Epistolarium*); and reviews of volume 1 by John Coakley, *Speculum* 68 (1993): 1132–1133, and volume 2 by Thomas H. Bestul, *Speculum* 70 (1995): 915.

4. Editorial changes other than stylistic polishing were also made in the Riesenkodex. Abbess Tenxwind of Andernach's sharp criticisms of dress practices and class distinctions at Rupertsberg were softened (see L. Van Acker, "Der Briefwechsel der hl. Hildegard von Bingen," 145). Hildegard's letter criticizing Philip of Heinsberg, archbishop of Cologne, for avarice was deleted, presumably

because by the time of the collection Philip had shifted his allegiance from the emperor to the pope (L. Van Acker, ibid., 148). Hildegard supported the papacy in the schism caused by the emperor's appointment of antipopes, but she corresponded with archbishops on both sides.

5. It is impossible to know whether certain letters ostensibly received by Hildegard were reassigned to more important correspondents or were even composed anew for the collection. "Forged" is a word that seems too strong for the context, since such letters may have been reconstructed from Hildegard's or Volmar's memory of what had originally been conveyed either in writing or orally. It is also possible that these letters had always existed but had not been included in the earlier collections. See Van Acker, "Briefwechsel der hl. Hildegard von Bingen."

6. Constable, *Letters*, 44, 48.

7. On the connections between Hildegard's interpretations of religious texts through interior illumination and the monastic "textual community" in the twelfth century, which valued a combination of divine wisdom, human intellect, and virtuous action for religious understanding in contrast to the more scholarly orientation of the schools, see Anne Clark Bartlett, "Miraculous Literacy and Textual Communities in Hildegard of Bingen's *Scivias*," *Mystics Quarterly* 18 (1992): 43–55.

8. For more on these letters to Bernard and Guibert and on Hildegard's correspondence and relations with her secretaries and helpers, see my "Scribe quae vides et audis: Hildegard: Her Language, and Her Secretaries," in David Townsend and Andrew Taylor, eds., *The Tongue of the Fathers: Gender and Ideology in Twelfth-Century Latin* (Philadelphia, 1998), 102–135.

9. On Hildegard's views of Adam and Eve, see my *To the Glory of Her Sex: Women's Roles in the Composition of Medieval Texts* (Bloomington, Ind., 1997), 166–173, particularly 170–172 for the letters in which she frequently mentions Adam's fall to male clergy.

10. For a more detailed discussion of references to Hildegard's prophetic gifts in her correspondence, see Sabina Flanagan, "Hildegard of Bingen as Prophet: The Evidence of Her Contemporaries," *Tjurunga* 32 (1987): 16–45, and Gillian Ahlgren, "Visions and Rhetorical Strategy in the Letters of Hildegard of Bingen," in Karen Cherewatuk and Ulrike Wiethaus, eds., *Dear Sister: Medieval Women and the Epistolary Genre* (Philadelphia, 1993), 46–63.

11. Epistle 27 in PL 197:186c.

12. *The Letters of John of Salisbury*, ed. W. J. Millor, H. E. Butler, and C. N. L. Brooke (Edinburgh, 1955), epistle 186.

13. Schrader and Führkötter, *Echtheit*, pp. 127, 129.

14. Epistle 112 in Pitra, p. 556.

15. Epistle 111 in Pitra, p. 556.

16. For the political context of these letters, see the essay "Prophet and Reformer" by Kathryn Kerby-Fulton in this volume.

17. Arnold, archbishop of Mainz: "If He made tillers of the field and dressers of sycamore trees into prophets and caused an ass to speak, how can we be surprised if He teaches you with his inspiration?" (epistle 20). Cf. Kerby-Fulton, "Prophet and Reformer," pp. 70–71 in this volume.

18. Hiltrud Rissel identifies another abbess as the recipient of this letter to Hazzecha. See "Hildegard von Bingen an Elisabeth von St. Thomas an der Kyll: Die heilige Hildegard und die frühesten deutschen Zisterzienserinnen," *Citeaux* 41 (1990): 5–44.

19. At every level of the religious life, Hildegard advises caution. To a nun, Luitburg of Trier, she suggests that she find herself a congregation suitable to her "infirmity" and not take on strict vows until she has proved herself in soul and body (epistle 222); and she advises a woman (through a priest who inquired on her behalf) that she is not yet ready to make a commitment, not yet inspired by the Holy Spirit, so she should stay where she is, wear a religious habit, and practice abstinence, alms, and prayers (ep. 70 in Pitra, p. 536).

20. Hildegard offers the same admonitions about mercy, justice, and correction of vice to popes (ep. 5 and 8) and archbishops (ep. 16r and 27r).

21. She emphasized the importance of confession as well as penance (see, for example, epistles 148r and 179), understanding that expressing guilt was an important step in the cure, just as she finally cured the possessed woman Sigewize by letting her demon talk itself out.

22. Guibert of Gembloux, *Epistolae,* ed. Albert Derolez, CCCM 66-66a (Turnhout, 1988, 1989), epistle 26, p. 278.

23. Guibert, *Epistolae,* epistle 38, pp. 367–368.

24. Guibert, *Epistolae,* epistle 38, p. 368.

25. PL 197:1053–1066; trans. Hugh Feiss, *Explanation of the Rule of Benedict* (Toronto, 1990).

26. Guibert, *Epistolae,* epistles 19 and 25.

27. See Kathryn Kerby-Fulton's essay "Prophet and Reformer" in this volume for the content of these prophetic sermons.

28. On this incident see "Sibyl of the Rhine," p. 23 in this volume, and Barbara Newman, "Three-Part Invention: The *Vita S. Hildegardis* and Mystical Hagiography," in Charles Burnett and Peter Dronke, eds., *Hildegard of Bingen: The Context of Her Thought and Art* (London, 1998): 183–203.

29. Epistle 8 in Dronke, *Women Writers,* 261–262.

30. Epistle 36 in Pitra, p. 521.

31. Epistle 161 in Pitra, p. 574.

32. Epistle 125 in Pitra, pp. 560–561.

33. Epistle 95 in Pitra, pp. 548–549.

34. Epistle 124 in Pitra, p. 560.

35. Epistle 36 in Pitra, p. 521. Cf. *Vita* III.10, p. 51, where the cure of this matron (Sibyl of Lausanne) is listed among Hildegard's miracles.

36. See the essay "Sibyl of the Rhine," pp. 26–27 above in this volume, and Anne Clark Bartlett, "Commentary, Polemic, and Prophecy in Hildegard of Bingen's *Solutiones Triginta Octo Quaestionum,*" *Viator* 23 (1992): 153–165.

37. Abbess Tenxwind also raises the question of Hildegard's snobbery (ep. 52); cf. the essay "Abbess" by John Van Engen in this volume, p. 36.

38. It is likely that his family had supported the convent, or had promised to, or that his death brought a legacy. But that is not mentioned and, while such an arrangement might have encouraged the burial in the first place, it would not, I think, have affected Hildegard's position once she had committed herself.

39. See the essay "Composer and Dramatist" by Margot Fassler in this volume for Hildegard's discussion of music.

40. Volmar had served as both provost and secretary to Hildegard, but Monika Klaes notes that by the end of her career, these positions probably entailed too much work to be handled by a single person. See *Vita*, pp. 88*, 90–91*.

41. Cf. the essay "Poet" in this volume by Barbara Newman, p. 191.

42. Hildegard implies that the monks of St. Disibod are like Lucifer, who did not praise God, while she is like Mary, a woman through whom God worked as he could not through angels or men.

43. See Newman, "Sibyl of the Rhine," p. 13 in this volume; Dronke, *Women Writers*, 150–159; and Flanagan, *A Visionary Life*, 180–184.

44. Schrader and Führkötter, *Echtheit*, 135.

45. Not all women approved of Hildegard! The abbess Tenxwind questioned Hildegard's exclusive admissions policy and her aristocratic dress code (ep. 52). Other people also wondered about her snobbery (abbot of Ilbenstadt, ep. 139) and the fancy dress: Guibert asked about the crowns and the diversity of the nuns in his epistle 17, *Epistolae*, p. 223.

46. For Elisabeth's letters to Hildegard see F. W. E. Roth, ed., *Die Visionen der hl. Elisabeth und die Schriften der Äbte Ekbert und Emecho von Schönau* (Brno, 1884), 70–75, epistles 19–21.

47. See Anne Clark, *Elisabeth of Schönau: A Twelfth-Century Visionary* (Philadelphia, 1992), 34–36, 95.

48. On these epistolary friendships, see Ulrike Wiethaus, "In Search of Medieval Women's Friendships: Hildegard of Bingen's Letters to Her Female Contemporaries," in Wiethaus, ed., *Maps of Flesh and Light: The Religious Experience of Medieval Women Mystics* (Syracuse, N.Y., 1993), 93–111.

49. Hildegard's nephew Wezelin also worked with her, but although she praises him highly in the epilogue to the *Book of Divine Works*, which he helped her complete, no letters between him and Hildegard are extant. There is one from his brother Arnold, archbishop of Trier, to their aunt, announcing his new position and asking if it was God's will—clearly wanting her reassurance, but also warning her against Wezelin, whom he calls a flatterer, while Arnold himself is a true friend (ep. 27). One does not know if this is jealousy of their close relation or sincere concern. According to Guibert (*Epistolae*, ep. 26, p. 293), Wezelin made off with his aunt's second set of solutions, supposedly to study them. Hildegard's answer to Arnold does not give him the assurance he asked of God's good will but suggests that he be more zealous in doing good works to win it; she warns him against pride like Satan's and against greed, and she tells him to have justice as his shield and truth as his breastplate and to heal the penitent with mercy. Did she have doubts about him or was she just being cautious? Hildegard's own brother Hugh, who served briefly as provost at Rupertsberg, was also involved in conflict with a brother, Roric, about which Hildegard admonishes him in the one letter to him (ep. 208). She had sisters as well, one of them a nun at Rupertsberg, but there are no extant identified letters to or from them. One wonders if only men in

her family wrote to her or if only their letters were kept because of their positions in the church.

50. In this letter Volmar lists many of Hildegard's books for the benefit of posterity; cf. the preface of her *Liber vite meritorum*, p. 8.

51. Epilogue to LDO, p. 464. There is a similar passage in the epilogue: "That blessed man also helped me in all my grief and desolation, consoling me himself and through other wise men . . . ," which may refer either to Wezelin, as Schrader and Führkötter think (*Echtheit*, 177–178), or to Ludwig. In any case, both of them helped her prepare the third book.

52. Translation by Dronke, *Women Writers*, 194. The correction Hildegard requests is the same kind of copyediting Volmar had always done for her. It does not give him license to tamper with the content, the word of God.

53. For Hildegard adversity serves a moral purpose. Compare ep. 146r, to a prelate of Kappenberg distressed by the present state of the church. Hildegard tells him, "If you always had prosperity, you would be like a crab which does not walk right."

54. One letter answers a specific question of Manegold's about lust: "Victory does not exhaust carnal desire in these cases . . . the bond of the flesh is stronger in that man than in the woman . . . But I see in you a whirlwind of heat which yet, with labor broken, disappears without deed" (ep. 136).

55. Guibert, *Epistolae*, ep. 22, p. 249.

CHAPTER 6: "ARTIST"

1. Detailed arguments will be found in four articles that I have written since 1990: "Anchoress, Abbess, and Queen: Donors and Patrons or Intercessors and Matrons?" in *Women's Literary and Artistic Patronage in the Middle Ages,* ed. June Hall McCash (Athens, Ga., 1996), 113–117; "Gender Symbolism and Text Image Relationships: Hildegard of Bingen's *Scivias,"* in *Translation Theory and Practice in the Middle Ages,* ed. Jeanette Beer (Kalamazoo, 1997), 71–111; "Hildegard of Bingen: German Author, Illustrator, and Musical Composer, 1098–1179," in *Dictionary of Women Artists,* ed. Delia Gaze (London, 1997), 685–687; "Hildegard as Designer of the Illustrations to Her Works," in *Hildegard of Bingen: The Context of Her Thought and Art,* ed. Charles Burnett and Peter Dronke (London, 1998): 29–62. I am also grateful to have been invited to participate in "Hildegard of Bingen: A Symposium," Yale Divinity School, February 1994, and for the opportunity it offered for discussion.

2. Adelgundis Führkötter, *The Miniatures from the Book Scivias—Know the Ways—of St. Hildegard of Bingen from the Illuminated Rupertsberg Codex* (Turnhout, 1977), 9–10, considered Hildegard the "spiritual inspiration behind the miniatures," while giving their execution to monks from a neighboring monastery, as also Karen Peterson and J. J. Wilson, *Women Artists: Recognition and Reappraisal from the Early Middle Ages to the Twentieth Century* (New York, 1976), 15. Christopher Reginald Dodwell, *The Pictorial Arts of the West 800–1200* (New Haven, 1993), 280–281, follows Lovis Baillet in

attributing the illuminations to the monastic house of St. Matthias in Trier,
though executed under Hildegard's direction, because of (unspecified) "affini-
ties with Trier works of c. 1180." Barbara Newman, *Sister of Wisdom* (Berkeley, 1987), 17–18, suggested the manuscript was produced under Hildegard's
supervision, "possibly by one of her nuns"; Carolyn Wörman Sur, *The Feminine Images of God in the Visions of Saint Hildegard of Bingen's "Scivias"*
(Lewiston, N.Y., 1993), 17–19 and 41, also gives Hildegard a supervisory role,
though acknowledging the primacy of her visual experience and the secondary
role of her text. "Hildegard's visions, and the illuminations which concretized
them, are her guidelines for the description of the text." Frances Beer, *Women
and Mystical Experience in the Middle Ages* (Woodbridge, Suffolk, 1992), 30,
leaves it open whether "she painted, or had paintings done, of these images." A
very recent publication, whose author was kind enough to send me a copy, dis-
tances Hildegard a priori from the artist (*der Maler*) of the visual images, in-
voking the time that elapsed between her visions and the production of the Rupertsberg manuscript: Keiko Suzuki, "Zum Strukturproblem in den
Visionsdarstellungen der Rupertsberger 'Scivias'-Handschrift," *Sacris Erudiri*
35 (1995): 221–291 (esp. 222, 232–233). Many of Suzuki's observations about
the interpretive value of the pictures, however, led me to the opposite conclusion, that they are the invention of the author.

   3. Rudolf Arnheim, *Visual Thinking* (Berkeley, 1969), v, 13–53.

   4. Otto Pächt, *Book Illumination in the Middle Ages: An Introduction*,
trans. Kay Davenport (London, 1986), 159–160, concludes that "the illustrator
has attempted to reinterpret the most important visions in her work, but in so
doing it was inevitable that his [*sic*] pictures would contain translations of non-
visual and purely symbolic elements" and that their allegorical character would
be foremost.

   5. W. Eugene Kleinbauer, *Modern Perspectives in Western Art History: An
Anthology of Twentieth-Century Writings on the Visual Arts* (New York,
1971), 13–36.

   6. Wilhelm Worringer, *Form in Gothic*, trans. Sir Herbert Read (London,
1927), illustrates a preponderance of German examples in all media (first published as *Formprobleme der Gotik*, 1912). Hanns Swarzenski's major work on
German manuscript illumination appeared just before he emigrated to the
United States: *Die lateinischen illuminierten Handschriften des XIII. Jahrhunderts in den Ländern an Rhein, Main, und Donau*, 2 vols. (Berlin, 1936). His
great study of "minor arts" highlights English, northern French and Mosan
works (from the Meuse valley) around 1200 and includes some German
thirteenth-century works as retardetaire Romanesque: *Monuments of Romanesque Art: The Art of Church Treasures in North-Western Europe*, 2d ed.
(London, 1967; original ed., 1954). Hans Jantzen, *High Gothic: The Classic
Cathedrals of Chartres, Reims, Amiens*, trans. James Palmes (New York,
1962), originally published as *Kunst der Gotik: Klassische Kathedralen
Frankreichs: Chartres, Reims, Amiens* (Hamburg, 1957); Otto von Simson,
*The Gothic Cathedral: Origins of Gothic Architecture and the Medieval Con-
cept of Order* (New York, 1956); Willibald Sauerländer, *Gothic Sculpture in*

France 1140–1270, trans. Janet Sondheimer (New York, 1972); and Florens Deuchler, *Gothic Art*, trans. Vivienne Menkes (New York, 1973), were among German-trained scholars who followed the same trend. Henri Focillon, *Art d'occident: Le Moyen âge, roman et gothique* (Paris, 1938), edited by Jean Bony and translated by Donald King as *The Art of the West in the Middle Ages* (New York, 1963), was the work of a French patriot who scarcely mentioned German monuments. Christopher Reginald Dodwell, *Painting in Europe 800 to 1200* (Harmondsworth, 1971), virtually ignores German painting after the Ottonian period.

7. The myth of the avant-garde that aided in the construction of modern geniuses like Picasso was exploded by Rosalind E. Krauss, *The Originality of the Avant-Garde and Other Modernist Myths* (Cambridge, Mass., 1985), esp. 151–170.

8. Walter Oakeshott, *The Artists of the Winchester Bible* (London, 1945), and *The Two Winchester Bibles* (Oxford, 1981).

9. Konrad Hoffmann, ed., *The Year 1200: A Centennial Exhibition at the Metropolitan Museum of Art* (New York, 1970); there were a few ivories (pp. 62–65), some metalwork (pp. 90, 104–123), several enamels (pp. 179–192), and a few stained glass panels (pp. 227–233), almost all from the Rhineland; the manuscripts were more numerous and diverse in origin, including several from Saxony, Westphalia, and Bavaria (pp. 266–289).

10. The Rheinisches Bildarchiv, Cologne, has some black-and-white negatives (ca. 1925) of the illustrations in the lost Rupertsberg manuscript; there is also a unique photographic copy of that era in the Abbey of St. Hildegard, Eibingen. Black-and-white photographs have been fully published only twice: Louis Baillet, "Les Miniatures du 'Scivias' de Sainte Hildegarde conservé à la bibliothèque de Wiesbaden," *Académie des inscriptions et belles lettres, monuments et mémoires* 19 (Paris, 1911): 49–149, and Maura Böckeler, *Hildegard von Bingen, Wisse die Wege, Scivias* (Salzburg, 1928). (Unfortunately, the 1954 and 1963 editions of Böckeler use the modern copy.) A complete copy of the Rupertsberg *Scivias* was made under the direction of Josepha Knips in 1927–1933 (Eibingen, Abtei St. Hildegard cod. 1); the illuminations have been reproduced in facsimile by Führkötter, *The Miniatures from the Book Scivias*, and they illustrate the CCCM *Scivias*.

11. Hiltgart L. Keller, *Mittelrheinische Buchmalereien in Handschriften aus dem Kreis der Hiltgart von Bingen* (Ph.D. diss., University of Frankfurt, 1933); Josef Schomer, *Die Illustrationen zu den Visionen der hl. Hildegard als künstlerische Neuschöpfung* (Ph.D. diss., University of Bonn, 1937). Unfortunately I have not had access to these works; I rely on the summary by Suzuki, "Zum Strukturproblem," 230–231.

12. Modern connoisseurs disregarded the prophetic negation of the unique qualities of the "original" by leftist writers such as Walter Benjamin, "The Work of Art in the Age of Mechanical Reproduction," in *Marxism and Art: Essays Classic and Contemporary*, ed. Maynard Solomon (New York, 1973), 550–561 (originally published as *Das Kunstwerk im Zeitalter seiner technischen Reproduzierbarkeit: Drei Studien zur Kunstsoziologie* [Frankfurt, 1963]).

13. Both Bernard Berenson and Max Friedländer supported themselves by passing judgment ("expertise") respectively on Italian and northern Renaissance paintings in the period before World War II, when photographic archives were also being formed.

14. Rita Otto, "Zu den gotischen Miniaturen einer Hildegardhandschrift in Lucca," *Mainzer Zeitschrift* 71–72 (1976–1977): 110–126.

15. Francis Wormald, "The Development of English Illumination in the Twelfth Century," *Journal of the British Archeological Association*, 3d ser. 8 (1943): 36–37, 48 (in relation to the Psalter of Christina of Markyate). Discerning the date and character of the lost original behind a series of copies was related to the philologists' establishment of a *stemma* for textual variants; among its major proponents was Kurt Weitzmann. My dissertation advisor, Hanns Swarzenski, was also expert in what I came to think of as "double connoisseurship": Swarzenski, "The Role of Copies in the Formation of the Styles of the Eleventh Century," in *Studies in Western Art: Acts of the Twentieth International Congress of the History of Art,* ed. Millard Meiss (Princeton, 1963), 1:7–13.

16. The book, formerly Wiesbaden, Württemburgische Landesbibliothek MS 1, had 235 leaves measuring 12.7 × 9.1 inches (32.1 × 23.1 cm); the framed area of the full-page illustrations measured about 9.6 × 6.8 inches (24.3 × 17.5 cm), according to *Scivias,* xxxiii.

17. *Scivias,* pl. 1 and p. 3. The free translation is my own; literally this is "say and write what you see and hear." At the end of the preface the command is rephrased: "Clama ergo et scribe sic" (therefore proclaim and write thus).

18. Pächt, *Book Illumination,* 160. He concludes that "the miniatures remain for the most part mere curiosities."

19. *Scivias,* preface, trans. Hart and Bishop, 59.

20. Barbara Newman, "Introduction," *Scivias,* trans. Hart and Bishop, 45.

21. Heidelberg, Universitätsbibliothek cod. Salem X, 16: Caviness, "Gender Symbolism," figs. 2, 3, 4. See also Reiner Haussherr, ed., *Die Zeit der Staufer: Geschichte-Kunst-Kultur,* exhibition catalog Württemburgisches Landesmuseum (Stuttgart, 1977), vol. 1, pp. 553–555, no. 732 (catalog entry by Renate Kroos, with bibliography). The most complete description and discussion of sources is still that of Adolf von Öchelhäuser, *Die Miniaturen der Universitäts-biobliothek zu Heidelberg* (Heidelberg, 1887–1895), vol. 1, pp. 75–107, pls. 11–17. Some sources are discussed by Clemencia Hand Kessler, "A Problematic Illumination of the Heidelberg Liber Scivias," *Marsyas* 8 (1957–1959): 7–21.

22. Charles Singer, "The Visions of Hildegard of Bingen," in *From Magic to Science: Essays on the Scientific Twilight* (London, 1928), pp. 199–239, pls. 1, 11–14, figs. 95, 97–99, 106–108. Oliver W. Sacks, *Migraine: Understanding a Common Disorder* (Berkeley, 1985), 57, 106–108, relied largely on Singer's analysis; he gives useful definitions of common aspects of migraine aura (pp. 248–249); see also Caviness, "Gender Symbolism," 95–99.

23. In the case of a strobe, one frequency affects migraine sufferers and another epileptics; at this stage of the attack the brain responds with an altered brain wave.

24. She might have seen some notable late-tenth-century examples in Regensburg, in a *Pericopes* from St. Emmeram, now in Pommersfelden, Graf von Schönborn Schloßbibliothek MS 340, and a monastic rule for the women at Niedermünster (Bamberg, Staatsbibliothek Msc. Lit. 142): *Regensburger Buchmalerei von frühkarolingischer Zeit bis zum Ausgang des Mittelalters*, exhibition catalog, Bayerischen Staatsbibliothek (Munich, 1987), pp. 30–31, nos. 12, 14, pls. 2–3. Tiny dots had also been used for the apocalyptic dragon: Émile-A. Van Moé, *L'Apocalypse de Saint-Sever, manuscrit latin 8878 de la Bibliothèque nationale (XIᵉ siècle)* (Paris, 1942), pls. 24, 28.

25. Frederick van der Meer, *Apocalypse: Visions from the Book of Revelation in Western Art* (New York, 1978), illus. on pp. 112, 123, 125; also Van Moé, *L'Apocalypse de Saint-Sever*, pls. 15, 22. For the large eight-pointed stars resembling flowers see also a drawing of the creation of the stars in a manuscript of Ambrosius, *Hexameron*, of about 1165–1170: *Regensburger Buchmalerei*, p. 51, no. 36, pl. 29.

26. Caviness, "Gender Symbolism," figs. 5, 14, 18.

27. Singer, *From Magic to Science*, 233, pls. 12, 14.

28. *Vita* II.5, p. 27.

29. In 1175, at the age of seventy-seven, Hildegard responded to Guibert of Gembloux's questioning about her visionary experiences in a letter, quoted here from Newman, *Sister of Wisdom*, 6. It is my own experience that auras often wake me at night and continue with my eyes open; migraine attacks often culminate in nausea as well as acute headaches and leave the patient limp and sometimes aphasic.

30. Verne S. Caviness Jr. and J. Patrick O'Brien, "Headache," *New England Journal of Medicine* 302 (1980): 446–450. For a synopsis of this biographical material see *Symphonia*, pp. 6–7.

31. The nineteenth-century neurologist Jean-Martin Charcot, who suffered occasionally from scintillating scotoma himself, published a drawing that he took from Hubert Airy (*Philosophical Transactions*, 1870, p. 147), but it and the description seem woefully inadequate to those of us who know the real thing. *Oeuvres complètes de J.-M. Charcot*, ed. Bernard Babinski et al. (Paris, 1890), vol. 3, pp. 74–75, fig. 12. See also the discussion and reproduction of the drawing by Georges Didi-Huberman, *Invention de l'hystérie: Charcot et l'iconographie photographique de la Salpêtrière* (Paris, 1982), pp. 131–132, fig. 55.

32. LVM VI.45, p. 292. The proscription, however, may not have been respected. The later Ghent manuscript of LDO demonstrates the extent of the changes and corrections made by Hildegard's assistants after Volmar's death: Albert Derolez, "The Genesis of Hildegard of Bingen's 'Liber divinorum operum': The Codicological Evidence," in *Texts and Manuscripts: Essays presented to G. I. Lieftinck* (Amsterdam, 1972), 2:23–33.

33. I have dealt with this problem at some length in "Gender Symbolism." Suzuki, "Zum Strukturproblem," 232, cites Keller, *Mittelrheinische Buchmalereien*, 127, to the effect that *scribere* was used to denote the total production of an illuminated manuscript.

34. *Symphonia*, p. 94. Most of the *Symphonia* lyrics were composed after the completion of the *Scivias* in 1151; Newman (p. 7) notes that Hildegard's

earlier songs were incorporated into the *Scivias,* constituting the last vision (III.13).

35. Paris, Bibliothèque nationale MS fr. 19093; see Caviness, "Gender Symbolism," fig. 21.

36. *Scivias,* preface, p. 3; *Scivias,* trans. Hart and Bishop, p. 59.

37. It has been more usual to view the range of colors symbolically, and no doubt they are given meanings in the context of Hildegard's writing: Christel Meier, "Die Bedeutung der Farben im Werk Hildegards von Bingen," *Frühmittelalterliche Studien* 6 (1972): 266–269; Roland Maisonneuve, "Le Symbolisme sacré des couleurs chez des mystiques médiévales: Hildegarde de Bingen; Julienne de Norwich," in *Les Couleurs au moyen âge* (Aix-en-Provence, 1988), 257–272.

38. Examples may be seen in Walter Cahn, *Romanesque Bible Illumination* (Ithaca, N.Y., 1982): Admont Bible from Salzburg ca. 1140 (fig. 121), Floreffe Bible ca. 1160 (figs. 154–155, 170–171).

39. For an example of the ornate imperial style see the Evangeliary of Henry IV or Henry V in Cracow, Cathedral Library MS 208, in *Regensburger Buchmalerei,* pls. 18–21.

40. *Scivias* II.1, pl. 10, pp. 110–112, cf. 116; *Scivias,* trans. Hart and Bishop, pp. 149–150, cf. 152.

41. Van Moé, *L'Apocalypse de Saint-Sever,* pl. 8 (fols. 108v–109). There are other commonalities: St. John holds a tablet to record his visions (pl. 5), and the dark recumbent devil is like the one in *Scivias* II.7 (pl. 22; cf. fig. 7 here).

42. Robert W. Scheller, *Exemplum: Model-Book Drawings and the Practice of Artistic Transmission in the Middle Ages (ca. 900–ca. 1470),* trans. Michael Hoyle (Amsterdam, 1995), 109–143, brings together a number of examples from the Romanesque period.

43. The Stammheim Missal, made for the Benedictine Abbey of St. Michael's, Hildesheim, about 1160, has been compared to the *Scivias* pictures for its iconography by Newman, *Sister of Wisdom,* 58, fig. 1, and also for the figural style by Caviness, "Gender Symbolism," fig. 6. A strong affinity with the *Clavis physicae* of Honorius Augustodunensis, Paris, Bibliothèque nationale MS lat. 6734, from the abbey of Michaelsberg near Bamberg, which Pächt attributed to the Meuse at mid-twelfth century, demonstrates the conservatism of Hildegard's style: Pächt, *Book Illumination,* p. 158, fig. 167. But an illustrated recension of Peter Lombard's *Commentary on the Psalms* made in Bamberg has been conservatively dated in the second half of the twelfth century: Gude Suckale-Redlefsen, *Der Buchschmuck zum Psalmenkommentar des Petrus Lombardus in Bamberg, Bamberg, Staatsbibliothek Msc. Bibl. 59* (Wiesbaden, 1986), 39–41. Despite its thoroughly rational pictorial organization, there are occasional resonances with the *Scivias* pictures, in the stiff figures, schematic drapery, carefully delineated masonry, and the use of inscribed scrolls.

44. The copies were reproduced by A. Straub and G. Keller, *Herrad of Landsberg: Hortus Deliciarum (Garden of Delights)* (New Rochelle, 1979). An excellent scholarly reconstruction with complete illustrations is Rosalie Green, Michael Evans, C. Bischoff, and M. Curschmann, *Hortus Deliciarum,* 2 vols. (London, 1979).

45. *Rhin-Meuse: Art et civilisation 800–1400*, exhibition catalog, Kunsthalle, Cologne (Cologne, 1972), nos. J20–48, pp. 292–312. Among conservative works are a lectionary from St.-Trond of the second half of the century, which followed an eleventh-century model, and the Life of St. Annon from Siegburg (J47, dated 1179–1181), but *Scivias* finds its closest parallels in a book from ca. 1130, the Lectionary of Archbishop Frederick of Cologne (J41).

46. Darmstadt, Hessische Landes- und Hochschulbibliothek MS 891; see Württembergisches Landesmuseum, *Die Zeit der Staufer: Geschichte—Kunst—Kultur*, exhibition catalog (Stuttgart, 1977), vol. 1, pp. 577–578, no. 749 (entry by Renate Kroos, with further bibliography).

47. Barbara Abou-El-Haj, *The Medieval Cult of Saints: Formations and Transformations*, (Cambridge, 1994), 107–130, 151–152; fig. 197 illustrates the typically Mosan page (Valenciennes, Bibliothèque municipale MS 500, fol. 68), which she plausibly dates 1160–1180, whereas she dates MS 501 to 1124–1145. Walter Cahn, *Romanesque Manuscripts: The Twelfth Century (A Survey of Manuscripts Illuminated in France)* (London, 1996), vol. 2, pp. 126–151, no. 126, and vol. 1, pl. 300, dates MS 501 in the third quarter of the twelfth century, despite comparisons with mid-twelfth-century works; he does not mention MS 500.

48. *Rhin-Meuse*, pp. 314–330, nos. K1–5, L1–4.

49. *Scivias* III.11, trans. Hart and Bishop, 493. This publication has plates by Mother Placid Dempsey, very freely redrawn from the copy of the Rupertsberg manuscript.

50. Norman Bryson, *Vision and Painting* (New Haven, 1982), 159–161, has remarked on the role of iconographic codes in the formation of a "community of recognition" throughout the Middle Ages, especially "if the stereotype were found at no point coincident with a reality outside it (the Trinity . . .)."

51. For an example of the bestial portrayal of the devil, see the late-twelfth-century English Huntingfield Psalter (New York, Pierpont Morgan Library M. 43, fol. 20v/23v), as described by Montague Rhodes James, *Catalogue of Manuscripts and Early Printed Books from the Libraries of William Morris, Richard Bennett, Bertram Fourth Earl of Ashburnham, and Other Sources, Now Forming Portions of the Library of J. Pierpont Morgan* (London, 1906), 35 (with old foliation).

52. *Scivias* III. 11.13–14, trans. Hart and Bishop, 497–498.

53. For examples of contemporary female artists' fragmented self-portrayal, see Francesca Woodman's photographs from the Providence series, 1975–1976, especially a frontal torso shot with a papier maché mask covering her genital area: Harm Lux and Friedrich Meschede, *Francesca Woodman: Photographische Arbeiten: Photographic Works* (Zurich and Münster, 1992), 68–69. See also *Kiki Smith: Unfolding the Body, an Exhibition of the Work in Paper*, exhibition catalog, Rose Art Museum, Brandeis University, catalog by Susan L. Stoops (Waltham, Brandeis University, 1992); and my "The Broken Mirror: Parts, Relics, Freaks," in Caviness, *Triangulating Medieval Art-Object, History, Feminism* (forthcoming).

54. A series of such domical buildings, from the Early Christian period through the Romanesque, was brought together by Richard Krautheimer, "Introduction to an Iconography of Medieval Architecture," *Journal of the Warburg*

and Courtauld Institutes 5 (1942): 1–33; reprinted in his *Studies in Early Christian, Medieval, and Renaissance Art* (New York, 1969), 115–150.

55. Caviness, "Hildegard of Bingen," *Dictionary of Women Artists,* 686–687.

56. *Scivias* III.7.9, trans. Hart and Bishop, 418.

57. *Scivias* III.7, trans. Hart and Bishop, 411–421. Ursula Nilgen, "Psalter der Christina von Markyate (sogenannter Albani-Psalter)," in *Der Schatz von St. Godehard,* exhibition catalog, Diözesan-Museum Hildesheim (Hildesheim, 1988), pp. 162–163, no. 69.

58. Personal letter, 10/10/1994; and see Walter Cahn, "Architectural Draftsmanship in Twelfth-Century Paris: The Illustrations of Richard of Saint-Victor's Commentary on Ezekiel's Temple Vision," *Gesta* 15 (1976): 247–254, figs. 1–4, and Cahn, "Architecture and Exegesis: Richard of St.-Victor's Ezekiel Commentary and Its Illustrations," *Art Bulletin* 76 (1994): 53–68, esp. 66–67.

59. Hans Erich Kubach, *Romanesque Architecture* (New York, 1975), 155–166, 279–284.

60. *Symphonia,* pp. 68–70, 193–199, 295–298.

61. *Vita S. Ruperti,* PL 197:1081–1094.

62. Erwin Panofsky, *Abbot Suger: On the Abbey Church of St.-Denis and Its Treasures,* 2d ed. (Princeton, 1979), 62–65. For glass colors and how they were made, see Madeline H. Caviness, *Stained Glass Windows* (Turnhout, 1996), 45–55.

63. The literal translation serves better: Rupert is simply "crowned with roses, lilies, and purple": *Symphonia,* p. 197.

64. *Symphonia,* pp. 193–197.

65. A facsimile of the illuminated pages exists: A. R. Calderoni Masetti and G. dalli Regoli, *Sanctae Hildegardis Revelationes Manoscritto 1942* (Lucca, 1973). These are also reproduced in the Derolez-Dronke edition of the LDO (CCCM 92). Less good color reproductions are in Hildegard von Bingen, *Welt und Mensch: Das Buch 'de operatione Dei' aus dem genter Kodex,* trans. Heinrich Schipperges (Salzburg, 1965). *Hildegard of Bingen's Book of Divine Works with Letters and Songs,* ed. Matthew Fox (a partial translation of Schipperges) (Santa Fe, N.M., 1987), contains incomplete illustrations redrawn by Angela Werneke.

66. Rita Otto, "Zu den gotischen Miniaturen einer Hildegardhandschrift in Lucca," *Mainzer Zeitschriften,* 71–72 (1976–1977): 110–126.

67. I have discussed the evidence for copying at length in "Hildegard as Designer of the Illustrations to Her Works."

68. I am grateful to have been able to examine the manuscript in order to make this original observation. Otto discussed the scrolls in some detail, treating them as an integral feature of the iconography: "Zu den gotischen Miniaturen," 113, 116, 117, 123, 125. My observations are recorded in detail in "Hildegard as Designer."

69. My numbering of the ten LDO visions follows the new edition in CCCM 92. In the old edition (PL 197) the visions are numbered consecutively from 1 to 10.

70. The symbolism of the cardinal directions in both works is discussed by Barbara Maurmann, *Die Himmelsrichtungen im Weltbild des Mittelalters: Hildegard von Bingen, Honorius Augustodunensis und andere Autoren* (Munich, 1976), 38–116. Yet in *Scivias* north is usually to the viewer's left, whereas it is more often toward the bottom of the folio in the LDO, and there are occasions in the later book where the pictorial sense of up and down has taken precedence. For instance, the text describes one of the strange composite figures in the upper left of the seventh vision as having its head to the north, yet both are upright.

71. The singular importance Hildegard attached to the winds in holding the cosmos in place has been emphasized by Barbara Obrist, "Wind Diagrams and Medieval Cosmology," *Speculum* 72 (1997): 33–84; this idea is matched, but not illustrated, by the novel beast heads.

72. Peter Lasko, *Ars Sacra: 800–1200* (Harmondsworth, 1972), pp. 156–168, 186–187, 240–252, pls. 161–165, 168–169, 288–294. Most dates are defined by the commissioning abbot; Nicholas is the only one with several signed and dated works that give him a kind of biography.

73. Dodwell, *Pictorial Arts*, pp. 341–344, pls. 346–347.

74. Madeline H. Caviness, *Sumptuous Arts at the Royal Abbeys in Reims and Braine* (Princeton, 1990), 69–70.

75. Theophilus, *De Diversis Artibus*, ed. Christopher R. Dodwell (London, 1961); reissued as Theophilus, *The Various Arts*, trans. Dodwell (Oxford, 1986).

76. Swarzenski, *Monuments of Romanesque Art*, 18. He notes that "donor and craftsman often appear as one and the same person and are recorded as *Auctor* as well as *Autor.*" This might also be expressed as *fecit* (s/he made x) or *fieri fecit* (s/he had x made).

77. Lambert of St.-Omer created his pictorial encyclopedia *Liber Floridus* about 1120 as a compendium for teaching. For a facsimile of the autograph manuscript, Ghent, Bibliothèque de l'Université de la Ville MS 16, see Albert Derolez, *Lamberti S. Audomari canonici Liber Floridus codex autographus Bibliothecae Universitatis Gandavensis* (Ghent, 1968). On Honorius, who may have served at the *alte Kapelle* of Regensburg, see Valerie I. J. Flint, *Honorius Augustodunensis of Regensburg* (Aldershot, 1995). For one of his pictorial works, see Pächt, *Book Illumination*, 160.

78. Hugh employs many vivid descriptions that demonstrate a knowledge of works of art of a variety of epochs and media (and of a community of recognition), but his exegetical cause célèbre is the mystical ark of Noah (PL 176:700–702). See Patrice Sicard, *Diagrammes médiévaux et exégèse visuelle: Le Libellus de formatione arche de Hugues de Saint-Victor* (Paris and Turnhout, 1993).

79. Michael Goodich, "The Politics of Canonization in the Thirteenth Century: Lay and Mendicant Saints," in *Saints and Their Cults: Studies in Religious Sociology, Folklore, and History*, ed. Stephen Wilson (Cambridge, 1983), 182, lays out the political reasons for the denial of canonization to Hildegard. See also Newman, "Sibyl of the Rhine," pp. 28–29 above.

80. Linda Nochlin, "Why Have There Been No Great Women Artists?" reprinted in her *Women, Art, and Power and Other Essays* (New York, 1988), 145–178; originally published in *Art News* 69 (January, 1971).

81. A very good recent review of the rise of the notions of originality and creative genius in the romantic period is given by Peter Jaszi and Martha Woodmansee, "The Ethical Reaches of Authorship," *South Atlantic Quarterly* 95, no. 4 (Fall 1996): 947–977.

CHAPTER 7: "MEDICAL WRITER"

1. Marianna Schrader and Adelgundis Führkötter, *Die Echtheit des Schrifttums der hl. Hildegard von Bingen* (Cologne, 1956), 4–5, 54–58. The volumes formerly preserved at the Rupertsberg, now lost, carried different titles, as Trithemius indicates in his *Hirsau Chronicle*, describing "a remarkable work on the causes and remedies of all diseases of the human body, which was entitled *Compound Medicine* and begins 'Deus ante creationem mundi absque initio fuit et est.' Another book on the natures of herbs which pertain to the cure of the human body, quite beautifully edited, which was entitled *Simple Medicine*." I employ the titles used by the editors of the texts for the sake of consistency. The title *Physica* does not appear in any of the manuscripts, but *Causae et curae* is the title given in the only extant manuscript of that text, written by the hand of one of the manuscript's rubricators. See my palaeographical analysis in "The Perforated Wall: An Inquiry into the Textual Traditions of Hildegard of Bingen's Medicine" (Ph.D diss., Duke University, 1998). The incipit given above by Trithemius for what he calls *Compound Medicine* is identical to that of the Copenhagen manuscript of the *Causes and Cures*.

2. The process of professionalization for male practitioners and the implications for women are broached in Luis Garcia-Ballester, Michael R. McVaugh, and Agustin Rubio-Vela, *Medical Licensing and Learning in Fourteenth-Century Valencia* (Philadelphia, 1989), and in Pearl Kibre, "The Faculty of Medicine at Paris, Charlatanism, and Unlicensed Medical Practices in the Later Middle Ages," *Bulletin of the History of Medicine* 27 (1953): 1–20. The "wondrous" nature of Hildegard's medical insights is additionally remarked in the preface to the sixteenth-century edition of the *Physica* by Johann Schott, *Physica S. Hildegardis. Elementorum, Fluminum aliquot Germaniae, Metallorum, Leguminum, Fructuum et Herbarum: Arborum et Arbustorum: Piscium denique, Volatilium et Animantium terrae naturas et operationes IV libris mirabili experientia posteritati tradens* (Strasbourg, 1533).

3. *Rule of St. Benedict*, trans. Anthony Meisel and M. L. del Mastro (New York, 1975), chaps. 36–37, pp. 78–79.

4. PL 197:1053–1066. Heinrich Schipperges, "Diätetische Lebensführung nach der 'Regula Benedicti' bei Hildegard von Bingen," *Arzt und Christ* 2 (1980): 87–97. As Barbara Newman has noted in "Sibyl of the Rhine," p. 7 in this volume, Hildegard's attitudes toward fasting and other unhealthy asceticism stand in contrast to those of her teacher Jutta.

5. See the analysis of monastic customaries and inventories in Donatella Nebbiai-Dalla Guarda, "Les Livres de l'infirmerie dans les monastères médié-

vaux," *Revue Mabillon* n.s. 5 (1994): 57–81, as well as my own analysis of early medieval library catalogs listing medical books in "The Perforated Wall."

6. Cf. the "Mulinen Rotulus" described by Augusto Beccaria, *I codici di medicina del periodo presalernitano (secoli IX, X, e XI)* (Rome, 1956), no. 124, pp. 358–359. Literature not kept in the monastic library probably suffered the fate of ephemera.

7. *The Letters of Abelard and Heloise*, trans. Betty Radice (Harmondsworth, 1974), no. 7, p. 215.

8. *The Letters of Gerbert* [of Rheims] *with His Papal Privileges as Sylvester II*, trans. Harriet Pratt Lattin (New York, 1961), letters 122, 159, 178. *The Letters and Poems of Fulbert of Chartres*, trans. Frederick Behrends (Oxford, 1976), letters 24, 47, 48. Jeffrey Richards, *Consul of God: The Life and Times of Gregory the Great* (London, 1980), 47.

9. Walter Horn and Ernest Born, *The Plan of St. Gall: A Study of the Architecture and Economy of and Life in a Paradigmatic Carolingian Monastery*, 3 vols. (Berkeley, 1979), 1:313–321, 2:175–188. See also the analysis of Loren C. MacKinney, *Early Medieval Medicine* (Baltimore, 1937), 53–55, and pl. 1. Despite its limitations, this study remains one of the better surveys of the period.

10. One good example is Warin, who entered St. Albans with his brother Matthew after both had studied medicine at Salerno. Warin was elected abbot of that house and died in 1195; there is no evidence, however, to suggest that either brother practiced medicine once they had taken their vows. See Charles H. Talbot and E. A. Hammond, *The Medical Practitioners of Medieval England: A Biographical Register* (London, 1965), 372–373.

11. For an analysis of the circumscriptions denying women access to formal theological study in the thirteenth century, see the fine essay by Alcuin Blamires, "The Limits of Bible Study for Medieval Women," in *Women, the Book, and the Godly*, ed. Lesley Smith and Jane H. M. Taylor (Cambridge, 1995), 1–12.

12. Darrel W. Amundsen, "Medieval Canon Law on Medical and Surgical Practice by the Clergy," *Bulletin of the History of Medicine* 52 (1978): 22–44.

13. *The Letters of St. Bernard of Clairvaux*, trans. Bruno Scott James (London, 1953), nos. 70 and 71, pp. 95–99.

14. *Letters of St. Bernard of Clairvaux*, no. 388, pp. 458–459.

15. Rare and largely unavailable works included Celsus's *On Medicine*, Caelius Aurelianus's *On Acute and Chronic Diseases*, and Caelius Aurelianus's *Gynecology*. See Beccaria, *I codici*, "Indici dei testi," 444–446; Ann Ellis Hanson and Monica H. Green, "Soranus of Ephesus: *Methodicorum princeps*," in Wolfgang Haase and Hildegard Temporini, eds., *Aufstieg und Niedergang der römischen Welt*, Teilband II, Band 37.2 (Berlin, 1994), 968–1075, esp. 1042–1061. On Gerbert of Rheims's search for a copy of the rare text *Ophthalmicus* by Demosthenes, see *Letters of Gerbert*, no. 16, p. 55; Heinrich von Staden, *Herophilus: The Art of Medicine in Early Alexandria* (Cambridge, 1989), 570–573.

16. *Cassiodori Senatoris Institutiones*, ed. R. A. B. Mynors (Oxford, 1937), 78–79.

17. For simplistic and uncritical assumptions about medical thought, literature, and practice, see Lucille B. Pinto, "The Folk Practice of Gynecology and

Obstetrics in the Middle Ages," *Bulletin of the History of Medicine* 47 (1973): 513–523, and Gertrude M. Engbring, "Saint Hildegard, Twelfth Century Physician," *Bulletin of the History of Medicine* 8 (1940): 770–784.

18. The best survey of medical literature before the twelfth century remains Beccaria's catalog (1956); for manuscripts pertaining to France, see also Ernest Wickersheimer, *Les Manuscrits latins de médecine du haut moyen âge dans les bibliothèques de France* (Paris, 1966). The survival of predominantly monastic medical literature may be a consequence of the greater stability and protection books in monastic collections enjoyed, as opposed to personal handbooks of practitioners outside the cloisters.

19. See the essays in *Le Latin médical: La Constitution d'un langage scientifique,* ed. Guy Sabbah, Centre Jean-Palerne Mémoires 10 (Saint Étienne: Université de Saint Étienne, 1991); Klaus-Dietrich Fischer, "Überlieferungs- und Verständnisprobleme im medizinischen Latein des frühen Mittelalters," *Berichte zur Wissenschaftsgeschichte* 17 (1994): 153–165; Michael Lapidge, "The Hermeneutic Style in Tenth-Century Anglo-Latin Literature," *Anglo-Saxon England* 4 (1975): 79–85, 103–105.

20. Augusto Beccaria, "Sulle tracce di un antico canone latino di Ippocrate e di Galeno," *Italia Medioevale e Umanistica* 2 (1959): 1–56, 4 (1961): 1–75, 14 (1971): 1–23. On the popularity of Hippocratic over Galenic gynecological theories, see Monica H. Green, *The Transmission of Ancient Theories of Female Physiology and Disease through the Early Middle Ages* (Ph.D. diss., Princeton University, 1985), esp. chaps. 1–4.

21. The Echternach manuscript is Paris, Bibliothèque nationale MS lat. 11219; Beccaria, *I codici,* no. 35, pp. 166–173. My thanks to Dr. Stephen Greenberg and the staff at the National Library of Medicine, History of Medicine Division (Bethesda, Md.), for granting me generous access to this and other microfilms in their keeping.

22. See the Old High German glossaries edited by Elias Steinmeyer and E. Sievers, *Die althochdeutschen Glossen,* vols. 3 and 5 (Berlin, 1895, 1922); two other important vernacular glossaries produced in the middle Rhine are found in Trier, Stadtbibliothek cod. 40, and Bonn, Universitätsbibliothek cod. 218. On the former, see Beccaria, *I codici,* 231–233, and F. W. E. Roth, "Althochdeutsches aus Trier," *Zeitschrift für deutsches Altertum und deutsche Literatur* 52 (1910): 169–176. On the latter see Rainer Reiche, *Ein rheinisches Schulbuch aus dem 11. Jahrhundert,* Münchener Beiträge zur Mediävistik und Renaissance-Forschung 24 (Munich, 1976); also Beccaria, *I codici,* 204–207; my thanks to the Hill Monastic Manuscript Library (Collegeville, Minn.) for allowing me to consult their microfilm of the Bonn manuscript, which was at one point owned by the monastery of Maria Laach, near Trier. An accessible account of Old German medical recipes and charms is Brian Murdoch, *Old High German Literature* (Boston, 1983), 45–54. Murdoch, however, does not discuss the medical glossaries of the Rhineland. See also Karl Sudhoff, "Die gedruckten mittelalterlichen medizinischen Texte in germanischen Sprachen," *Sudhoffs Archiv für Geschichte der Medizin* 3 (1910): 273–300.

23. Jerome J. Bylebyl, "The Medical Meaning of *Physica*," *Osiris,* 2d ser. 6 (1990): 16–41; John J. Contreni, "Masters and Medicine in Northern France

during the Reign of Charles the Bald," in *Charles the Bald: Court and Kingdom*, ed. Margaret Gibson and Janet Nelson, with the assistance of David Ganz (Oxford, 1981), 333–346.

24. Charles Burnett, "The Contents and Affiliation of the Scientific Manuscripts Written at, or Brought to, Chartres in the Time of John of Salisbury," in *The World of John of Salisbury*, ed. Michael Wilks (Oxford, 1984), 127–160; Mary Wack, "Ali ibn al-Abbas al-Magusi and Constantine on Love, and the Evolution of the *Practica Pantegni*," in *Constantine the African and 'Ali ibn al-Abbas al-Magusi: The* Pantegni *and Related Texts*, ed. Charles Burnett and Danielle Jacquart (Leiden, 1994), 197–199. Wack's essay introduces important new evidence exposing textual manipulations of the new literature, undertaken by the monk-physician Northungus of Hildesheim (fl. ca. 1140).

25. Danielle Jacquart, "The Introduction of Arabic Medicine into the West: The Question of Etiology," in *Health, Disease, and Healing in Medieval Culture*, ed. Sheila Campbell, Bert Hall, and David Klausner (New York, 1992), 186–195. For an up-to-date and accessible survey, see Vivian Nutton, "Medicine in Medieval Western Europe, 1100–1500," in *The Western Medical Tradition, 800 B.C. to A.D. 1800*, ed. Lawrence I. Conrad, Michael Neve, Vivian Nutton et al. (Cambridge, 1995), 139–143.

26. Paul Kaiser's edition of *Causae et curae* (Leipzig, 1903) numbers the prognostics and lunar horoscope together as book 5, following the fifteenth-century hand that assigned numbers to each chapter and designated book numeration at the tops of pages (as well as a table of chapters, in five books, at the end of the manuscript). There are, however, six large foliated decorative initials in the text itself, suggesting a six-book division. On the compatibility of the lunar horoscope with other elements of Hildegard's thought, see Peter Dronke, *Women Writers of the Middle Ages* (Cambridge, 1984), 177–179.

27. *Physica*, ed. Charles Daremberg and F. A. Reuss, in PL 197:1118–1352. The text begins at col. 1125.

28. Jerry Stannard, "Natural History," in *Science in the Middle Ages*, ed. David C. Lindberg (Chicago, 1978), 429–460. See also the lengthy title of the *Hermeneumata*, or glossary of medicinal categories, given in the ninth-century Echternach manuscript, Paris, Bibliothèque nationale MS lat. 11219, described above in this article at note 21.

29. This idea was expressed in the preface to the *Physica*, PL 197:1125–1128. Compare Adam's arranging of creatures in Hildegard's *Expositio Evangeliorum*: see Peter Dronke, "Platonic-Christian Allegories in the Homilies of Hildegard of Bingen," in *From Athens to Chartres: Neoplatonism and Medieval Thought: Studies in Honor of Edouard Jeauneau*, ed. Haijo J. Westra (Leiden, 1992), 391–392.

30. *Lingua Ignota*, partially edited by Jean-Baptiste Pitra, *Analecta Sacra*, vol. 8 (Monte Cassino, 1882), 496–502. See Jeffrey T. Schnapp, "Virgin Words: Hildegard of Bingen's *Lingua Ignota* and the Development of Imaginary Languages Ancient to Modern," *Exemplaria* 3 (1991): 267–298. I would like to thank the curators of the Berlin Staatsbibliothek, Preussischer Kulturbesitz, for granting me access to their manuscript, cod. lat. quarto 674, and Jeffrey

Schnapp for sharing his views with me prior to our respective papers at Yale Divinity School's "Hildegard of Bingen: A Symposium" (February 1994).

31. For a persuasive analysis of early medieval female scribal activity, see Rosamund McKitterick, "Women and Literacy in the Early Middle Ages," in her *Books, Scribes, and Learning in the Frankish Kingdoms, Sixth–Ninth Centuries* (Aldershot, 1994).

32. Constantine's text appears in Isaac Israeli, *Omnia opera Ysaac,* part 2 (Lyon, 1515), as well as in *Constantini . . . opera* (Basel, 1536/1539), which is considered the better edition. Although the *Theorica* and *Practica* should have had ten books each, the great majority of the *Practica* was lost before Constantine began his translation and it was only reconstructed by others much later. See the essays of Monica Green, Mary Wack, and Mark Jordan in Burnett and Jacquart, *Constantine the African.*

33. Conrad et al., *Western Medical Tradition,* 170, 174–175. Regrettably the editors did not catch the typographical error that gives the year of Hildegard's death as 1197 rather than 1179. For timely remarks on the significance of encyclopedic twelfth-century medical compilation, see the recent news story by William H. Honan, "Library and Dealer Dispute Custody of Medieval Text," *The New York Times,* 1 September 1997, p. A-9. The text in question, National Library of Medicine MS 8, copied ca. 1150, offers a mixture of both early medieval and Salernitan literature, including excerpts from Constantine's *Pantegni.*

34. Hildegard's pharmacopoeia combines the *Dynamidia* tradition, which characterized medicines by their hot, cold, dry, or moist "powers" or "virtues," with the *Physiologus* tradition characterizing animals. The former was broadened by Constantine the African's pharmacopoeia, especially the *De gradibus,* sometimes called *De dynamidibus.* See Loren C. MacKinney, " 'Dynamidia' in Medieval Medical Literature," *Isis* 24 (1935–1936): 400–414; *Bibliographie des textes médicaux latins: Antiquité et haut moyen âge,* ed. Guy Sabbah, Pierre-Paul Corsetti, Klaus-Dietrich Fischer, Centre Jean Palerne Mémoires 6 (Saint Étienne, 1987), 73–75, 83–84. On the *Physiologus* and animals, see Laurence Moulinier, *Le Manuscrit perdu à Strasbourg: Enquête sur l'œuvre scientifique de Hildegarde* (Paris, 1995), 227–233; Moulinier, "L'Ordre du monde animal selon Hildegarde de Bingen," in *L'Homme, l'animal domestique, et l'environnement du moyen âge au XVIIIᵉ siècle,* ed. R. Durant (Nantes, 1993), 119–134.

35. One possible exception to Hildegard's exclusive position as a female medical writer is a brief series of medical recipes in Old English copied into a manuscript of devotional texts associated with the Benedictine convent of Nunnaminster (Winchester); it is not clear to me whether the nuns owned the manuscript at the time the additions were made. See N. R. Ker, *A Catalogue of Manuscripts Containing Anglo-Saxon* (Oxford, 1957), 157; Stephanie Hollis and Michael Wright, "The Remedies in British Library MS Cotton Galba A.xiv, fols. 139 and 136r," *Notes and Queries* 239, n.s. 41, no. 2 (June 1994): 146–147; and the bibliographical survey in Hollis and Wright, *Old English Prose of Secular Learning* (Cambridge, 1992), 234–238.

36. Hildegard's efforts to present a balanced view of the human experience, addressing both male and female issues equally, sets her apart from the majority of medical authors who routinely discussed women chiefly in their reproductive capacity. See Joan Cadden, *Meanings of Sex Difference in the Middle Ages: Medicine, Science, and Culture* (Cambridge, 1993), 70–88.

37. It is interesting that the *Trotula* ascribed to Trota of Salerno was printed together with Hildegard's *Physica* in the Schott edition of 1533 (see n. 2 above, this chapter). See also Monica H. Green, "Documenting Medieval Women's Medical Practice," in *Practical Medicine from Salerno to the Black Death*, ed. Luis Garcia-Ballester, Roger French, Jon Arrizabalaga, and Andrew Cunningham (Cambridge, 1994), 322–352; Green, "The Development of the *Trotula*," *Revue d'histoire des textes* 26 (1996): 119–203; Green, "A Handlist of the Latin and Vernacular Manuscripts of the So-Called *Trotula* Texts," *Scriptorium* 50 (1996): 137–175. See also the overview of women and medicine in Conrad et al., *Western Medical Tradition*, 168–175.

38. LDO; see especially the cosmological visions of the "Pars prima." Hildegard's cosmological thought is discussed and placed in context in Hans Liebeschütz, *Das allegorische Weltbild der hl. Hildegard von Bingen* (Leipzig, 1930), esp. 86–107.

39. In many cases Hildegard seemed to prefer a plurality of expressions, not always entirely consistent with one another but cumulatively conveying a more evocative exposition than would simple "straight" discourse. See Barbara Newman's analysis of Hildegard's use of metaphor and image in *Symphonia*, 40–45.

40. *Causae et curae*, 45.

41. *Causae et curae*, 2.

42. *Causae et curae*, 10.

43. Ernst Wickersheimer, "Figures médico-astrologiques des IXe, X^e, et XIe siècles," *Janus* 19 (1914): 157–177; Byrhtferth of Ramsey's "Manual," in *Anglo-Saxon Prose*, trans. Michael Swanton (London, 1993), 265–267; Lapidge, "Hermeneutic Style," 90–94; "Sapientia artis medicinae," ed. M. Wlaschky, *Kyklos* 1 (1928): 104–105. On Hildegard and the winds, see Barbara Obrist, "Wind Diagrams and Medieval Cosmology," *Speculum* 72 (1997): 75–84. My thanks to the keepers of the Southern Historical Collection at the University of North Carolina for granting me access to films and photographs collected by the late Loren C. MacKinney containing many of these images, especially the photographs of Chartres MS 62, which was destroyed in World War II.

44. *Causae et curae*, 3, 40–41. The "quartered sphere" of the earth and the *homo microcosmus*, both subject to cosmological influences, are best represented in the Lucca manuscript of the *Book of Divine Works* (Lucca, Biblioteca governativa cod. 1942). See the plates and discussion in the CCCM edition of the *Liber divinorum operum*, and Liebeschütz, *Das allegorische Weltbild*. As Madeline Caviness persuasively argues in chapter 6, "Artist," in this volume, the Lucca manuscript, though from the thirteenth century, almost certainly preserves significant elements of Hildegard's original designs.

45. *Causae et curae*, 49–50.

46. The fullest analysis is Sue Spencer Cannon, "The Medicine of Hildegard of Bingen: Her Twelfth-Century Theories and Their Twentieth-Century Appeal as a Form of Alternative Medicine" (Ph.D. diss., UCLA, 1993), 76–117; see also Sabina Flanagan, "Hildegard and the Humors: Medieval Theories of Illness and Personality," in *Madness, Melancholy, and the Limits of the Self: Studies in Culture, Law, and the Sacred*, ed. Andrew D. Weiner and Leonard V. Kaplan (Madison, Wisc., 1996), 14–23. Humoral doctrine was a theory developed only by the ancient Dogmatists or Rationalists, one of the three most influential philosophical medical sects. The Hippocratic writers had not developed an entirely uniform or consistent doctrine, and several early medieval treatises speak of the humors only in general terms. See Erich Schoner, "Das Viererschema in der Antiken Humoralpathologie," *Sudhoffs Archiv*, suppl. 4 (Wiesbaden, 1964).

47. *Causae et curae*, 42, 50, 57, 59.

48. *Causae et curae*, 36; Dronke, "Platonic-Christian Allegories," 390.

49. Rudolph Arbesmann, "The Concept of 'Christus Medicus' in St. Augustine," *Traditio* 10 (1954): 1–26.

50. Prayer does not figure prominently in the medical writings. Occasionally Hildegard writes that cures are accomplished through medicines with God's permission, in much the same way that knowledge is achieved through human effort met by divine cooperation. On charms, amulets, and the like, see George Radimersky, "Magic in the Works of Hildegard von Bingen," *Monatshefte* 49 (1957): 353–360. Burchard of Worms's penitential *Decretum* (ca. 1008–1012) approved the chanting of the Creed or the Lord's Prayer during the collection of medicinal herbs; John T. McNeill and Helena M. Gamer, *Medieval Handbooks of Penance* (New York, 1938), 42. See also Vivian Nutton, "From Medical Certainty to Medical Amulets: Three Aspects of Ancient Therapeutics," *Clio Medica* 22 (1991): 13–22.

51. Wickersheimer, *Les Manuscrits*, pp. 89–91, pl. 7: Paris, Bibliothèque nationale cod. lat. 9332.

52. Cf. "The Defense of the Art of Medicine" in "Das 'Lorscher Arzneibuch,' " ed. Ulrich Stoll, *Sudhoffs Archiv*, suppl. 28 (Stuttgart, 1992), 48–62.

53. M. Wellmann, ed., *Die Fragmente der Sikelischen Ärzte Akron, Philistion und des Diokles von Karystos* (Berlin, 1901), 208–234, from Brussels, Bibliothèque royale cod. lat. 1342–1350, a manuscript of the twelfth century owned by the Benedictines of St. Panthaleon, Cologne. Beccaria, *I codici*, 109–112.

54. *Causae et curae*, 109–110; Wellmann, *Fragmente*, 223, 215.

55. This is not to suggest that Hildegard's medical ideas were inspired by distinct experiential visions but that her perpetual, overarching *visio* played a pivotal role in her own epistemological processes.

56. Cadden, *Meanings of Sex Difference*, part 1; Cadden, "It Takes All Kinds: Sexuality and Gender Differences in Hildegard of Bingen's 'Book of Compound Medicine,' " *Traditio* 40 (1984): 149–174; Dronke, *Women Writers*, 171–183.

57. Vindician, *Gynaecia*, ed. Valentin Rose, *Theodori Prisciani Euporiston libri III . . . [et] Vindiciani Afri quae feruntur reliquiae* (Leipzig, 1894), 426–466. The rather evocative phrase "omnes compagines membrorum," used

to signify the integral body composed of different organs, appears variously in Hildegard's sequence "O ignis Spiritus Paracliti," in the *Causes and Cures,* and in the *Book of Divine Works.* The phrase was, I think, inspired by the opening lines of Vindician's *Gynaecia,* where the human body is "composed" or "bound together" from bones, nerves, etc. For the text of the sequence see Barbara Newman's essay "Poet," pp. 186–188 in this volume.

58. Katharine Park, "The Criminal and the Saintly Body: Autopsy and Dissection in Renaissance Italy," *Renaissance Quarterly* 47 (1994): 1–33; Park, "The Life of the Corpse: Division and Dissection in Late Medieval Europe," *Journal of the History of Medicine* 50 (1995): 111–132.

59. On Hildegard and the *Pantegni,* see Peter Dronke, Introduction 2 to LDO, xv–xvi.

60. *Causae et curae,* 99–100, 179–180; *Pantegni, Theorica,* IX, 39.

61. *Causae et curae,* 99–100.

62. Mark Jordan has noted that manuscripts of the *Pantegni,* though numerous, stand relatively devoid of annotations, with only occasional glosses or underlinings added by medieval readers. The practice of excerpting *sententiae,* or pithy definitions of terms, was far more common among the *Pantegni*'s readers; see Jordan's essay in Burnett and Jacquart, *Constantine the African.* Hildegard's use represents a somewhat more casual, less reverential approach to this medical blockbuster of a text.

63. Hanson and Green, "Soranus of Ephesus," 1054–1055, on the "De passionibus mulierum" B. See also my analysis in "The Development of Gariopontus of Salerno's 'Passionarius': Preliminary Findings and a List of Manuscripts" (forthcoming).

64. Peter Dronke, "Problemata Hildegardiana," *Mittellateinisches Jahrbuch* 16 (1981): 97–131, esp. 107–117; Barbara Newman, "Hildegard of Bingen: Visions and Validation," *Church History* 54 (1985): 163–175.

65. *Causae et curae,* 66–67.

66. There is, however, no way to "decode" her miraculous healings as masking some sort of efficacious medical practice by Hildegard herself. Both in her *Vita* and in the *Acta inquisitionis* compiled for her canonization bid, Hildegard's cures are all couched in purely miraculous terms, many of them effected through her hair, her clothing, river water, and even the wearing of written amulets. These cures continued, moreover, at her burial and beyond her death. To interpret Hildegard's miracles as medical activity would beg the question of whether we ought to do the same for the cures effected, for instance, at Thomas Becket's shrine in Canterbury or at Bury St. Edmunds, two pilgrimage sites and ecclesiastical centers that owned numerous influential medical texts, as well as hospices for the care of the sick. The truth is surely more complex.

67. Melitta Weiss-Amer, "Die Physica Hildegards von Bingen als Quelle für das Kochbuch Meister Eberhards," *Sudhoffs Archiv* 76 (1992): 87–96; Melitta Weiss Adamson [Weiss-Amer], "A Reevaluation of St. Hildegard's 'Physica' in Light of the Latest Manuscript Finds," in *Manuscript Sources of Medieval Medicine,* ed. Margaret Schleissner (New York, 1995), 55–80.

68. Barbara Fehringer, *Das Speyerer Kräuterbuch mit den Heilpflanzen Hildegards von Bingen: Eine Studie zur mittelhochdeutschen Physica-Rezeption*

mit Kritischer Ausgabe des Textes (Würzburg, 1994). Other sources used by the compiler were Macer Floridus and the *Circa instans*.

69. Laurence Moulinier, "Fragments inédits de la 'Physica': Contribution à l'étude de la transmission des manuscrits scientifiques de Hildegarde de Bingen," *Mélanges de l'École française de Rome* 105, no. 2 (1993): 629–650.

70. Schrader and Führkötter, *Echtheit*, 56. Dr. Barbatus's medical manuscripts are described in Hermann Hagen, *Catalogus Codicum Bernensium* (Bern, 1875), 93, 276, 287, 353, 377, 439–440, 455–457. My thanks to Marlis Stahli, curator of manuscripts at Bern, for generously allowing me to examine the medical manuscripts as well as the Hagen catalog.

71. Weiss Adamson, "A Reevaluation."

72. The one possible exception to the independent circulation of the *Physica* and the *Causes and Cures* is presented by Meritta Weiss Adamson, "Der deutsche Anhang zu Hildegard von Bingens 'Liber simplicis medicinae' in codex 6952 der Bibliothèque nationale in Paris (fols. 232v–238v)," *Sudhoffs Archiv* 79 (1995): 173–192.

73. LVM, preface, p. 8. See also LDO III.3.2, p. 381.

74. *Vita* II.1, p. 20.

75. Medicinal exotica like cinnamon, pepper, and zituar (zedoary) figure especially in *Physica*, book 1. On their purchase and use by early medieval monastic communities, see John M. Riddle, "The Introduction and Use of Eastern Drugs in the Early Middle Ages," *Sudhoffs Archiv* 49 (1965): 185–198; Jerry Stannard, "Greco-Roman Materia Medica in Medieval Germany," *Bulletin of the History of Medicine* 46 (1972): 455–468.

76. Talbot and Hammond, *Medical Practitioners*, 45–46.

77. John H. Newell Jr., "William of Conches," *Dictionary of Literary Biography*, ed. J. Hackett (Detroit, 1992), vol. 115, pp. 353–359; Italo Ronca, "The Influence of the *Pantegni* on William of Conches' 'Dragmaticon,' " in Burnett and Jacquart, *Constantine the African*, 266–285.

78. Schrader and Führkötter, *Echtheit*, 54–58.

79. Derolez, Introduction 4, LDO, xcvii–ci.

80. Charles Singer, "The Scientific Views and Visions of Saint Hildegard," in *Studies in the History and Method of Science*, 2d ed. (London, 1955), 1:1–55. A better overview and critique of Singer is Lynn Thorndike, "Saint Hildegard of Bingen," chap. 40 in *A History of Magic and Experimental Science* (New York, 1923), 2:124–154. See also Liebeschütz, *Das allegorische Weltbild*, and Peter Dronke's response to the arguments of Heinrich Schipperges in "Problemata Hildegardiana," 112–117.

81. Irmgard Müller, "Zur Verfasserfrage der medizinisch-naturkundlichen Schriften Hildegards von Bingen," in *Tiefe des Gotteswissens—Schönheit der Sprachgestalt bei Hildegard von Bingen*, ed. Margot Schmidt (Stuttgart, 1995), 1–18; I think Müller's interpretation overreaches the evidence. Compare the more thoughtful discussion of the same evidence in Moulinier, *Le Manuscrit*, 113–138.

82. For the details of this argument, and a proposed reconstruction of the chronology of Hildegard's various steps in writing down, revising, and editing her medical ideas, see my "The Perforated Wall."

83. For Trithemius, see note 1 above, this chapter. Hildegard's involvement in the editing of her treatises is discussed in Albert Derolez, "The Genesis of Hildegard of Bingen's 'Liber divinorum operum': The Codicological Evidence," in *Litterae textuales. Texts and Manuscripts: Essays Presented to G. I. Lieftinck* (Amsterdam, 1972), 2:23–33; and Derolez, "Die Bedeutung der neuen Edition von Hildegards 'Liber divinorum operum,' " in Schmidt, ed., *Tiefe des Gotteswissens,* 29–48.

84. *Symphonia,* pp. 9–11, 68–73.

CHAPTER 8: "COMPOSER AND DRAMATIST"

This paper is dedicated to the memory of Anne Zirkle (1972–1997), beloved and brilliant student at Yale Divinity School and the Yale Institute of Sacred Music. Requiescat in pace.

1. *Letters* 23, p. 79. For the Latin of this passage, see *Epistolarium* 23, p. 64.

2. For an introduction to the central importance of liturgy in monastic life, see Jean Leclercq, *The Love of Learning and the Desire for God,* trans. Catharine Misrahi (New York, 1961). A discussion of liturgical trends specifically related to twelfth-century monasticism is found in Giles Constable, *The Reformation of the Twelfth Century* (Cambridge, 1996), 199–208.

3. We leave to one side men such as the fourteenth-century composer Guillaume de Machaut, who wrote many polyphonic compositions, the majority of which are secular works.

4. For an explanation of the problems with recovering Notker's sequence melodies, see Richard Crocker, *The Early Medieval Sequence* (Berkeley, 1977); important recent research on Notker's life and work is found as part of the commentary by Wulf Arlt and Susan Rankin for the facsimile editions of *Stiftsbibliothek Sankt Gallen Codices 484 & 381,* 3 vols. (Winterthur, Switz., 1996). I have discussed which of the Victorine sequences may have been by Adam in *Gothic Song: Victorine Sequences and Augustinian Reform in Twelfth-Century Paris* (Cambridge, 1993), 290–320. Other significant composers from the twelfth century are Peter Abelard, much of whose music unfortunately does not survive (see Chrysogonus Waddell, " 'Epithalamica': An Easter Sequence by Peter Abelard," *Musical Quarterly* 72 [1986]: 239–271), and Nicholas of Clairvaux (see note 23 below, this chapter). A great composer of polyphonic works and a contemporary of Hildegard's was Leoninus of Notre Dame and St. Victor, who is credited with having created the first great cycle of polyphonic chants in the Middle Ages. See Craig Wright, *Music and Ceremony at Notre Dame of Paris (500–1550)* (Cambridge, 1989).

5. For the texts of the *Symphonia,* with a very useful introduction, see Barbara Newman, ed. and trans., *Symphonia* (Ithaca, N.Y., 1988; rev. ed., 1998). For the *Ordo virtutum,* I have followed the text edited and translated by Peter Dronke in his *Nine Medieval Latin Plays* (Cambridge, 1994), 147–184. Hildegard's music has not been published in a critical edition, which has severely hampered its study. Each scholar makes her/his own transcriptions, time permitting, so one has a hodge-podge of editorial decisions and no careful and accurate body of repertory to study. I have been unwilling to add yet another

handful of works by preparing transcriptions for this essay. Instead, I have used the transcriptions of the *Symphonia* prepared by Pudentiana Barth, M. Immaculata Ritscher, and Joseph Schmidt-Görg, *Lieder* (Salzburg, 1969). I have also consulted Audrey Davidson, *The 'Ordo Virtutum' of Hildegard of Bingen* (Kalamazoo, 1985), Christopher Page, *Abbess Hildegard of Bingen: Sequences and Hymns* (Newton Abbot, Devon, 1983), and Ian Bent, "Hildegard of Bingen," *New Grove Dictionary of Music and Musicians,* ed. Stanley Sadie (London, 1980), 8:553–556.

6. For further information regarding singing by nuns, including a summary discussion of Hildegard, see Anne Bagnall Yardley, " 'Ful weel she soong the service dyvyne': The Cloistered Musician in the Middle Ages," in *Women Making Music,* ed. Jane Bowers and Judith Tick (Urbana, Ill., 1986), 15–38.

7. Tropes are additions of newly composed texts and music to preexisting chants. For necessary further refinements and bibliography, see the opening chapters of my *Gothic Song.* For analysis of one of Hildegard's sequences, the text and the music, see Janet Martin and Greta Mary Hair, " 'O Ecclesia': The Text and Music of Hildegard of Bingen's Sequence for St. Ursula," *Tjurunga* 30 (1986): 3–62.

8. An exchange of letters between Hildegard and Abbot Kuno of the Disibodenberg shows a commissioning of liturgical chants for the patron saint of this place, Hildegard's former abbey, and her positive reply to the request. That Kuno would ask Hildegard for these chants, even after they had struggled persistently over a variety of issues, testifies to his respect for and knowledge of her compositional prowess. See Barbara Newman's chapter 9, "Poet," p. 191, and *Letters* 74–74r, pp. 158–162.

9. For a brief explanation of the great responsories as a genre of chant, see David Hiley, *Western Plainchant: A Handbook* (Oxford, 1993), 69–76.

10. The authority on the music for late medieval rhymed offices is Andrew Hughes. A ready-to-hand explanation of musical styles within this category of chants is his article "Rhymed Offices," in *The Dictionary of the Middle Ages,* ed. Joseph Strayer (New York, 1988), 10:366–377. Hughes comments (p. 375) on the features of this musical style, all of which are pertinent to Hildegard's music:

> The most obviously novel features are an increase in range, so that a twelfth or more is not uncommon, incorporating both plagal and authentic versions of the mode, and melodic movement in the same direction for longer motives, giving a sense of direction to the melodies that is quite foreign to standard plainsong. Such chants must surely have been written with the abilities of specific choirs in mind. On rare occasions, the new style is clearly for the purposes of blatant word painting.

11. A doxology is a formulaic closing prayer to the Trinity, normally the *Gloria Patri*: "Glory be to the Father and to the Son and to the Holy Spirit."

12. Hiley, *Western Plainchant,* 88.

13. The most frequently heard music within any medieval monastery was that of intoned psalm or canticle texts, introduced and followed by the singing of an antiphon. The intonation formulae are simple and fairly easy to learn, and monks and nuns in the Middle Ages knew a substantial group of them by heart. Using the tones, texts are proclaimed, verse by verse, and singers punctu-

ate the ends of lines with brief turnings, or melodic formulae, followed by a return to the stability of the reciting tone for each subsequent verse. Hildegard's Psalter antiphons were sung in conjunction with intoned psalms, although, unfortunately, they are usually not performed this way on modern recordings or in concerts. Because her music, almost all of which is liturgical and written for specific purposes, is taken out of context, we get a skewed sense of how her compositions functioned and the great amounts of very simple music that operated in conjunction and in contrast with her antiphons and responsories.

14. Detailed histories of these two chants remain to be written. They are, however, apparently earlier than the other two most famous works of their kind, "Regina celi" and "Salve regina." "Ave regina celorum" and "Alma redemptoris" are already well established in early-twelfth-century sources from a variety of northern European regions. Early attributions to Hermann of Reichenau are no longer tenable, but they do testify to the importance of these works in German regions.

15. For a discussion of some of the most famous Marian chants of the Middle Ages, see Hiley, *Western Plainchant,* 104–108.

16. It should be noted that the concept of pitch, as we moderns think of it, did not operate in the Middle Ages. What mattered about the pitches were the half step/whole step progressions below and above them, the determinant features of mode (or scale). The idea of tuning A, for example, to a particular number of oscillations per second and then singing or playing to this precisely established sound pattern arose only in the course of the eighteenth and nineteenth centuries, the tuning fork having been invented in the early eighteenth century. More extensive definitions for many of the musical terms used in this article can be found in *The New Harvard Dictionary of Music,* ed. Don M. Randel (Cambridge, Mass., 1986), a standard reference tool available in most libraries. The most extensive study of mode in Hildegard's compositions is Marianne Richert Pfau, "Hildegard von Bingen's *Symphonia armonie celestium revelationum:* An Analysis of Musical Process, Modality, and Text-Music Relations" (Ph.D. diss., State University of New York at Stony Brook, 1990).

17. The melodic phrases indicated here do not resemble the formulae used frequently in responsorial genres of Gregorian chant. Repeating phrases such as these are, however, characteristic of the sequence repertory.

18. These pieces, which formed such important musical models for Hildegard the composer, were also shaping forces for Hildegard the liturgical poet. Barbara Newman says of "Alma redemptoris mater": "Sprung from its meter, [it] yields a syntactic structure close to that of Hildegard's lyrics, though somewhat more sophisticated." Newman offers examples of this famous text both in its hexameters, and "sprung," as the music would demand (*Symphonia,* p. 35).

19. *Scivias* III.13.12, trans. Hart and Bishop, p. 533. For a discussion of this concept as it related to alleluias and sequences see my *Gothic Song,* 44–58. The themes regarding music and text and the interrelationships between them resonate strongly with Hildegard's ideas: "Early medieval sequences written in what is now France were most often statements about the angelic 'speech' of their music, whose mode of communication was believed superior to that of the texts themselves. In these repertories, texts are magnificently wrought shades,

placed for human convenience over the dazzling expressivity of the melodies" (*Gothic Song*, p. 58).

20. One gets the sense of how she may have composed from nuns who remembered her walking through the cloister and singing "O virga ac diadema" while illumined by the Holy Spirit. See Newman, chapter 9 below, "Poet," p. 176.

21. For a comparative study of select repertories of sequences sung and newly composed by Benedictines, Augustinians, and cathedral canons in the twelfth century, see my *Gothic Song*, 85–134.

22. For comparison of "Victimae paschali" to a late sequence that uses it as a model, see my *Gothic Song*, 164–170 and 419–420.

23. Nicholas of Clairvaux, a maverick composer who was a Cistercian, wrote a significant body of sequences, although twelfth-century Cistercians made no place for sequences in their liturgies. See John Benton, "Nicholas of Clairvaux and the Twelfth-Century Sequence, with Special Reference to Adam of St. Victor," *Traditio* 18 (1962): 149–180, and especially the forthcoming study of Professor Calvin Bower, Department of Music, University of Notre Dame.

24. Hildegard apparently conceived of much of her liturgical music for women to sing. Her emphases on women religious and on the Virgin Mary do not, however, stand in the way of her central theme, the universal church and its incarnational power. We can say the same of her that we can of Victorine sequence composers: her liturgical songs, with the exception of those for local saints, are not so narrowly specified as to be useless for any community but her own. Quite the contrary, there is evidence that Hildegard was willing to make changes in her works to make them more widely useful. See Newman, chapter 9 below, "Poet," p. 182.

25. The role of music in monastic education is treated at length in Susan Boynton, "Glossed Hymns in Eleventh-Century Continental Hymnaries" (Ph.D. diss., Brandeis University, 1997).

26. For details regarding this fifth decade of Hildegard's life see Newman, chapter 1, "Sibyl of the Rhine," pp. 12–16.

27. Using the evidence of Hildegard's writings and the major manuscripts, Barbara Newman has sketched a tentative chronological framework for three layers of Hildegard's seventy-seven songs: early, middle, and late. For further information see the introduction to the sources and to these arguments in her *Symphonia*, pp. 6–12 and 60–73, and the discussion in Peter Dronke, "The Composition of Hildegard of Bingen's *Symphonia*," *Sacris Erudiri* 19 (1969–70): 381–393. Yet another source has subsequently been reported by Audrey Ekdahl Davidson, "Another Manuscript of the *Ordo Virtutum* of Hildegard von Bingen," *Early Drama, Art, and Music Review* 13 (1991): 36–41. The musical portion of the Dendermonde codex (ca. 1175) has been published in facsimile: Peter van Poucke, ed., *Symphonia harmoniae caelestium revelationum* (Peer, 1991). The other major manuscript of Hildegard's liturgical music is the so-called Riesenkodex (Giant Codex), produced at the Rupertsberg in the final years before Hildegard's death.

28. The Parisian master Odo of Soissons in a letter of ca. 1147 says to Hildegard: "It is reported that, exalted, you see many things in the heavens and record

them in your writing, and that you bring forth the melody of a new song, although you have studied nothing of such things" (*Letters* 40, p. 110). In Latin the crucial phrase reads "atque modus noui carminis edas," which is usually rendered as above. I suggest as just as plausible "a type of new song." If this were the sense, Odo would be recognizing Hildegard's compositions as innovative.

29. This penchant for systematic and large-scale modes of organization is characteristic of many twelfth-century thinkers. Hugh of St. Victor, for example, used pictograms (which do not survive) as models for teaching and contemplation, the most famous of which is described in the opening of his *Mystical Ark of Noah*, PL 176:681–682. Graphic representations used to organize information and aid the memory are discussed from two different angles in Mary Carruthers, *The Book of Memory: A Study of Memory in Medieval Culture* (Cambridge, 1990), and Anna Esmeijer, *Divina quaternitas: A Preliminary Study in the Method and Application of Visual Exegesis* (Amsterdam, 1978). I have discussed the Victorine sequences and their modes of organization as an art of memory in *Gothic Song*, 290–296.

30. If one takes her liturgical songs and the play as a whole, other large-scale images become equally important to Hildegard, and all of them work as representations of the church: the Heavenly Jerusalem, constructed with living stones, of 1 Peter 2.5; the Garden of the Song of Songs, type of the restored Garden of Eden in Paradise, with the Tree of Life at the center. There are many ways in which the complexes of images associated with the Jesse tree, the Song of Songs, and the Tree of Life are interdependent.

31. The classic depiction of the tree of Jesse is that found in the northern lancet window of the west facade at Chartres cathedral, dated to the mid-twelfth century and seen as modeled on the Jesse tree window (now heavily restored) from the same period at St. Denis. Here Jesse sleeps at the bottom, while rising from his loins, phalluslike, is the tree of his lineage; to both sides of the tree stand prophets with their scrolls, who point to the messianic heritage on display within the tree itself. For the window at Chartres and other early depictions of the Jesse tree, see Arthur Watson, *The Early Iconography of the Jesse Tree* (London, 1934).

32. The *Speculum virginum* appears in a critical edition by Jutta Seyfarth, CCCM 5 (Turnhout, 1990).

33. From Isaiah 11.1–2: "A shoot shall come out from the stump of Jesse, and a branch shall grow out of his roots. The spirit of the Lord shall rest on him, the spirit of wisdom and understanding, the spirit of counsel and might, the spirit of knowledge and the fear of the Lord" (*New Revised Standard Version*). The flower and the rod are typified as well by the flowering rod of Aaron, which brought forth flowers and fruit (Numbers 17), and the flowering rod of Joseph from the Apocrypha, which indicated that he was the man destined to be Mary's husband. A twelfth-century fusing of these images is found in the Victorine sequence for Christmas, "In excelsis canitur," for which see my *Gothic Song*, 286–287.

34. Watson, *Early Iconography*, 131; see also his plates 16 and 29.

35. See John Van Engen, chapter 2 above, "Abbess," pp. 46–48. An excellent collection of essays concerning the Rule and its history is found in *RB*

1980: The Rule of St. Benedict in Latin and English, ed. Timothy Fry (Collegeville, Minn., 1980); the volume also contains an edition of the Rule in Latin and the English translation referred to here.

36. Apparently the nuns in Hildegard's convent dressed in elaborate veils and wore jewels and crowns on high feast days. Her liturgical poetry and the play, filled with allusions to garments, emphasize the newness of flesh made possible through the Incarnation. See Peter Dronke, *Women Writers of the Middle Ages* (Cambridge, 1984), 165–169.

37. From *Scivias* II.5.18-20, trans. Hart and Bishop, pp. 212-213.

> For the monks are the girdle of the Church and strongly encircle her, since they are concerned with My Son's Incarnation and also exercise the function of the angels; that is, they do not cease at any hour to sing melodiously or pray in compunction, with the freshness of remorse . . . their garment is unlike that of other people, for it symbolizes the incorrupt Incarnation of My Son, which is completely different from the procreation of other people. . . . And this garment flies with wings of subtlety like the glitter of supernal spirits, and points to the Incarnation and burial of My Son . . . [God proclaims: I brought forth Benedict,] whom I passed by in burning fire, teaching him to honor the Incarnation of my Son in the garment of his way of life, and imitate His Passion in the abnegation of his will. For Benedict is like a second Moses . . .

38. For Hildegard's own commentary on the Rule, see her *Explanation of the Rule of Benedict,* trans. Hugh Feiss (Toronto, 1990).

39. *The Rule of St. Benedict,* prologue, in *RB 1980,* 165:

> Brothers, now that we have asked the Lord who will dwell in his tabernacle, we have heard the instructions for dwelling in it, but only if we fulfill the obligations of those who live there. We must, then, prepare our hearts and bodies for the battle of holy obedience to his instructions. What is not possible to us by nature, let us ask the Lord to supply by the help of his grace. If we wish to reach eternal life, even as we avoid the torments of hell, then—while there is still time, while we are in this body and have time to accomplish all these things by the light of life—we must run and do now what will profit us forever.

40. *The Rule of St. Benedict,* chap. 7, in *RB 1980,* 193:

> Accordingly, brothers, if we want to reach the highest summit of humility, if we desire to attain speedily that exaltation in heaven to which we climb by the humility of this present life, then by our ascending actions we must set up that ladder on which Jacob in a dream saw "angels descending and ascending" (Gen. 28.12). Without doubt, this descent and ascent can signify only that we descend by exaltation and ascend by humility. Now the ladder erected is our life on earth, and if we humble our hearts the Lord will raise it to heaven. We may call our body and soul the sides of this ladder, into which our divine vocation has fitted the various steps of humility and discipline as we ascend.

41. *Scivias* III.8.13, trans. Hart and Bishop, p. 435.

> "But in the pillar, there is an ascent like a ladder from bottom to top." This is to say that in the incarnate Son of God all the virtues work fully, and that He left in Himself the way of salvation; so that faithful people both small and great can find in Him the right step on which to place their foot in order to ascend to virtue, so that they can reach the best place to exercise all the virtues. . . . They see the manifestation of the true Incarnation, in which the Son of God was truly shown in the flesh; and that is where the certain ascent to the heavenly places is to be found. Therefore, "you see all the virtues of God descending and ascending, laden down

with stones"; for in God's Only-Begotten the lucent virtues descend in His Humanity and ascend in His Divinity.

(The quotations in the passage are from the prologue to vision 8.)

42. *Scivias* III.8.15, trans. Hart and Bishop, pp. 436–439.

"And there shall come forth a branch out of the root of Jesse; and a flower shall rise up out of his root. And the Spirit of the Lord will rest upon him; the spirit of wisdom and of understanding, the spirit of knowledge and of piety; and the spirit of the fear of the Lord shall fill him." This is to say: The Virgin Mary came forth from the troubles of earthly oppression into the sweetness of moral life, as a person might come forth from a house in which he was imprisoned . . . And why a branch? Because it is not thorny in its manner, or knotted with worldly desires, but straight, unconnected with carnal lusts; arisen, therefore, from the root of Jesse, who was the foundation of the royal race from which the stainless mother had her origin. And so from the root of that branch arose the sweet fragrance of the Virgin's intact fecundity; and when it had so arisen, the Holy Spirit inundated it so that the tender flower was born from her. How? Like a flower born in a field though its seed was not sown there, the Bread of Heaven arose in her without originating in a mingling with a man and without any human burden; it was born in the sweetness of divinity, untouched by sin, without the knowledge and utterly without the influence of the devious serpent. Hence this Flower deceived the serpent; He ascended on high and lifted up with Him the sinful human race, which the serpent had seduced and drawn down with him into perdition. And because this Flower was the Son of God, the Spirit of the Lord rested on Him . . . Piety is rightly linked with knowledge; for the Son of God fulfilled the will of His Father knowingly and in great piety. For He, the only Son, born of the Virgin, scattered among the peoples the seed of heavenly virtue; and so He made it possible for them to follow the company of the angels in the modesty of chastity, since this virtue arose in supernal piety. And so, in the branch that came forth from Jesse, the virtues of this Flower put forth buds. The first woman had fled from these virtues by consenting to the counsel she heard from the serpent, and the whole human race fell in her and was cut off from supernal joy and glory; but the blossoming of this branch uplifted the human race in knowledge through piety to the holiness of salvation. How? The fortitude that conquers the Devil and is joined to knowledge is inspired by the Holy Spirit when faithful people devoutly acknowledge God with ardent desire and embrace Him eagerly in the very depths of their souls.

43. In a forthcoming study I will explore the liturgical context of the songs more fully, using the liturgical practices of Hildegard's own region as context.

44. The antiphons, in contrast, provide the image of building the church as the New Jerusalem with living stones. By juxtaposing the Jesse tree and the New Jerusalem with some consistency in these early antiphon/responsory pairs, Hildegard made two of her favored complexes of images resonate together, building the vast edifice of the church as she depicted it in song, drama, and visionary text.

45. Hildegard describes green as it relates to the crown of Humility, Queen of the Virtues: "For the Humanity of the Savior manifests the high and profound goodness of His works; the Son of God wrought them in the greenness of the blossoming of the virtues in His teachings, and in the redness of His blood when He suffered death on the cross to save humanity, and in the whiteness of His resurrection and ascension" (*Scivias* III.8.18, trans. Hart and Bishop, p. 442). Mary too, of course, is identified with Queen Humility in the *Ordo virtutum*. The three colors in her crown (green, red, and white) are the colors emphasized in the songs. These are important liturgical colors used for vestments

and other draperies to underscore the seasons. Red is for Passiontide and white for Eastertide; green is for the time after Pentecost.

46. See Marianne Richert Pfau, "Mode and Melody Types in Hildegard von Bingen's *Symphonia*," *Sonus* 11 (1990): 53–71. This entire issue is dedicated to Hildegard and contains provocative papers on a variety of issues, including an analysis by Robert Cogan of Hildegard's antiphon "O quam mirabilis." Cogan identifies the musical "cells" in the piece and explains how they are organized: "Hildegard's Fractal Antiphon," 1–19.

47. For a useful critique of various theories regarding Hildegard's use of stock phrases, see the opening chapters of Pfau's dissertation, "Hildegard von Bingen's *Symphonia*."

48. Hildegard lived in the world of the sundial rather than of the mechanical clock. Fixed perceptions of time units, as developed in the course of the late twelfth and thirteenth centuries, had profound effects on the art of music. It is during this period that the rhythmic modes were invented and that musicians first learned to notate units of sound with some precision. For an introduction to the shifts in time sense taking place in this period, see my article, "The Role of the Parisian Sequence in the Evolution of Notre-Dame Polyphony," *Speculum* 62 (1987): 345–374. A general introduction to time shifts in the centuries after Hildegard is Alfred W. Crosby, *The Measure of Reality: Quantification and Western Society, 1250–1600* (New York, 1995).

49. This responsory has been recorded twice: by the Ensemble Mediatrix on the CD *Feminea Forma Maria* (Calig 50982), a Solesmes-style "Gregorian" performance, and by Sequentia on *Canticles of Ecstasy* (DHM 05472-77320-2), a much freer performance. For full details, see the discography at the end of this volume.

50. Text and translation as found in Newman's *Symphonia*, 1998 ed., pp. 132–133.

51. For the sake of convenience I have used the conventions for representing pitches in specific octaves as found in *The New Harvard Dictionary of Music*, p. 640. Here middle C is represented as c′ and the octave above it as c″; the octave below middle C is expressed as c. Hence, the pitch D above middle C will be written as d′. Which C one actually used as middle C is an arbitrary decision. What really matters, as I have said, is not the actual number of oscillations per second but the relationships between notes. As long as these relationships are preserved, one can place the music in the range best suited to the voices singing it.

52. In fact, several of the songs in the *Scivias* cycle traverse the same distance on a single downward melisma.

53. For an introduction to the erotic nature of Hildegard's lyrics, see Bruce Holsinger, "The Flesh of the Voice: Embodiment and the Homoerotics of Devotion in the Music of Hildegard of Bingen (1098–1179)," *Signs* 19 (1993): 92–125.

54. For analyses that emphasize the importance of phrase repetition in Hildegard's composition, see Marianne Richert Pfau, "Music and Text in Hildegard's Antiphons," in *Symphonia*, 74–94. Pfau acknowledges a debt that I share to the writings of Ritva Jonsson [Jacobsson] and Leo Treitler and to other members of the Corpus Troporum, especially Gunilla Björkvall and Gu-

nilla Iversen. For bibliography and an early position paper, see Jonsson [Jacobsson] and Treitler, "Medieval Music and Language: A Reconsideration of the Relationship," in *Studies in the History of Music*, vol. 1, *Music and Language* (New York, 1983), 1–23. For continuing work in this vein, see Gunilla Björkvall and Andreas Haug, "Early Versified Offices," in *The Divine Office in the Latin Middle Ages: Source Studies and Methodology, Regional Developments, Hagiography*, ed. Rebecca Baltzer and Margot Fassler (forthcoming from Oxford University Press).

55. "O splendidissima gemma" can be heard on the disk by Ensemble Mediatrix, *Feminea Forma Maria*.

56. For a more tightly controlled example of Hildegard's use of preexisting melody, see Karlheinz Schlager, "Hildegard von Bingen im Spiegel der Choralforschung: Rückschau und Ausblick," in *De Musica et Cantu: Studien zur Geschichte der Kirchenmusik und der Oper*, ed. Peter Cahn and Ann-Katrin Heimer (Hildesheim, 1993), 309–323. The analysis on pp. 313–315 compares the melody of "O magne Pater" to a Gloria melody.

57. Recorded by Sequentia on the disk *Canticles of Ecstasy*.

58. The images of light and flowering are characteristic of almost every piece Hildegard wrote in celebration of the Virgin. See for example "O quam preciosa" (*Symphonia*, no. 22): "Thus the tender shoot / that is her Son / opened paradise / through the cloister of her womb. // And the Son of God came forth / from her secret chamber / like the dawn."

59. An analysis of the entire song and its interaction with the model will appear in my study (now in progress) of Hildegard's use of preexisting melodies. Here I have presented only the first section of the song. In the example, notes from the model, "Ave regina celorum," are found on the first line of the three-line system, written in black noteheads. The lines of "O nobilissima viriditas" are positioned below, with the borrowed material rendered in white noteheads to make the extent of borrowing within each passage clearer.

60. For an analysis of complex systems of meaning arising from the resetting of symbolically charged melodies to several different but interrelated texts, see my *Gothic Song*, 161–184 and 290–320.

61. Here too I would argue that both text and music of this early version of the play existed by the time the *Scivias* was complete. Peter Dronke has argued that the skeleton form of the play was extracted from the entire play, which already, if he is correct, existed by 1151. "Problemata Hildegardiana," *Mittellateinisches Jahrbuch* 16 (1981): 97–131.

62. See Dronke's commentary in *Ordo virtutum*, 148.

63. The classic study of medieval prophets' plays is that of Karl Young in *The Drama of the Medieval Church* (Oxford, 1933). For a more recent look at the genre, see Regula Meyer Evitt, "Anti-Judaism and the Medieval Prophet Plays: Exegetical Contexts for the 'Ordines prophetarum' " (Ph.D. diss., University of Virginia, 1992).

64. In the responsory for patriarchs and prophets (*Symphonia*, no. 32), Hildegard makes a powerful connection between these men and the virtues who now continue their work: "O you happy roots, / with whom the work of miracles / was planted— / and not the work of crimes." This is an instructive

example of the connections Hildegard made between her liturgical songs for the Divine Office and her morality play.

65. *Ordo virtutum*, 161.

66. Charity is the Virtue who actually makes the connection with the Jesse tree and the blossoming branch first alluded to by the prophets (the roots) in the play: "I am Charity, the flower of love— / come to me, Virtues, and I'll lead you / into the radiant light of the flower of the rod." *Ordo virtutum*, 167.

67. The bedchamber, the *thalamus*, would have been well established in Hildegard's mind through the long and beautiful processional antiphon "Adorna thalamum," which has its beginnings in the East and was sung throughout Western Europe on the Feast of the Purification of the Virgin (February 2).

68. The prototypical battle of vices and virtues is laid out in the fifth-century *Psychomachia* by Prudentius, ed. and trans. H. J. Thompson (London, 1949). The idea of the *Ordo virtutum* as a forerunner of the later tradition of morality plays is explored and rejected by Robert Potter, "The *Ordo Virtutum*: Ancestor of the English Moralities?" in Audrey Davidson, ed., *The* Ordo Virtutum *of Hildegard of Bingen: Critical Studies* (Kalamazoo, 1992), 31–41.

69. For imagery used to describe the virtues/virgins in the play and the songs, see *Scivias* II.3.23, trans. Hart and Bishop, p. 178.

70. For the heat imagery associated with sexual intercourse, see, for example, *Scivias* II.3.22, trans. Hart and Bishop, p. 177. In the largest sense Hildegard's Anima is Everysoul. The Virgin Mary, type of the church, is the Bride of Christ and the Mother of the Faithful. See *Scivias* I.3, trans. Hart and Bishop, p. 169: "Her womb was pierced like a net with many openings, with a huge multitude of people running in and out . . ."

71. See *Scivias* I.4.30, trans. Hart and Bishop, p. 128. The wounds described are those sustained by Anima: "There are many who accept penance for their sins only with difficulty; but, though with much effort, they nonetheless carry it out for fear of death. But I give them My hand, and change their bitterness into sweetness . . . He who neglects repentance for his sins . . . does not want to look at himself, or seek a physician, or have his wounds healed."

72. *Ordo virtutum*, 165.

73. At the opening of *Scivias*, Hildegard the prophet is charged by God to teach: "O human, who are fragile dust of the earth . . . Cry out and speak of the origin of pure salvation until those people are instructed . . . Unlock for them the enclosure of mysteries": *Scivias* I.1, trans. Hart and Bishop, p. 67.

74. Humility, who is Queen of the Virtues in Hildegard's play, is also the crowning virtue in the Rule of St. Benedict, where the acquisition of humility is laid out in a series of steps. These steps play a major role in *Scivias* as well, as discussed above.

75. Missing only is the harshness of poverty. The ways in which the Virtues' speeches reinforce monastic life according to the Rule are discussed in Pamela Sheingorn, "The Virtues of Hildegard's *Ordo Virtutum*; or, It *Was* a Woman's World," in Davidson, ed., *The* Ordo Virtutum *of Hildegard of Bingen: Critical Studies*, 43–62, esp. 49, and in Julia Bolton Holloway's paper in the same collection, "The Monastic Context of Hildegard's *Ordo Virtutum*," 63–77.

76. I am grateful to Gunilla Iversen for sharing her paper with me before its publication; this idea was proposed earlier by Julia Holloway in "The Monastic Context" and by Barbara Newman in *Sister of Wisdom*, 222–224. The context of the play has been analyzed by other scholars as well: Peter Dronke believes the drama was performed to celebrate the dedication of the new church at the Rupertsberg (see his discussion in *Ordo virtutum*, 152–155), and Pamela Sheingorn sees it as connected with the medieval ceremony of taking the veil ("The Virtues"). See also Patricia Kazarow, "Text and Context in Hildegard of Bingen's *Ordo Virtutum*," in *Maps of Flesh and Light: The Religious Experience of Medieval Women Mystics*, ed. Ulrike Wiethaus (Syracuse, N.Y., 1993), 127–151 and 174–182.

77. *Ordo virtutum*, 151.

78. This is not the only place Hildegard's liturgical writings are interactive with the visual arts. See Madeline Caviness, chapter 6, "Artist," p. 120, for possible allusions to stained glass in the *Symphonia*.

79. *Scivias* III.13.1, trans. Hart and Bishop, p. 525.

80. For a useful introduction to musical unity and development of scene and character, see Audrey Davidson, "Music and Performance: Hildegard of Bingen's *Ordo Virtutum*," in Davidson, ed., *The* Ordo Virtutum *of Hildegard of Bingen: Critical Studies*, 1–29.

81. For a discussion of the various social forces working beneath the surface of the Beauvais *Play of Daniel*, see Margot Fassler, "The Feast of Fools and *Danielis Ludus:* Popular Tradition in a Medieval Cathedral Play," in *Plainsong in the Age of Polyphony*, ed. Thomas Forrest Kelly (Cambridge, 1992).

CHAPTER 9: "POET"

1. *Acta* 4, PL 197:133c.

2. "O virga ac diadema," *Symphonia* 20, pp. 128–131. All texts of Hildegard's poetry are taken from this 1988 edition (identical to texts and verse translations in the 1998 revised edition). My translations in this essay are based on the verse translations in *Symphonia*, modified at times in the direction of stricter fidelity

3. "O Fili dilectissime," *Symphonia*, pp. 260–261. Ironically, this lyric praising Christ as the Song of God and Mary is one of at least four songs by Hildegard for which no music survives. Their melodies were either lost or never composed; see *Symphonia*, p. 11.

4. *Scivias* III.13.12, p. 631.

5. Lyrics probably created at the request or for the use of male monasteries include the compositions honoring St. Disibod (*Symphonia*, nos. 41 through 45), St. Matthias (no. 50), St. Boniface (no. 51), St. Eucharius (nos. 52–53), and St. Maximin (no. 54). Hildegard wrote three of the pieces for St. Disibod at the request of her abbot, Kuno, in 1155. St. Eucharius was the patron of a monastery in Trier (rededicated to St. Matthias in 1148), where Hildegard had several correspondents and a close friend, Abbot Ludwig. Around 1175 she sent a complete manuscript of her *Symphonia* to the Cistercian monks of Villers in Brabant (this is the manuscript now at Dendermonde, St.-Pieters-&-Paulusabdij

cod. 9). Since notation is carefully included, it is likely that the monks performed at least some of the lyrics.

6. See Patrick Diehl, *The Medieval European Religious Lyric: An Ars Poetica* (Berkeley, 1985), 32–34.

7. The bibliography on Hildegard's poetry is not extensive. Aside from the *Symphonia* introduction and commentaries, it consists chiefly of Peter Dronke's contributions: *The Medieval Lyric* (London, 1968), 75–78; "Hildegard of Bingen as Poetess and Dramatist," in *Poetic Individuality in the Middle Ages* (Oxford, 1970), 150–179; and "Tradition and Innovation in Medieval Western Colour-Imagery," *Eranos Jahrbuch* 41 (1972): 82–88. Two essays by Peter Walter address the treatment of Mary and the saints in the *Symphonia* lyrics: "*Virgo filium dei portasti:* Maria in den Gesängen der hl. Hildegard von Bingen," *Archiv für mittelrheinische Kirchengeschichte* 29 (1977): 75–96, and "Die Heiligen in der Dichtung der hl. Hildegard von Bingen," in Anton Brück, ed., *Hildegard von Bingen, 1179–1979* (Mainz, 1979), 211–237. For a controversial perspective see Bruce Holsinger, "The Flesh of the Voice: Embodiment and the Homoerotics of Devotion in the Music of Hildegard of Bingen," *Signs* 19 (1993): 92–125.

8. Born in Lavardin, Hildebert was an outstanding classical scholar and poet who became bishop of Le Mans (1096–1125), then archbishop of Tours (1125–1133). His most famous poem, "De sancta Trinitate," and many short poems and epigrams can be found in A. Brian Scott, ed., *Hildeberti Carmina minora* (Leipzig, 1969). See also PL 171 and Helen Waddell, ed. and trans., *More Latin Lyrics: From Virgil to Milton* (New York, 1976), 260–287.

9. Few biographical details are known about Adam, an Augustinian canon of St.-Victor and cantor (or precentor) at Notre Dame cathedral in Paris. For the poetry traditionally ascribed to him, see Adam von Sankt Viktor, *Sämtliche Sequenzen*, ed. Franz Wellner (Munich, 1955). On the Victorine musical repertoire see Margot Fassler, *Gothic Song: Victorine Sequences and Augustinian Reform in Twelfth-Century Paris* (Cambridge, 1993), esp. 206–210 on Adam.

10. Diehl, *Religious Lyric*, 88. Sequences were to be sung before the Gospel reading at Mass; the other liturgical genres discussed here were intended for the monastic Office of the Hours.

11. I thank my former colleague Catherine Wallace for this observation.

12. See John Stevens, *Words and Music in the Middle Ages: Song, Narrative, Dance, and Drama, 1051–1350* (Cambridge, 1986), 100–109; and for a more detailed account of twelfth-century contrafacta, see Fassler, *Gothic Song,* 161–184.

13. The complete text can be found in the Roman missal or *Liber Usualis* (with melody); or in Waddell, *More Latin Lyrics*, 298–300. "Veni Sancte Spiritus" was one of only five medieval sequences in the Roman liturgy to survive the great purge of the Council of Trent, the others being "Victimae paschali" (for Easter), "Lauda Syon Salvatorem" (for Corpus Christi), "Stabat mater" (for Passiontide), and "Dies irae" (for the requiem mass).

14. Sequence 1 in *Sämtliche Sequenzen*, ed. Wellner, 30–32.

15. Joseph Szövérffy, ed., *Peter Abelard's Hymnarius Paraclitensis* (Albany, N.Y., 1975), 1:54.

16. Szövérffy, *Hymnarius Paraclitensis*, 2:239–241, no. 118.

17. For this terminology see Diehl, *Religious Lyric*, 93, 101–102. The classical sequence (poetically very different from the twelfth-century regular sequence) is best represented in the poetry of the ninth-century monk Notker of St. Gall. See his *Liber ymnorum*, ed. Wolfram von den Steinen (Bern, 1960), and Richard Crocker, *The Early Medieval Sequence* (Berkeley, 1977).

18. Hildebert, "In laudem Spiritus sancti," PL 171:1413–1416; Waddell, *More Latin Lyrics*, 270. Translations are my own.

19. The only English poet indebted to the Latin "filigree stanza" appears to be John Skelton (ca. 1460–1529), whose "skeltonics" are based on this verse form. See for example "To Mistress Margaret Hussey": "Merry Margaret, / As midsummer flower, / Gentle as falcon / Or hawk of the tower; / With solace and gladness, / Much mirth and no madness, / All good and no badness; / So joyously, / So maidenly, / So womanly / Her demeaning / In every thing, / Far, far passing / That I can endite, / Or suffice to write / Of merry Margaret . . ."

20. For dismissive assessments of Hildegard's poetry see G. M. Dreves and Clemens Blume, *Analecta hymnica medii aevi* (Leipzig, 1886–1922), vol. 50, part 2, p. 484; F. J. E. Raby, *A History of Christian-Latin Poetry from the Beginnings to the Close of the Middle Ages* (Oxford, 1927), 294; Joseph de Ghellinck, *L'Essor de la littérature latine au XIIe siècle* (Paris, 1946), 1:198. Brief but more respectful treatments can be found in Joseph Szövérffy, *Die Annalen der lateinischen Hymnendichtung* (Berlin, 1965), 2:139–142, and Stevens, *Words and Music*, 398–399.

21. Margot Fassler points out that the regular sequence, a genre first promoted by the Augustinian canons, was little used among Benedictines during Hildegard's lifetime. See Fassler's chapter 8, "Composer and Dramatist," p. 155 above.

22. Diehl, *Religious Lyric*, 103.

23. See Fassler, chapter 8, pp. 166–168 above.

24. These lyrics include "O viridissima virga" (no. 19), "O dulcissime amator" (no. 57), "O Pater omnium" (no. 58), and "O Ierusalem" (no. 49), which begins stanzaically but ends in free form.

25. See Albert Derolez, introduction to LDO, lxxxvi–xcvi; Derolez, "The Genesis of Hildegard of Bingen's *Liber divinorum operum:* The Codicological Evidence," in *Litterae Textuales: Essays Presented to G. I. Lieftinck* (Amsterdam, 1972), 2:23–33; and Derolez, "Die Bedeutung der neuen Edition von Hildegards *Liber divinorum operum*," in Margot Schmidt, ed., *Tiefe des Gotteswissens—Schönheit der Sprachgestalt bei Hildegard von Bingen* (Stuttgart, 1995), 19–28.

26. This manuscript is Vienna, Nationalbibliothek cod. 963, from S. Maria in Rommersdorf. Although it dates from the thirteenth century, it appears to be based on a lost exemplar from Hildegard's lifetime, as the same miscellany appears in the late-twelfth-century Riesenkodex (Wiesbaden, Hessische Landesbibliothek cod. 2), fols. 404rb–407va. It was published in Pitra's *Analecta S. Hildegardis*, 358–368, under the misleading title "Epilogus ad Vitam S. Ruperti."

27. For a fuller and more technical version of this argument see *Symphonia*, pp. 9–11, 68–73.

28. The exception is that in the Dendermonde manuscript songs in praise of the Father precede the Marian songs, while those honoring the Holy Spirit follow them. As I argued in *Symphonia* (p. 59), this anomaly suggests that Hildegard understood her Marian lyrics as christological and therefore followed the tripartite order: Father and Son, Mother and Son, Holy Spirit.

29. "O spectabiles viri," *Symphonia* 31, pp. 158–159. The last line means literally "from the entrance of the light taking root"—but this light is itself the "root" of all being. *Radix* (root) has the metaphorical sense of "origin" or "source," permitting Hildegard a kind of conceptual pun.

30. "O nobilissima viriditas, / que radicas in sole": *Symphonia* 56, p. 218.

31. "O vos felices radices / cum quibus opus miraculorum / . . . per torrens iter / perspicue umbre / plantatum est": *Symphonia* 32, p. 160.

32. "O viridissima virga . . . / que in ventoso flabro sciscitationis / sanctorum prodisti": *Symphonia* 19, p. 126.

33. "Vos flores rosarum," *Symphonia* 38, p. 172.

34. "O orzchis Ecclesia," *Symphonia* 68, p. 252.

35. "O Ierusalem," *Symphonia* 49, pp. 192–199.

36. "O splendidissima gemma / et serenum decus solis": *Symphonia* 10, p. 114.

37. "Et te Verbo suo / auream materiam, / o laudabilis Virgo, fecit": "O virga ac diadema," *Symphonia* 20, pp. 128–131.

38. See Barbara Newman, *Sister of Wisdom: St. Hildegard's Theology of the Feminine* (Berkeley, 1987), 17, 60, and Dronke, *Medieval Lyric*, 77.

39. I borrow this distinction from C. S. Lewis. On Hildegard's "naturalism," see also chapter 3 above, "Religious Thinker," by Constant Mews.

40. "Spiritus sanctus vivificans vita," *Symphonia* 24, p. 140.

41. "O ignis Spiritus Paracliti," *Symphonia* 28, pp. 148–151.

42. This is the language of Christian Platonism common among twelfth-century theologians. The "forms" are the exemplars of created beings, existing eternally in the mind of God.

43. On the nexus linking the Holy Spirit with the World Soul and the divine feminine figures Hildegard called Caritas and Sapientia (Love and Wisdom), see Newman, *Sister of Wisdom*, 64–71.

44. Dronke, *Poetic Individuality*, 157.

45. Notker, *Liber ymnorum*, 54.

46. "O ignee Spiritus," *Symphonia* 27, pp. 142–147.

47. The tent, or *tabernaculum*, of the soul is its body. Hildegard uses the same image in the lament of the pilgrim soul to her mother Zion (*Scivias* I.4). Its biblical source is the description of the tabernacle or "tent of meeting" (Exodus 25–26) as the locus of God's presence, containing the ark of testimony and the mercy seat.

48. See my "Sibyl of the Rhine," chapter 1, p. 13 in this volume.

49. The manuscripts have *confringis*, "break in pieces," which makes little sense and would be an easy scribal error for *constringis*, "constrain."

50. All these are ways of saying "But when," "And yet . . ."

51. "O mirum admirandum," *Symphonia* 41, p. 180.

52. *Vita S. Disibodi,* PL 197:1095–1116. See also *Epistolarium* 74–74r and 77, pp. 160–162, 166–167.

53. Cf. John Van Engen, "Abbess," chapter 2, p. 41 in this volume.

54. *succurrente flore / omnium ramorum mundi:* "with the aid of the flower of all the branches of the world." The meaning is obscure, but I take this flower to be Christ and its appearance on "all the branches of the world" to signify the glory of the saints at the Last Judgment.

Bibliography of Works by and about Hildegard of Bingen

LATIN EDITIONS, FACSIMILES, AND MUSIC

Analecta Sanctae Hildegardis. Ed. Jean-Baptiste Pitra. *Analecta sacra,* vol. 8. Monte Cassino, 1882. Includes *Expositiones evangeliorum,* 145 *epistolae,* and other works.

Causae et curae. Ed. Paul Kaiser. Leipzig, 1903.

"Epistolae S. Hildegardis secundum codicem Stuttgartensem." Ed. Francis Haug. *Revue bénédictine* 43 (1931): 59–71.

Epistolarium. Ed. Lieven Van Acker. CCCM 91–91a. Turnhout, 1991, 1993. Third volume forthcoming, ed. Monika Klaes.

Gottfried of Disibodenberg and Theoderic of Echternach. *Vita Sanctae Hildegardis.* Ed. Monika Klaes. CCCM 126. Turnhout, 1993.

Guibert of Gembloux. *Epistolae.* Ed. Albert Derolez et al. CCCM 66–66a. Turnhout, 1988, 1989.

Hildegardis opera omnia. Ed. J.-P. Migne. PL 197. Paris, 1855.

Liber divinorum operum. Ed. Albert Derolez and Peter Dronke. CCCM 92. Turnhout, 1996.

Liber vite meritorum. Ed. Angela Carlevaris. CCCM 90. Turnhout, 1995.

Lieder. Ed. Pudentiana Barth, M.-I. Ritscher, and Joseph Schmidt-Görg. Musical edition. Salzburg, 1969.

Mainzer Urkundenbuch. Vol. 2, part 1. Ed. Peter Acht. Darmstadt, 1968.

Ordo virtutum. Ed. and trans. Peter Dronke. In *Nine Medieval Latin Plays,* 147–184. Cambridge, 1994.

Ordo virtutum. Ed. Audrey Ekdahl Davidson. Performance edition. Kalamazoo, 1985.

Sanctae Hildegardis revelationes, MS 1942. Ed. Anna Calderoni Masetti and Gigetta dalli Regoli. Facsimile of LDO illuminations. Lucca, 1973.

Schipperges, Heinrich, ed. "Ein unveröffentlichtes Hildegard Fragment." *Sudhoffs Archiv für Geschichte der Medizin* 40 (1956): 41–77.

Scivias. Ed. Adelgundis Führkötter and Angela Carlevaris. CCCM 43-43a. Turnhout, 1978.

Sequences and Hymns. Ed. Christopher Page. Performance edition. Newton Abbot, Devon: Antico Church Music, 1983.

Symphonia armonie celestium revelationum. Ed. and trans. Barbara Newman. Ithaca, N.Y., 1988. Rev. ed., 1998.

Symphonia harmoniae caelestium revelationum. Ed. Peter van Poucke. Facsimile edition with music. Peer, 1991.
"Vita domnae Juttae inclusae." Ed. Franz Staab. In Stefan Weinfurter, ed., *Reformidee und Reformpolitik im spätsalisch-frühstaufischen Reich,* 172–187. Mainz, 1992.
Wörterbuch der Unbekannten Sprache [Lingua ignota]. Ed. Marie-Louise Portmann and Alois Odermatt. Basel, 1986.

ENGLISH TRANSLATIONS

Book of Divine Works, with Letters and Songs. Abridged. Ed. Matthew Fox, trans. Robert Cunningham et al. Santa Fe, 1987.
Book of the Rewards of Life. Trans. Bruce Hozeski. New York, 1994.
Explanation of the Rule of Benedict. Trans. Hugh Feiss. Toronto, 1990.
Hildegard of Bingen: Mystical Writings. Ed. Fiona Bowie and Oliver Davies, trans. Robert Carver. New York, 1990.
Letters of Hildegard of Bingen. Trans. Joseph Baird and Radd Ehrman. Oxford, 1994, 1998. Two additional volumes to appear.
Life of the Saintly Hildegard. Trans. Hugh Feiss. Toronto, 1996.
Play of the Virtues. Trans. Peter Dronke. In *Nine Medieval Latin Plays,* 161–181. Cambridge, 1994.
Scivias. Trans. Columba Hart and Jane Bishop. Paulist Classics of Western Spirituality. New York, 1990.
Secrets of God: Writings of Hildegard of Bingen. Trans. Sabina Flanagan. Boston, 1996.
Symphonia [Symphony of the Harmony of Celestial Revelations]. Trans. Barbara Newman. Ithaca, N.Y., 1988. Rev. ed., 1998.

HISTORICAL FICTION

Lachman, Barbara. *The Journal of Hildegard of Bingen* (novel). New York, 1993.
Ohanneson, Joan. *Scarlet Music. Hildegard of Bingen: A Novel.* New York, 1997.
Ulrich, Ingeborg. *Hildegard of Bingen: Mystic, Healer, Companion of the Angels* (novel). Trans. Linda Maloney. Collegeville, Minn., 1993.

SCHOLARSHIP

Adamson, Melitta Weiss [aka Melitta Weiss-Amer]. "A Reevaluation of St. Hildegard's 'Physica' in Light of the Latest Manuscript Finds." In Margaret Schleissner, ed., *Manuscript Sources of Medieval Medicine,* 55–80. New York, 1995.
———. "Der deutsche Anhang zu Hildegard von Bingens 'Liber simplicis medicinae' in Codex 6952 der Bibliothèque Nationale in Paris." *Sudhoffs Archiv* 79 (1995): 173–192.

Ahlgren, Gillian. "Visions and Rhetorical Strategy in the Letters of Hildegard of Bingen." In Karen Cherewatuk and Ulrike Wiethaus, eds., *Dear Sister: Medieval Women and the Epistolary Genre*, 46–63. Philadelphia, 1993.

Arduini, Maria Lodovica. "Der Einfluss Ruperts auf die Werke Hildegards von Bingen." In M. L. Arduini, *Rupert von Deutz (1076–1129) and der "Status christianitatis" seiner Zeit*, 308–324. Cologne, 1987.

Baillet, Louis. *Les Miniatures du* Scivias *de Sainte Hildegarde.* Paris, 1911.

Bartlett, Anne Clark. "Commentary, Polemic, and Prophecy in Hildegard of Bingen's *Solutiones Triginta Octo Quaestionum.*" *Viator* 23 (1992): 153–165.

———. "Miraculous Literacy and Textual Communities in Hildegard of Bingen's *Scivias.*" *Mystics Quarterly* 18 (1992): 43–55.

Barton, Julie, and Constant Mews, eds. *Hildegard of Bingen and Gendered Theology in Judaeo-Christian Tradition.* Clayton, Victoria, Australia, 1995.

Beer, Frances. *Women and Mystical Experience in the Middle Ages.* Woodbridge, Suffolk, 1992.

Berg, Ludwig. "Die Mainzer Kirche und die heilige Hildegard." *Archiv für mittelrheinische Kirchengeschichte* 27 (1975): 49–70.

Böckeler, Maura. *Das Grosse Zeichen (Apok. 12,1): Die Frau als Symbol göttlicher Wirklichkeit.* Salzburg, 1941.

Braun, Johannes. *Die heilige Hildegard, Äbtissin vom Rupertsberg.* Regensburg, 1918.

Brede, Maria. "Die Klöster der hl. Hildegard Rupertsberg und Eibingen." In Anton Brück, ed., *Hildegard von Bingen*, 77–94.

Brück, Anton, ed. *Hildegard von Bingen, 1179–1979: Festschrift zum 800. Todestag der Heiligen.* Mainz, 1979.

Bund, Konrad. "Die 'Prophetin,' ein Dichter und die Niederlassung der Bettelorden in Köln." *Mittellateinisches Jahrbuch* 23 (1988): 171–260.

Burnett, Charles, and Peter Dronke, eds. *Hildegard of Bingen: The Context of Her Thought and Art.* London, 1998.

Büttner, Heinrich. "Studien zur Geschichte von Disibodenberg." *Studien und Mitteilungen zur Geschichte des Benediktinerordens und seiner Zweige* 52 (1934): 1–46.

Cadden, Joan. "It Takes All Kinds: Sexuality and Gender Differences in Hildegard of Bingen's 'Book of Compound Medicine.' " *Traditio* 40 (1984): 149–174.

Cannon, Sue Spencer. "The Medicine of Hildegard of Bingen: Her Twelfth-Century Theories and Their Twentieth-Century Appeal as a Form of Alternative Medicine." Ph.D. dissertation, University of California, Los Angeles, 1993.

Carlevaris, Angela. "*Scripturas subtiliter inspicere subtiliterque excribrare.*" In Margot Schmidt, ed., *Tiefe des Gotteswissens*, 29–48.

Caviness, Madeline. "Gender Symbolism and Text Image Relationships: Hildegard of Bingen's *Scivias.*" In Jeanette Beer, ed., *Translation Theory and Practice in the Middle Ages*, 71–111. Kalamazoo, 1997.

———. "Hildegard as Designer of the Illustrations to Her Works." In Charles Burnett and Peter Dronke, eds., *Hildegard of Bingen*, 29–62.

Chávez Alvarez, Fabio. *"Die brennende Vernunft"*: *Studien zur Semantik der "rationalitas" bei Hildegard von Bingen.* Stuttgart, 1991.

Clark, Anne. *Elisabeth of Schönau: A Twelfth-Century Visionary.* Philadelphia, 1992.

Clausberg, Karl. *Kosmische Visionen: Mystische Weltbilder von Hildegard von Bingen bis heute.* Cologne, 1980.

Cogan, Robert. "Hildegard's Fractal Antiphon." *Sonus* 11 (1990): 1–19.

Craine, Renate. *Hildegard: Prophet of the Cosmic Christ.* New York, 1997.

Czarski, Charles. "The Prophecies of St. Hildegard of Bingen." Ph.D. dissertation, University of Kentucky, 1983.

Davidson, Audrey Ekdahl. "Another Manuscript of the *Ordo Virtutum* of Hildegard von Bingen." *Early Drama, Art, and Music Review* 13 (1991): 36–41.

———. "Music and Performance: Hildegard of Bingen's *Ordo Virtutum.*" In Audrey Davidson, ed., *The Ordo Virtutum,* 1–29.

———, ed. *The Ordo Virtutum of Hildegard of Bingen: Critical Studies.* Kalamazoo, 1992.

———, ed. *"Wisdom Which Encircles Circles"*: *Papers on Hildegard von Bingen.* Kalamazoo, 1996.

Derolez, Albert. "Die Bedeutung der neuen Edition von Hildegards *Liber divinorum operum.*" In Margot Schmidt, ed., *Tiefe des Gotteswissens,* 19–28.

———. "The Genesis of Hildegard of Bingen's *Liber divinorum operum*: The Codicological Evidence." In *Litterae Textuales: Essays Presented to G. I. Lieftinck,* 2:23–33. Amsterdam, 1972.

Dreyer, Elizabeth. *Passionate Women: Two Medieval Mystics.* New York, 1989.

Dronke, Peter. "Arbor Caritatis." In P. L. Heyworth, ed., *Medieval Studies for J. A. W. Bennett,* 207–253. Oxford, 1981.

———. "The Composition of Hildegard of Bingen's *Symphonia.*" *Sacris Erudiri* 19 (1969–1970): 381–393.

———. "Hildegard of Bingen." In *Women Writers of the Middle Ages: A Critical Study of Texts from Perpetua (d. 203) to Marguerite Porete (d. 1310),* 144–201. Cambridge, 1984.

———. "Hildegard of Bingen as Poetess and Dramatist." In *Poetic Individuality in the Middle Ages: New Departures in Poetry, 1000–1150,* 150–179. Oxford, 1970.

———. "Platonic-Christian Allegories in the Homilies of Hildegard of Bingen." In Haijo Jan Westra, ed., *From Athens to Chartres: Neoplatonism and Medieval Thought,* 381–396. Leiden, 1992.

———. "Problemata Hildegardiana." *Mittellateinisches Jahrbuch* 16 (1981): 97–131.

Fegers, Hans. "Die Bilder im *Scivias* der Hildegard von Bingen." *Das Werk des Künstlers* 1 (1939): 109–145.

Fehringer, Barbara. *Das Speyerer Kräuterbuch mit den Heilpflanzen Hildegards von Bingen: Eine Studie zur mittelhochdeutschen Physica-Rezeption mit Kritischer Ausgabe des Textes.* Würzburg, 1994.

Felten, Franz. "Frauenklöster und -stifte im Rheinland im 12. Jahrhundert: Ein Beitrag zur Geschichte der Frauen in der religiösen Bewegung des hohen Mittelalters." In Stefan Weinfurter, ed., *Reformidee und Reformpolitik,* 189–300.

Ferrante, Joan. "Scribe quae vides et audis: Hildegard, Her Language, and Her Secretaries." In David Townsend and Andrew Taylor, eds., *The Tongue of the Fathers: Gender and Ideology in Twelfth-Century Latin*, 102–135. Philadelphia, 1998.

———. *To the Glory of Her Sex: Women's Roles in the Composition of Medieval Texts*. Bloomington, Ind., 1997.

Flanagan, Sabina. "Hildegard and the Gendering of Sanctity." In Julie Barton and Constant Mews, eds., *Hildegard of Bingen*, 81–92.

———. "Hildegard and the Humors: Medieval Theories of Illness and Personality." In Andrew Weiner and Leonard Kaplan, eds., *Madness, Melancholy, and the Limits of the Self*, 14–23. Madison, Wisc., 1996.

———. *Hildegard of Bingen, 1098–1179: A Visionary Life*. London, 1989. Rev. ed. 1998.

———. "Hildegard of Bingen as Prophet: The Evidence of Her Contemporaries." *Tjurunga* 32 (1987): 16–45.

———. "Oblation or Enclosure: Reflections on Hildegard of Bingen's Entry into Religion." In Audrey Davidson, ed., *"Wisdom Which Encircles Circles,"* 1–14.

Fleischmann, Hildebrand. *Hildegard-Eigenoffizium*. Freiburg, 1952.

Forster, Edeltraud, ed. *Hildegard von Bingen: Prophetin durch die Zeiten. Zum 900. Geburtstag*. Freiburg, 1997.

Fox, Matthew. *Illuminations of Hildegard of Bingen*. Santa Fe, N.M., 1985.

Franche, Paul. *Sainte Hildegarde*. Paris, 1903.

Führkötter, Adelgundis. *Hildegard von Bingen*. Salzburg, 1972.

———, ed. *Hildegard von Bingen: Briefwechsel*. Rev. ed. Salzburg, 1990.

———, ed. *Kosmos und Mensch aus der Sicht Hildegards von Bingen*. Mainz, 1987.

Glaze, Florence Eliza. "The Perforated Wall: An Inquiry into the Textual Traditions of Hildegard of Bingen's Medicine." Ph.D. dissertation, Duke University, 1998.

Gössmann, Elisabeth. *Hildegard of Bingen: Four Papers*. Toronto, 1995.

———. *Hildegard von Bingen: Versuche einer Annäherung*. Munich, 1995.

———. "Zyklisches und lineares Geschichtsbewusstsein im Mittelalter: Hildegard von Bingen, Johannes von Salisbury und Andere." In Christian Wenin, ed., *L'Homme et son univers au moyen âge*, 2:882–892. Louvain, 1986.

Gouguenheim, Sylvain. *La Sibylle du Rhin: Hildegarde de Bingen, abbesse et prophétesse rhénane*. Paris, 1996.

Gronau, Eduard. *Hildegard von Bingen, 1098–1179: prophetische Lehrerin der Kirche an der Schwelle und am Ende der Neuzeit*. Stein-am-Rhein, Switzerland, 1985.

Grundmann, Herbert. "Zur Vita S. Gerlaci Eremitae." In *Ausgewählte Aufsätze*, 1:187–194. Stuttgart, 1976.

Haverkamp, Alfred. "Tenxwind von Andernach und Hildegard von Bingen: Zwei 'Weltanschauungen' in der Mitte des 12. Jahrhunderts." In Lutz Fenske et al., eds., *Institutionen, Kultur und Gesellschaft im Mittelalter*, 515–548. Sigmaringen, 1984.

Herwegen, Ildefons. "Les Collaborateurs de sainte Hildegarde." *Revue bénédictine* 21 (1904): 192–204.

Hilpisch, Stephanus. "Der Kult der hl. Hildegard." *Pastor bonus* 45 (1934): 118–133.

Hinkel, Helmut. "St. Hildegards Verehrung im Bistum Mainz." In Anton Brück, ed., *Hildegard von Bingen*, 385–411.

Holloway, Julia Bolton. "The Monastic Context of Hildegard's *Ordo Virtutum*." In Audrey Davidson, ed., The Ordo Virtutum, 63–77.

Holsinger, Bruce. "The Flesh of the Voice: Embodiment and the Homoerotics of Devotion in the Music of Hildegard of Bingen." *Signs* 19 (1993): 92–125.

Hotchin, Julie. "Enclosure and Containment: Jutta and Hildegard at St. Disibod." *Magistra* 2 (1996): 103–123.

———. "Images and Their Places: Hildegard of Bingen and Her Communities." *Tjurunga* 49 (1996): 23–38.

Jenks, Stuart. "Die Prophezeiung von Ps.-Hildegard von Bingen: Eine vernachlässigte Quelle über die Geisslerzüge von 1348–1349." *Mainfrankisches Jahrbuch für Geschichte und Kunst* 29 (1977): 9–38.

Kazarow, Patricia. "Text and Context in Hildegard of Bingen's *Ordo Virtutum*." In Ulrike Wiethaus, ed., *Maps of Flesh and Light*, 127–151.

Kerby-Fulton, Kathryn. "Hildegard and the Male Reader: A Study in Insular Reception." In Rosalynn Voaden, ed., *Prophets Abroad: The Reception of Continental Holy Women in Late-Medieval England*, 1–18. Cambridge, 1996.

———. "Hildegard of Bingen and Antimendicant Propaganda." *Traditio* 43 (1987): 386–399.

———. *Reformist Apocalypticism and* Piers Plowman. Cambridge, 1989.

———. "A Return to 'the First Dawn of Justice': Hildegard's Visions of Clerical Reform and the Eremitical Life." *American Benedictine Review* 40 (1989): 383–407.

———, and Dyan Elliott. "Self-Image and the Visionary Role in Two Letters from the Correspondence of Elizabeth of Schönau and Hildegard of Bingen." *Vox benedictina* 2 (1985): 204–223.

Kessler, Clemencia Hand. "A Problematic Illumination of the Heidelberg *Liber Scivias*." *Marsyas* 8 (1957–1959): 7–21.

Kienzle, Beverly Mayne. "*Operatrix in vinea Domini*: Hildegard's Public Preaching and Polemics against the Cathars." *Heresis* 26–27 (1996): 43–56.

———, and Pamela J. Walker, eds. *Women Preachers and Prophets through Two Millennia of Christianity*. Berkeley, 1998.

Klaes, Monika. "Zur Schau und Deutung des Kosmos bei Hildegard von Bingen." In Adelgundis Führkötter, ed., *Kosmos und Mensch*, 37–115.

Kraft, Kent. "The Eye Sees More than the Heart Knows: The Visionary Cosmology of Hildegard of Bingen." Ph.D. dissertation, University of Wisconsin, 1977.

Lautenschläger, Gabriele. *Hildegard von Bingen: Die theologische Grundlegung ihrer Ethik und Spiritualität*. Stuttgart, 1993.

Lauter, Werner. *Hildegard-Bibliographie*. 2 vols. Alzey, 1970, 1984. Third volume forthcoming.

Lehrbach, Heike. *Katalog zur internationalen Ausstellung "Hl. Hildegard von Bingen, 1179–1979."* Bingen-am-Rhein, 1979.

Liebeschütz, Hans. *Das allegorische Weltbild der hl. Hildegard von Bingen.* Leipzig, 1930.

Maisonneuve, Roland. "Le Symbolisme sacré des couleurs chez des mystiques médiévales: Hildegarde de Bingen, Julienne de Norwich." In *Les Couleurs au moyen âge,* 257–272. Aix-en-Provence, 1988.

Manselli, Raoul. "Amicizia spirituale ed azione pastorale nella Germania del sècolo XII: Ildegarda di Bingen, Elisabetta ed Ecberto di Schönau contro l'eresia catara." *Studi e materiali di storia delle religioni* 38 (1967), fasc. 1–2: 302–313.

Martin, Janet, and Greta Mary Hair. " 'O Ecclesia': The Text and Music of Hildegard of Bingen's Sequence for St. Ursula." *Tjurunga* 30 (1986): 3–62.

Maurmann, Barbara. *Die Himmelsrichtungen im Weltbild des Mittelalters: Hildegard von Bingen, Honorius Augustodunensis und andere Autoren.* Munich, 1976.

May, Johannes. *Die heilige Hildegard von Bingen.* Kempten, 1911.

Meier-Staubach, Christel [aka Christel Meier]. "Die Bedeutung der Farben im Werk Hildegards von Bingen." *Frühmittelalterliche Studien* 6 (1972): 245–355.

———. "Eriugena im Nonnenkloster? Überlegungen zum Verhältnis von Prophetentum und Werkgestalt in den 'figmenta prophetica' Hildegards von Bingen." *Frühmittelalterliche Studien* 19 (1985): 466–497.

———. " 'Nostris temporibus necessaria': Wege und Stationen der mittelalterlichen Hildegard-Rezeption." In Ulrich Ernst and Bernhard Dowinski, eds., *Architectura Poetica: Festschrift für Johannes Rathofer,* 307–326. Cologne, 1990.

———. "Prophetentum als literarische Existenz: Hildegard von Bingen (1098–1179), Ein Portrait." In Gisela Brinker-Gabler, ed., *Deutsche Literatur von Frauen,* 76–87. Munich, 1988.

———. "*Scientia Divinorum Operum:* Zu Hildegards von Bingen visionär-künstlerischer Rezeption Eriugenas." In Werner Beierwaltes, ed., *Eriugena redivivus,* 89–141. Heidelberg, 1987.

———. "Vergessen, Erinnern, Gedächtnis im Gott-Mensch-Bezug: Zu einem Grenzbereich der Allegorese bei Hildegard von Bingen und anderen Autoren des Mittelalters." In Hans Fromm, Wolfgang Harms, and Uwe Ruberg, eds., *Verbum et Signum: Beiträge zur mediävistischen Bedeutungsforschung,* 1:143–194. Munich, 1975.

———. "*Virtus* und *operatio* als Kernbegriffe einer Konzeption der Mystik bei Hildegard von Bingen." In Margot Schmidt and Dieter Bauer, eds., *Grundfragen christlicher Mystik,* 73–101. Stuttgart, 1987.

———. "Zwei Modelle von Allegorie im 12. Jahrhundert: Das allegorische Verfahren Hildegards von Bingen und Alans von Lille." In Walter Haug, ed., *Formen und Funktionen der Allegorie,* 70–89. Stuttgart, 1979.

Mews, Constant. "Hildegard of Bingen: Gender, Nature and Visionary Experience." In Julie Barton and Constant Mews, eds., *Hildegard of Bingen,* 63–80.

———. "Hildegard of Bingen: The Virgin, the Apocalypse, and the Exegetical Tradition." In Audrey Davidson, ed., *"Wisdom Which Encircles Circles,"* 22–42.

―――. "Seeing Is Believing: Hildegard of Bingen and the *Life of Jutta, Scivias,* and the *Commentary on the Rule of Benedict.*" *Tjurunga* 51 (1996): 9–40.

Moulinier, Laurence. "Fragments inédits de la 'Physica': Contribution à l'étude de la transmission des manuscrits scientifiques de Hildegarde de Bingen." *Mélanges de l'École française de Rome* 105 (1993): 629–650.

―――. "La Botanique d'Hildegarde de Bingen." *Médiévales* 16–17 (1989): 113–129.

―――. *Le Manuscrit perdu à Strasbourg: Enquête sur l'oeuvre scientifique de Hildegarde.* Paris, 1995.

―――. "Les Merveilles de la nature vues par Hildegarde de Bingen (XIIᵉ siècle)." In *Miracles, prodiges, et merveilles au Moyen Âge,* 115–131. XXVᵉ Congrès de la Société des Historiens Médiévistes de l'Enseignement Supérieur. Paris, 1995.

―――. "L'Ordre du monde animal selon Hildegarde de Bingen." In R. Durant, ed., *L'Homme, l'animal domestique, et l'environnement du Moyen Âge au XVIIIᵉ siècle,* 119–134. Nantes, 1993.

Müller, Irmgard. "Zur Verfasserfrage der medizinisch-naturkundlichen Schriften Hildegards von Bingen." In Margot Schmidt, ed., *Tiefe des Gotteswissens,* 1–17.

Newman, Barbara. "Hildegard and Her Hagiographers: The Remaking of Female Sainthood." In Catherine M. Mooney, ed., *Gendered Voices: Medieval Saints and Their Interpreters.* Philadelphia, forthcoming.

―――. "Hildegard of Bingen and the 'Birth of Purgatory.' " *Mystics Quarterly* 19 (1993): 90–97.

―――. "Hildegard of Bingen: Visions and Validation." *Church History* 54 (1985): 163–175.

―――. *Sister of Wisdom: St. Hildegard's Theology of the Feminine.* Berkeley, 1987. 2d ed. 1997.

―――. "Three-Part Invention: The Making of the *Vita S. Hildegardis.*" In Charles Burnett and Peter Dronke, eds., *Hildegard of Bingen: The Context of Her Thought and Art,* 183–203. London, 1998.

Nolan, Edward Peter. *Cry Out and Write: A Feminine Poetics of Revelation.* New York, 1994.

Otto, Rita. "Zu den gotischen Miniaturen einer Hildegardhandschrift in Lucca." *Mainzer Zeitschriften* 71–72 (1976–1977): 110–126.

―――. "Zu einigen Miniaturen einer *Scivias*handschrift des 12. Jahrhunderts." *Mainzer Zeitschriften* 67–68 (1972–1973): 128–137.

Pereira, Michela. "Maternità e sessualità femminile in Ildegarda di Bingen: Proposte di Lettura." *Quaderni storici* 44 (1980): 564–579.

Pernoud, Régine. *Hildegarde de Bingen: Conscience inspirée du XIIᵉ siècle.* Monaco, 1994.

Pfau, Marianne Richert. "Hildegard von Bingen's *Symphonia armonie celestium revelationum:* An Analysis of Musical Process, Modality, and Text-Music Relations." Ph.D. dissertation, State University of New York, Stony Brook, 1990.

―――. "Mode and Melody Types in Hildegard von Bingen's *Symphonia.*" *Sonus* 11 (1990): 53–71.

Potter, Robert. "The *Ordo Virtutum*: Ancestor of the English Moralities?" In Audrey Davidson, ed., *The* Ordo Virtutum, 31–41.

Radimersky, George. "Magic in the Works of Hildegard von Bingen." *Monatshefte* 49 (1957): 353–360.

Rauh, H. D. "Hildegard von Bingen." In *Das Bild des Antichrist im Mittelalter: Von Tychonius zum deutschen Symbolismus,* 474–527. Munich, 1973.

Rissel, Hiltrud. "Hildegard von Bingen an Elisabeth von St. Thomas an der Kyll: Die hl. Hildegard und die frühesten deutschen Zisterzienserinnen." *Cîteaux* 41 (1990): 5–44.

Sancy, Danièle. "Iconographie de la prophétie: L'Image d'Hildegarde de Bingen dans le *Liber divinorum operum.*" *Mélanges de l'École française de Rome* 102 (1990): 405–416.

Schipperges, Heinrich. "Diatetische Lebensführung nach der 'Regula Benedicti' bei Hildegard von Bingen." *Arzt und Christ* 2 (1980): 87–97.

———. "Die Engel in Weltbild Hildegards von Bingen." In Hans Fromm et al., eds., *Verbum et Signum,* 2: 99–117. Munich, 1975.

———. *Hildegard of Bingen.* Trans. Eva Jauntzems. New York, 1989.

———. *Hildegard of Bingen: Healing and the Nature of the Cosmos.* Trans. John Broadwin. Princeton, 1997.

———. "Das Schöne in der Welt Hildegards von Bingen." *Jahrbuch für Ästhetik und allgemeine Kunstwissenschaft* 4 (1958–1959): 83–139.

Schlager, Karlheinz. "Hildegard von Bingen im Spiegel der Choralforschung: Rückschau und Ausblick." In Peter Cahn and Ann-Katrin Heimer, eds., *De Musica et Cantu: Studien zur Geschichte der Kirchenmusik und der Oper,* 309–323. Hildesheim, 1993.

Schmeidler, Bernhard. "Bemerkungen zum Corpus der Briefe der hl. Hildegard von Bingen." In *Corona Quernea: Festgabe Karl Strecker,* 335–366. Leipzig, 1941.

Schmelzeis, J. P. *Das Leben und Wirken der heiligen Hildegardis.* Freiburg, 1879.

Schmidt, Margot. *Die fragende Schau der hl. Hildegard.* Leutesdorf, 1992.

———. "Die Kirche—'Eine Erde der Lebendigen': Zum Kirchenbild bei Hildegard von Bingen." Bischöflichen Ordinariat, aktuelle information, no. 16. Mainz, 1980.

———, ed. *Tiefe des Gotteswissens—Schönheit der Sprachgestalt bei Hildegard von Bingen.* Stuttgart, 1995.

Schmitt, Miriam. "Blessed Jutta of Disibodenberg: Hildegard of Bingen's Magistra and Abbess." *American Benedictine Review* 40 (1989): 170–189.

Schnapp, Jeffrey. "Virgin Words: Hildegard of Bingen's *Lingua ignota* and the Development of Imaginary Languages Ancient to Modern." *Exemplaria* 3 (1991): 267–298.

Scholz, Bernhard. "Hildegard von Bingen on the Nature of Woman." *American Benedictine Review* 31 (1980): 361–383.

Schrader, Marianna. *Die Herkunft der heiligen Hildegard.* 2d ed. Mainz, 1981.

———, and Adelgundis Führkötter. *Die Echtheit des Schrifttums der hl. Hildegard von Bingen.* Cologne and Graz, 1956.

Seibrich, Wolfgang. "Geschichte des Klosters Disibodenberg." In Anton Brück, ed., *Hildegard von Bingen,* 55–75.

Sheingorn, Pamela. "The Virtues of Hildegard's *Ordo Virtutum;* or, It *Was* a Woman's World." In Audrey Davidson, ed., *The* Ordo Virtutum, 43–62.

Singer, Charles. "The Scientific Views and Visions of Saint Hildegard." In *Studies in the History and Method of Science,* 1:1–55. Oxford, 1917.

Sommerfeld, G. "Die Prophetien der hl. Hildegard in einem Schreiben des Meisters Heinrich von Langenstein." *Historisches Jahrbuch* 30 (1909): 43–61, 297–307.

Stanzl, Günther. *Die Klosterruine Disibodenberg: Neue baugeschichtliche und archäologische Untersuchungen.* Worms, 1992.

Sur, Carolyn Wörman. *The Feminine Images of God in the Visions of Saint Hildegard of Bingen's 'Scivias.'* Lewiston, N.Y., 1993.

Suzuki, Keiko. "Zum Strukturproblem in den Visionsdarstellungen der Rupertsberger 'Scivias'-Handschrift." *Sacris Erudiri* 35 (1995): 221–291.

Thompson, Augustine. "Hildegard of Bingen on Gender and the Priesthood." *Church History* 63 (1994): 349–364.

Ungrund, Magna. *Die metaphysische Anthropologie der hl. Hildegard von Bingen.* Münster, 1938.

Van Acker, Lieven. "Der Briefwechsel der hl. Hildegard von Bingen: Vorbemerkungen zu einer kritischen Edition." *Revue bénédictine* 98 (1988): 141–168; 99 (1989): 118–154.

Walter, Peter. "Die Heiligen in der Dichtung der hl. Hildegard von Bingen." In Anton Brück, ed., *Hildegard von Bingen,* 211–237.

———. "*Virgo filium dei portasti:* Maria in den Gesängen der hl. Hildegard von Bingen." *Archiv für mittelrheinische Kirchengeschichte* 29 (1977): 75–96.

Weinfurter, Stefan, ed. *Reformidee und Reformpolitik im spätsalisch-frühstaufischen Reich.* Mainz, 1992.

Weiss-Amer, Melitta [aka Melitta Weiss Adamson]. "Die 'Physica' Hildegards von Bingen als Quelle für das Kochbuch Meister Eberhards." *Sudhoffs Archiv* 76 (1992): 87–96.

Widmer, Bertha. *Heilsordnung und Zeitgeschehen in der Mystik Hildegards von Bingen.* Basel, 1955.

Wiethaus, Ulrike. "In Search of Medieval Women's Friendships: Hildegard of Bingen's Letters to Her Female Contemporaries." In Ulrike Wiethaus, ed., *Maps of Flesh and Light,* 93–111.

———, ed. *Maps of Flesh and Light: The Religious Experience of Medieval Women Mystics.* Syracuse, N.Y., 1993.

Yardley, Anne Bagnall. " 'Ful weel she soong the service dyvyne': The Cloistered Musician in the Middle Ages." In Jane Bowers and Judith Tick, eds., *Women Making Music,* 15–38. Urbana, Ill., 1986.

Discography

This discography excludes the many CDs containing only one or two pieces from Hildegard's Symphonia as well as New Age adaptations of her music.

Anonymous 4. *11,000 Virgins: Chants for the Feast of St. Ursula.* 1997. Harmonia mundi 907200.

Early Music Institute, dir. Thomas Binkley. *The Lauds of St. Ursula.* 1991. Focus 911.

Ensemble für frühe Musik, Augsburg. *Hildegard von Bingen und ihre Zeit: Geistliche Musik des 12. Jahrhunderts.* 1990. Christophorus 74584. Music of Hildegard and Abelard.

Ensemble Mediatrix, dir. Johannes Göschl. *Feminea Forma Maria.* 1996. Calig 50982. Marian songs of the Dendermonde codex.

Ensemble Organum, dir. Marcel Pérès. *Hildegard von Bingen: Laudes de Ste. Ursule.* 1997. Harmonia mundi 901626.

Norma Gentile. *Unfurling Love's Creation: Chants by Hildegard von Bingen.* 1997. Lyrichord Early Music Series (LEMS) 8027.

Gothic Voices, dir. Christopher Page. *A Feather on the Breath of God.* 1984. Hyperion CDA 66039. Sequences and hymns.

Instrumentalkreis Helga Weber, with Almut Teichert-Hailperin. *Geistliche Musik des Mittelalters und der Renaissance.* 1980, 1993. Christophorus CHE 0041-2. Music of Hildegard, Dunstable, Dufay, and Brassart.

Musica Sacra, dir. Richard Westenburg. *Monk and the Abbess.* 1996. BMG Catalyst 09026-68329-2. Music of Hildegard and Meredith Monk.

Ellen Oak. *Hildegard of Bingen: The Harmony of Heaven.* 1995. Bison Tales 0001.

Oxford Camerata, dir. Jeremy Summerly. *Hildegard von Bingen: Heavenly Revelations.* 1994. Naxos 8.550998.

Schola der Benediktinerinnenabtei St. Hildegard, dir. M.-I. Ritscher. *Gesänge der hl. Hildegard von Bingen.* 1979. Bayer 100116.

Catherine Schroeder et al. *O nobilissima viriditas.* 1995. Champeaux CSM 0006.

Sequentia, dir. Barbara Thornton. *Canticles of Ecstasy.* 1994. Deutsche Harmonia mundi 05472-77320-2.

Sequentia, dir. Barbara Thornton. *O Jerusalem.* 1997. Deutsche Harmonia mundi 05472-77353-2.

Sequentia, dir. Barbara Thornton. *Ordo virtutum.* 2 disks, 1982. Deutsche Harmonia mundi 77051-2-RG. Re-recorded 1998. DHM 05472-77394-2.

Sequentia, dir. Barbara Thornton. *Saints.* 1998. Deutsche Harmonia mundi 05472-77378-2.

Sequentia, dir. Barbara Thornton. *Symphoniae: Geistliche Gesänge.* 1985. Deutsche Harmonia mundi 77020-2-RG.

Sequentia, dir. Barbara Thornton. *Voice of the Blood.* 1995. Deutsche Harmonia mundi 05472-77346-2.

Sinfonye, dir. Stevie Wishart. *Symphony of the Harmony of Celestial Revelations.* Vol. 1. 1996. Celestial Harmonies 13127-2.

Tapestry, dir. Laurie Monahan. *Hildegard von Bingen: Celestial Light.* 1997. Telarc 80456. Music of Hildegard and Robert Kyr, with Notre Dame polyphony.

Viriditas, dir. Juliette Hughes. *Jouissance.* 1993. Spectrum/Cistercian Publications, ISBN 0-86786-344-7. Music of Hildegard and Abelard.

Voices of Ascension, dir. Dennis Keene. *Voices of Angels: Music of Hildegard von Bingen.* 1997. Delos 3219.

Notes on Contributors

MADELINE CAVINESS   is Mary Richardson Professor and Professor of Art History at Tufts University, where she has taught since 1972. She has published extensively on medieval stained glass and served eight years as president of the International Board of the Corpus Vitrearum Medii Aevi; she was also president of the Medieval Academy of America in 1993–1994. Her book *The Sumptuous Arts at the Royal Abbeys in Reims and Braine* (Princeton, 1990) won the Haskins Medal of the Medieval Academy. She is currently working on a book that investigates medieval works in a variety of media in light of current feminist theories.

MARGOT FASSLER   specializes in the chant and liturgy of the Latin Middle Ages. She teaches at Yale University, where she also directs the Yale Institute of Sacred Music. She is the author of *Gothic Song: Victorine Sequences and Augustinian Reform in Twelfth-Century Paris* (Cambridge, 1993). Having recently finished a series of articles on medieval Marian veneration, Professor Fassler is now writing a book on the Virgin at Chartres in the eleventh and twelfth centuries.

JOAN FERRANTE   has been a professor of Comparative Literature at Columbia University for thirty-five years. She has written widely on medieval literature and on women in the Middle Ages. Her books include *Woman as Image in Medieval Literature from the Twelfth Century to Dante* (New York, 1975); a commentary and translation with Robert Hanning, *Lais of Marie de France* (New York, 1978); and most recently *To the Glory of Her Sex: Women's Roles in the Composition of Medieval Texts* (Bloomington, 1997). She is a past president of the Dante Society of America.

FLORENCE ELIZA GLAZE   received her doctorate from Duke University in 1998, specializing in the history of medicine, medieval history, and Latin palaeography. Her doctoral thesis, "The Perforated Wall: An Inquiry into the Textual Traditions of Hildegard of Bingen's Medicine," examines Hildegard's medical writings in light of contemporary medical thought. She is currently composing a descriptive and photographic inventory of approximately fifty fragments from medieval and Renaissance manuscripts which she discovered at Duke, including a fragment of Constantine the African's *Pantegni*. She has also undertaken an extensive analysis of the *Passionarius* of Gariopontus of Salerno, an eleventh-century physician.

KATHRYN KERBY-FULTON   is associate professor of English and Medieval Studies at the University of Victoria (Canada). She has published on Hildegard's prophecy and ideas of church reform in *Reformist Apocalypticism and* Piers Plowman (Cambridge, 1990) and in various articles, most recently in Rosalynn Voaden's *Prophets Abroad: The Reception of Continental Holy Women in Late-Medieval England* (Woodbridge, Suffolk, 1996). Her most recent books are *Written Work: Langland, Labor, and Authorship,* (Philadelphia, 1997), coedited with Steven Justice, and *Iconography and the Professional Reader: The Politics of Book Production in the Douce Piers Plowman* (Minneapolis, 1998), coauthored with Denise Despres.

CONSTANT MEWS   is senior lecturer in the Department of History and director of the Centre for Studies in Religion and Theology at Monash University, Australia. He has edited Peter Abelard's *Theologia* in Corpus Christianorum: Continuatio Mediaeualis 13 (Turnhout, 1987) and is author of *Peter Abelard,* Authors of the Middle Ages 5 (London, 1995), as well as of numerous articles about scholasticism. He is coeditor with Julie Barton of *Hildegard of Bingen and Gendered Theology in Judaeo-Christian Tradition* (Clayton, Victoria, Australia, 1995).

BARBARA NEWMAN   is professor of English and Religion at Northwestern University, specializing in medieval religious women. She is the author of *Sister of Wisdom: St. Hildegard's Theology of the Feminine* (Berkeley, 1987) and editor and translator of Hildegard's *Symphonia* (Ithaca, N.Y., 1988; rev. ed., 1998). Her most recent book is *From Virile Woman to WomanChrist: Studies in Medieval Religion and Literature* (Philadelphia, 1995).

JOHN VAN ENGEN   served for more than ten years as director of the Medieval Institute and is currently professor of history at the University of Notre Dame, where he specializes in religious and intellectual history of the Middle Ages. His first book, *Rupert of Deutz* (Berkeley, 1983), treated a twelfth-century Benedictine. He has also published a collection of texts in translation, *Devotio Moderna: Basic Writings* (New York, 1988). He is currently at work on a general book about Christianization in medieval Europe, to be called *The Christening of Europe,* and is editing texts from the first house of the Brothers of the Common Life.

Index